TOR

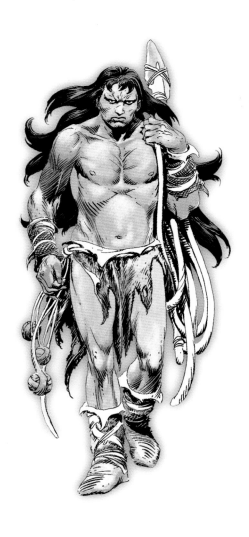

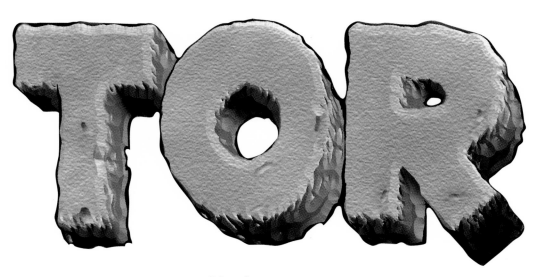

Volume 3

BY JOE KUBERT

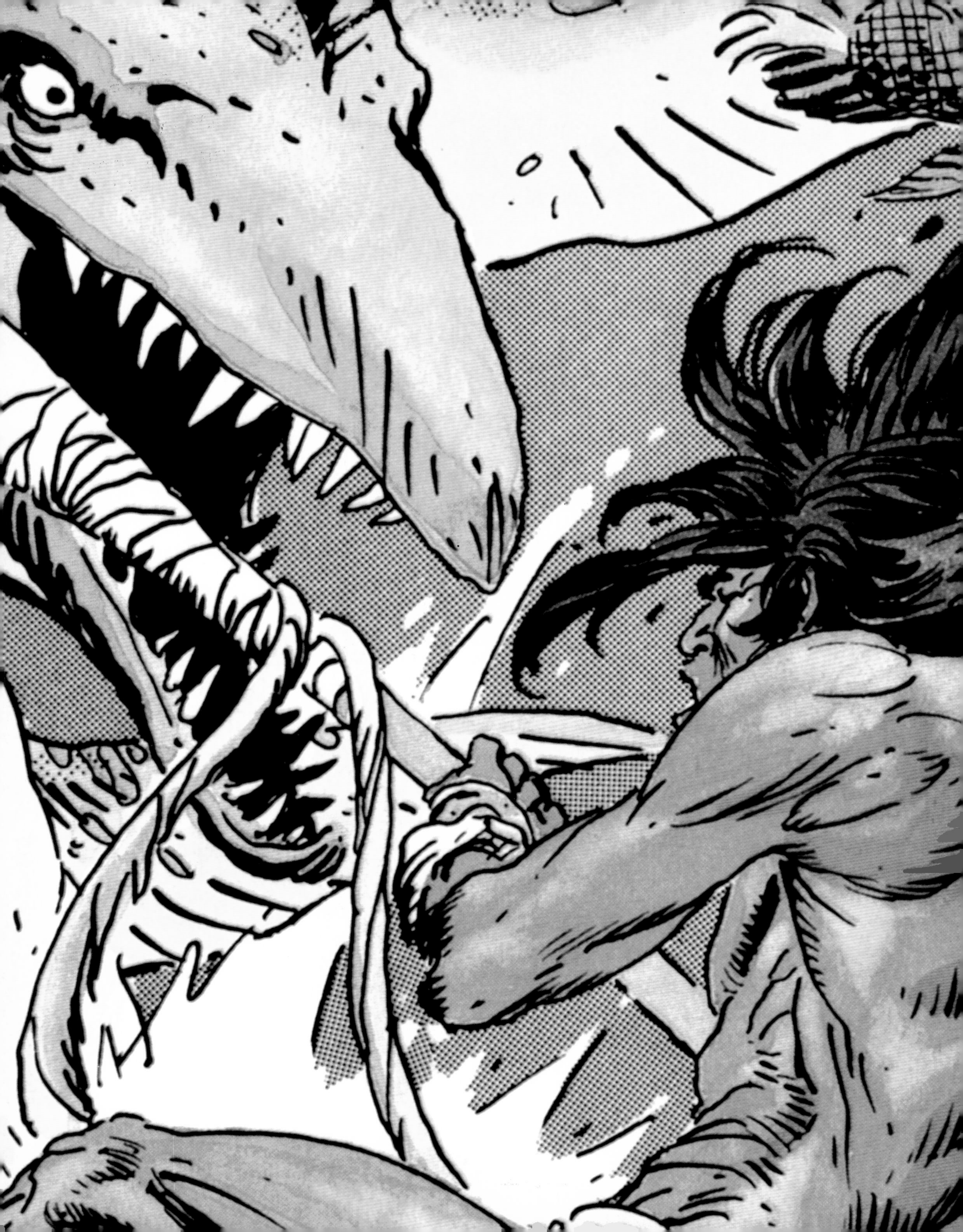

TOR

Volume 3

BY JOE KUBERT

The Joe Kubert Library

DC Comics New York, New York

DC Comics

TOR by Joe Kubert
Volume 3

Published by DC Comics
Cover and compilation copyright © 2003 Joe Kubert.
Foreword and introduction copyright © 2003 DC Comics.
Originally published as TOR Volume 1 No. 1 (May-June 1975), TOR Volume 1 No. 1 (June 1993),
TOR Volume 1 No. 2 (July 1993), TOR Volume 1 No. 3 (August 1993) and TOR Volume 1 No. 4 (September 1993).
Copyright © 1975, 1993 by Joe Kubert. All Rights Reserved.

The stories, characters, and incidents featured in this publication are entirely fictional.
DC Comics does not read or accept unsolicited submissions of ideas, stories or artwork..

DC Comics, 1700 Broadway, New York, NY 10019.
A Warner Bros. Entertainment Company
Printed in Hong Kong.
ISBN 1-56389-998-1
First Printing.

Cover illustration by Joe Kubert.
Art & color reconstruction on selected stories by Telegraphics.

Special thanks to:

Norman Maurer, Leonard Maurer, Bob Bean, Robert Bernstein,
Alex Toth, Russ Heath, Leonard Stern, Carmine Infantino, Tatjana Wood,
Roy Thomas, J. Guinta, Pete Carlsson, and Archer St. John.

*Information relating to Joe Kubert, The Joe Kubert School of Cartoon Art
and his correspondence courses can be found at the website www.joekubert.com
or www.kubertsworld.com, or via e-mail at kubert@intrepid.net.*

TOR
JOE KUBERT
volume three

Foreword by Joe Kubert

YOU CAN'T GO HOME AGAIN.

This statement has been made to describe the fact that situations and circumstances once visited can never again be repeated. Not in the same way or intensity. My own personal experiences deny that statement. Or is it that I continue to be one lucky ol' codger? The book you hold in your hands lends validity to my denial.

TOR has been a source of personal pleasure and friendship to me for over fifty years. A strange thing to say about an imaginary character? A being that is only a figment of my imagination? Well, perhaps not so strange. From his inception aboard a troopship bound for Germany in the early '50s to the present day, TOR has always been an important part of my life. And, like a true friend, his patience with me and my sometimes ineptitude is boundless.

At times I cringe at my early drawings, proportions that are not quite right, dinosaurs that look more like plastic toys, but he never complained. When I placed him in situations that would embarrass or even frighten a less hearty soul, not a word of recrimination. When months or sometimes years passed between publications, he still remained my friend and although unseen, my companion.

His company has always been a pleasurable experience for me. He's done all the things I've only dreamed of doing. I shivered and sweated when he faced powerful opponents bent on tearing him apart. I took deep breaths as he narrowly escaped erupting volcanoes and boulder-shattering earthquakes. I consistently tried to improve my drawings in order to truly convey the makeup of the man. The heavy brow, the squinting eyes, the thick nose, the strong jaw reflected the hard life into which he was born. His muscled torso scarred in past battles was the mark of his survival. He survived through strength of mind and body, and I tried to show these elemental basics in my drawings.

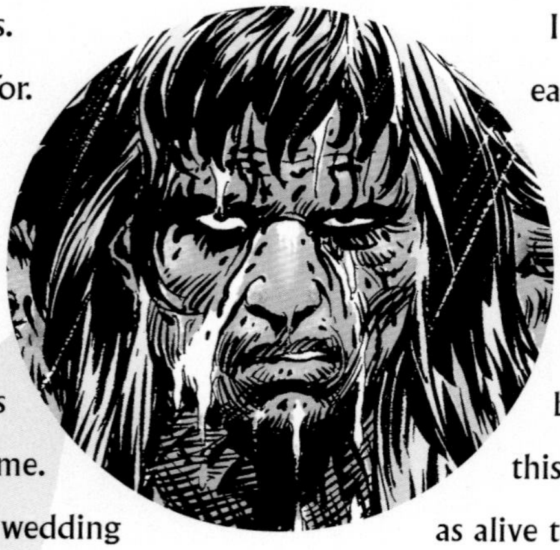

I believe others feel as I do about Tor. During his tenure as president and publisher of DC Comics, Carmine Infantino asked if I'd be interested in seeing TOR republished.

Carmine and I have been friends and associates for a long period of time. In fact, Carmine was an usher at my wedding eons ago. We've worked together on many projects, Carmine pencilling and my inking his pencils. Projects like "Jesse James" and "The Flash" come to mind. It was always a treat for me to ink his wonderful drawings. Before Carmine took up the reins of editorial director at DC Comics, I had suggested the possibility of doing TOR as a newspaper strip. I asked Carmine if he'd be interested in writing the script, and he agreed to do it. His writing is contained in this archive publication, within the pages of the twenty-five-cent version of TOR number one, dated June 1975. Originally, the script was written and drawn in strip form, consisting of newspaper dailies. (The original strip concept was printed in the first archive volume of TOR.) When Carmine gave me the opportunity to have TOR reappear for DC, I converted the dailies into the sixteen-page story contained herein. I added panels, pages and designed page layouts that I felt were more applicable to a comic book. I heard no complaints from Carmine — or TOR. We had a good run.

Then, TOR lay dormant for a number of years before I was contacted by Carl Potts, an executive editor at Marvel Comics. He was setting up a series of publications featuring "creator owned" characters. This 1993 version of TOR comprised four volumes, all contained herein.

I have revisited TOR many times, and each time with undiminished pleasure. He is a reminder of the times I spent as a youngster, wrapped in the newspaper strip "Tarzan," swinging through jungle foliage and fighting bull apes. Hal Foster was the artist for this Burroughs creation, and Tarzan was as alive to me then as TOR is to me now. After all, TOR is an apeman in a prehistoric Stone Age setting.

There are a number of projects which demand my attention at present, but I still look forward to the next opportunity of getting back to my old friend in the fur shorts, writing and drawing future adventures about a man who lived a million years ago, and who, for me, is alive today.

— Joe Kubert

April, 2003

Introduction by Roy Thomas

A TOR FOR ALL SEASONS

Clearly, Joe Kubert is a pack rat... someone who, if he can help it, never throws anything away.

Including ideas.

Especially ideas.

As proof, look at the two previous volumes of this series — as if I could *stop* anyone who's picked up *this* one from immediately running out and moving heaven and earth to locate the preceding pair, in the unlikely event that he/she hasn't already long since added them to his/her library.

Along with the art and story for all six issues of *Tor/1,000,000 Years Ago* that were published during 1953-54 by St. John Publishing Company, those two beautiful hardcover volumes contain promotional drawings

and storyboards for a possible *Tor* animated TV series, scripts for a "Tor" story, projected children's-book artwork, sample comic strip continuity, warm-up sketches, drawings done for fanzines and comics convention program books — even an illustration done for the World Health Organization. Timewise, these varied artistic visions were produced between the early 1950s and at least 1990.

In fact, 'twould seem that the one thing that thus far has eluded Joe is the batch of original sketches of Tor (with notes) that he did on a U.S. troopship bound for Europe in 1950, as he related in Volume 1. More's the pity. To dyed-in-the-woolly-mammoth *Tor* fans like myself (I bought that first issue hot off the newsstand back in

1953 and still have it), locating those initial concept sketches — would be like finding a new cave full of primordial art, *à la* Lascaux or Altamont. A Rosetta Stone that would need no deciphering, only enjoying.

Of course, those of us who lusted after more *Tor* for the first decade or so after St. John folded didn't know about the 1950 sketches — or the storyboards or children's-book illustrations.

The first clue I ever had that there might be life after St. John for Tor was during the week or so in 1965 that I worked on staff for DC Comics. That's when I met Joe for the first time, and he regaled me with news of a top-secret idea he had for a magazine, one that would feature episodes of Tor and other characters by other creators. He wondered aloud if I might be willing to help him, when the time came, to drum up enthusiasm for this mag among the network of comics fans of which I was very much a part. Naturally, I responded in the affirmative — it would've been an honor to help promote one of my favorite comics heroes, done by my all-time favorite comics artist — but it was destined to be another decade-plus till the handsome oversize publication he had envisioned would briefly emerge: *Sojourn*, with Tor, plus features by John Severin, Dick Giordano, and Sergio Aragones.

Luckily, neither I nor other eager fans had to wait that long to see more of Tor.

You could've knocked me over with a Stone Age feather when I learned in the late '60s, through my friend Mark Hanerfeld — another true-blue Tor *and* Kubert fan, if ever there was one! — that Joe possessed the artwork for two weeks' worth of dailies of an unsold *Tor* newspaper comic strip, done a couple of years before. More: Joe was amenable to allowing me to publish them in my fanzine *Alter Ego*, which I was planning to revive even though by then I'd been writing and editing for Stan Lee at Marvel for several years. And so those twelve strips (reprinted in Volume 1 of this series) first saw the light of day at the turn of 1969-70...

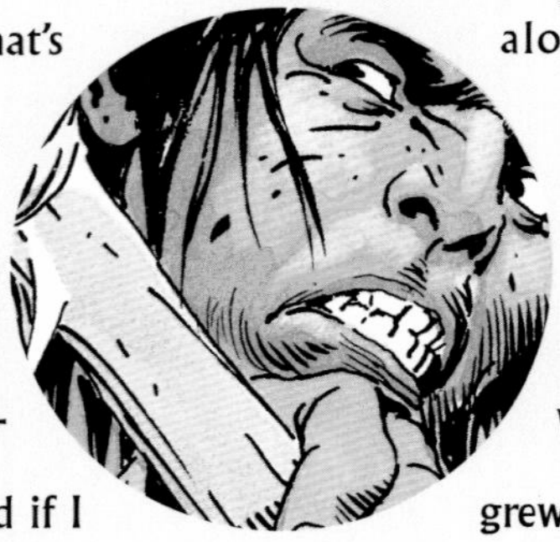

along with a gorgeous Tor and Chee-Chee illustration Joe had done for Mark, which he let us make the issue's back cover.

Everyone I know who saw those strips, which starred a young Tor, years before he grew into the hero we'd known in the comic books, wanted to read the entire story... sometime... somewhere... somehow.

The time turned out to be only a few years later... and the place was Joe's longtime publisher of choice, DC Comics. As for the *how*...

For a new "*Tor*, Vol. 1, No. 1," cover-dated June 1975, Joe reworked the art from those dozen comic strips into the fabric of a new and expanded story, seen as a flashback through the adult Tor's eyes after a fierce tussle with a smallish dinosaur. But Joe, being Joe, wasn't content simply to turn those strips into a few pages of the new comic. Instead, he integrated them into spanking-new pages designed with a comic *book* in mind. The little box-panels unrelentingly demanded by newspapers were accompanied, often even surrounded and engulfed, by sprawling vistas that depicted Tor striding up a cliff-side, or being beaten by a deerskin-wearing youth (now given a name, Kobar, in yet another new panel) while pterosaurs wheel in the sky like prehistoric vultures. Do yourself a favor and peruse this volume's reprinting of that tale from the 1975 *Tor* alongside the twelve strips that appeared in the first one. It'll show you an artist, a writer, a creator at work.

At last, Mark and I and other Torophiles got to see the finish of the battle between Kobar and the "water devil," which had lain uncompleted for nearly a decade. We saw the establishment of a bond between Kobar and Tor... though this was only a tantalizing hint of yet *another* story, still to come. For that's what Joe does with his writing and his art... he draws you into his world, be it primeval ooze or World War II or the super-science of Thanagar, and you don't surface again until he's good and ready to *let* you.

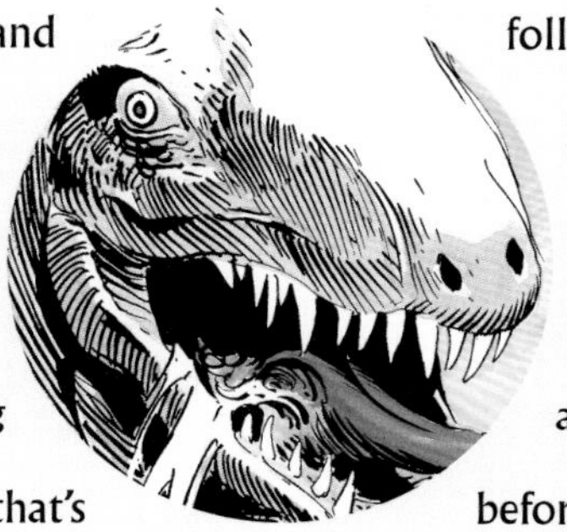

We Tor-fans were pleased, too, that Joe chose in the 1970s to continue a fondly remembered tradition of *Tor* from the 1950s, by depicting himself at the drawing board at the beginning and end of the new stories, talking to the reader — to you, to *me* — in that same straight-from-the-shoulder, no-nonsense way that had made the St. John Tor so much more than just another comic book.

In fact, I'll admit there was only one tiny, nitpicking aspect of the DC *Tor* I didn't like (besides all those paid ads that kept breaking up the stories, but that was unavoidable in that day and age): Joe had chosen to give Tor *brown hair* this time around. This was probably done, I guessed, to decrease any slight visual similarity between Tor and Tarzan, whom Joe had been drawing so magnificently only months before. Still, those of us who "*knew Tor when*" were fully aware that his hair was jet-black (and is again in this volume's reprinting), albeit sometimes with bluish highlights.

The rest of that first DC issue, and the five that followed, were composed of reprints of the St. John material, albeit behind new covers; but that was fine by us. For one thing, several of those original stories, having appeared in "3-D" issues in 1953, had never before been printed in color. Besides, ere long, the 1950s material would all be happily back in print — and then we'd glory in new "Tor" stories and art.

Alas, it was not to be. The mid-'70s were a tough time for new comic books, and after six issues *Tor* went back into mothballs until 1986, when Eclipse Comics published two issues of *Tor 3-D*, featuring new red-and-green separations by the indefatigable Ray Zone... again behind new (non-3-D) Kubert covers.

Then, in the early 1990s, Joe took Tor to yet a fourth company (a fifth, if you count his own, that had published *Sojourn*): none other than Marvel Comics, as part of its "Heavy Hitters" line.

For four issues in 1993, forty years after the St. John days, Joe gave us a new continued epic, in which he introduced strains of fantasy that went a bit beyond where Tor had stalked before. In stories prepared since 1954, Joe had elected not to ask readers to suspend their disbelief concerning the possibility that vintage dinosaurs like T. rex and bronto/apatosaurus had coexisted with early mankind. Instead, even in drawings done for convention program books and the like, he utilized only lesser saurians that seemed to be "survivals," specimens of a last remnant of dinosaurs, dying out as human beings inherited the earth.

But, in the quartet of "Heavy Hitters" issues, he introduced a mottled, slightly-less-than-human race as his villains... then another species that straddled the line between anthropoid and reptilian... and finally a multi-legged worm-thing that might have slithered out of one of Robert E. Howard's fabled stories of Conan the Cimmerian. The result took Tor to the next level, and made him a viable hero for a new era.

As for "we happy few" (and perhaps more-than-few) who had accepted the years that yawned between appearances of Tor as merely the price we had to patiently pay for the wonderment that would from time to time beckon to us, we took it all in stride, content to follow Tor — and Joe Kubert — wherever they led.

As this final hardcover volume of the collected *Tor* is published, including all the material produced for DC and Marvel and even *Sojourn*, plus an armful of other antediluvian goodies besides, it's been precisely ten years since the stone-axe-wielding hero's last new outing... and *half a century* since his first one.

But we know there'll be another new adventure, one of these days. We have to believe that we haven't seen the last of Tor the Hunter. And when he returns, we'll be there. Waiting.

We're sure glad Joe Kubert never throws anything away.

Maybe, one of these days, he'll even find those 1950 Tor sketches...!

— Roy Thomas
February, 2002

Roy Thomas has been a writer and editor in the comic–book field since 1965, primarily for DC and Marvel. A winner of the Alley, Eagle, Shazam, Alfred (Angoulême, France), and Haxtur (Gijon, Spain) awards, he is perhaps most noted for major stints as the writer (at Marvel) of Conan the Barbarian, The Avengers, The X-Men, et al., and (at DC) of ALL-STAR SQUADRON, INFINITY, INC., and others. He currently edits Alter Ego, *a magazine dealing with the history of heroic comic books, and is writing Prestige Format books and limited series which are forthcoming from DC.*

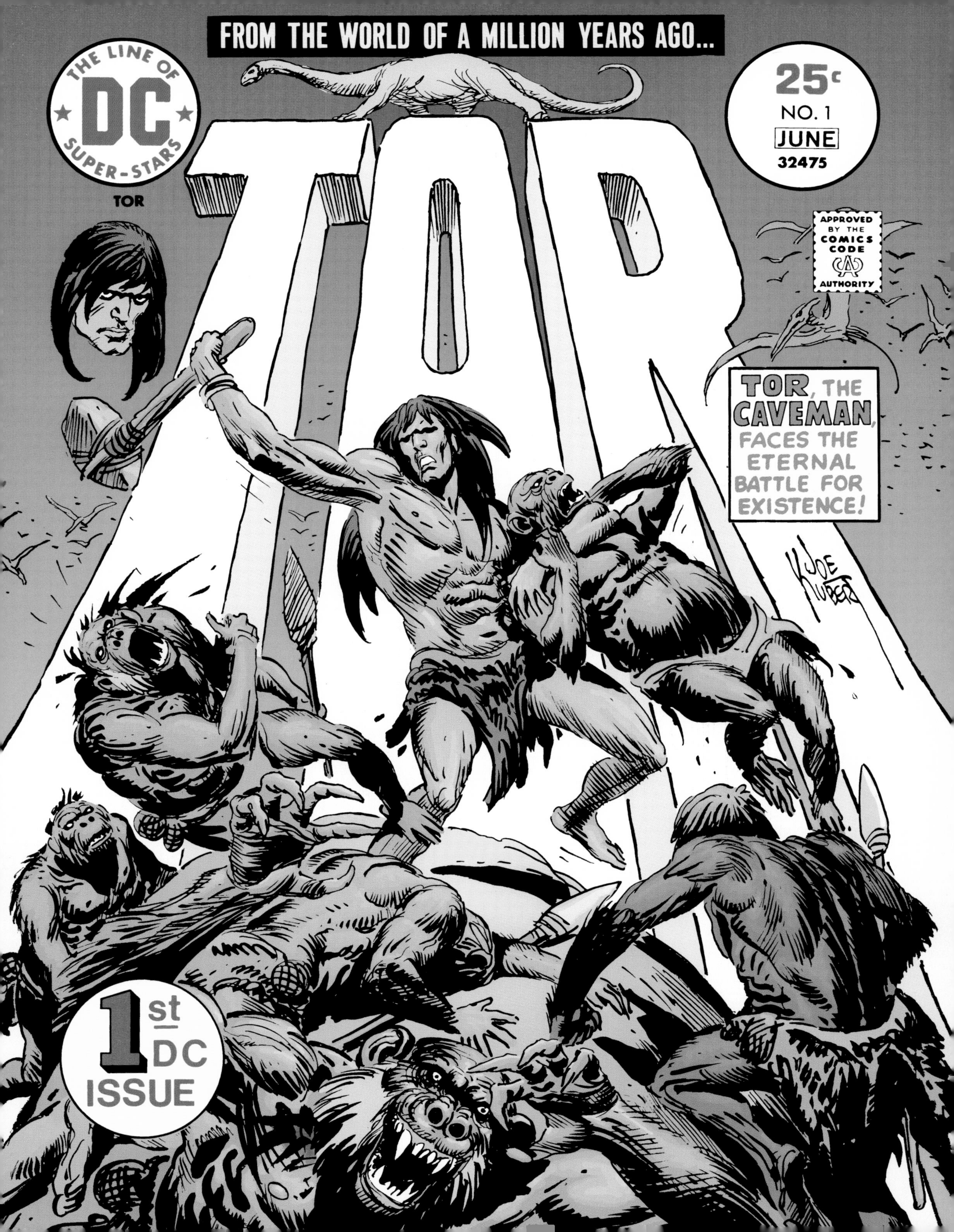
FROM THE WORLD OF A MILLION YEARS AGO...
THE LINE OF DC SUPER-STARS
TOR
25¢
NO. 1
JUNE
32475
TOR
APPROVED BY THE COMICS CODE AUTHORITY
TOR, THE CAVEMAN, FACES THE ETERNAL BATTLE FOR EXISTENCE!
JOE KUBERT
1st DC ISSUE

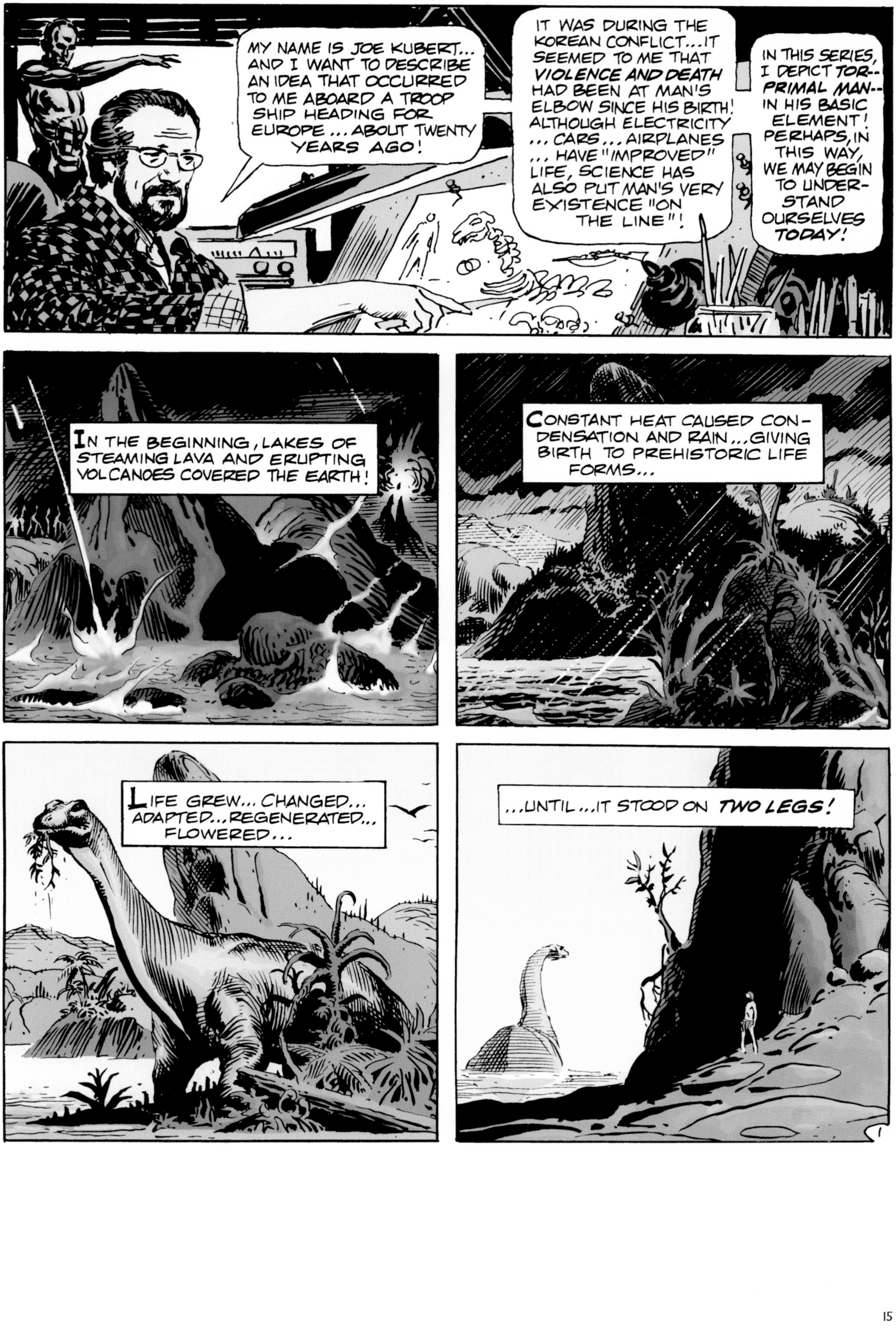
MY NAME IS JOE KUBERT... AND I WANT TO DESCRIBE AN IDEA THAT OCCURRED TO ME ABOARD A TROOP SHIP HEADING FOR EUROPE ... ABOUT TWENTY YEARS AGO!
IT WAS DURING THE KOREAN CONFLICT...IT SEEMED TO ME THAT VIOLENCE AND DEATH HAD BEEN AT MAN'S ELBOW SINCE HIS BIRTH! ALTHOUGH ELECTRICITY ... CARS ... AIRPLANES ... HAVE "IMPROVED" LIFE, SCIENCE HAS ALSO PUT MAN'S VERY EXISTENCE "ON THE LINE"!
IN THIS SERIES, I DEPICT TOR-- PRIMAL MAN-- IN HIS BASIC ELEMENT! PERHAPS, IN THIS WAY, WE MAY BEGIN TO UNDERSTAND OURSELVES TODAY!
IN THE BEGINNING, LAKES OF STEAMING LAVA AND ERUPTING VOLCANOES COVERED THE EARTH!
CONSTANT HEAT CAUSED CONDENSATION AND RAIN...GIVING BIRTH TO PREHISTORIC LIFE FORMS...
LIFE GREW... CHANGED... ADAPTED...REGENERATED... FLOWERED...
...UNTIL...IT STOOD ON TWO LEGS!
1

THE SHAGGY-MANED FIGURE TURNS FROM THE WALLOWING *THUNDER LIZARD*... NOSTRILS DILATED... *TOR* TENSES!

FOOD! IF HE MUST, *TOR* WILL IMPERIL HIS LIFE -- TO ACQUIRE LIFE'S SUSTENANCE!

ACTION IS TAKEN WITHOUT HESITATION!

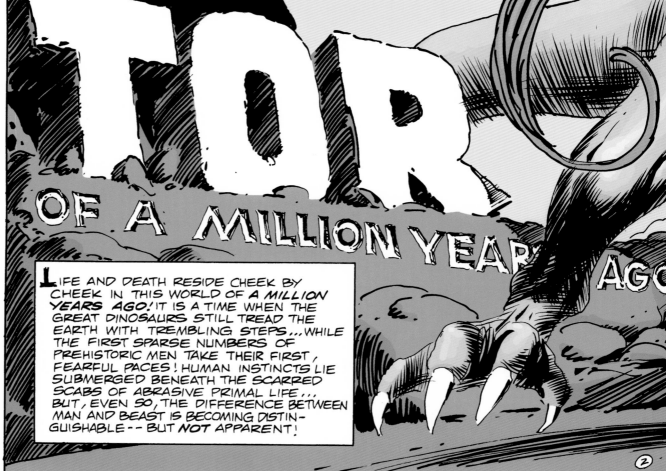

TOR
OF A MILLION YEARS AGO

LIFE AND DEATH RESIDE CHEEK BY CHEEK IN THIS WORLD OF *A MILLION YEARS AGO!* IT IS A TIME WHEN THE GREAT DINOSAURS STILL TREAD THE EARTH WITH TREMBLING STEPS... WHILE THE FIRST SPARSE NUMBERS OF PREHISTORIC MEN TAKE THEIR FIRST, FEARFUL PACES! HUMAN INSTINCTS LIE SUBMERGED BENEATH THE SCARRED SCABS OF ABRASIVE PRIMAL LIFE... BUT, EVEN SO, THE DIFFERENCE BETWEEN MAN AND BEAST IS BECOMING DISTINGUISHABLE -- BUT *NOT* APPARENT!

2

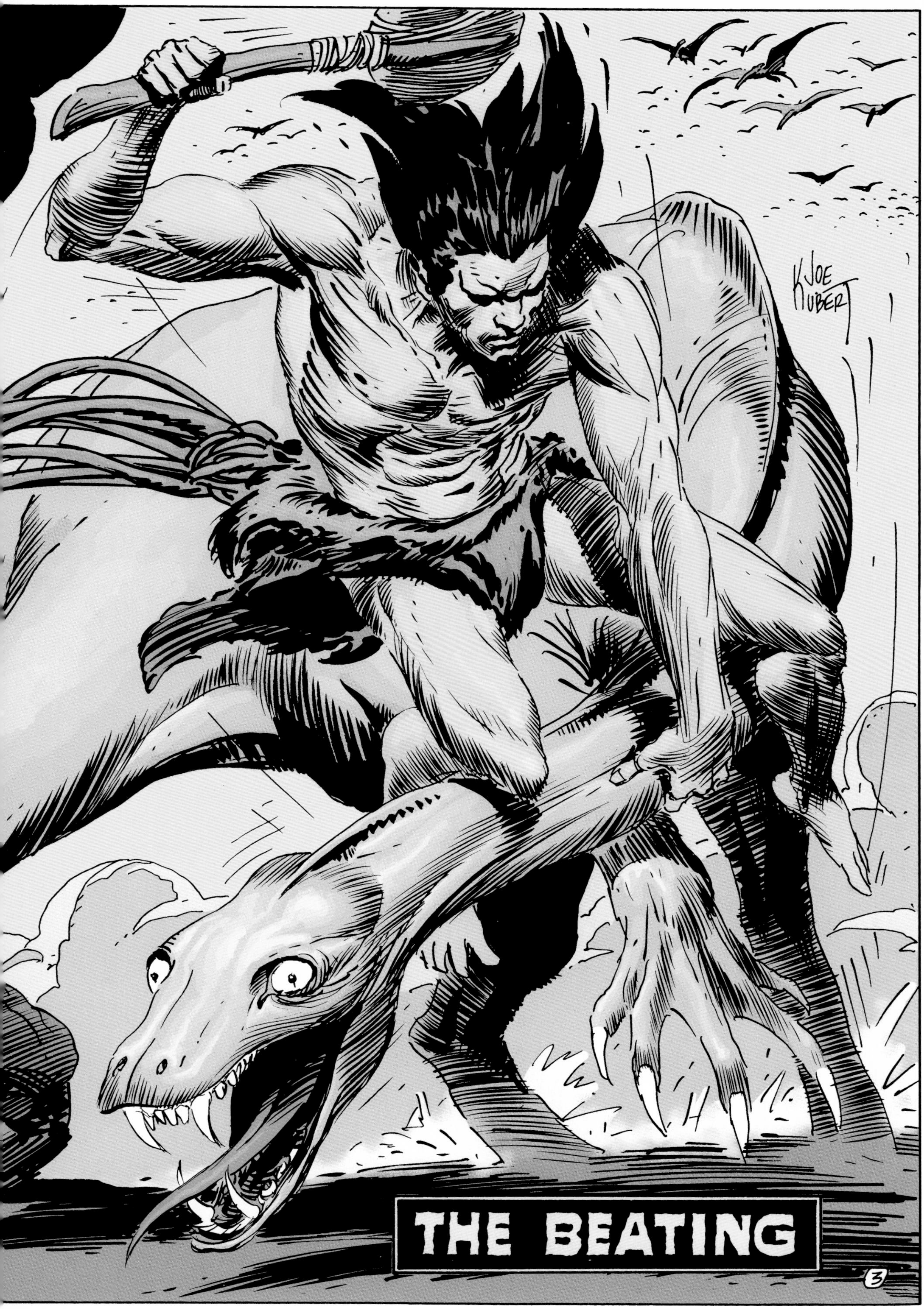
JOE KUBERT
THE BEATING
3

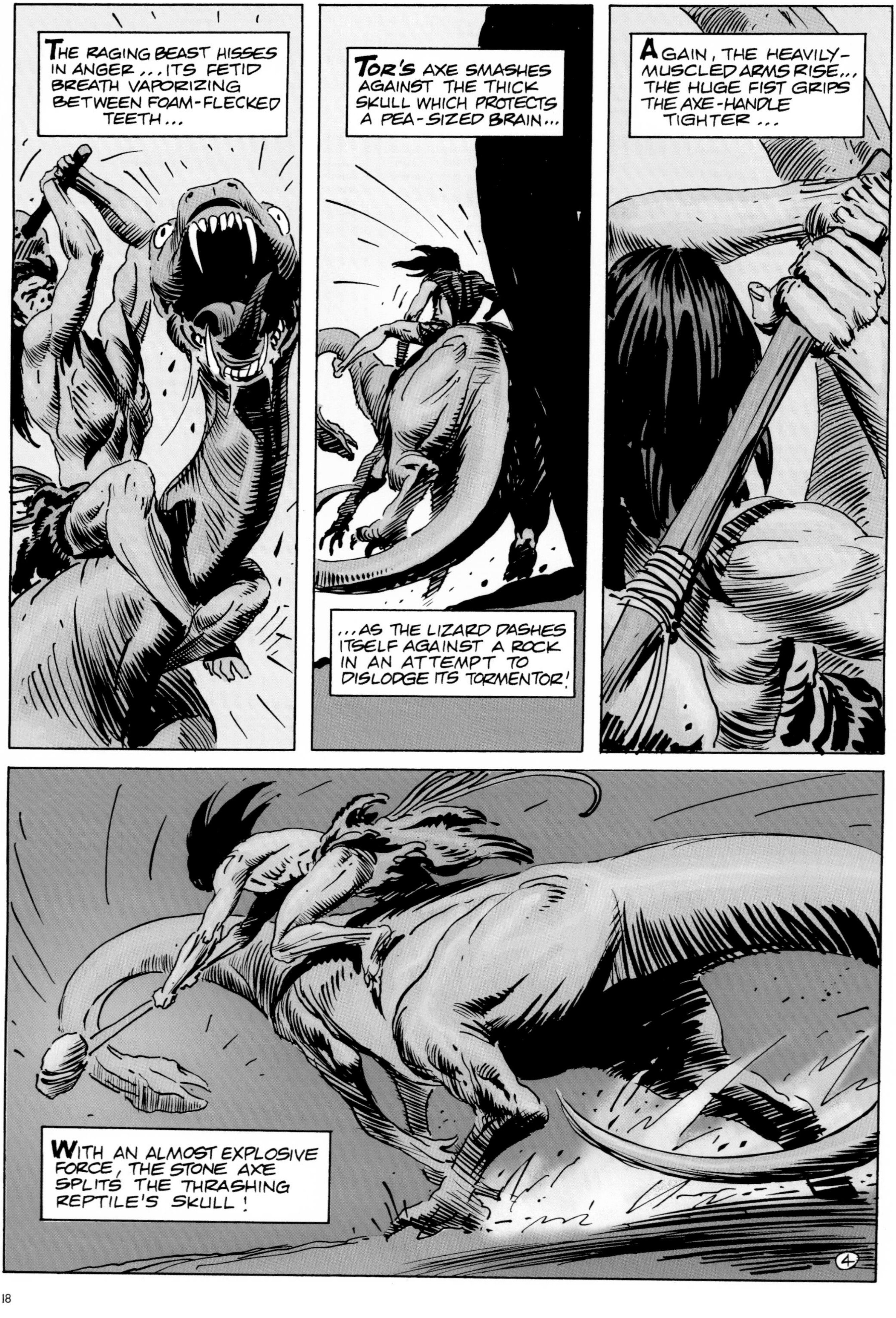
THE RAGING BEAST HISSES IN ANGER... ITS FETID BREATH VAPORIZING BETWEEN FOAM-FLECKED TEETH...
TOR'S AXE SMASHES AGAINST THE THICK SKULL WHICH PROTECTS A PEA-SIZED BRAIN...
...AS THE LIZARD DASHES ITSELF AGAINST A ROCK IN AN ATTEMPT TO DISLODGE ITS TORMENTOR!
AGAIN, THE HEAVILY-MUSCLED ARMS RISE... THE HUGE FIST GRIPS THE AXE-HANDLE TIGHTER...
WITH AN ALMOST EXPLOSIVE FORCE, THE STONE AXE SPLITS THE THRASHING REPTILE'S SKULL!
4

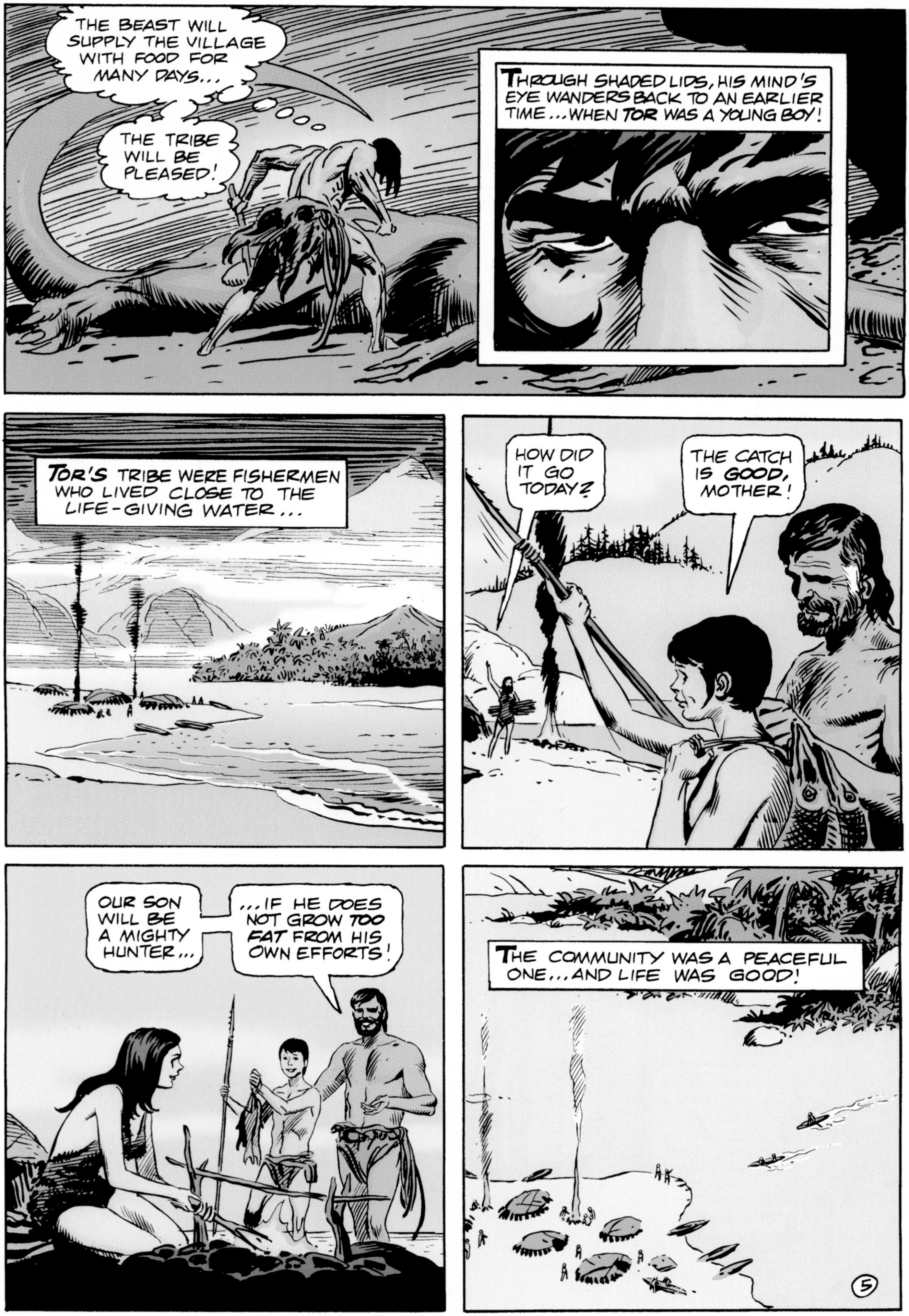
THE BEAST WILL SUPPLY THE VILLAGE WITH FOOD FOR MANY DAYS...
THE TRIBE WILL BE PLEASED!
THROUGH SHADED LIDS, HIS MIND'S EYE WANDERS BACK TO AN EARLIER TIME...WHEN TOR WAS A YOUNG BOY!
TOR'S TRIBE WERE FISHERMEN WHO LIVED CLOSE TO THE LIFE-GIVING WATER...
HOW DID IT GO TODAY?
THE CATCH IS GOOD, MOTHER!
OUR SON WILL BE A MIGHTY HUNTER...
...IF HE DOES NOT GROW TOO FAT FROM HIS OWN EFFORTS!
THE COMMUNITY WAS A PEACEFUL ONE...AND LIFE WAS GOOD!
5

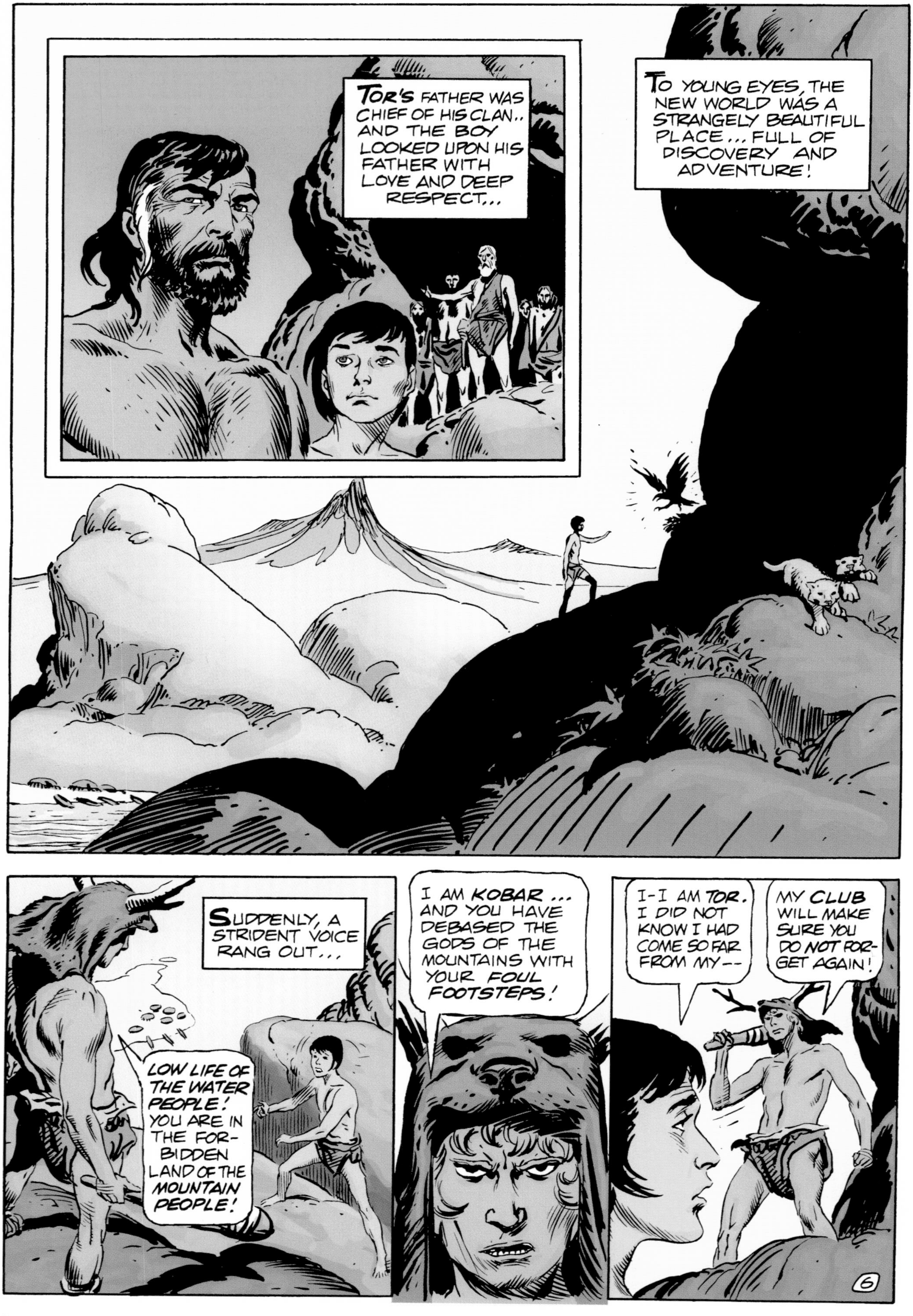
TOR'S FATHER WAS CHIEF OF HIS CLAN.. AND THE BOY LOOKED UPON HIS FATHER WITH LOVE AND DEEP RESPECT...
TO YOUNG EYES, THE NEW WORLD WAS A STRANGELY BEAUTIFUL PLACE... FULL OF DISCOVERY AND ADVENTURE!
SUDDENLY, A STRIDENT VOICE RANG OUT...
LOW LIFE OF THE WATER PEOPLE! YOU ARE IN THE FOR-BIDDEN LAND OF THE MOUNTAIN PEOPLE!
I AM KOBAR... AND YOU HAVE DEBASED THE GODS OF THE MOUNTAINS WITH YOUR FOUL FOOTSTEPS!
I-I AM TOR. I DID NOT KNOW I HAD COME SO FAR FROM MY--
MY CLUB WILL MAKE SURE YOU DO NOT FOR-GET AGAIN!
6

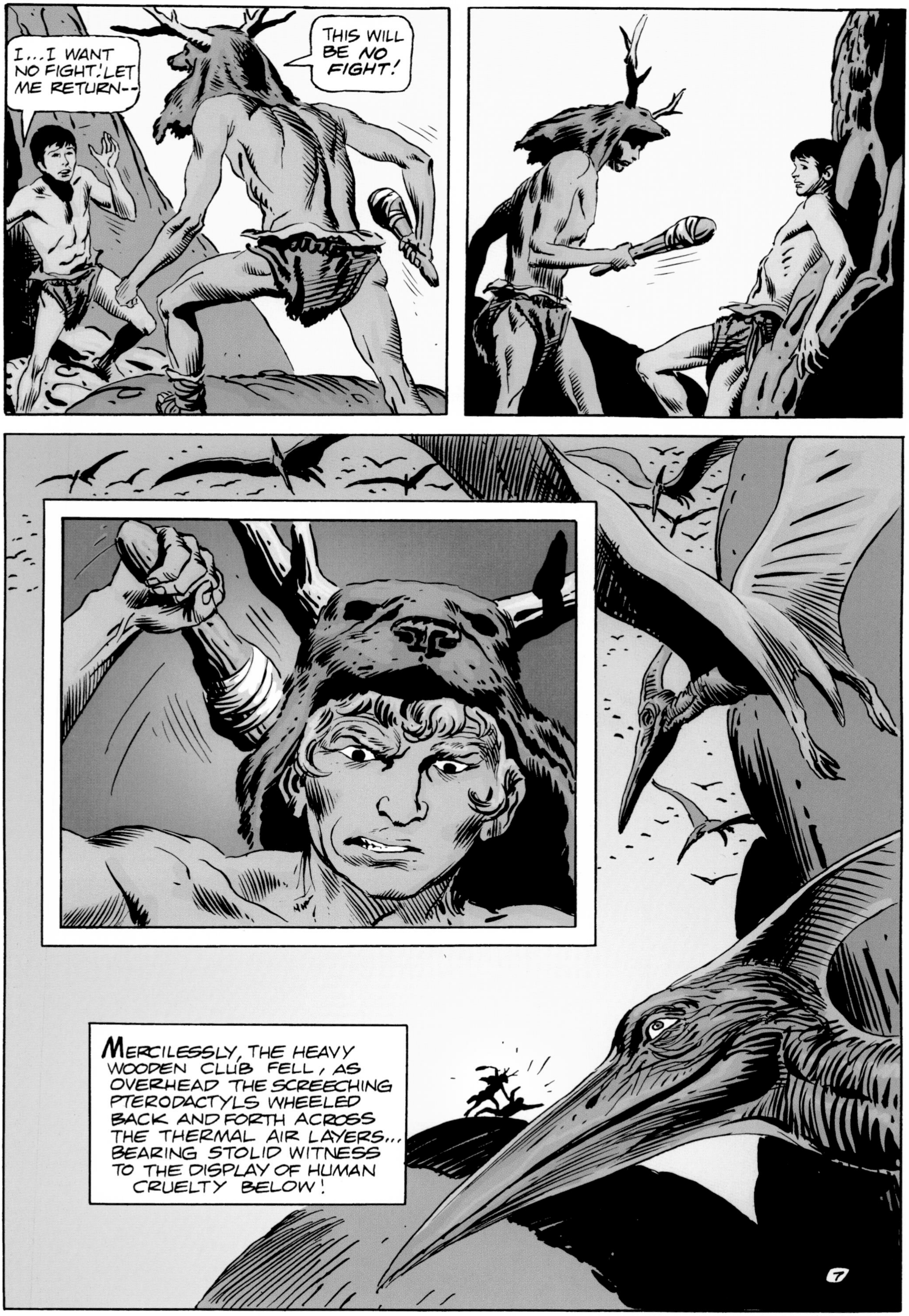
I...I WANT NO FIGHT! LET ME RETURN--
THIS WILL BE NO FIGHT!
MERCILESSLY, THE HEAVY WOODEN CLUB FELL, AS OVERHEAD THE SCREECHING PTERODACTYLS WHEELED BACK AND FORTH ACROSS THE THERMAL AIR LAYERS... BEARING STOLID WITNESS TO THE DISPLAY OF HUMAN CRUELTY BELOW!
7

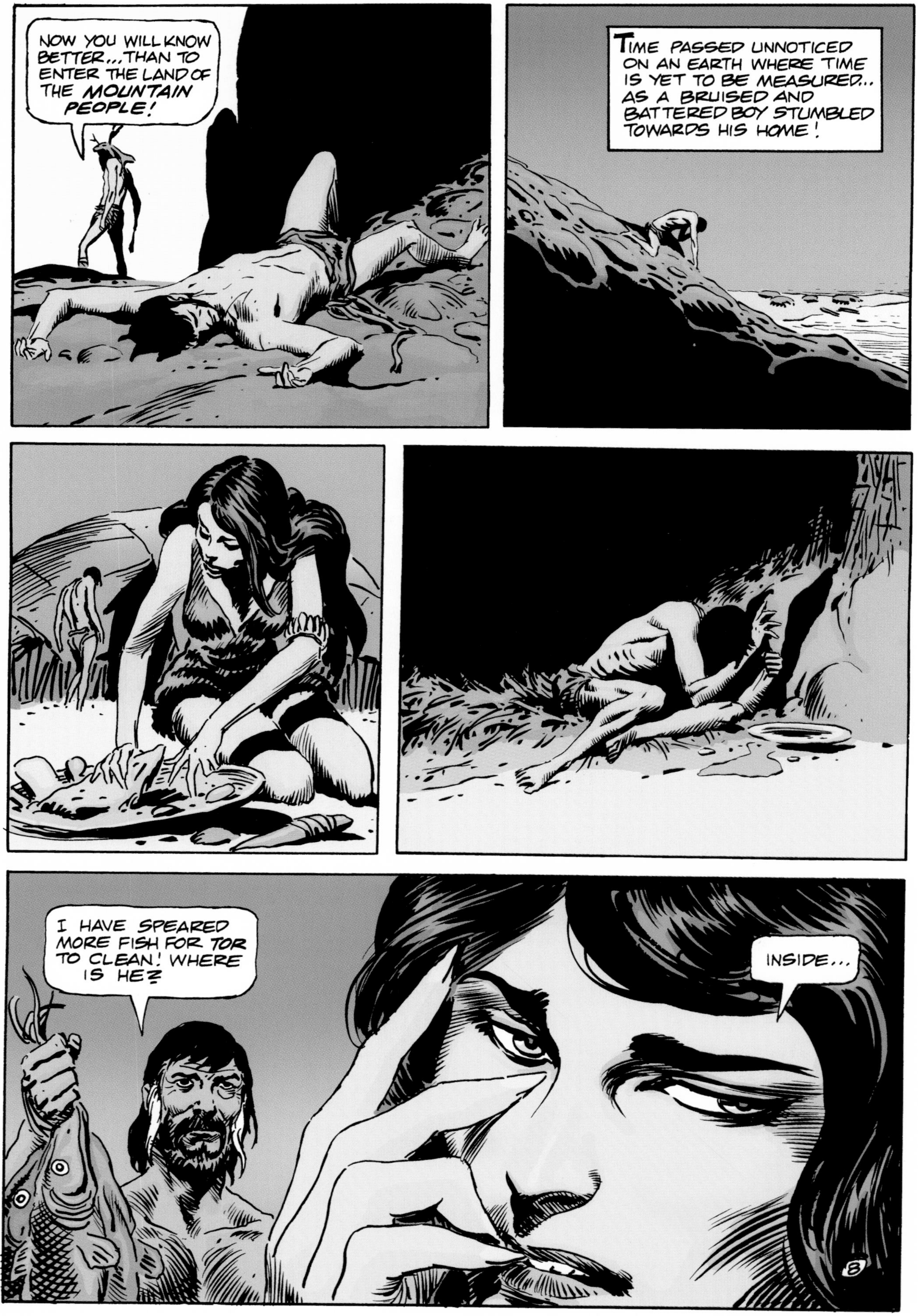
NOW YOU WILL KNOW BETTER... THAN TO ENTER THE LAND OF THE MOUNTAIN PEOPLE!
TIME PASSED UNNOTICED ON AN EARTH WHERE TIME IS YET TO BE MEASURED... AS A BRUISED AND BATTERED BOY STUMBLED TOWARDS HIS HOME!
I HAVE SPEARED MORE FISH FOR TOR TO CLEAN! WHERE IS HE?
INSIDE...
8

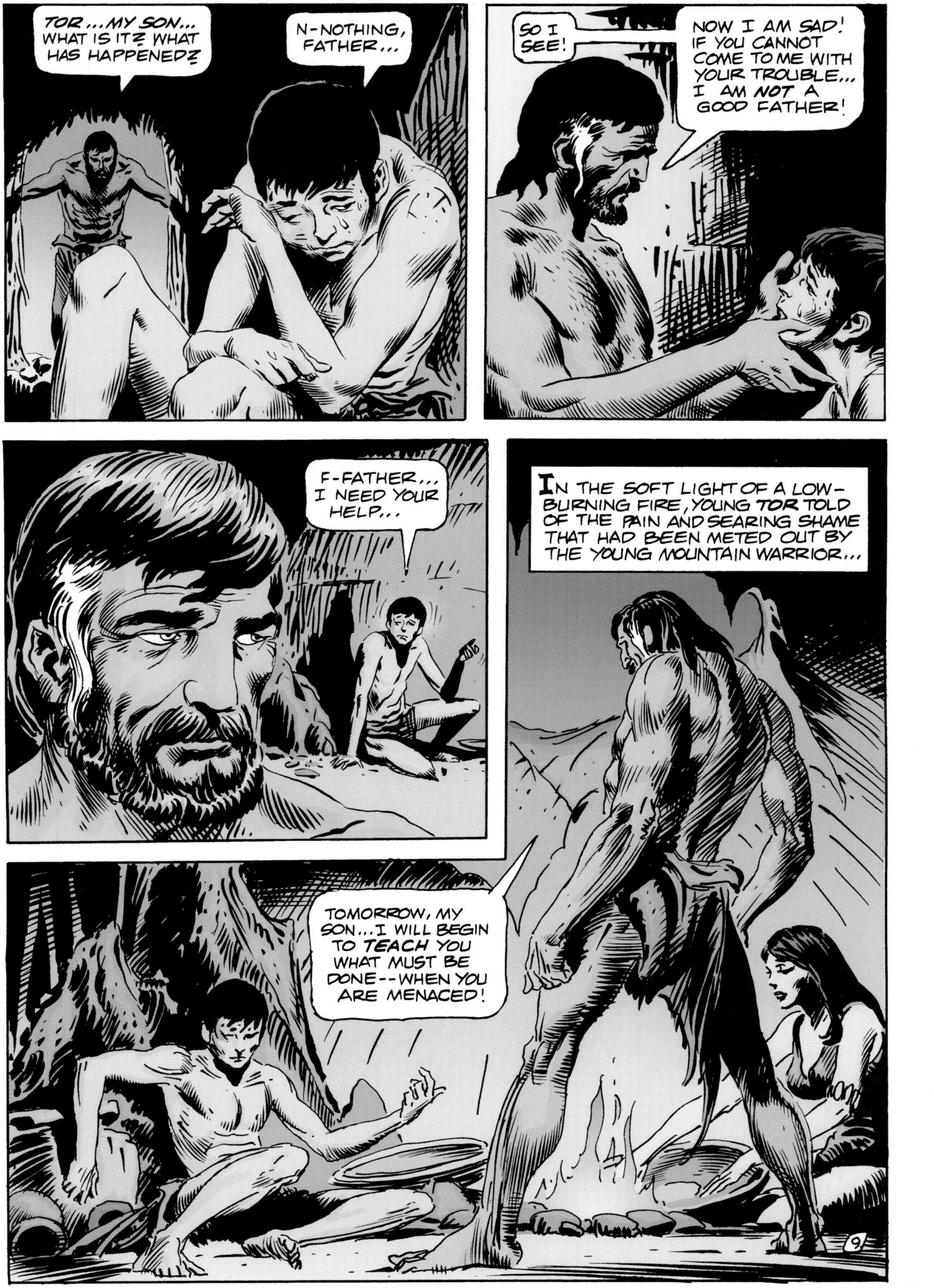
TOR... MY SON... WHAT IS IT? WHAT HAS HAPPENED?
N-NOTHING, FATHER...
SO I SEE!
NOW I AM SAD! IF YOU CANNOT COME TO ME WITH YOUR TROUBLE... I AM NOT A GOOD FATHER!
F-FATHER... I NEED YOUR HELP...
IN THE SOFT LIGHT OF A LOW-BURNING FIRE, YOUNG TOR TOLD OF THE PAIN AND SEARING SHAME THAT HAD BEEN METED OUT BY THE YOUNG MOUNTAIN WARRIOR...
TOMORROW, MY SON... I WILL BEGIN TO TEACH YOU WHAT MUST BE DONE--WHEN YOU ARE MENACED!
9

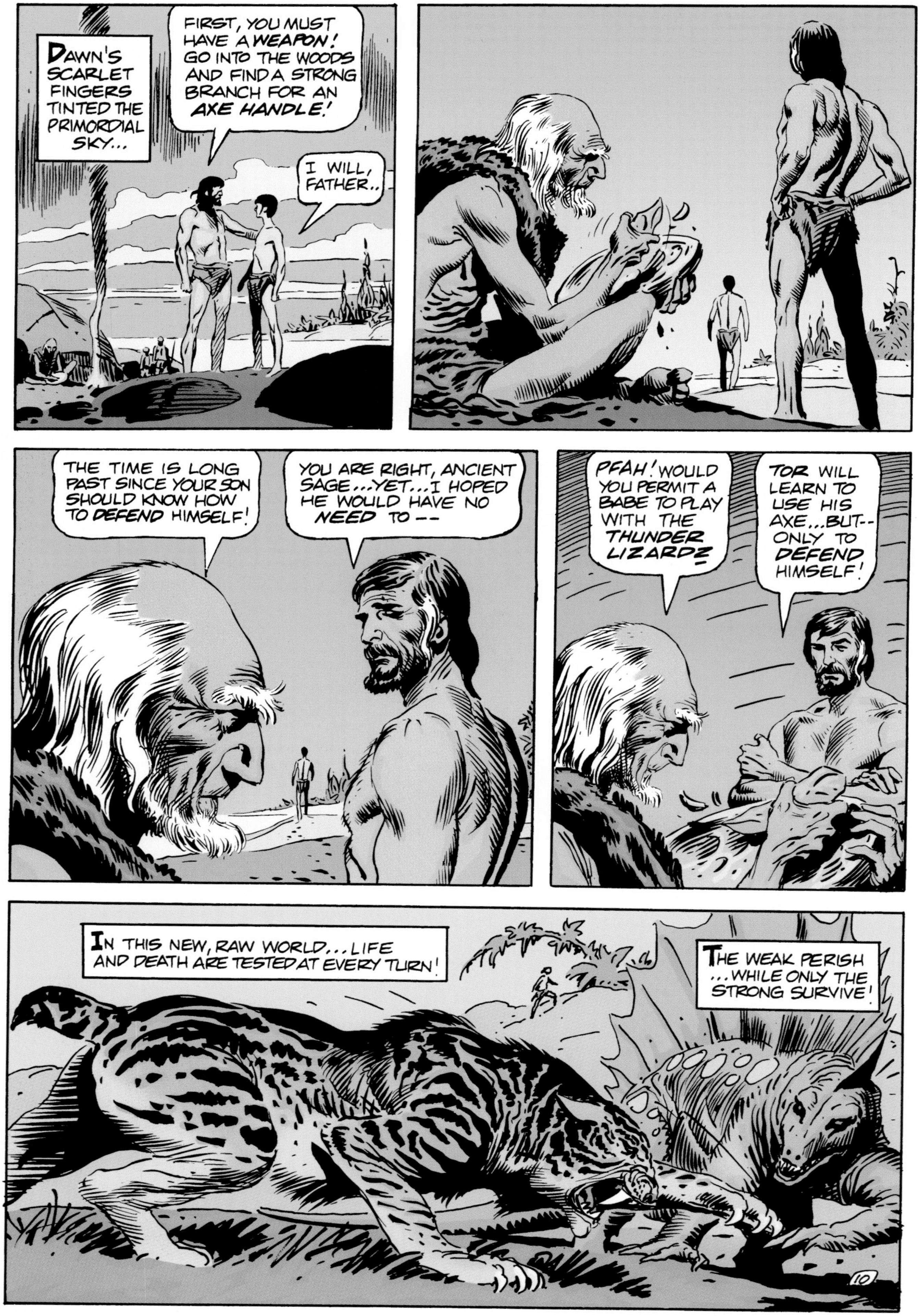
DAWN'S SCARLET FINGERS TINTED THE PRIMORDIAL SKY...
FIRST, YOU MUST HAVE A WEAPON! GO INTO THE WOODS AND FIND A STRONG BRANCH FOR AN AXE HANDLE!
I WILL, FATHER..
THE TIME IS LONG PAST SINCE YOUR SON SHOULD KNOW HOW TO DEFEND HIMSELF!
YOU ARE RIGHT, ANCIENT SAGE...YET...I HOPED HE WOULD HAVE NO NEED TO --
PFAH! WOULD YOU PERMIT A BABE TO PLAY WITH THE THUNDER LIZARDS?
TOR WILL LEARN TO USE HIS AXE...BUT-- ONLY TO DEFEND HIMSELF!
IN THIS NEW, RAW WORLD...LIFE AND DEATH ARE TESTED AT EVERY TURN!
THE WEAK PERISH ...WHILE ONLY THE STRONG SURVIVE!
10

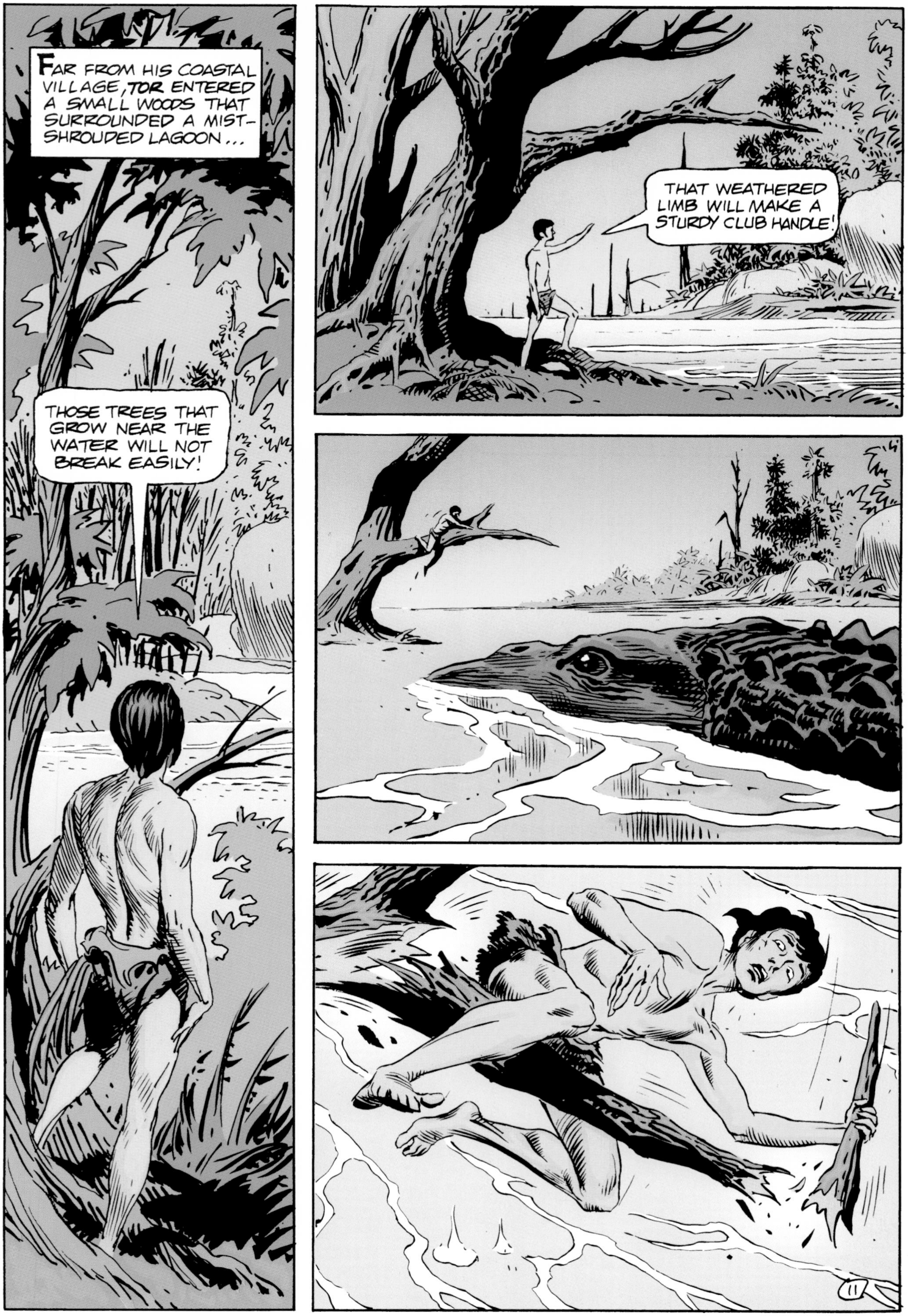
FAR FROM HIS COASTAL VILLAGE, TOR ENTERED A SMALL WOODS THAT SURROUNDED A MIST-SHROUDED LAGOON...
THOSE TREES THAT GROW NEAR THE WATER WILL NOT BREAK EASILY!
THAT WEATHERED LIMB WILL MAKE A STURDY CLUB HANDLE!
11

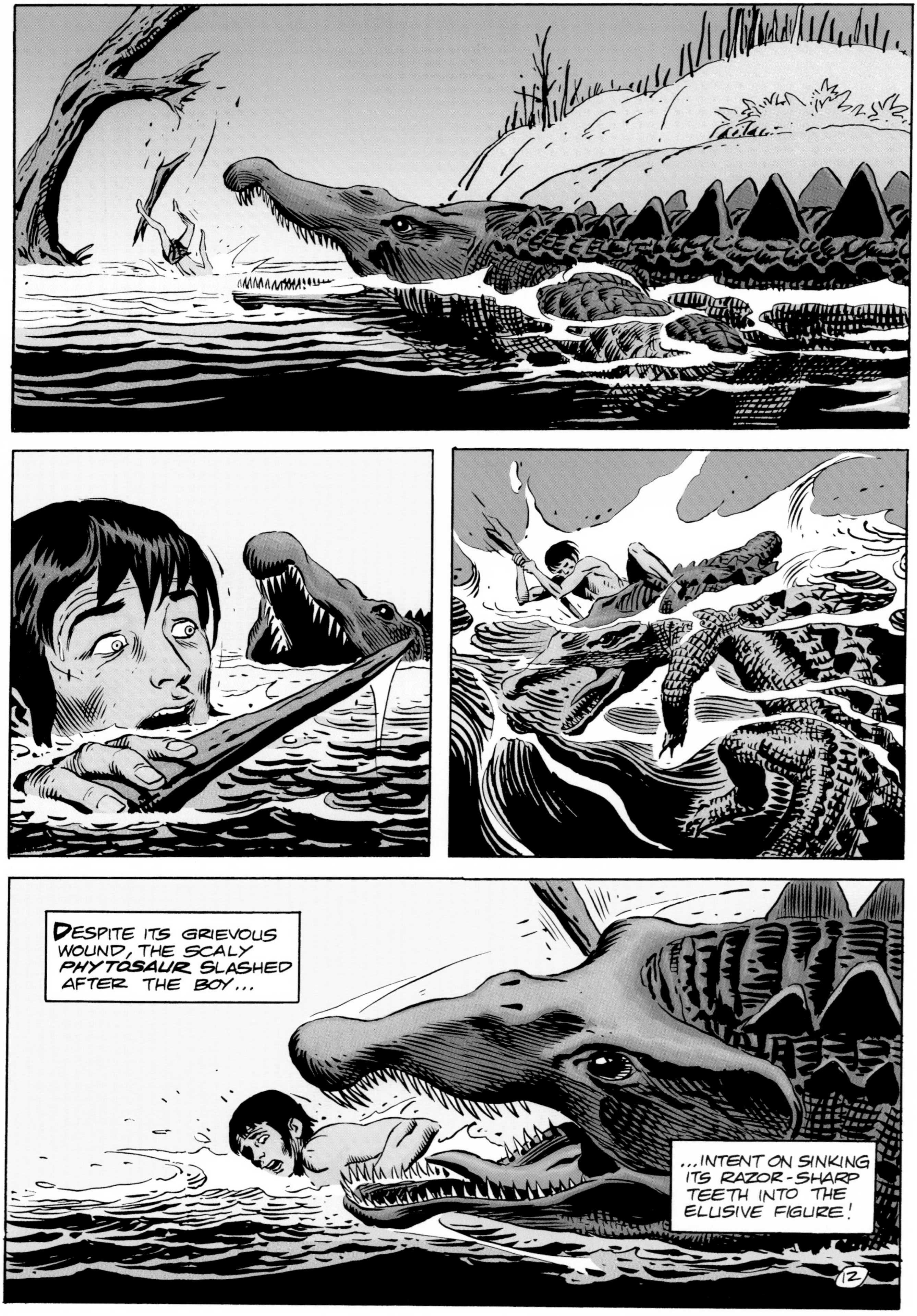
DESPITE ITS GRIEVOUS WOUND, THE SCALY PHYTOSAUR SLASHED AFTER THE BOY...
...INTENT ON SINKING ITS RAZOR-SHARP TEETH INTO THE ELUSIVE FIGURE!
12

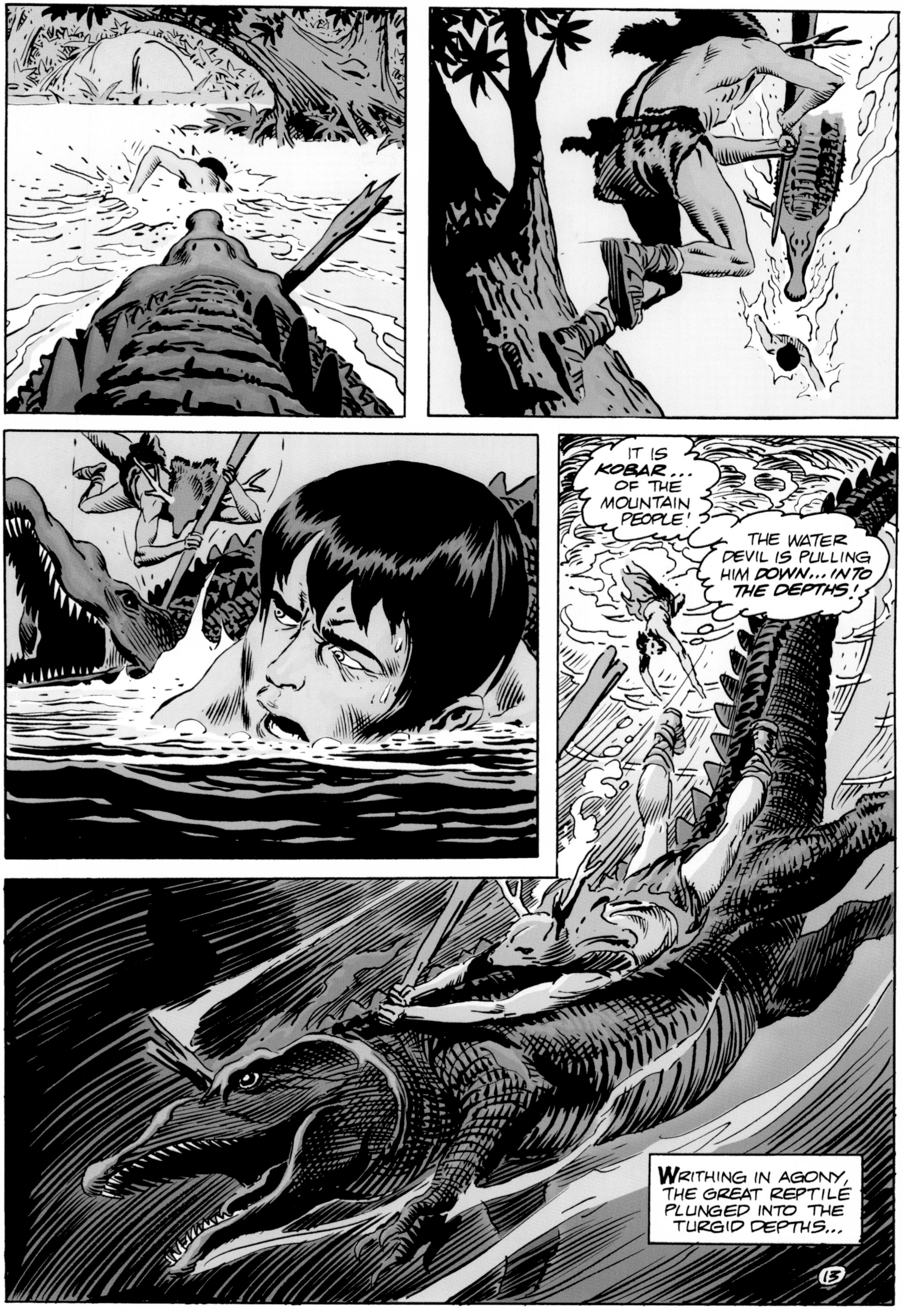
IT IS KOBAR... OF THE MOUNTAIN PEOPLE!
THE WATER DEVIL IS PULLING HIM DOWN... INTO THE DEPTHS!
WRITHING IN AGONY, THE GREAT REPTILE PLUNGED INTO THE TURGID DEPTHS...
13

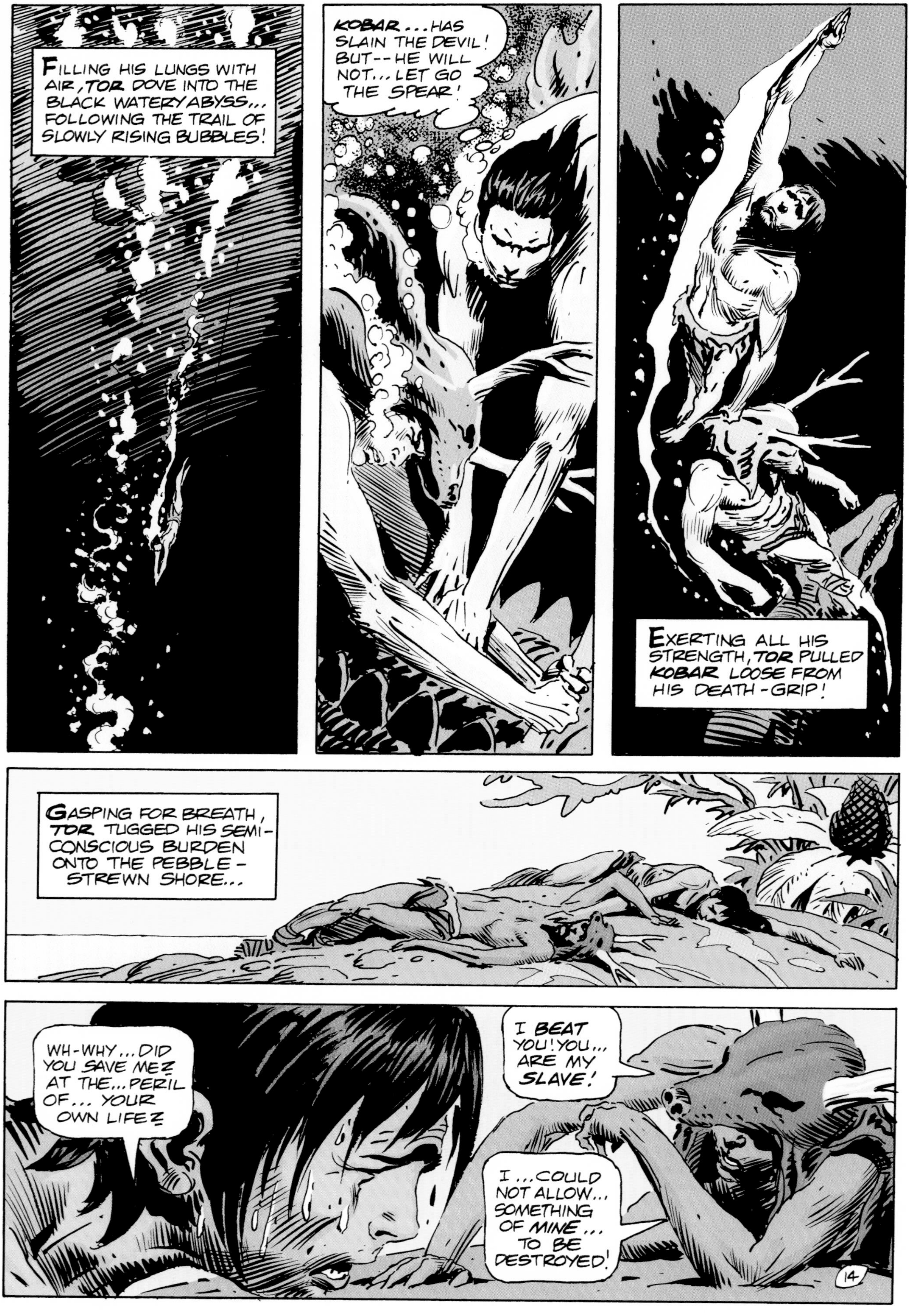
FILLING HIS LUNGS WITH AIR, TOR DOVE INTO THE BLACK WATERY ABYSS... FOLLOWING THE TRAIL OF SLOWLY RISING BUBBLES!
KOBAR...HAS SLAIN THE DEVIL! BUT--HE WILL NOT...LET GO THE SPEAR!
EXERTING ALL HIS STRENGTH, TOR PULLED KOBAR LOOSE FROM HIS DEATH-GRIP!
GASPING FOR BREATH, TOR TUGGED HIS SEMI-CONSCIOUS BURDEN ONTO THE PEBBLE-STREWN SHORE...
WH-WHY...DID YOU SAVE ME? AT THE...PERIL OF... YOUR OWN LIFE?
I BEAT YOU! YOU... ARE MY SLAVE!
I...COULD NOT ALLOW... SOMETHING OF MINE... TO BE DESTROYED!
14

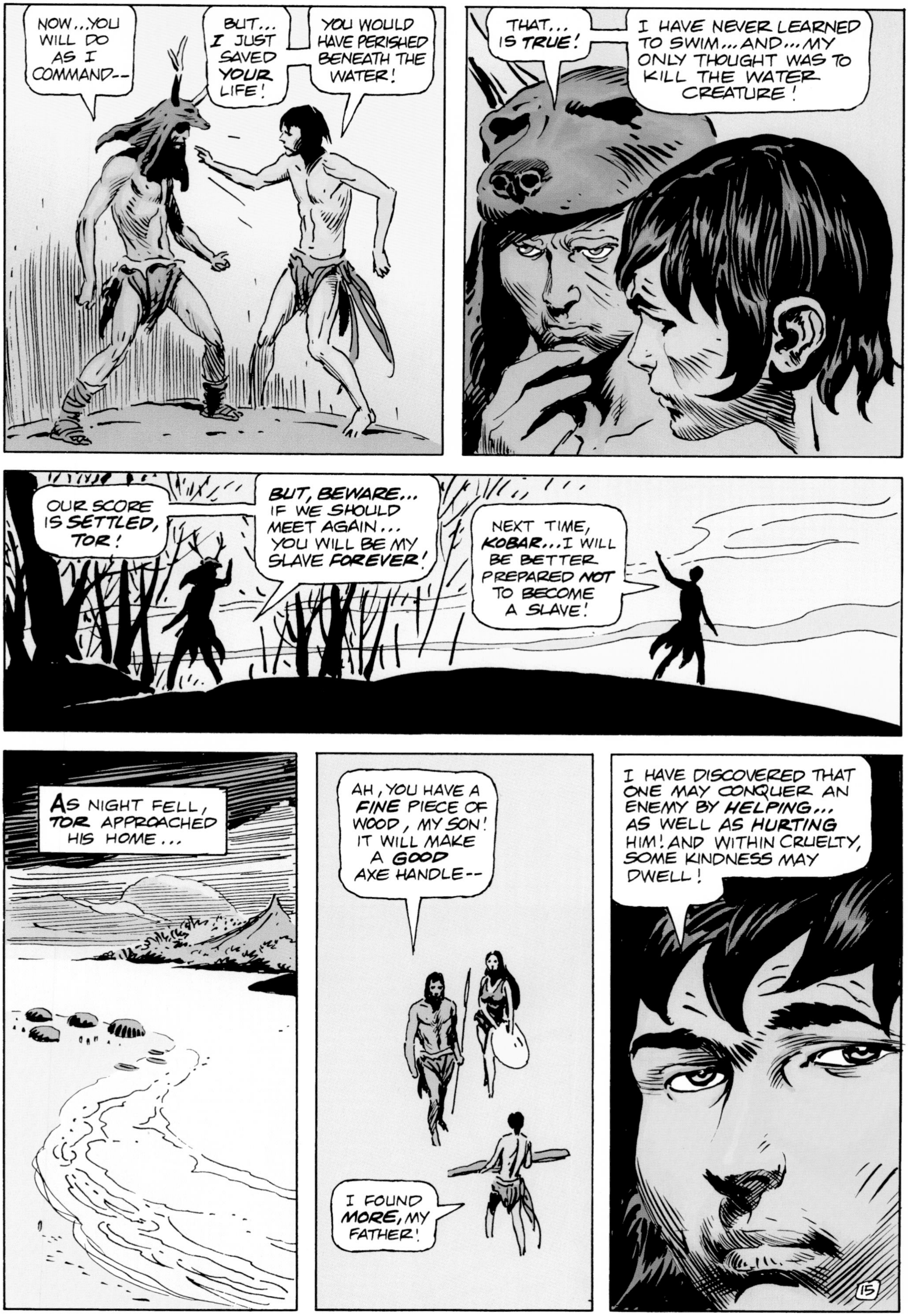
NOW...YOU WILL DO AS I COMMAND--
BUT... I JUST SAVED YOUR LIFE!
YOU WOULD HAVE PERISHED BENEATH THE WATER!
THAT... IS TRUE!
I HAVE NEVER LEARNED TO SWIM...AND...MY ONLY THOUGHT WAS TO KILL THE WATER CREATURE!
OUR SCORE IS SETTLED, TOR!
BUT, BEWARE... IF WE SHOULD MEET AGAIN... YOU WILL BE MY SLAVE FOREVER!
NEXT TIME, KOBAR...I WILL BE BETTER PREPARED NOT TO BECOME A SLAVE!
AS NIGHT FELL, TOR APPROACHED HIS HOME...
AH, YOU HAVE A FINE PIECE OF WOOD, MY SON! IT WILL MAKE A GOOD AXE HANDLE--
I FOUND MORE, MY FATHER!
I HAVE DISCOVERED THAT ONE MAY CONQUER AN ENEMY BY HELPING... AS WELL AS HURTING HIM! AND WITHIN CRUELTY, SOME KINDNESS MAY DWELL!
15

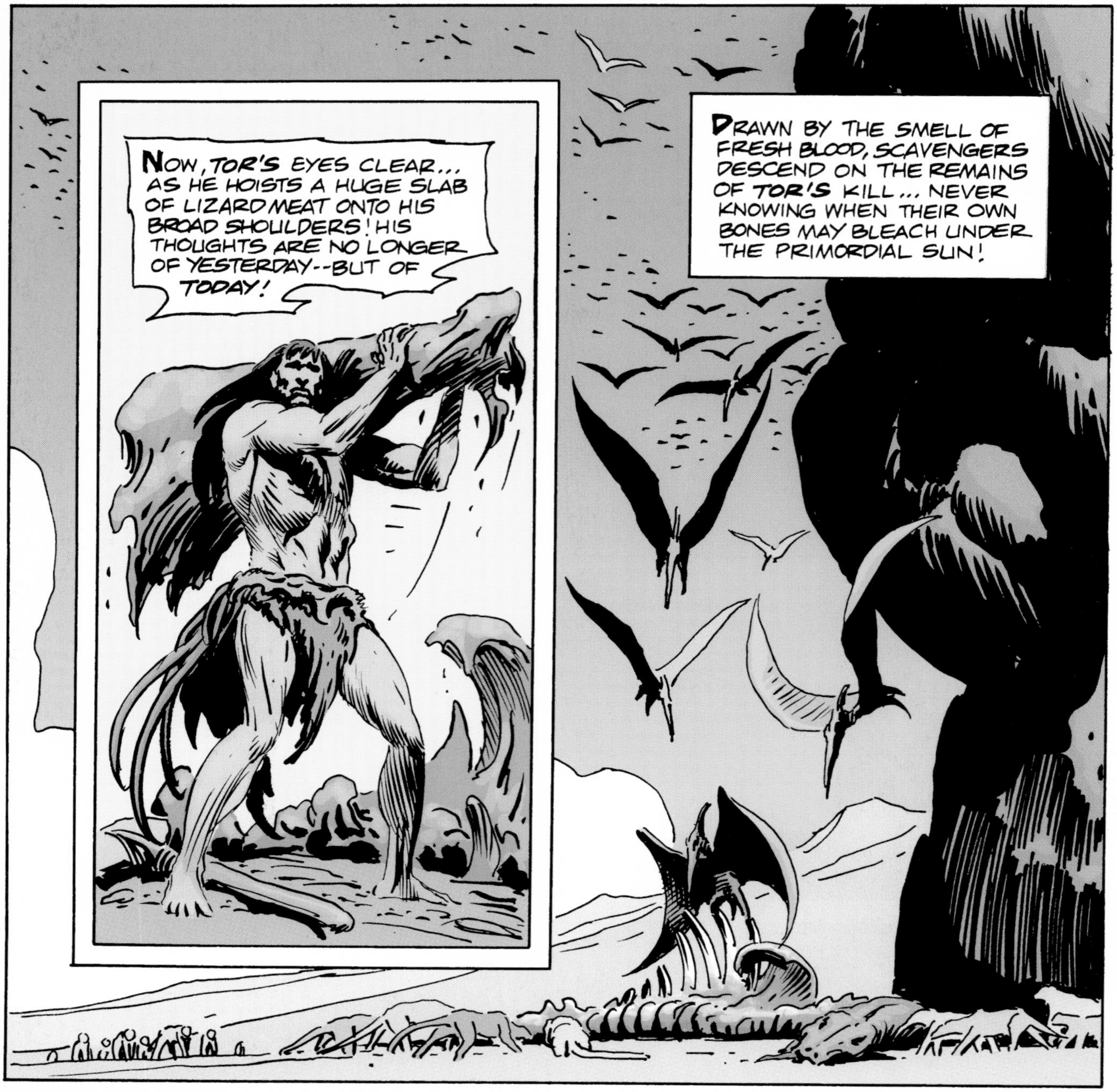
NOW, TOR'S EYES CLEAR... AS HE HOISTS A HUGE SLAB OF LIZARD MEAT ONTO HIS BROAD SHOULDERS! HIS THOUGHTS ARE NO LONGER OF YESTERDAY--BUT OF TODAY!
DRAWN BY THE SMELL OF FRESH BLOOD, SCAVENGERS DESCEND ON THE REMAINS OF TOR'S KILL... NEVER KNOWING WHEN THEIR OWN BONES MAY BLEACH UNDER THE PRIMORDIAL SUN!

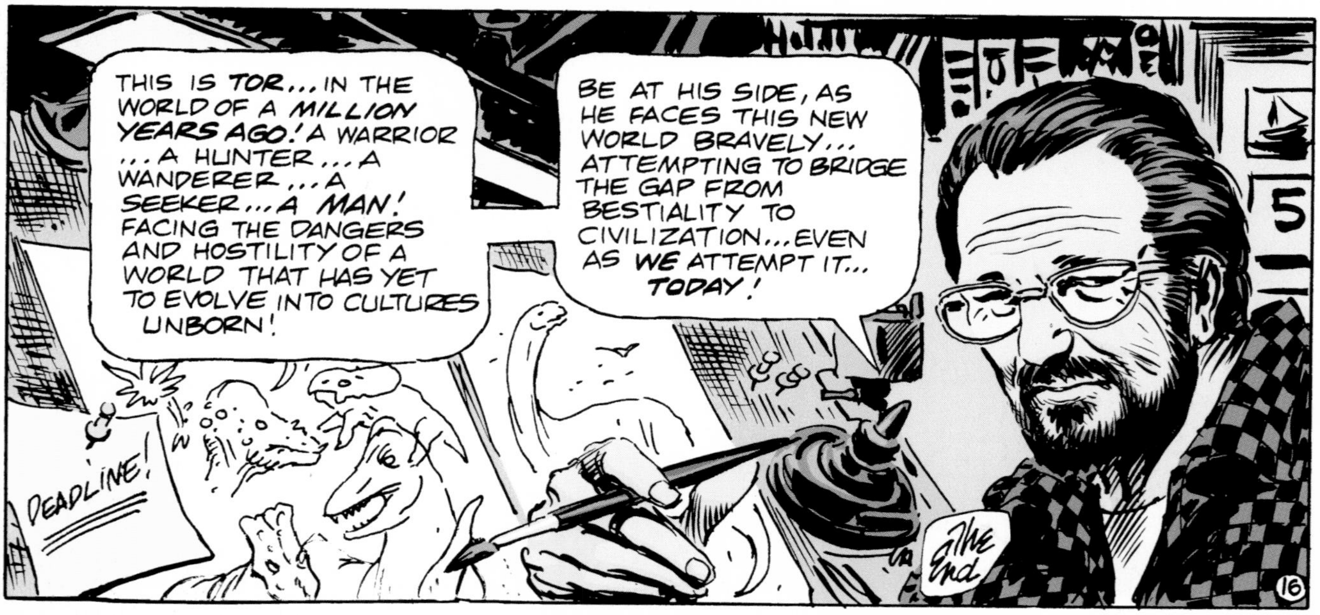
THIS IS TOR... IN THE WORLD OF A MILLION YEARS AGO! A WARRIOR ...A HUNTER... A WANDERER... A SEEKER... A MAN! FACING THE DANGERS AND HOSTILITY OF A WORLD THAT HAS YET TO EVOLVE INTO CULTURES UNBORN!
BE AT HIS SIDE, AS HE FACES THIS NEW WORLD BRAVELY... ATTEMPTING TO BRIDGE THE GAP FROM BESTIALITY TO CIVILIZATION... EVEN AS WE ATTEMPT IT... TODAY!
DEADLINE!
5
The End
16

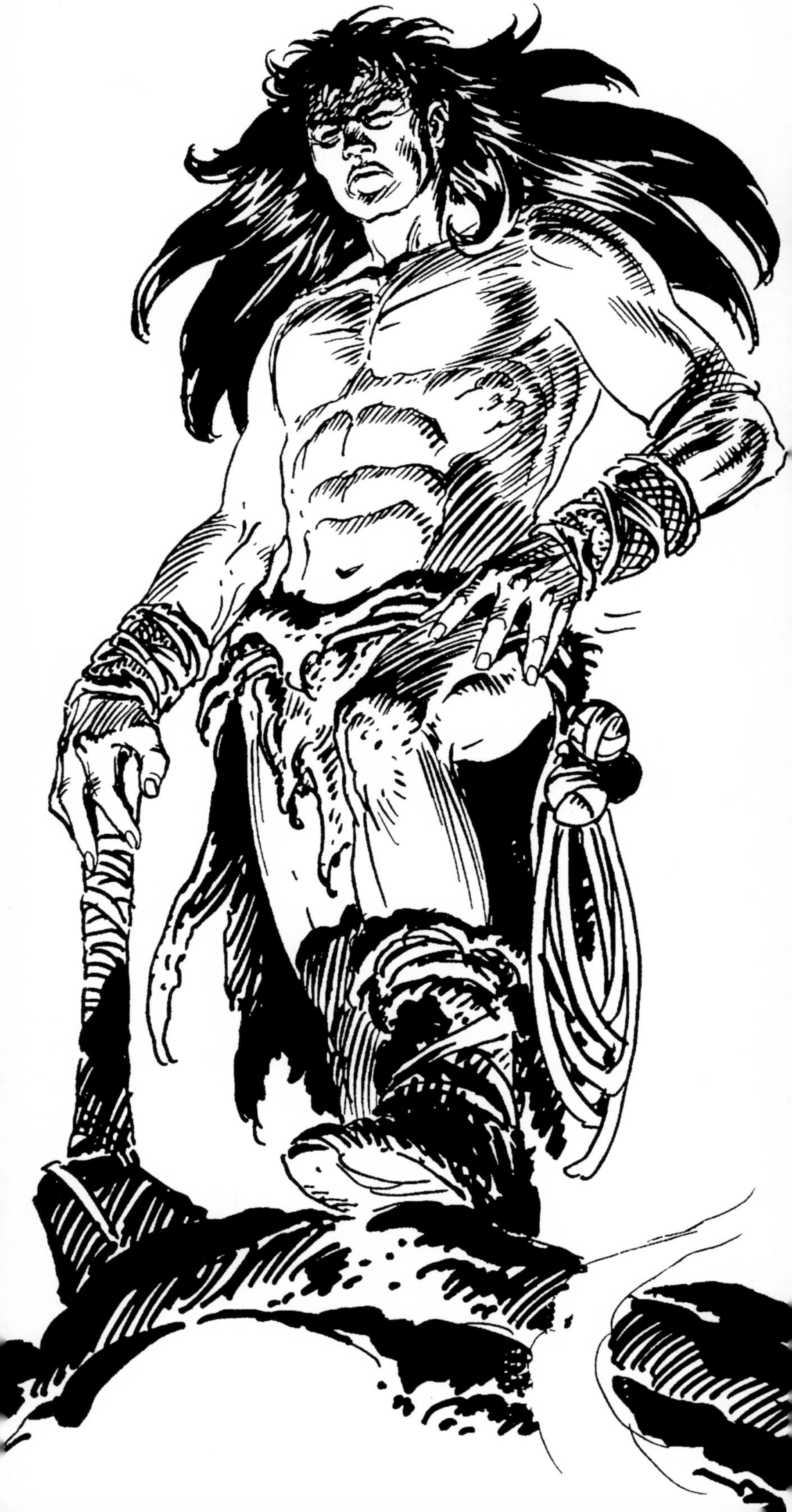

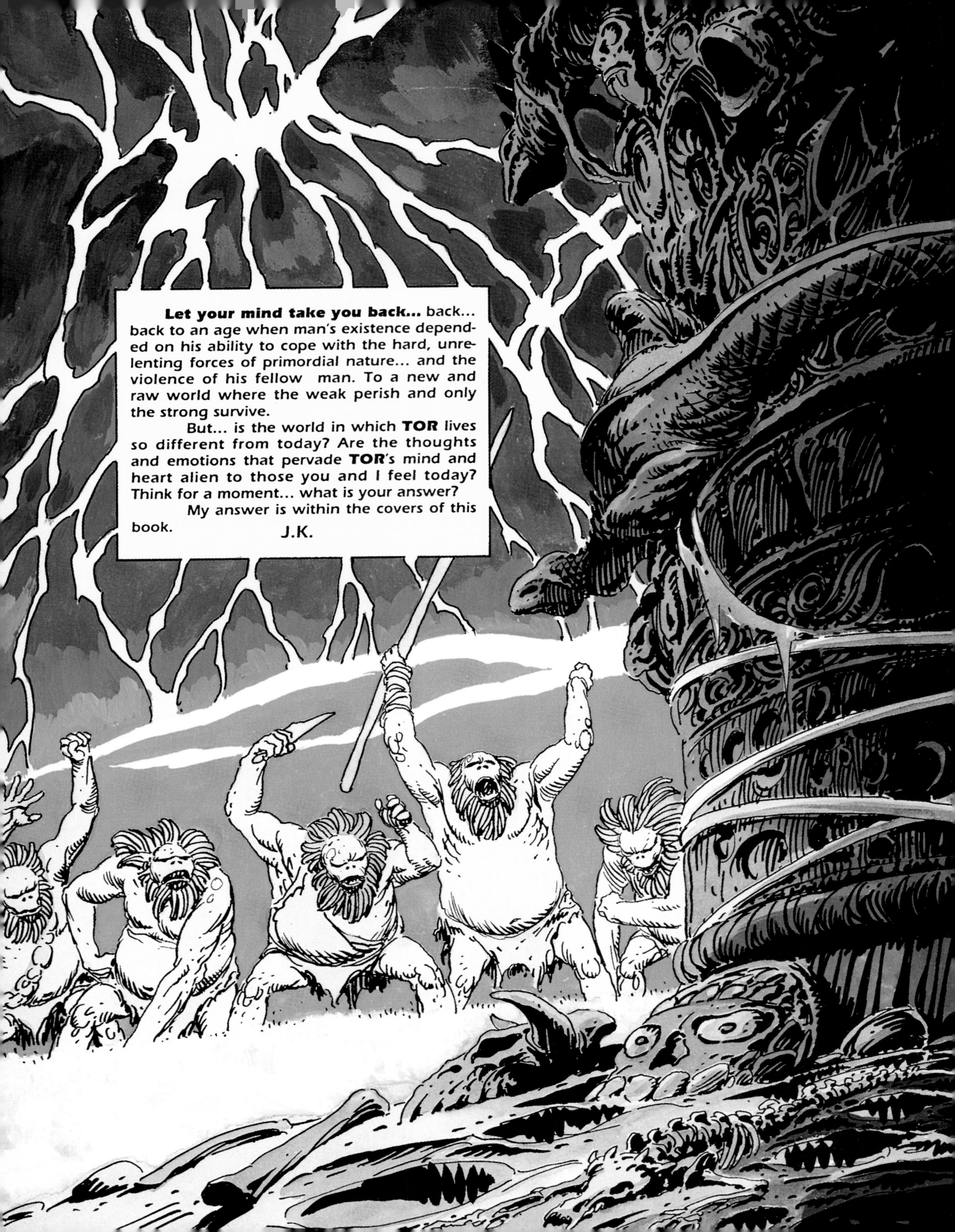
Let your mind take you back... back... back to an age when man's existence depended on his ability to cope with the hard, unrelenting forces of primordial nature... and the violence of his fellow man. To a new and raw world where the weak perish and only the strong survive.
But... is the world in which **TOR** lives so different from today? Are the thoughts and emotions that pervade **TOR**'s mind and heart alien to those you and I feel today? Think for a moment... what is your answer?
My answer is within the covers of this book.
J.K.

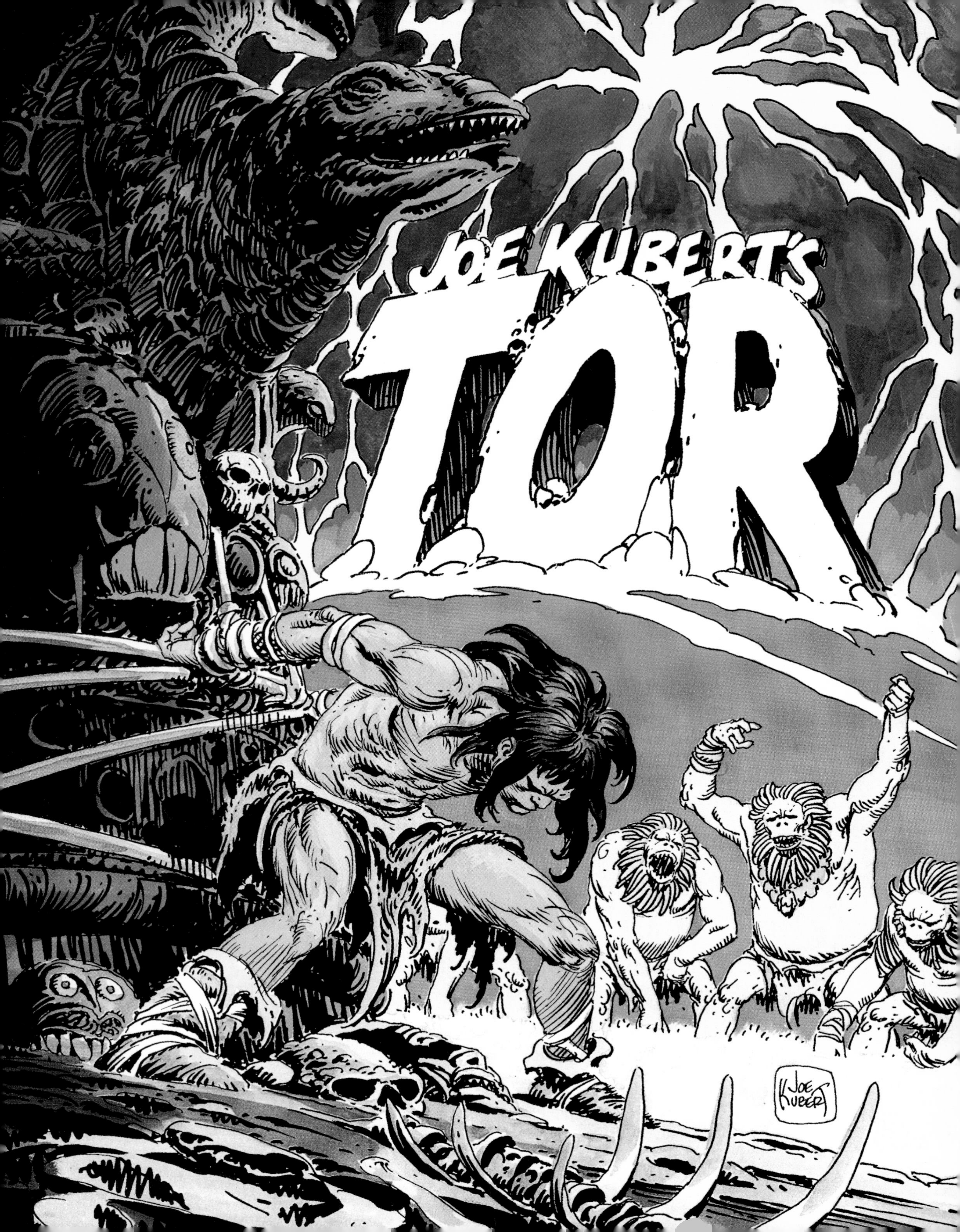
JOE KUBERT'S
TOR
JOE KUBERT

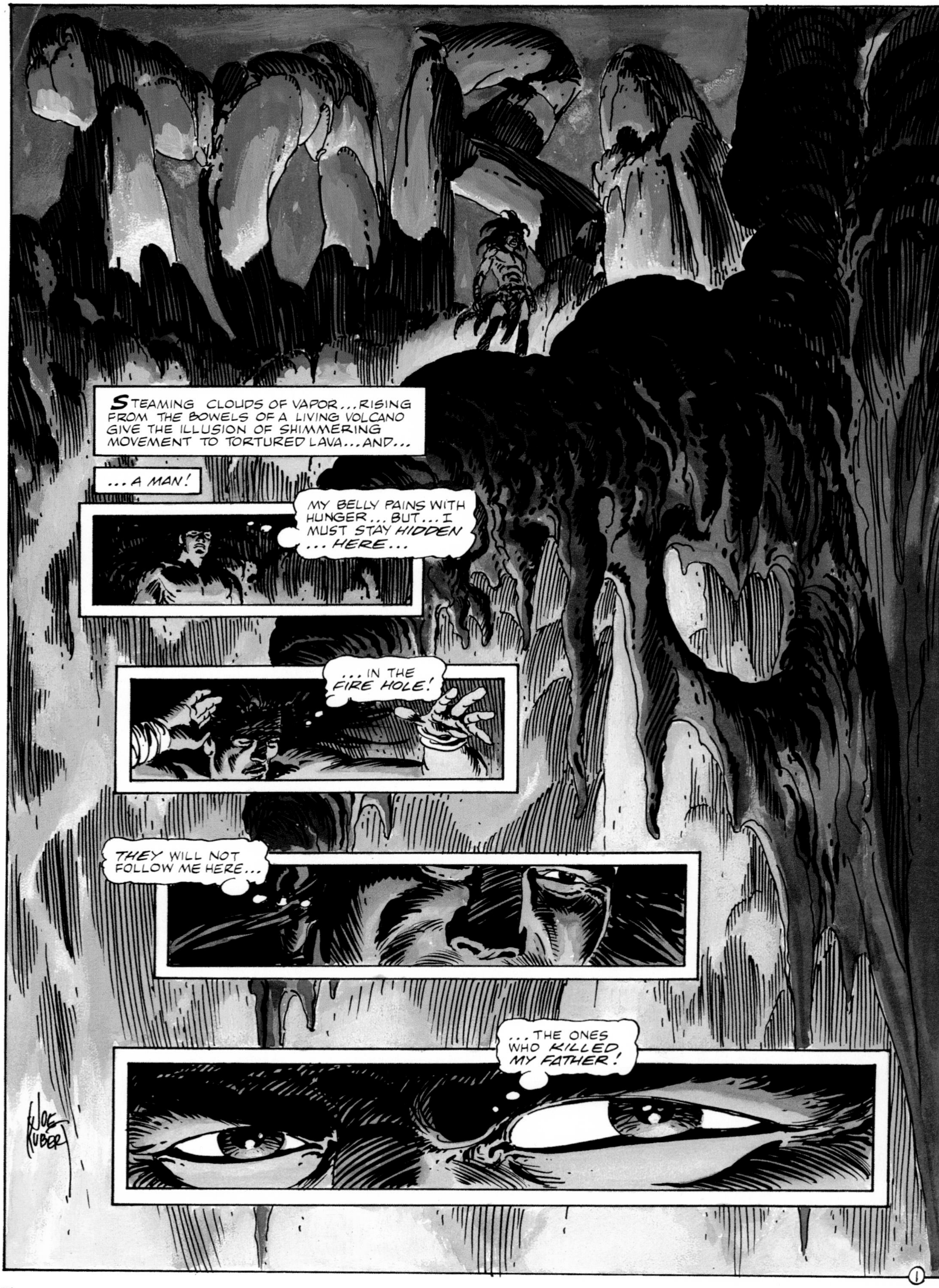

STEAMING CLOUDS OF VAPOR... RISING FROM THE BOWELS OF A LIVING VOLCANO GIVE THE ILLUSION OF SHIMMERING MOVEMENT TO TORTURED LAVA... AND...
...A MAN!
MY BELLY PAINS WITH HUNGER... BUT... I MUST STAY HIDDEN ... HERE...
...IN THE FIRE HOLE!
THEY WILL NOT FOLLOW ME HERE...
...THE ONES WHO KILLED MY FATHER!
JOE KUBERT
1

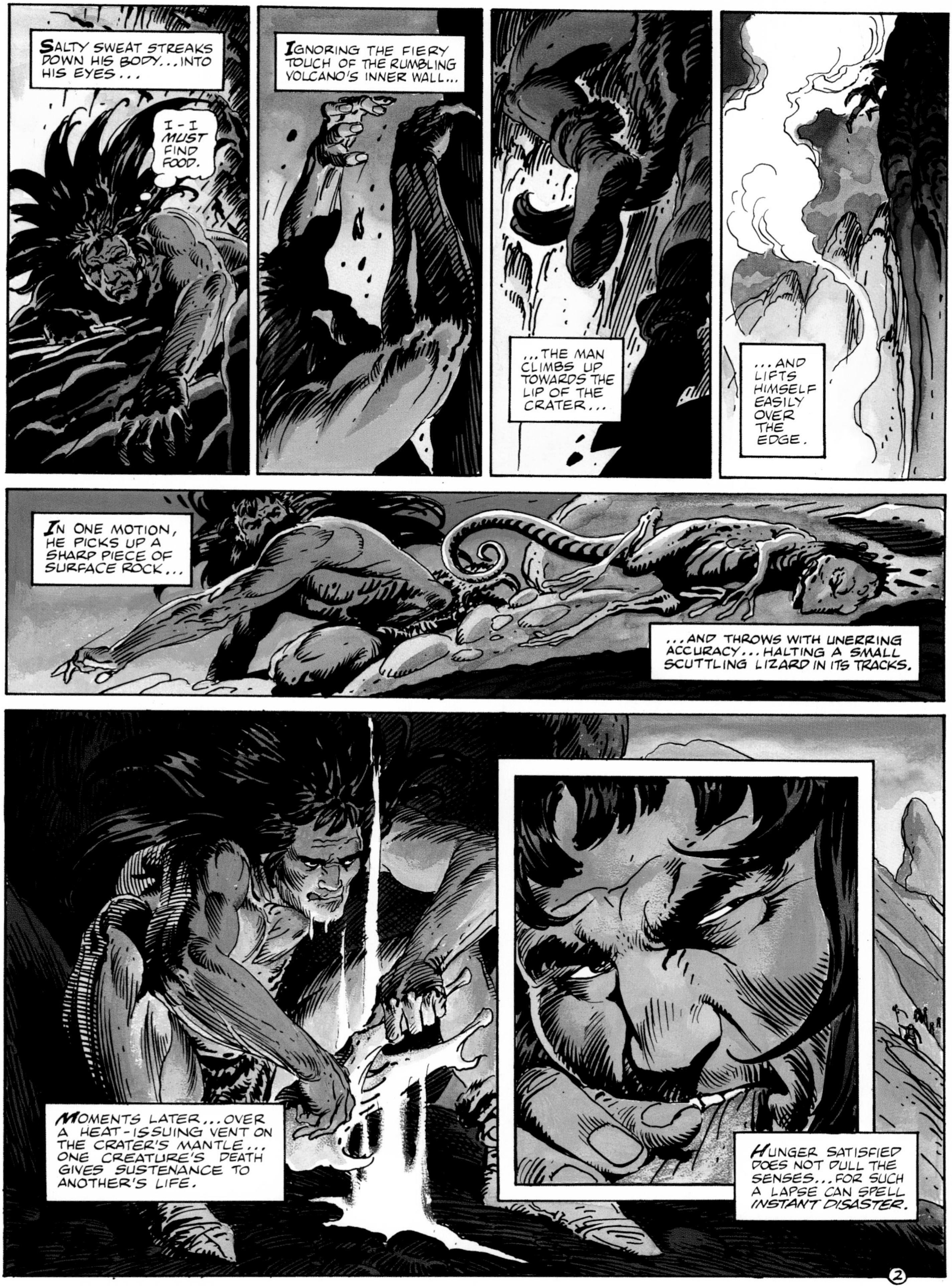
SALTY SWEAT STREAKS DOWN HIS BODY... INTO HIS EYES...
I-I MUST FIND FOOD.
IGNORING THE FIERY TOUCH OF THE RUMBLING VOLCANO'S INNER WALL...
...THE MAN CLIMBS UP TOWARDS THE LIP OF THE CRATER...
...AND LIFTS HIMSELF EASILY OVER THE EDGE.
IN ONE MOTION, HE PICKS UP A SHARP PIECE OF SURFACE ROCK...
...AND THROWS WITH UNERRING ACCURACY... HALTING A SMALL SCUTTLING LIZARD IN ITS TRACKS.
MOMENTS LATER... OVER A HEAT-ISSUING VENT ON THE CRATER'S MANTLE... ONE CREATURE'S DEATH GIVES SUSTENANCE TO ANOTHER'S LIFE.
HUNGER SATISFIED DOES NOT DULL THE SENSES... FOR SUCH A LAPSE CAN SPELL INSTANT DISASTER.
2

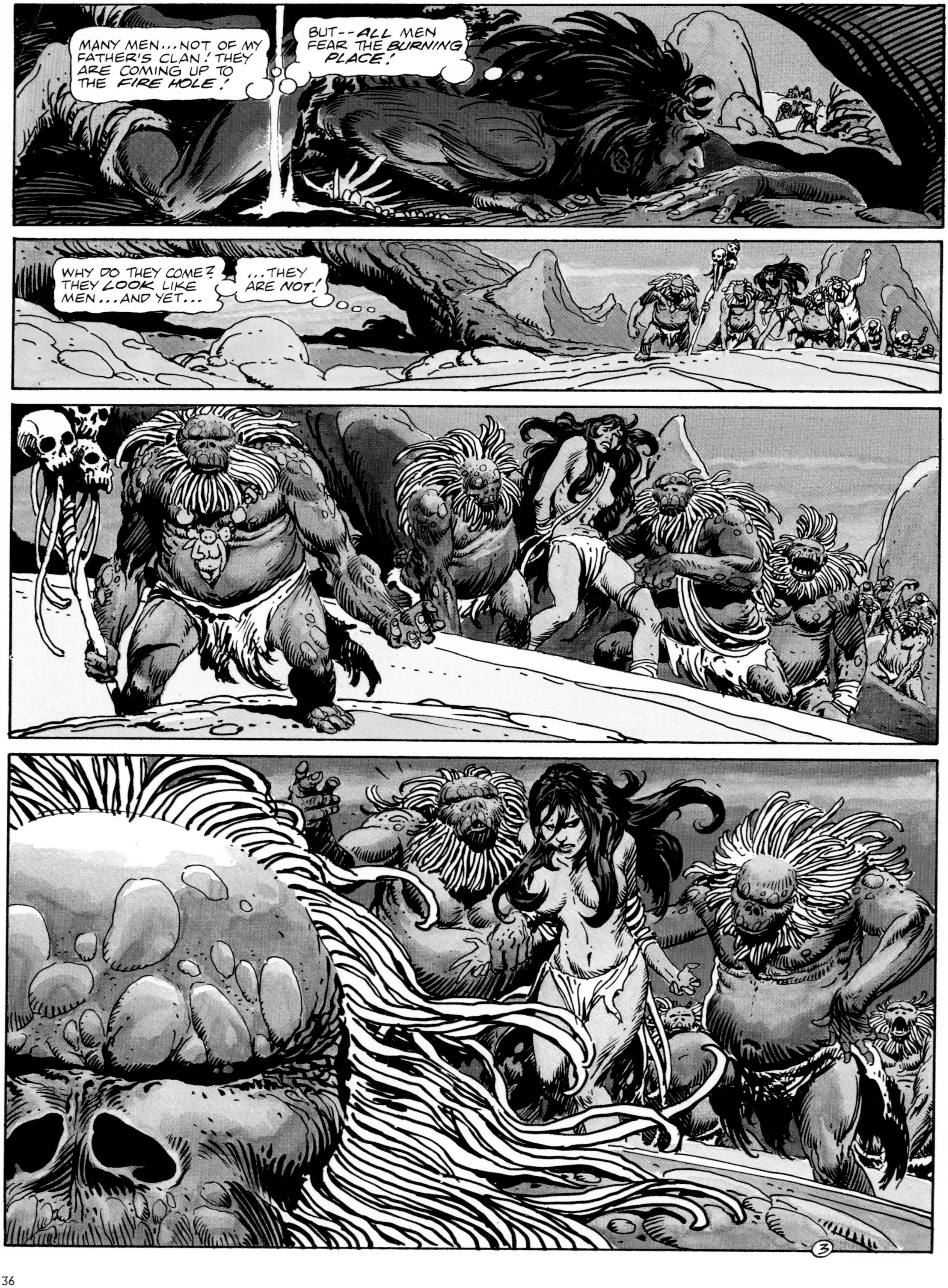
MANY MEN... NOT OF MY FATHER'S CLAN! THEY ARE COMING UP TO THE FIRE HOLE!
BUT--ALL MEN FEAR THE BURNING PLACE!
WHY DO THEY COME? THEY LOOK LIKE MEN... AND YET...
...THEY ARE NOT!
3

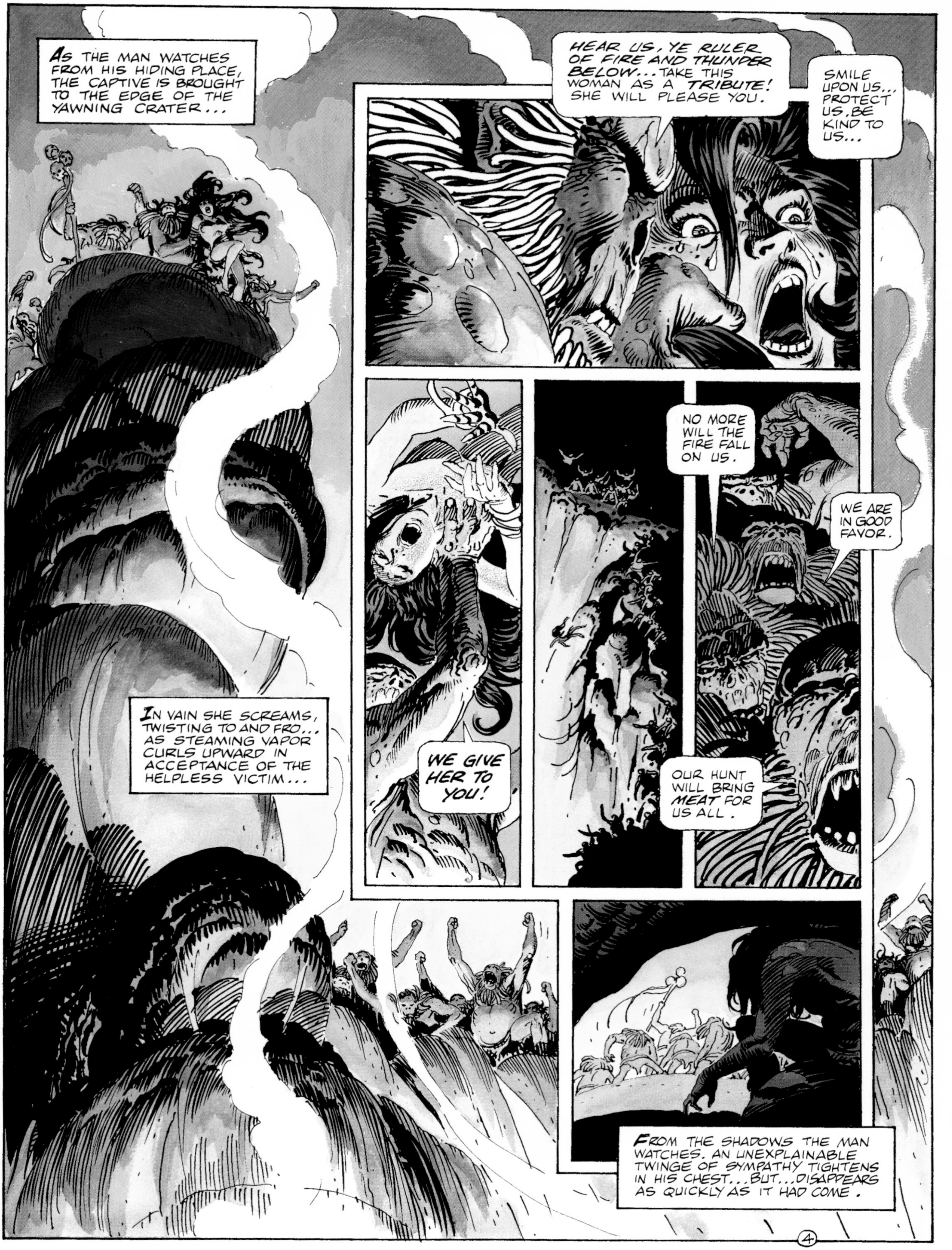
AS THE MAN WATCHES FROM HIS HIDING PLACE, THE CAPTIVE IS BROUGHT TO THE EDGE OF THE YAWNING CRATER...
HEAR US, YE RULER OF FIRE AND THUNDER BELOW... TAKE THIS WOMAN AS A TRIBUTE! SHE WILL PLEASE YOU.
SMILE UPON US... PROTECT US, BE KIND TO US...
NO MORE WILL THE FIRE FALL ON US.
WE ARE IN GOOD FAVOR.
IN VAIN SHE SCREAMS, TWISTING TO AND FRO... AS STEAMING VAPOR CURLS UPWARD IN ACCEPTANCE OF THE HELPLESS VICTIM...
WE GIVE HER TO YOU!
OUR HUNT WILL BRING MEAT FOR US ALL.
FROM THE SHADOWS THE MAN WATCHES. AN UNEXPLAINABLE TWINGE OF SYMPATHY TIGHTENS IN HIS CHEST... BUT... DISAPPEARS AS QUICKLY AS IT HAD COME.
4

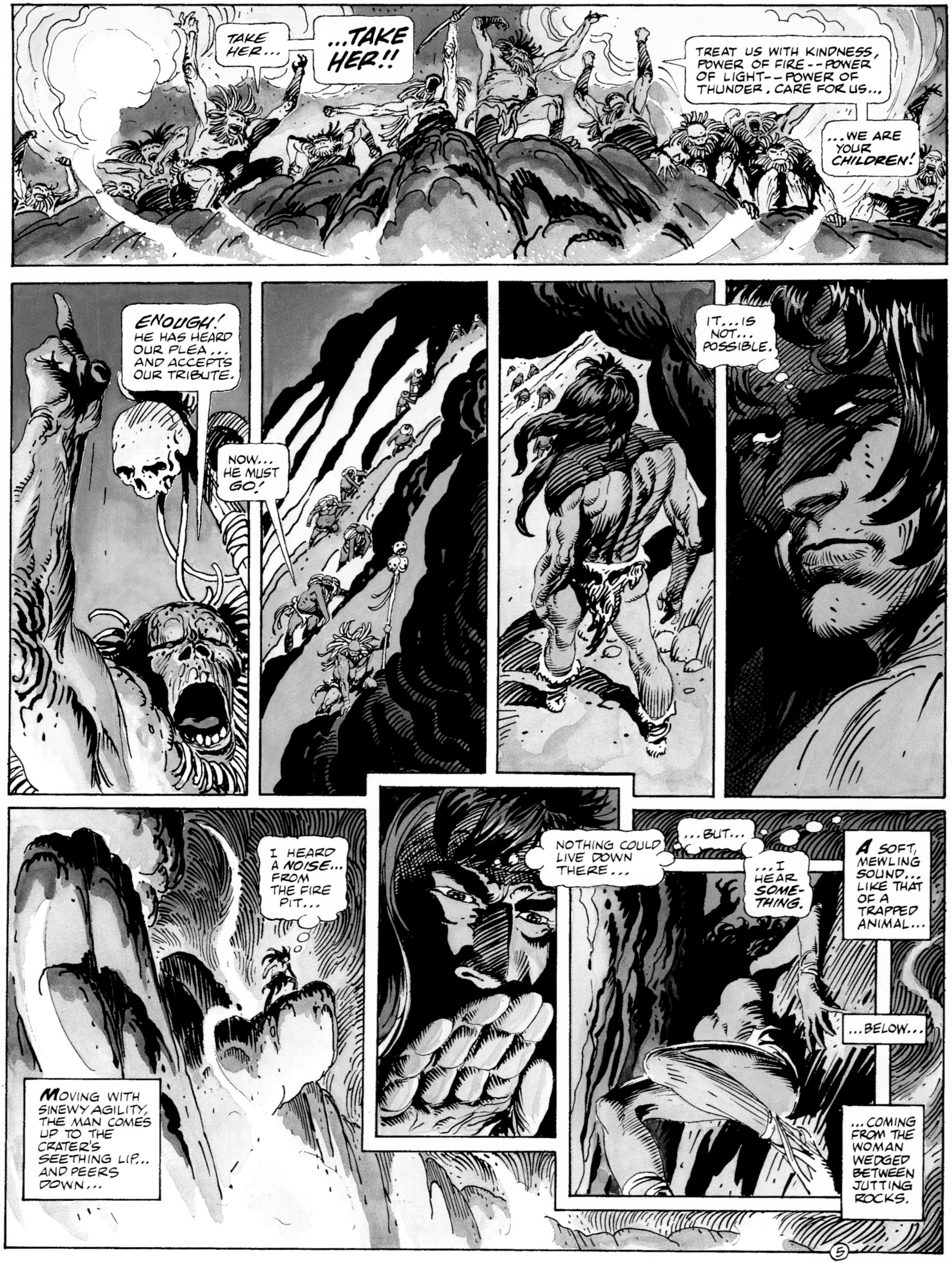
TAKE HER...
...TAKE HER!!
TREAT US WITH KINDNESS, POWER OF FIRE--POWER OF LIGHT--POWER OF THUNDER. CARE FOR US...
...WE ARE YOUR CHILDREN!
ENOUGH! HE HAS HEARD OUR PLEA... AND ACCEPTS OUR TRIBUTE.
NOW... HE MUST GO!
IT... IS NOT... POSSIBLE.
I HEARD A NOISE... FROM THE FIRE PIT...
MOVING WITH SINEWY AGILITY, THE MAN COMES UP TO THE CRATER'S SEETHING LIP... AND PEERS DOWN...
NOTHING COULD LIVE DOWN THERE...
...BUT...
...I HEAR SOMETHING.
A SOFT, MEWLING SOUND... LIKE THAT OF A TRAPPED ANIMAL...
...BELOW...
...COMING FROM THE WOMAN WEDGED BETWEEN JUTTING ROCKS.
5

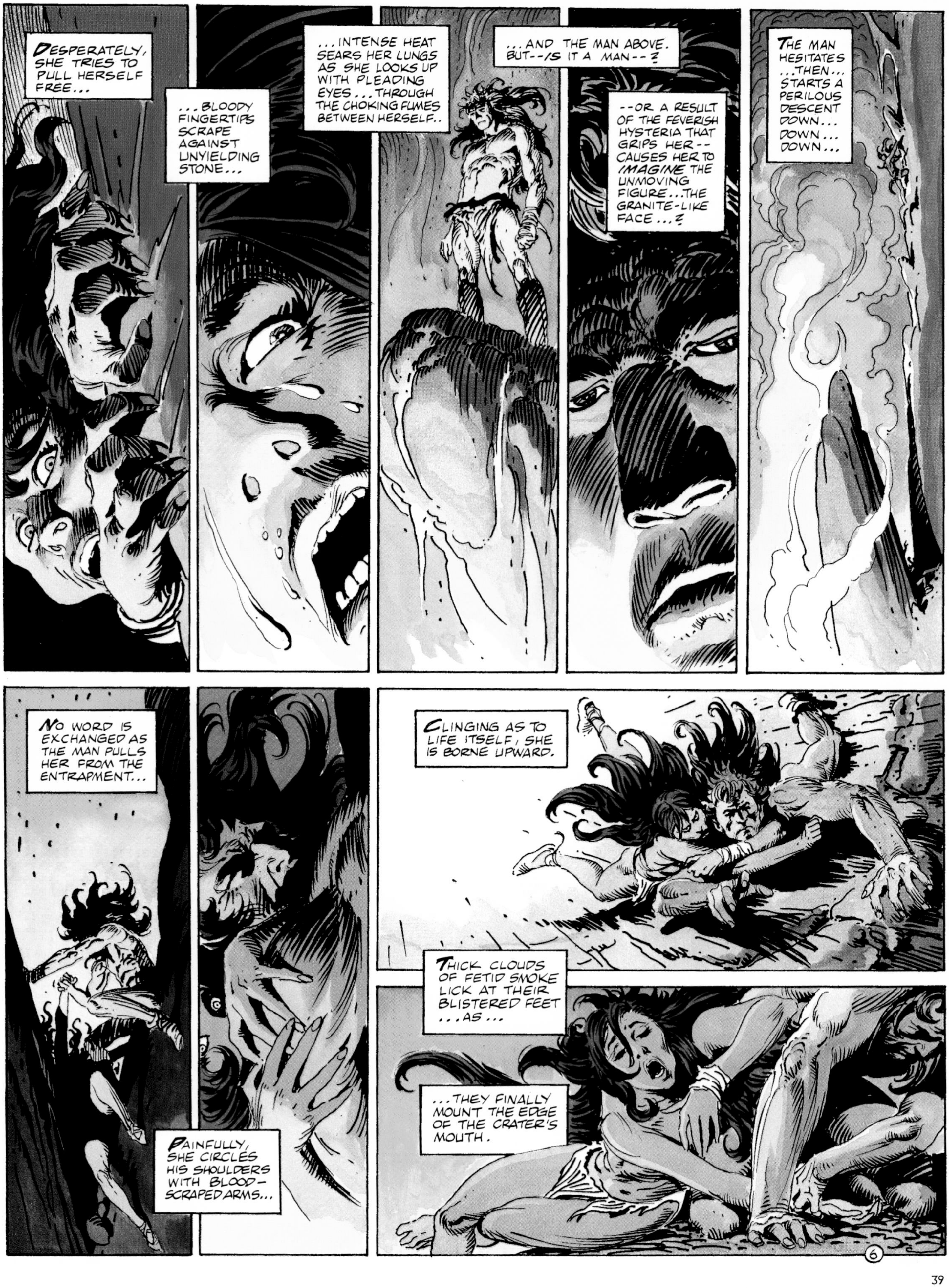
DESPERATELY, SHE TRIES TO PULL HERSELF FREE...
...BLOODY FINGERTIPS SCRAPE AGAINST UNYIELDING STONE...
...INTENSE HEAT SEARS HER LUNGS AS SHE LOOKS UP WITH PLEADING EYES...THROUGH THE CHOKING FUMES BETWEEN HERSELF..
...AND THE MAN ABOVE. BUT--IS IT A MAN--?
--OR A RESULT OF THE FEVERISH HYSTERIA THAT GRIPS HER--CAUSES HER TO IMAGINE THE UNMOVING FIGURE...THE GRANITE-LIKE FACE...?
THE MAN HESITATES...THEN...STARTS A PERILOUS DESCENT DOWN...DOWN...DOWN...
NO WORD IS EXCHANGED AS THE MAN PULLS HER FROM THE ENTRAPMENT...
PAINFULLY, SHE CIRCLES HIS SHOULDERS WITH BLOOD-SCRAPED ARMS...
CLINGING AS TO LIFE ITSELF, SHE IS BORNE UPWARD.
THICK CLOUDS OF FETID SMOKE LICK AT THEIR BLISTERED FEET...AS...
...THEY FINALLY MOUNT THE EDGE OF THE CRATER'S MOUTH.
6

Panel 2 caption: *T*EAR-STREAKED EYES CONVEY GRATITUDE -- AND FEAR -- WITH SILENT ELOQUENCE.

Panel 3 caption: *R*ESOLUTELY, THE MAN STEPS AWAY.

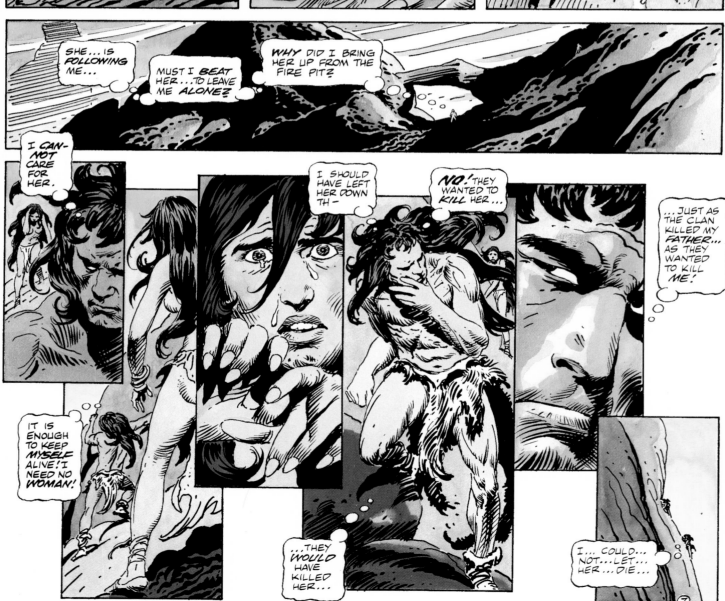

SHE...IS FOLLOWING ME...

MUST I *BEAT* HER...TO LEAVE ME *ALONE?*

WHY DID I BRING HER UP FROM THE FIRE PIT?

I *CAN-NOT* CARE FOR HER.

I SHOULD HAVE LEFT HER DOWN TH--

NO! THEY WANTED TO *KILL* HER...

...JUST AS THE CLAN KILLED MY *FATHER*... AS THEY WANTED TO KILL *ME!*

IT IS ENOUGH TO KEEP *MYSELF* ALIVE! I NEED NO *WOMAN!*

...THEY *WOULD* HAVE KILLED HER...

I...COULD... NOT...LET... HER...DIE...

⑦

40

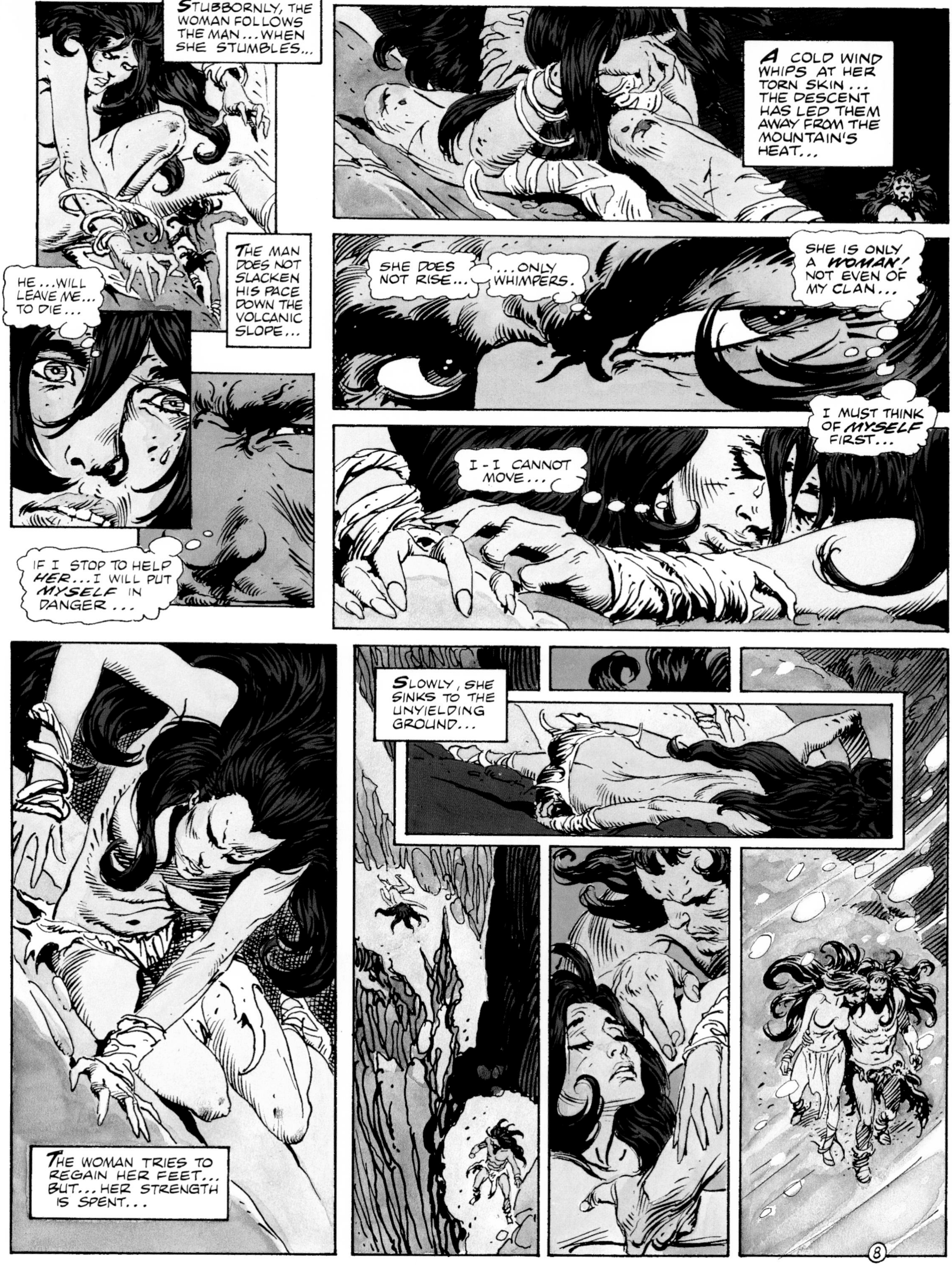
STUBBORNLY, THE WOMAN FOLLOWS THE MAN... WHEN SHE STUMBLES...
A COLD WIND WHIPS AT HER TORN SKIN... THE DESCENT HAS LED THEM AWAY FROM THE MOUNTAIN'S HEAT...
THE MAN DOES NOT SLACKEN HIS PACE DOWN THE VOLCANIC SLOPE...
HE... WILL LEAVE ME... TO DIE...
SHE DOES NOT RISE...
...ONLY WHIMPERS.
SHE IS ONLY A WOMAN! NOT EVEN OF MY CLAN...
IF I STOP TO HELP HER... I WILL PUT MYSELF IN DANGER...
I MUST THINK OF MYSELF FIRST...
I - I CANNOT MOVE...
THE WOMAN TRIES TO REGAIN HER FEET... BUT... HER STRENGTH IS SPENT...
SLOWLY, SHE SINKS TO THE UNYIELDING GROUND...
8

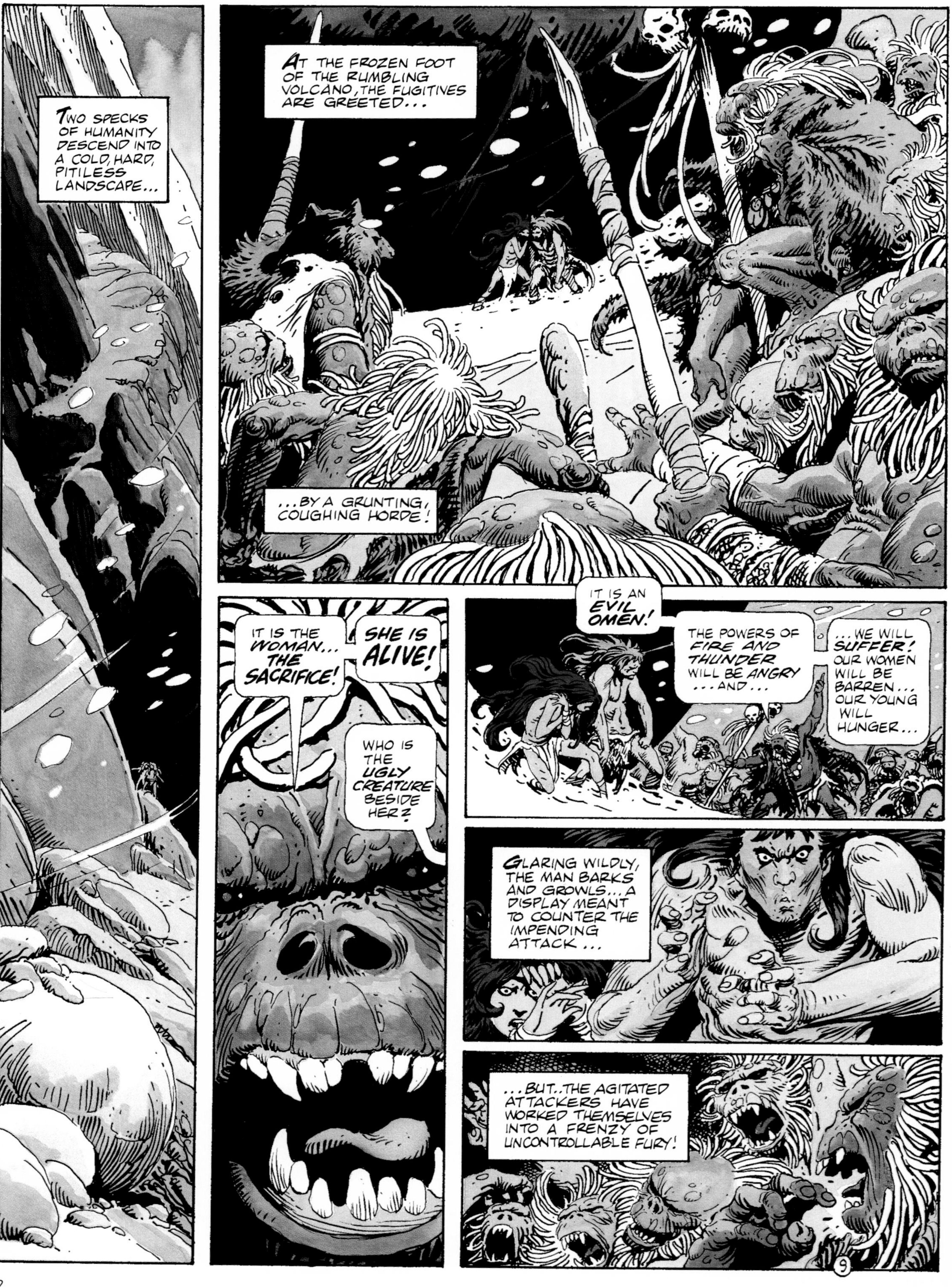
TWO SPECKS OF HUMANITY DESCEND INTO A COLD, HARD, PITILESS LANDSCAPE...
AT THE FROZEN FOOT OF THE RUMBLING VOLCANO, THE FUGITIVES ARE GREETED...
...BY A GRUNTING, COUGHING HORDE!
IT IS THE WOMAN... THE SACRIFICE!
SHE IS ALIVE!
WHO IS THE UGLY CREATURE BESIDE HER?
IT IS AN EVIL OMEN!
THE POWERS OF FIRE AND THUNDER WILL BE ANGRY ...AND...
...WE WILL SUFFER! OUR WOMEN WILL BE BARREN... OUR YOUNG WILL HUNGER...
GLARING WILDLY, THE MAN BARKS AND GROWLS... A DISPLAY MEANT TO COUNTER THE IMPENDING ATTACK...
...BUT..THE AGITATED ATTACKERS HAVE WORKED THEMSELVES INTO A FRENZY OF UNCONTROLLABLE FURY!
9

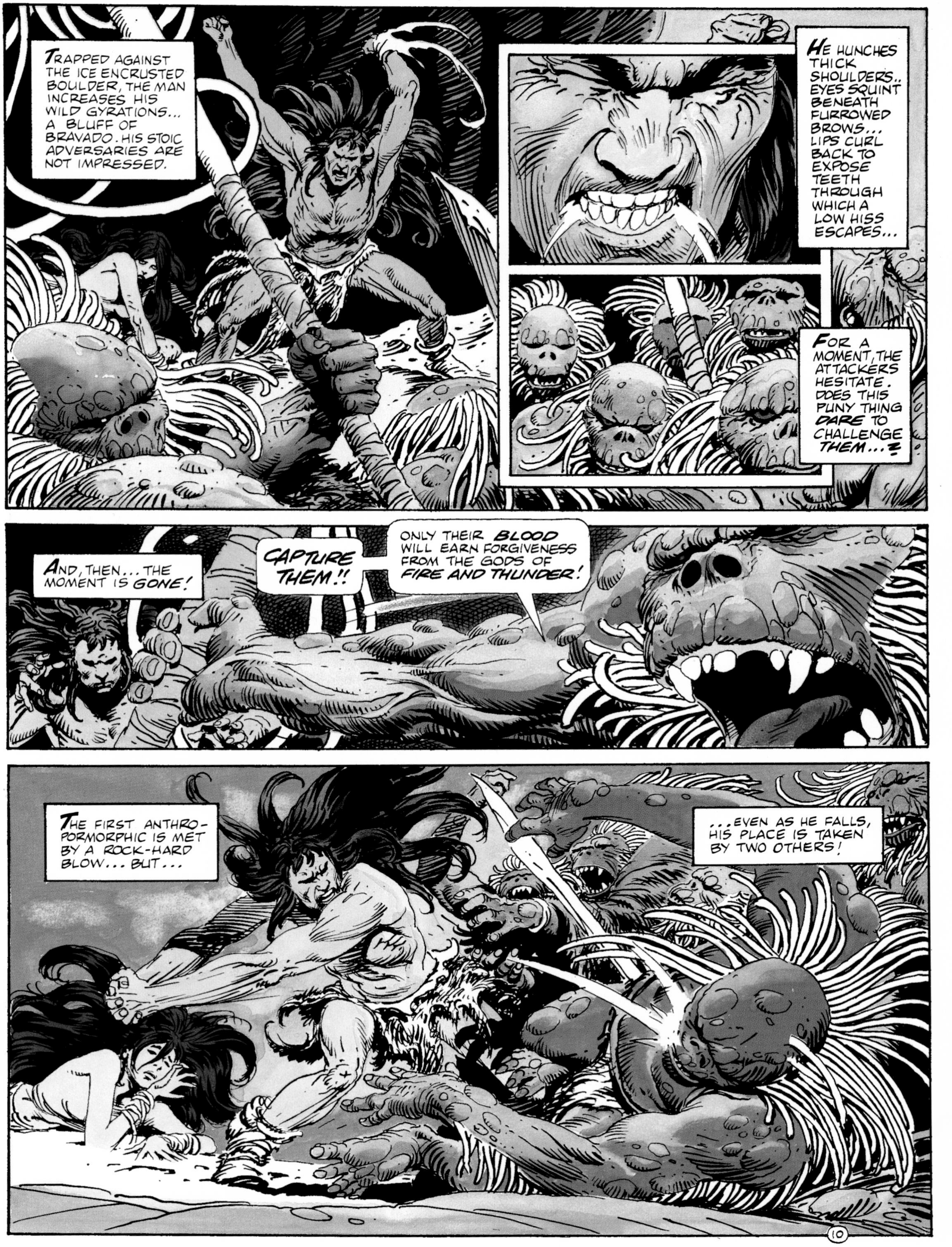
TRAPPED AGAINST THE ICE ENCRUSTED BOULDER, THE MAN INCREASES HIS WILD GYRATIONS... A BLUFF OF BRAVADO. HIS STOIC ADVERSARIES ARE NOT IMPRESSED.
HE HUNCHES THICK SHOULDERS.. EYES SQUINT BENEATH FURROWED BROWS... LIPS CURL BACK TO EXPOSE TEETH THROUGH WHICH A LOW HISS ESCAPES...
FOR A MOMENT, THE ATTACKERS HESITATE. DOES THIS PUNY THING DARE TO CHALLENGE THEM...?
AND, THEN... THE MOMENT IS GONE!
CAPTURE THEM!!
ONLY THEIR BLOOD WILL EARN FORGIVENESS FROM THE GODS OF FIRE AND THUNDER!
THE FIRST ANTHRO-PORMORPHIC IS MET BY A ROCK-HARD BLOW... BUT...
...EVEN AS HE FALLS, HIS PLACE IS TAKEN BY TWO OTHERS!
10

MUSCLES AND TENDONS KNOT AS THE MAN STRAINS AGAINST CLAWING NAILS AND SLATHERING JAWS...

THE SMELL OF DEATH---HIS DEATH--FILLS HIS NOSTRILS...

SUMMONING RAW STRENGTH BRED OF DESPERATION, HE DISLODGES A BLOOD-FLECKED ATTACKER... INHALES A BREATH OF SWEET AIR...

...AND FOR A MOMENT CASTS AN EYE ON HIS HELPLESS COMPANION.

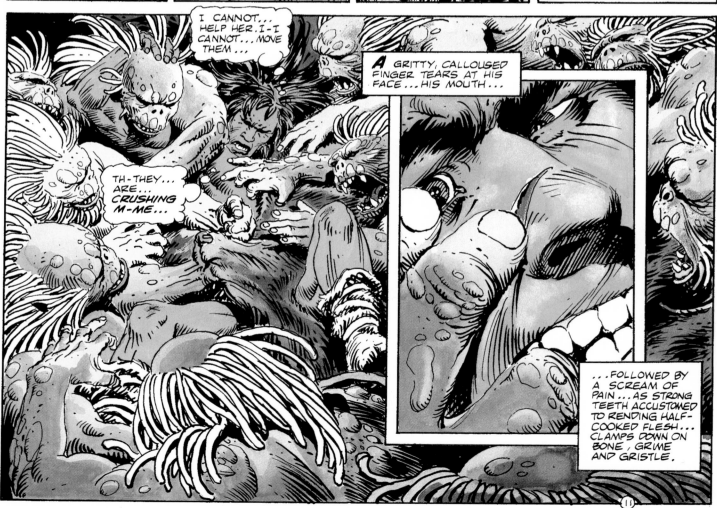

I CANNOT... HELP HER. I-I CANNOT... MOVE THEM...

TH-THEY... ARE... CRUSHING M-ME...

A GRITTY, CALLOUSED FINGER TEARS AT HIS FACE... HIS MOUTH...

...FOLLOWED BY A SCREAM OF PAIN...AS STRONG TEETH ACCUSTOMED TO RENDING HALF-COOKED FLESH... CLAMPS DOWN ON BONE, GRIME AND GRISTLE.

11

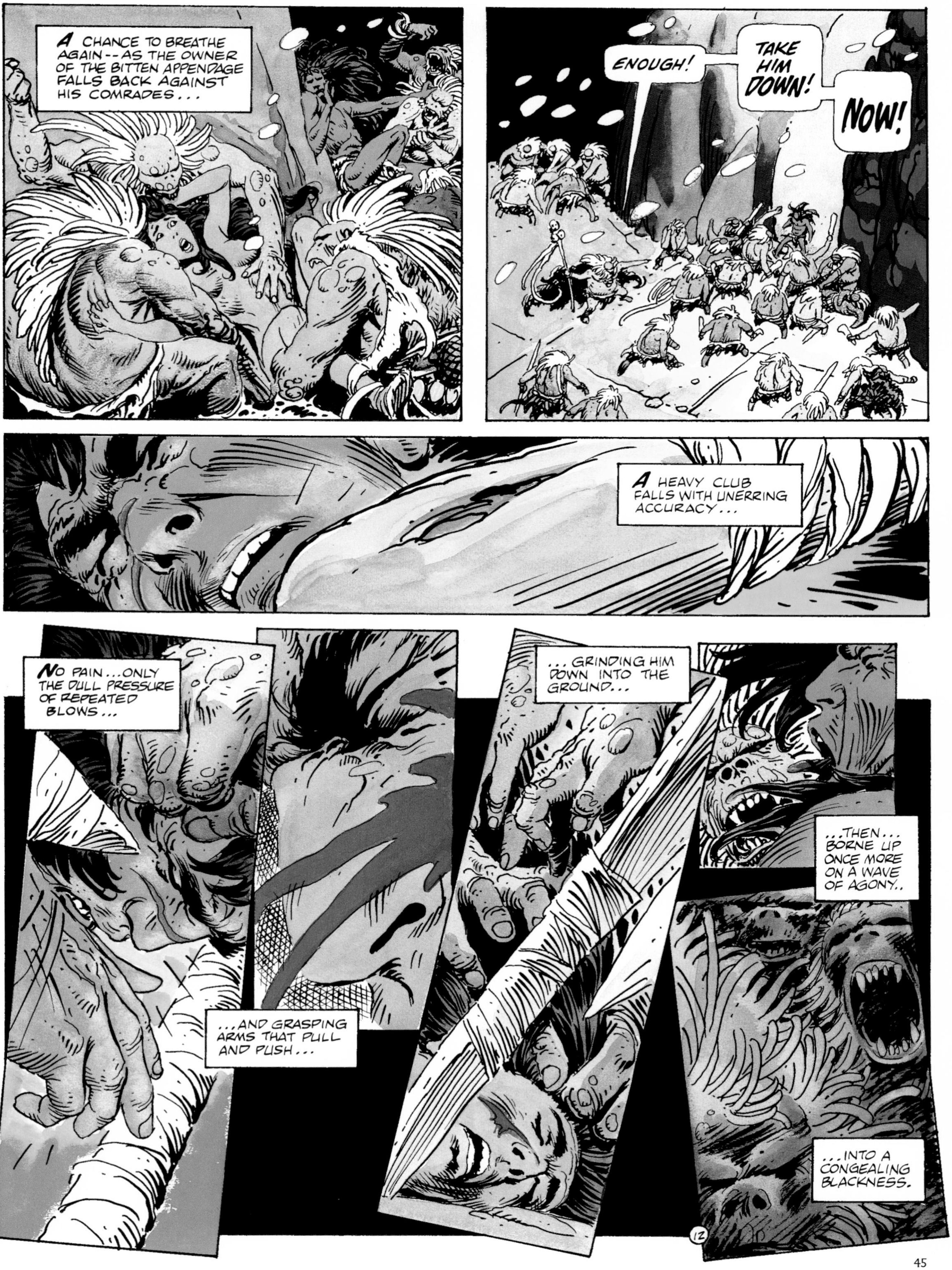
A CHANCE TO BREATHE AGAIN--AS THE OWNER OF THE BITTEN APPENDAGE FALLS BACK AGAINST HIS COMRADES...
ENOUGH!
TAKE HIM DOWN!
NOW!
A HEAVY CLUB FALLS WITH UNERRING ACCURACY...
NO PAIN...ONLY THE DULL PRESSURE OF REPEATED BLOWS...
...AND GRASPING ARMS THAT PULL AND PUSH...
...GRINDING HIM DOWN INTO THE GROUND...
...THEN... BORNE UP ONCE MORE ON A WAVE OF AGONY..
...INTO A CONGEALING BLACKNESS.
12

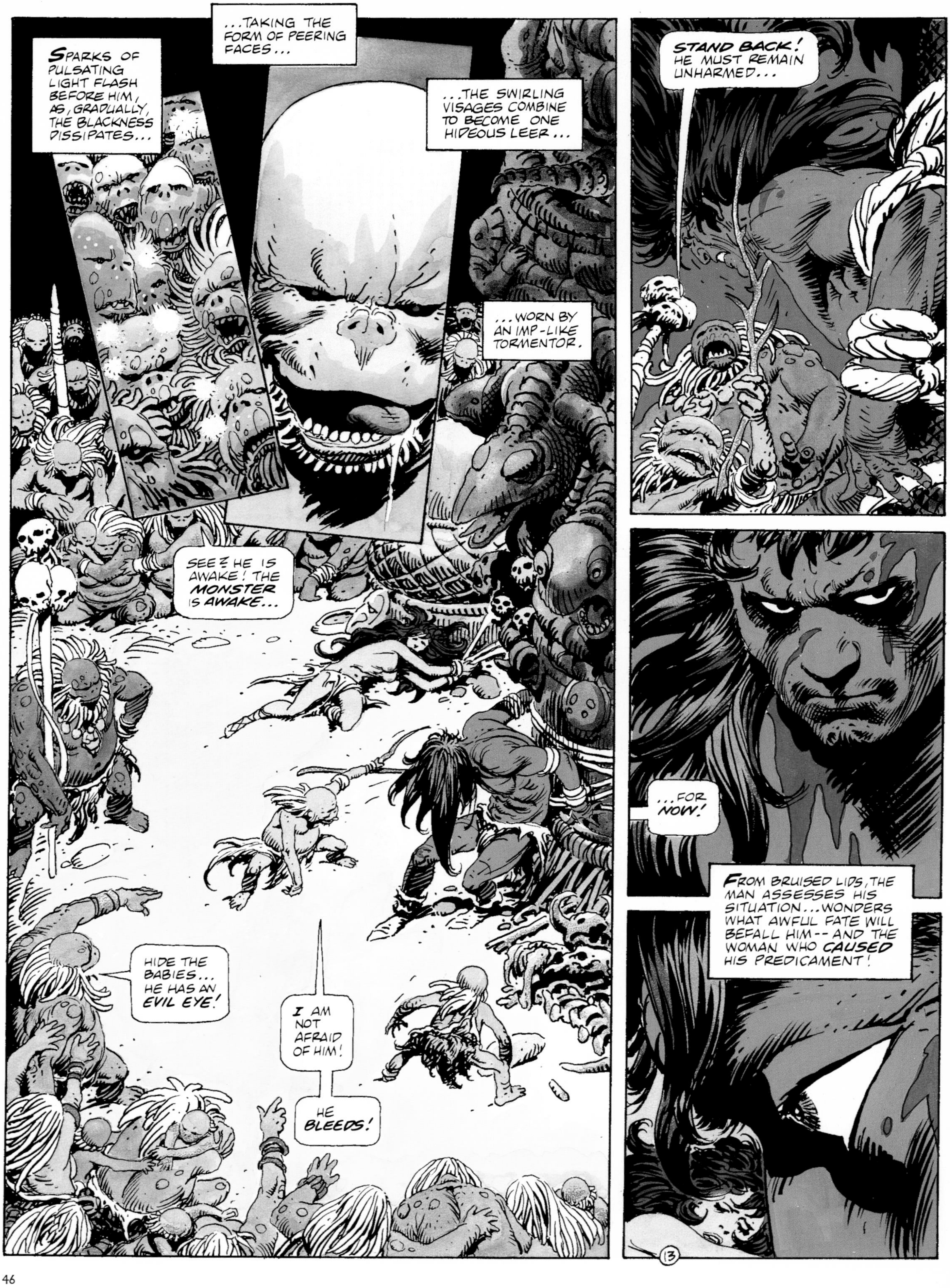
SPARKS OF PULSATING LIGHT FLASH BEFORE HIM, AS, GRADUALLY, THE BLACKNESS DISSIPATES...
...TAKING THE FORM OF PEERING FACES...
...THE SWIRLING VISAGES COMBINE TO BECOME ONE HIDEOUS LEER...
...WORN BY AN IMP-LIKE TORMENTOR.
SEE? HE IS AWAKE! THE MONSTER IS AWAKE...
HIDE THE BABIES... HE HAS AN EVIL EYE!
I AM NOT AFRAID OF HIM!
HE BLEEDS!
STAND BACK! HE MUST REMAIN UNHARMED...
...FOR NOW!
FROM BRUISED LIDS, THE MAN ASSESSES HIS SITUATION... WONDERS WHAT AWFUL FATE WILL BEFALL HIM -- AND THE WOMAN WHO CAUSED HIS PREDICAMENT!
13

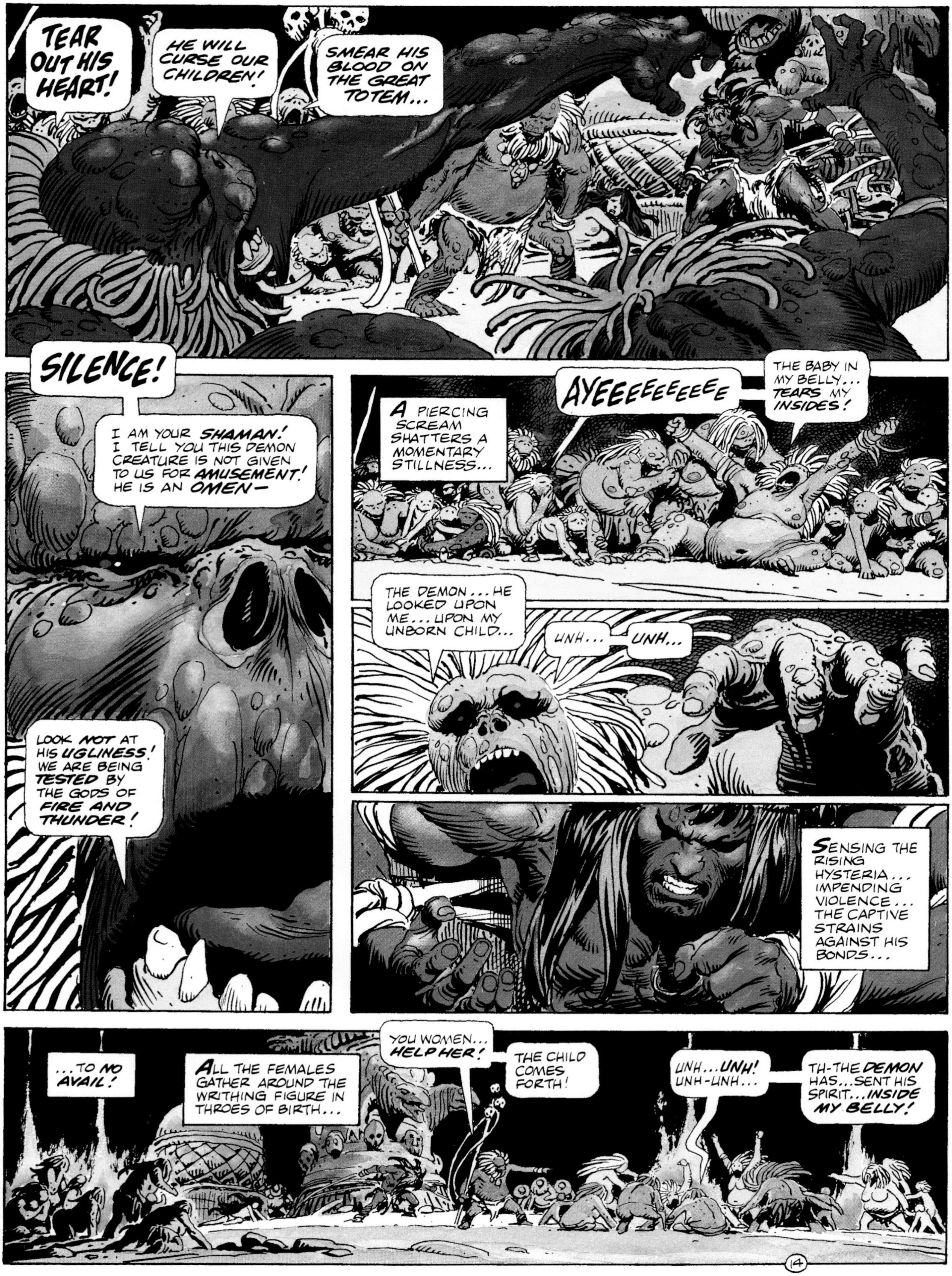
TEAR OUT HIS HEART!
HE WILL CURSE OUR CHILDREN!
SMEAR HIS BLOOD ON THE GREAT TOTEM...
SILENCE!
I AM YOUR SHAMAN! I TELL YOU THIS DEMON CREATURE IS NOT GIVEN TO US FOR AMUSEMENT! HE IS AN OMEN—
LOOK NOT AT HIS UGLINESS! WE ARE BEING TESTED BY THE GODS OF FIRE AND THUNDER!
A PIERCING SCREAM SHATTERS A MOMENTARY STILLNESS...
AYEEEEEEEEEE
THE BABY IN MY BELLY... TEARS MY INSIDES!
THE DEMON... HE LOOKED UPON ME... UPON MY UNBORN CHILD...
UNH...
UNH...
SENSING THE RISING HYSTERIA... IMPENDING VIOLENCE... THE CAPTIVE STRAINS AGAINST HIS BONDS...
...TO NO AVAIL!
ALL THE FEMALES GATHER AROUND THE WRITHING FIGURE IN THROES OF BIRTH...
YOU WOMEN... HELP HER!
THE CHILD COMES FORTH!
UNH...UNH! UNH-UNH...
TH-THE DEMON HAS...SENT HIS SPIRIT...INSIDE MY BELLY!
14

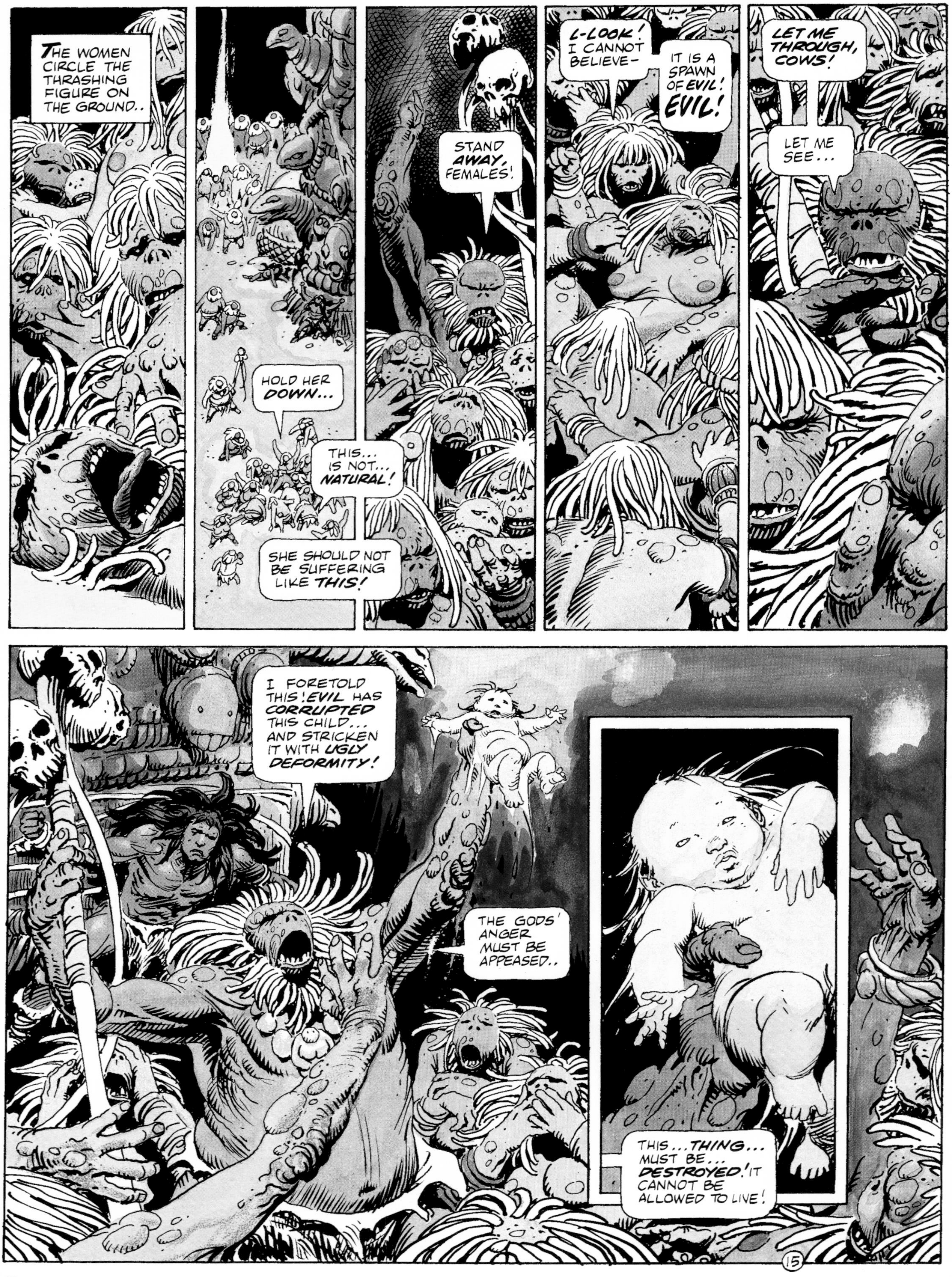
THE WOMEN CIRCLE THE THRASHING FIGURE ON THE GROUND..
HOLD HER DOWN...
THIS... IS NOT... NATURAL!
SHE SHOULD NOT BE SUFFERING LIKE THIS!
STAND AWAY, FEMALES!
L-LOOK! I CANNOT BELIEVE-
IT IS A SPAWN OF EVIL! EVIL!
LET ME THROUGH, COWS!
LET ME SEE...
I FORETOLD THIS! EVIL HAS CORRUPTED THIS CHILD... AND STRICKEN IT WITH UGLY DEFORMITY!
THE GODS' ANGER MUST BE APPEASED..
THIS... THING... MUST BE... DESTROYED! IT CANNOT BE ALLOWED TO LIVE!
15

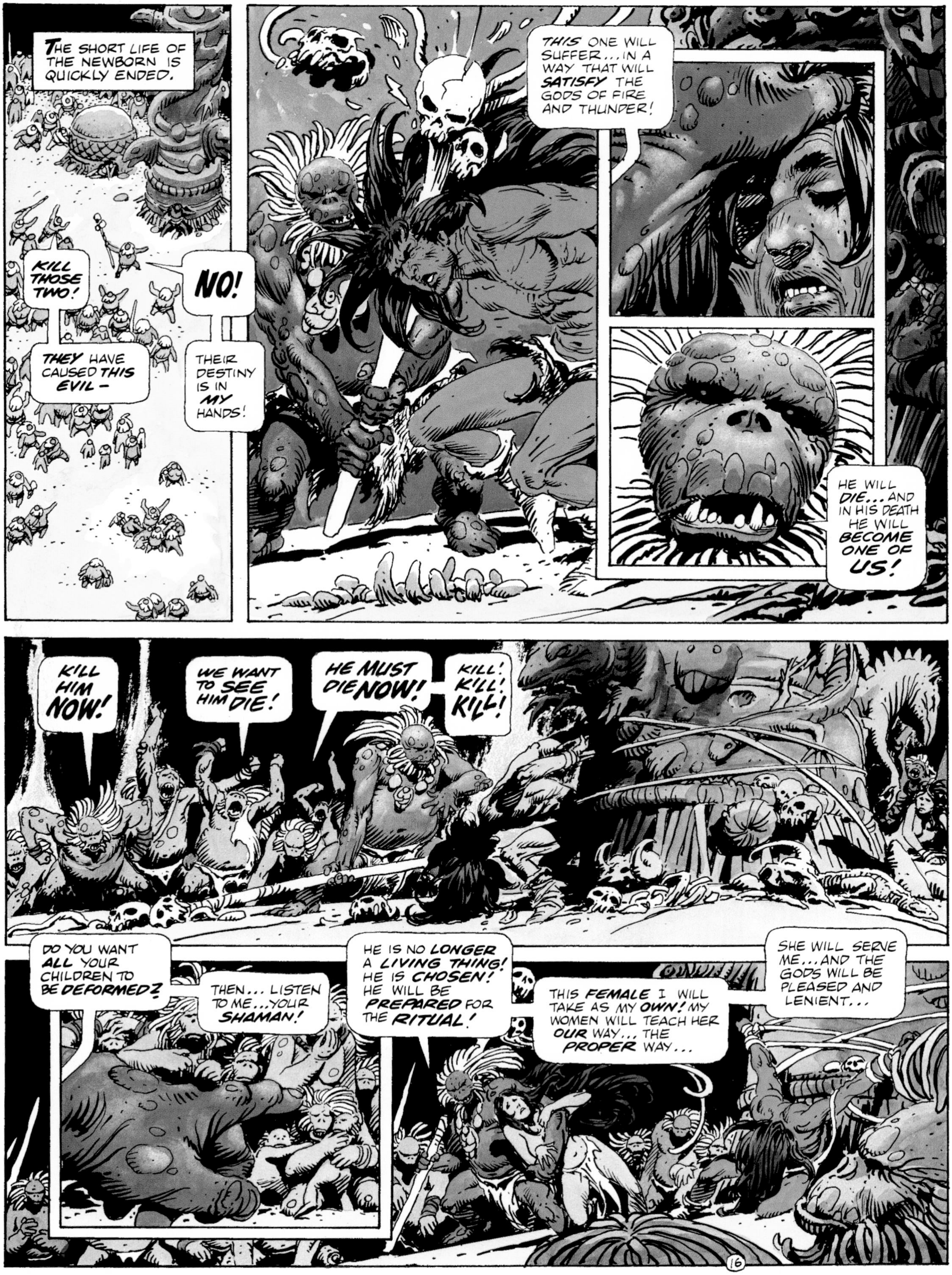

THE SHORT LIFE OF THE NEWBORN IS QUICKLY ENDED.
KILL THOSE TWO!
THEY HAVE CAUSED THIS EVIL—
NO!
THEIR DESTINY IS IN MY HANDS!
THIS ONE WILL SUFFER... IN A WAY THAT WILL SATISFY THE GODS OF FIRE AND THUNDER!
HE WILL DIE... AND IN HIS DEATH HE WILL BECOME ONE OF US!
KILL HIM NOW!
WE WANT TO SEE HIM DIE!
HE MUST DIE NOW!
KILL! KILL! KILL!
DO YOU WANT ALL YOUR CHILDREN TO BE DEFORMED?
THEN... LISTEN TO ME... YOUR SHAMAN!
HE IS NO LONGER A LIVING THING! HE IS CHOSEN! HE WILL BE PREPARED FOR THE RITUAL!
THIS FEMALE I WILL TAKE AS MY OWN! MY WOMEN WILL TEACH HER OUR WAY... THE PROPER WAY...
SHE WILL SERVE ME... AND THE GODS WILL BE PLEASED AND LENIENT...
16

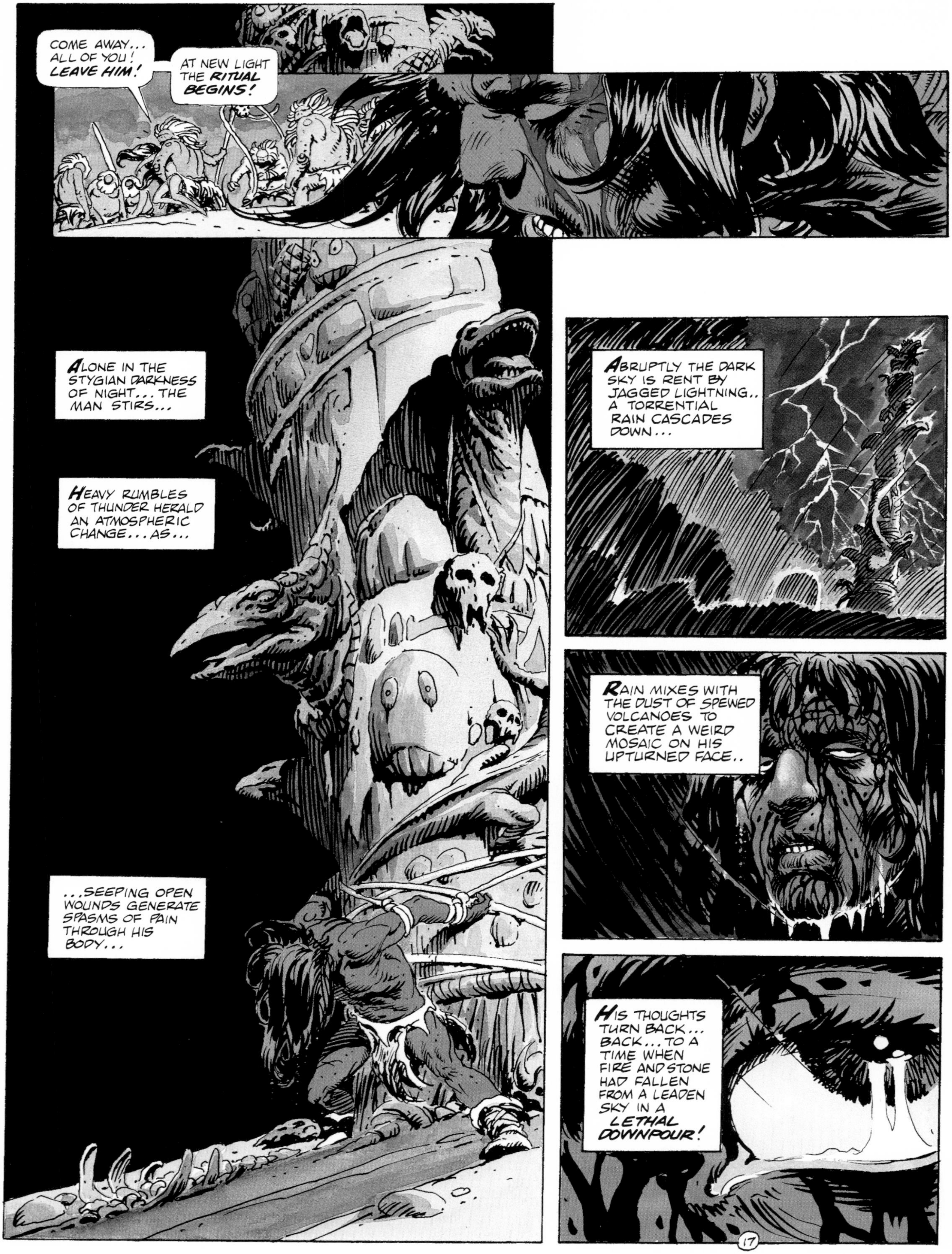
COME AWAY... ALL OF YOU! LEAVE HIM!
AT NEW LIGHT THE RITUAL BEGINS!
ALONE IN THE STYGIAN DARKNESS OF NIGHT... THE MAN STIRS...
HEAVY RUMBLES OF THUNDER HERALD AN ATMOSPHERIC CHANGE... AS...
...SEEPING OPEN WOUNDS GENERATE SPASMS OF PAIN THROUGH HIS BODY...
ABRUPTLY THE DARK SKY IS RENT BY JAGGED LIGHTNING.. A TORRENTIAL RAIN CASCADES DOWN...
RAIN MIXES WITH THE DUST OF SPEWED VOLCANOES TO CREATE A WEIRD MOSAIC ON HIS UPTURNED FACE..
HIS THOUGHTS TURN BACK... BACK... TO A TIME WHEN FIRE AND STONE HAD FALLEN FROM A LEADEN SKY IN A LETHAL DOWNPOUR!
17

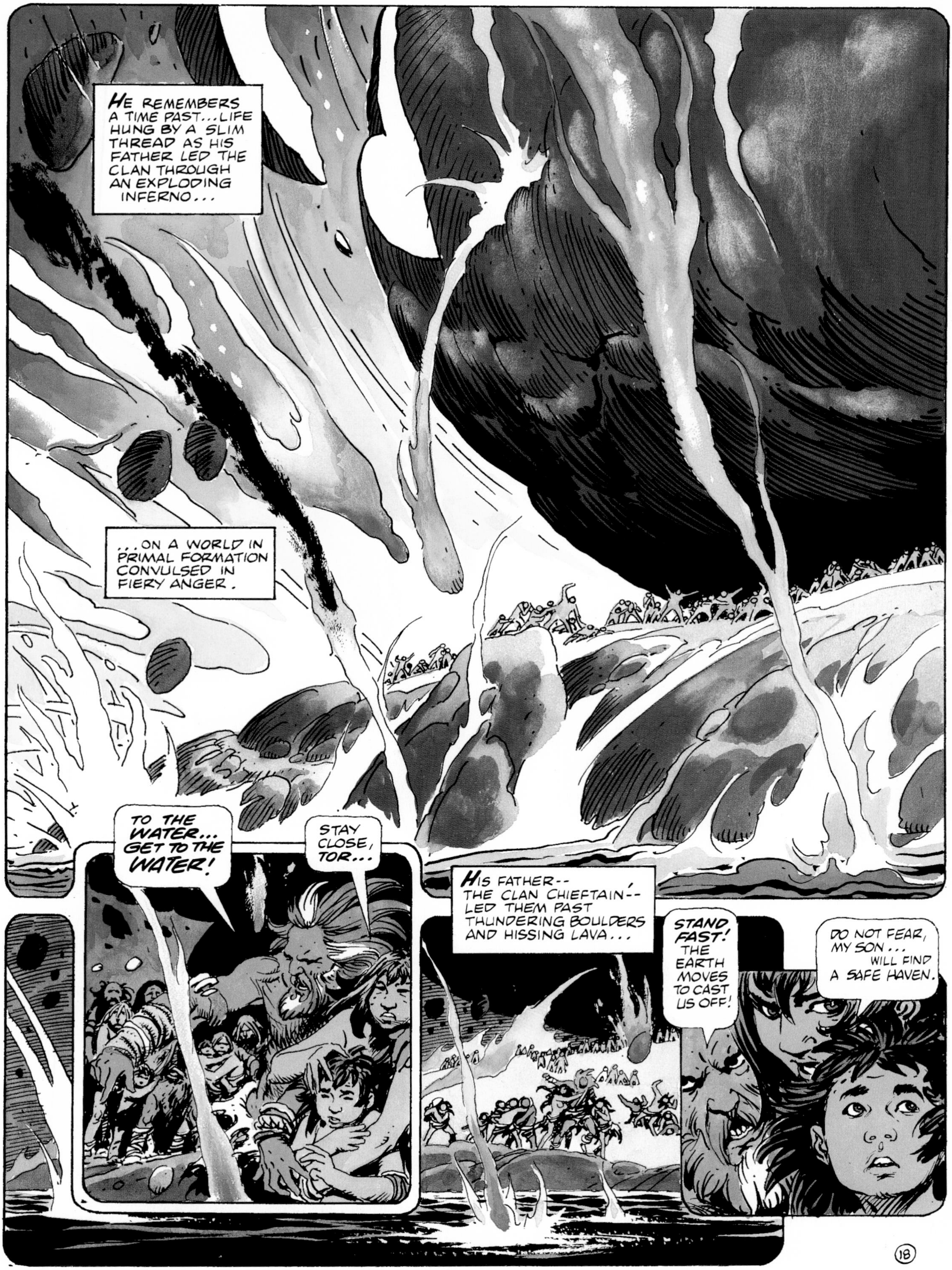
HE REMEMBERS A TIME PAST... LIFE HUNG BY A SLIM THREAD AS HIS FATHER LED THE CLAN THROUGH AN EXPLODING INFERNO...
...ON A WORLD IN PRIMAL FORMATION CONVULSED IN FIERY ANGER.
TO THE WATER... GET TO THE WATER!
STAY CLOSE, TOR...
HIS FATHER-- THE CLAN CHIEFTAIN!-- LED THEM PAST THUNDERING BOULDERS AND HISSING LAVA...
STAND FAST! THE EARTH MOVES TO CAST US OFF!
DO NOT FEAR, MY SON... WILL FIND A SAFE HAVEN.
18

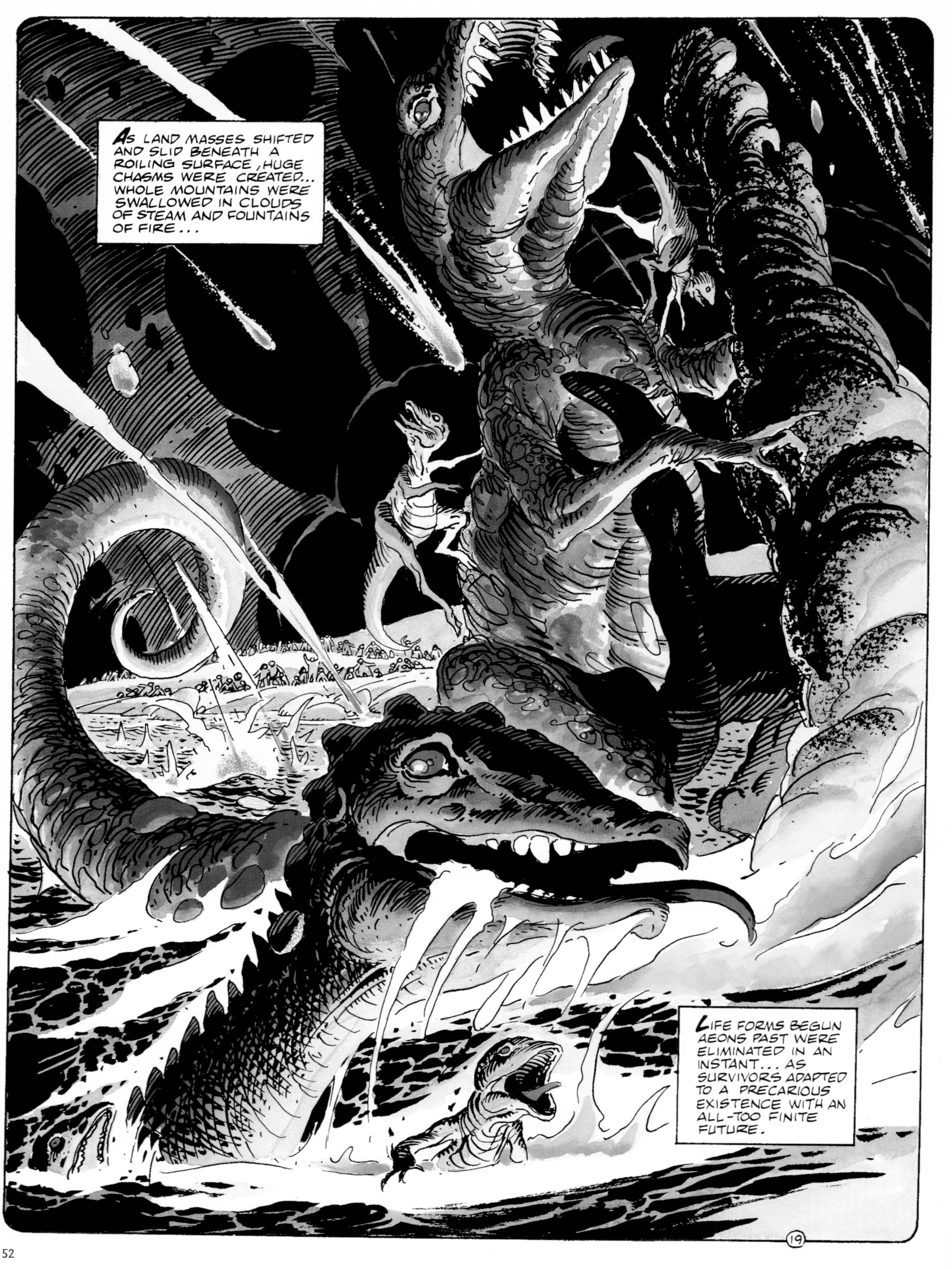
As land masses shifted and slid beneath a roiling surface, huge chasms were created... whole mountains were swallowed in clouds of steam and fountains of fire...
Life forms begun aeons past were eliminated in an instant... as survivors adapted to a precarious existence with an all-too finite future.
19

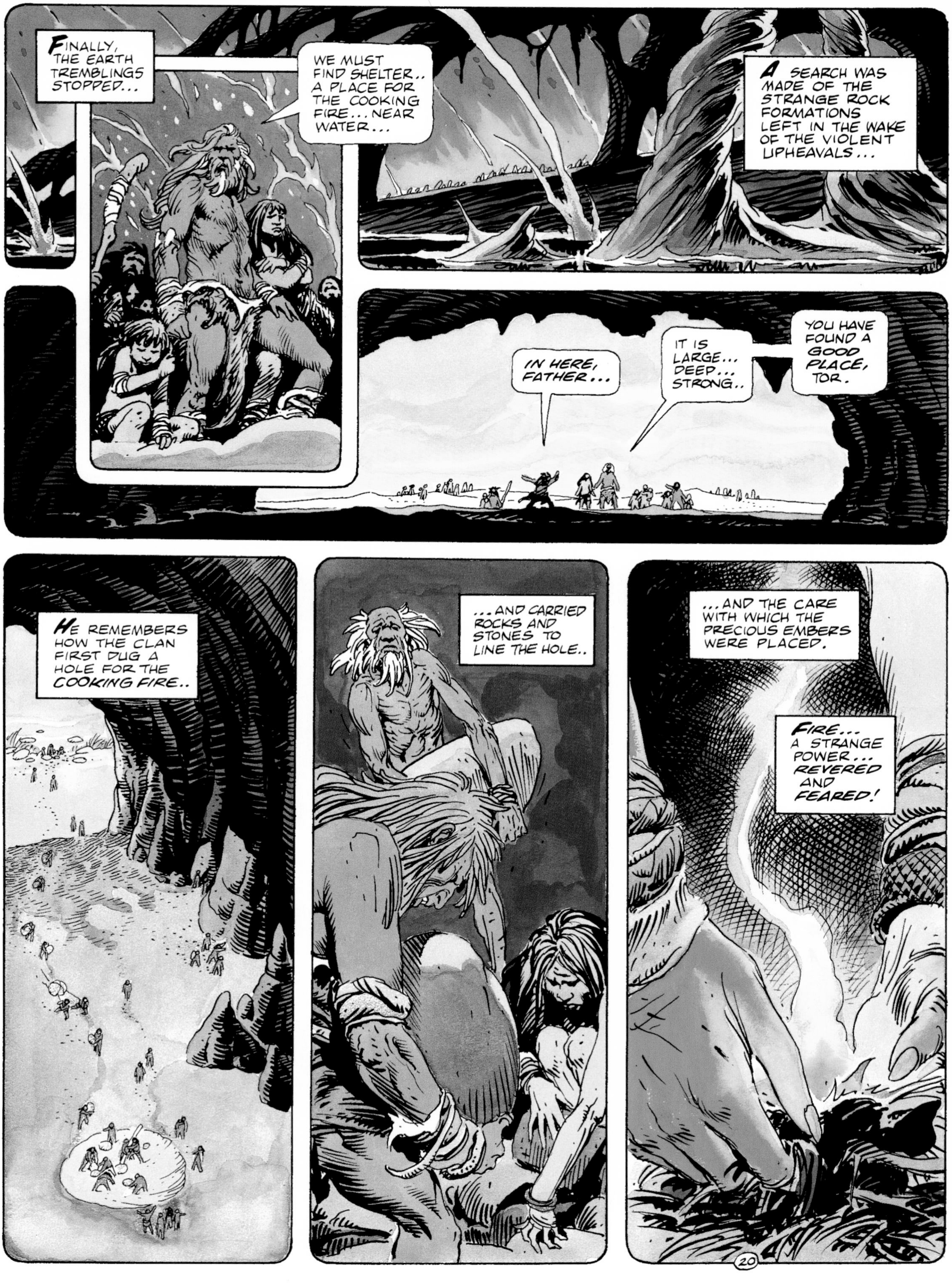
FINALLY, THE EARTH TREMBLINGS STOPPED...
WE MUST FIND SHELTER.. A PLACE FOR THE COOKING FIRE... NEAR WATER...
A SEARCH WAS MADE OF THE STRANGE ROCK FORMATIONS LEFT IN THE WAKE OF THE VIOLENT UPHEAVALS...
IN HERE, FATHER...
IT IS LARGE... DEEP... STRONG..
YOU HAVE FOUND A GOOD PLACE, TOR.
HE REMEMBERS HOW THE CLAN FIRST DUG A HOLE FOR THE COOKING FIRE..
...AND CARRIED ROCKS AND STONES TO LINE THE HOLE..
...AND THE CARE WITH WHICH THE PRECIOUS EMBERS WERE PLACED.
FIRE... A STRANGE POWER... REVERED AND FEARED!
20

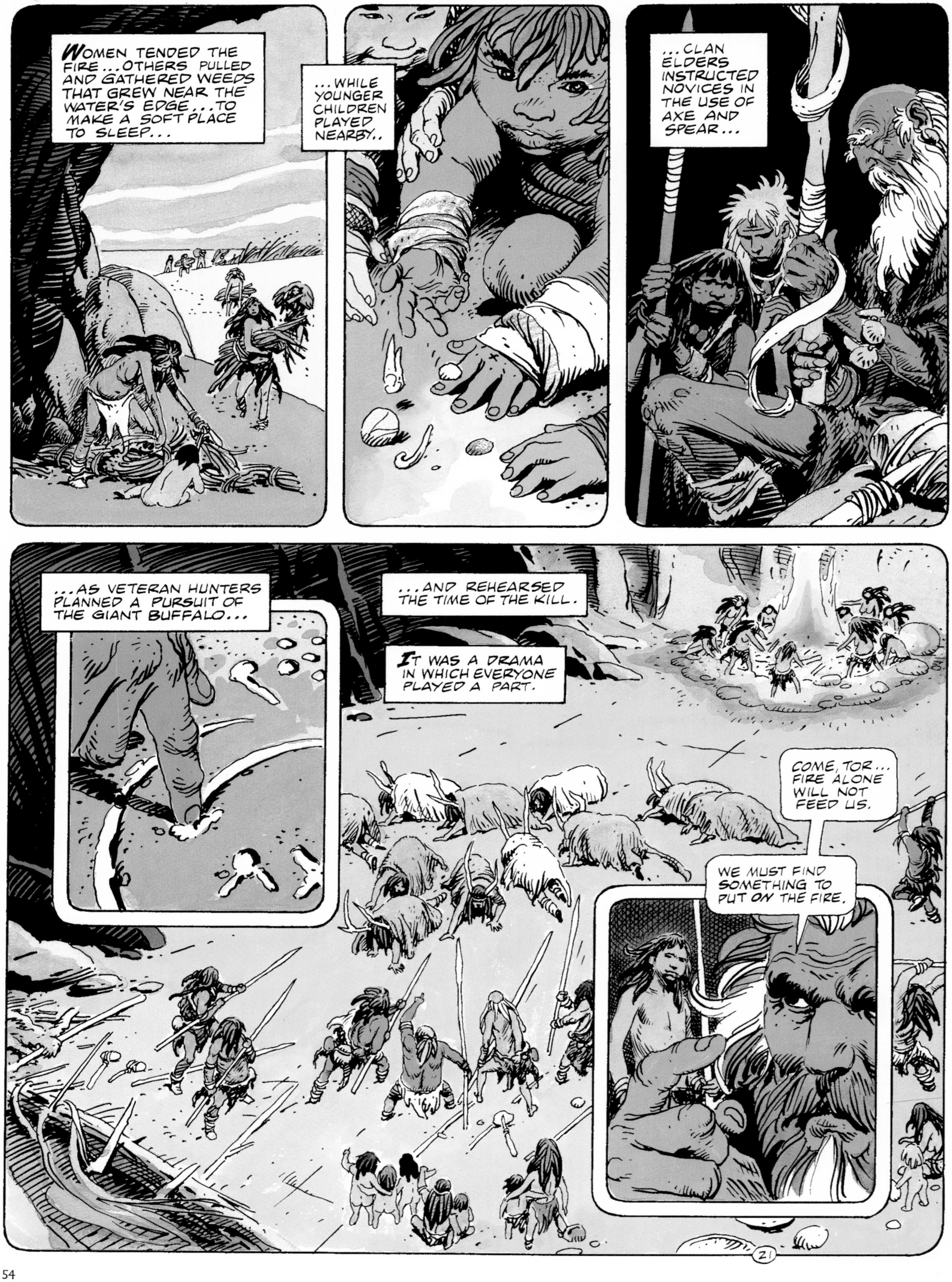
WOMEN TENDED THE FIRE... OTHERS PULLED AND GATHERED WEEDS THAT GREW NEAR THE WATER'S EDGE... TO MAKE A SOFT PLACE TO SLEEP...
...WHILE YOUNGER CHILDREN PLAYED NEARBY..
...CLAN ELDERS INSTRUCTED NOVICES IN THE USE OF AXE AND SPEAR...
...AS VETERAN HUNTERS PLANNED A PURSUIT OF THE GIANT BUFFALO...
...AND REHEARSED THE TIME OF THE KILL.
IT WAS A DRAMA IN WHICH EVERYONE PLAYED A PART.
COME, TOR... FIRE ALONE WILL NOT FEED US.
WE MUST FIND SOMETHING TO PUT ON THE FIRE.
21

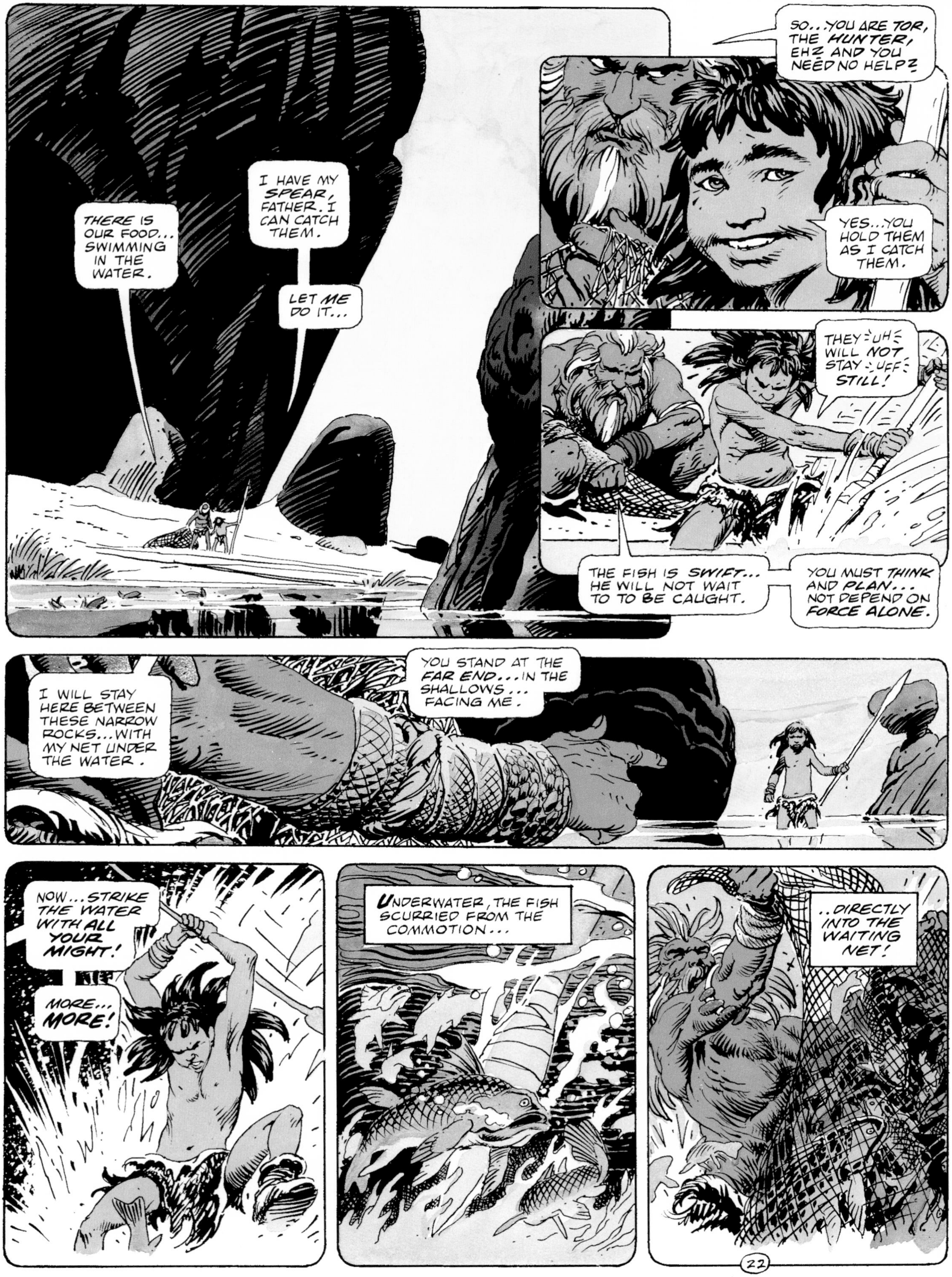
THERE IS OUR FOOD... SWIMMING IN THE WATER.
I HAVE MY SPEAR, FATHER. I CAN CATCH THEM.
LET ME DO IT...
SO... YOU ARE TOR, THE HUNTER, EHZ AND YOU NEED NO HELP?
YES... YOU HOLD THEM AS I CATCH THEM.
THEY -UH- WILL NOT STAY -UFF- STILL!
THE FISH IS SWIFT... HE WILL NOT WAIT TO TO BE CAUGHT.
YOU MUST THINK AND PLAN... NOT DEPEND ON FORCE ALONE.
I WILL STAY HERE BETWEEN THESE NARROW ROCKS... WITH MY NET UNDER THE WATER.
YOU STAND AT THE FAR END... IN THE SHALLOWS... FACING ME.
NOW... STRIKE THE WATER WITH ALL YOUR MIGHT!
MORE... MORE!
UNDERWATER, THE FISH SCURRIED FROM THE COMMOTION...
..DIRECTLY INTO THE WAITING NET!
22

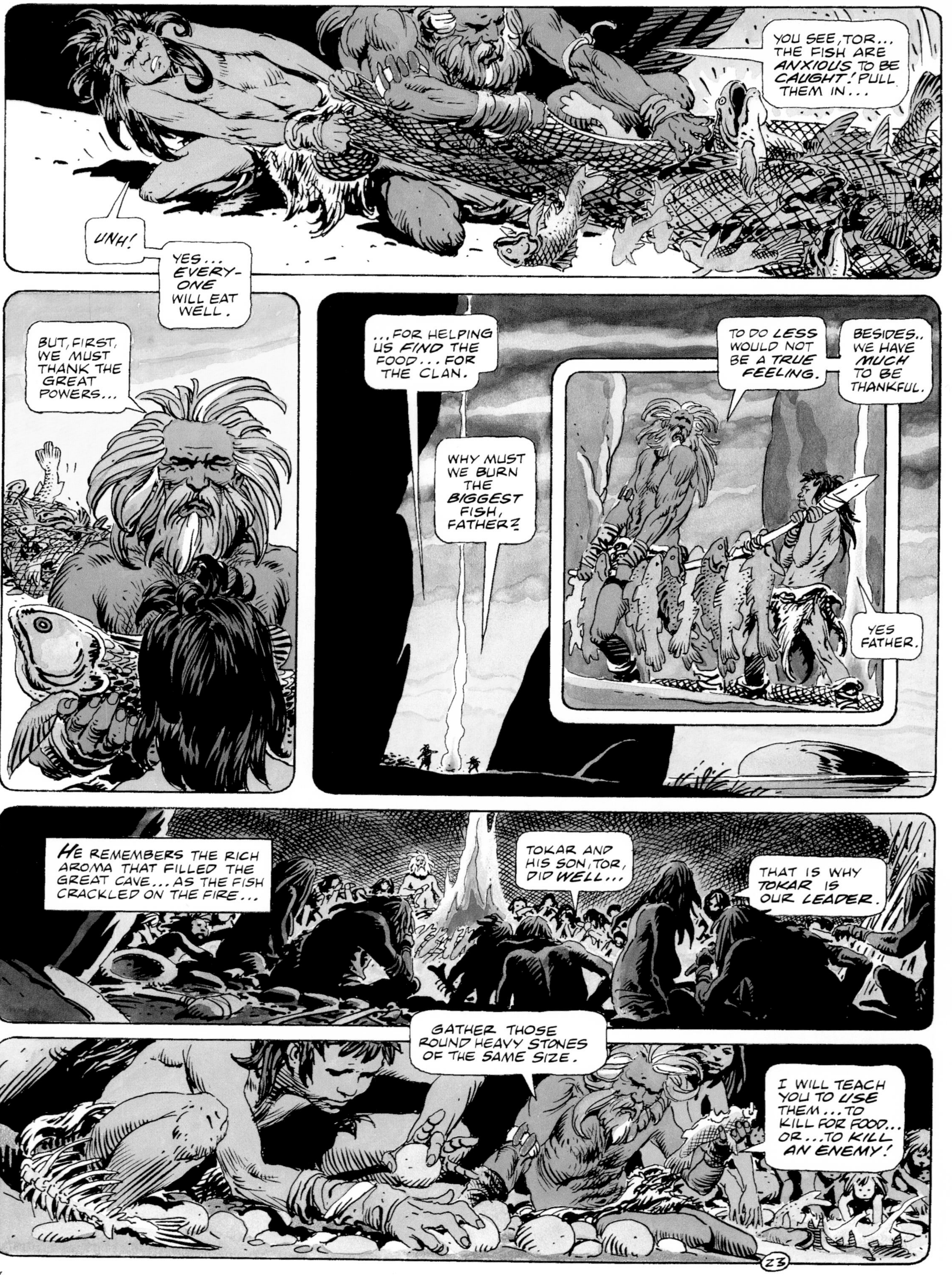
YOU SEE, TOR... THE FISH ARE ANXIOUS TO BE CAUGHT! PULL THEM IN...
UNH!
YES... EVERY-ONE WILL EAT WELL.
BUT, FIRST, WE MUST THANK THE GREAT POWERS...
...FOR HELPING US FIND THE FOOD... FOR THE CLAN.
WHY MUST WE BURN THE BIGGEST FISH, FATHER?
TO DO LESS WOULD NOT BE A TRUE FEELING.
BESIDES.. WE HAVE MUCH TO BE THANKFUL.
YES FATHER.
HE REMEMBERS THE RICH AROMA THAT FILLED THE GREAT CAVE... AS THE FISH CRACKLED ON THE FIRE...
TOKAR AND HIS SON, TOR, DID WELL...
THAT IS WHY TOKAR IS OUR LEADER.
GATHER THOSE ROUND HEAVY STONES OF THE SAME SIZE.
I WILL TEACH YOU TO USE THEM... TO KILL FOR FOOD... OR... TO KILL AN ENEMY!
23

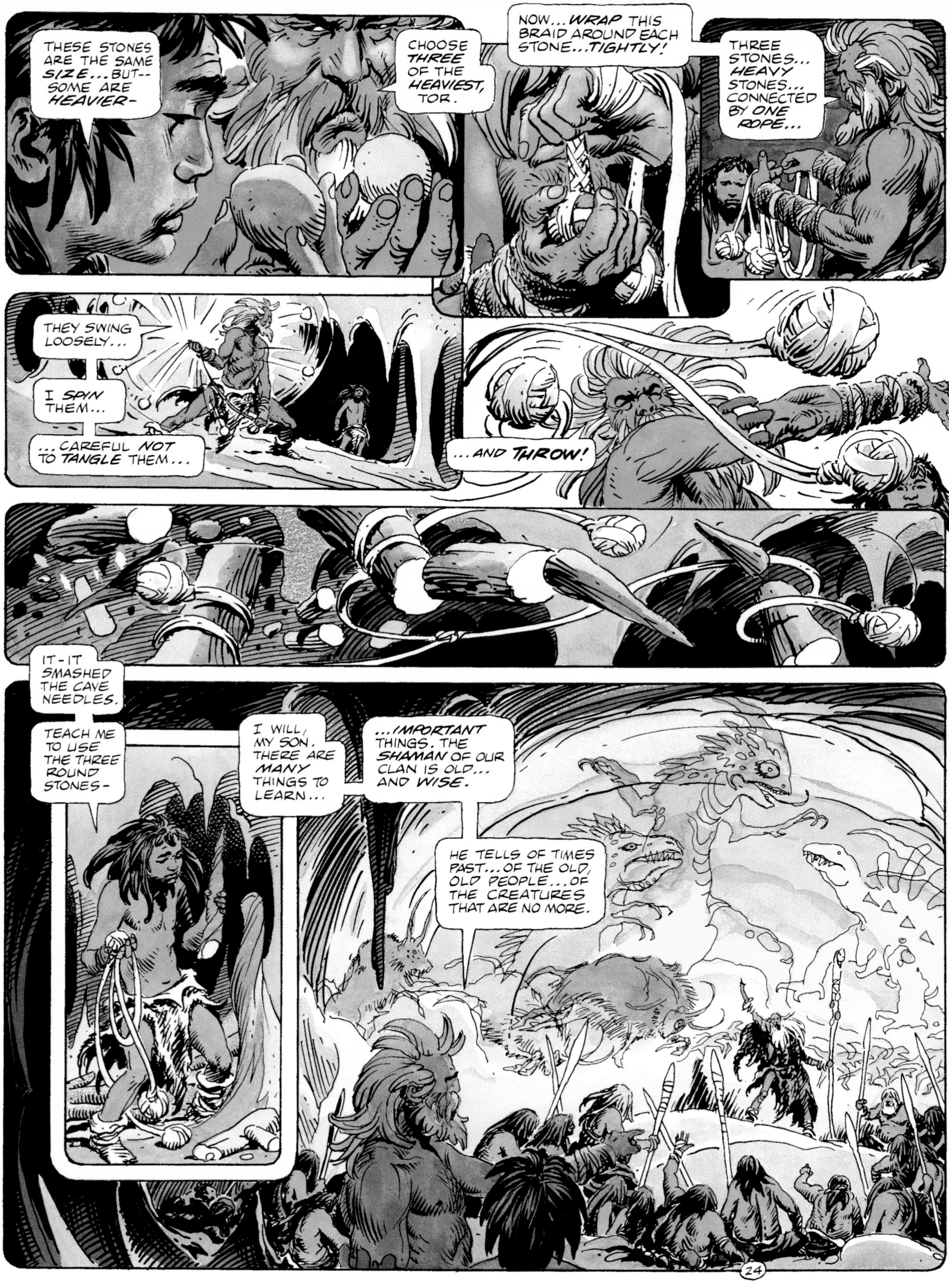
THESE STONES ARE THE SAME SIZE... BUT-- SOME ARE HEAVIER-
CHOOSE THREE OF THE HEAVIEST, TOR.
NOW... WRAP THIS BRAID AROUND EACH STONE... TIGHTLY!
THREE STONES... HEAVY STONES... CONNECTED BY ONE ROPE...
THEY SWING LOOSELY...
I SPIN THEM...
...CAREFUL NOT TO TANGLE THEM...
...AND THROW!
IT-IT SMASHED THE CAVE NEEDLES.
TEACH ME TO USE THE THREE ROUND STONES-
I WILL, MY SON. THERE ARE MANY THINGS TO LEARN...
...IMPORTANT THINGS. THE SHAMAN OF OUR CLAN IS OLD... AND WISE.
HE TELLS OF TIMES PAST... OF THE OLD, OLD PEOPLE... OF THE CREATURES THAT ARE NO MORE.
24

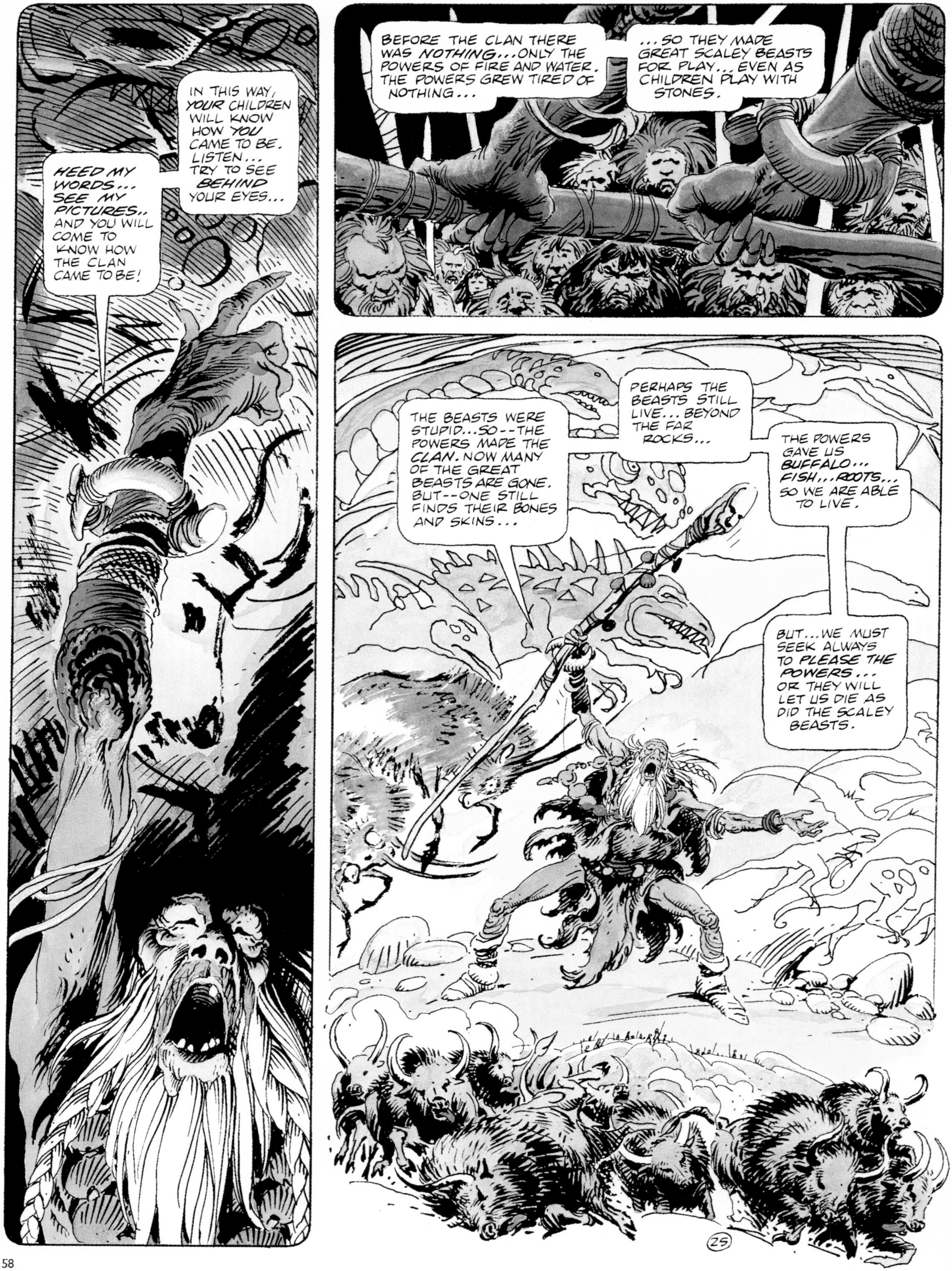
HEED MY WORDS... SEE MY PICTURES.. AND YOU WILL COME TO KNOW HOW THE CLAN CAME TO BE!
IN THIS WAY, YOUR CHILDREN WILL KNOW HOW YOU CAME TO BE. LISTEN... TRY TO SEE BEHIND YOUR EYES...
BEFORE THE CLAN THERE WAS NOTHING... ONLY THE POWERS OF FIRE AND WATER. THE POWERS GREW TIRED OF NOTHING...
...SO THEY MADE GREAT SCALEY BEASTS FOR PLAY... EVEN AS CHILDREN PLAY WITH STONES.
THE BEASTS WERE STUPID...SO--THE POWERS MADE THE CLAN. NOW MANY OF THE GREAT BEASTS ARE GONE. BUT--ONE STILL FINDS THEIR BONES AND SKINS...
PERHAPS THE BEASTS STILL LIVE... BEYOND THE FAR ROCKS...
THE POWERS GAVE US BUFFALO... FISH... ROOTS... SO WE ARE ABLE TO LIVE.
BUT... WE MUST SEEK ALWAYS TO PLEASE THE POWERS... OR THEY WILL LET US DIE AS DID THE SCALEY BEASTS.
25

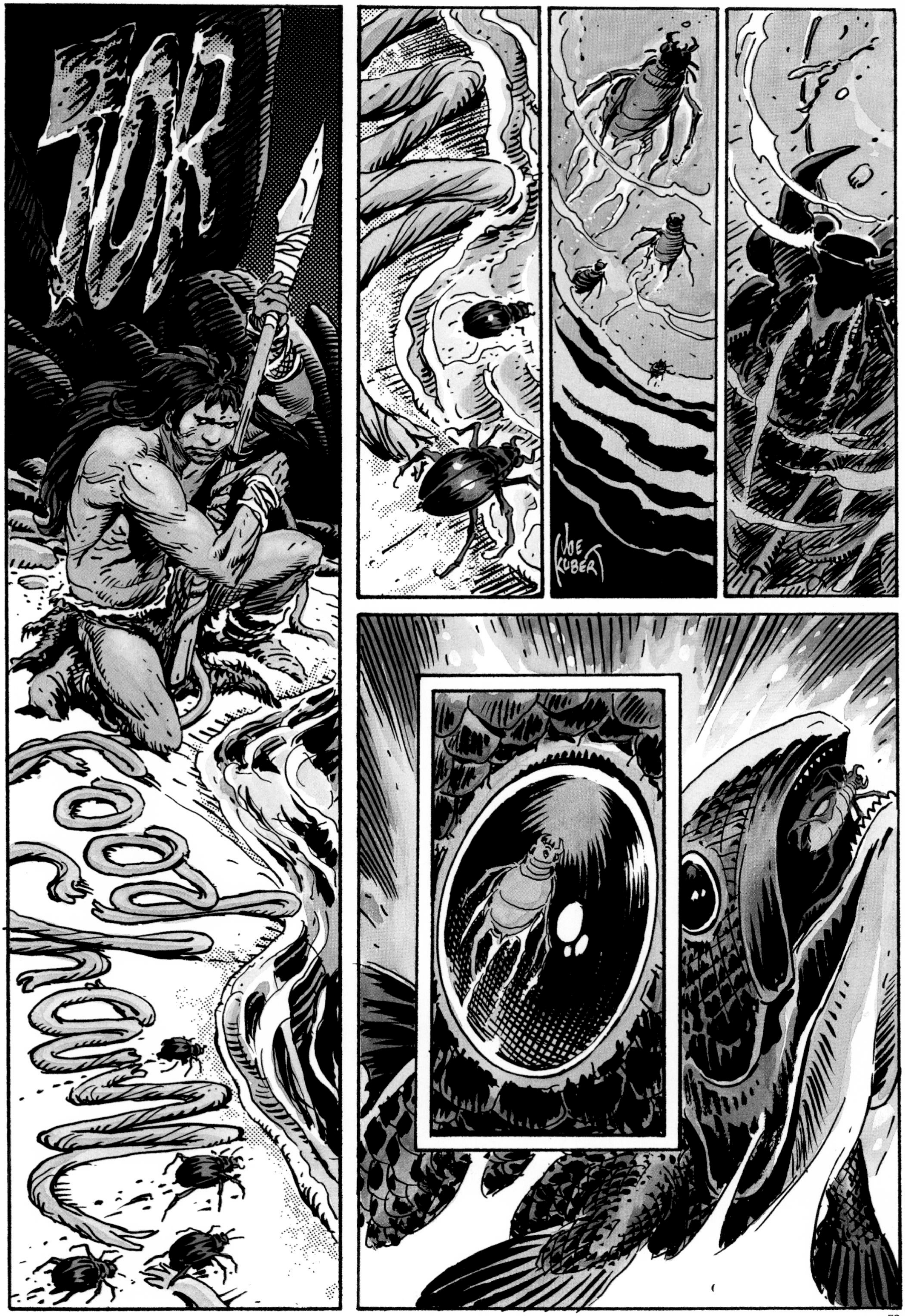
TOR
JOE KUBERT

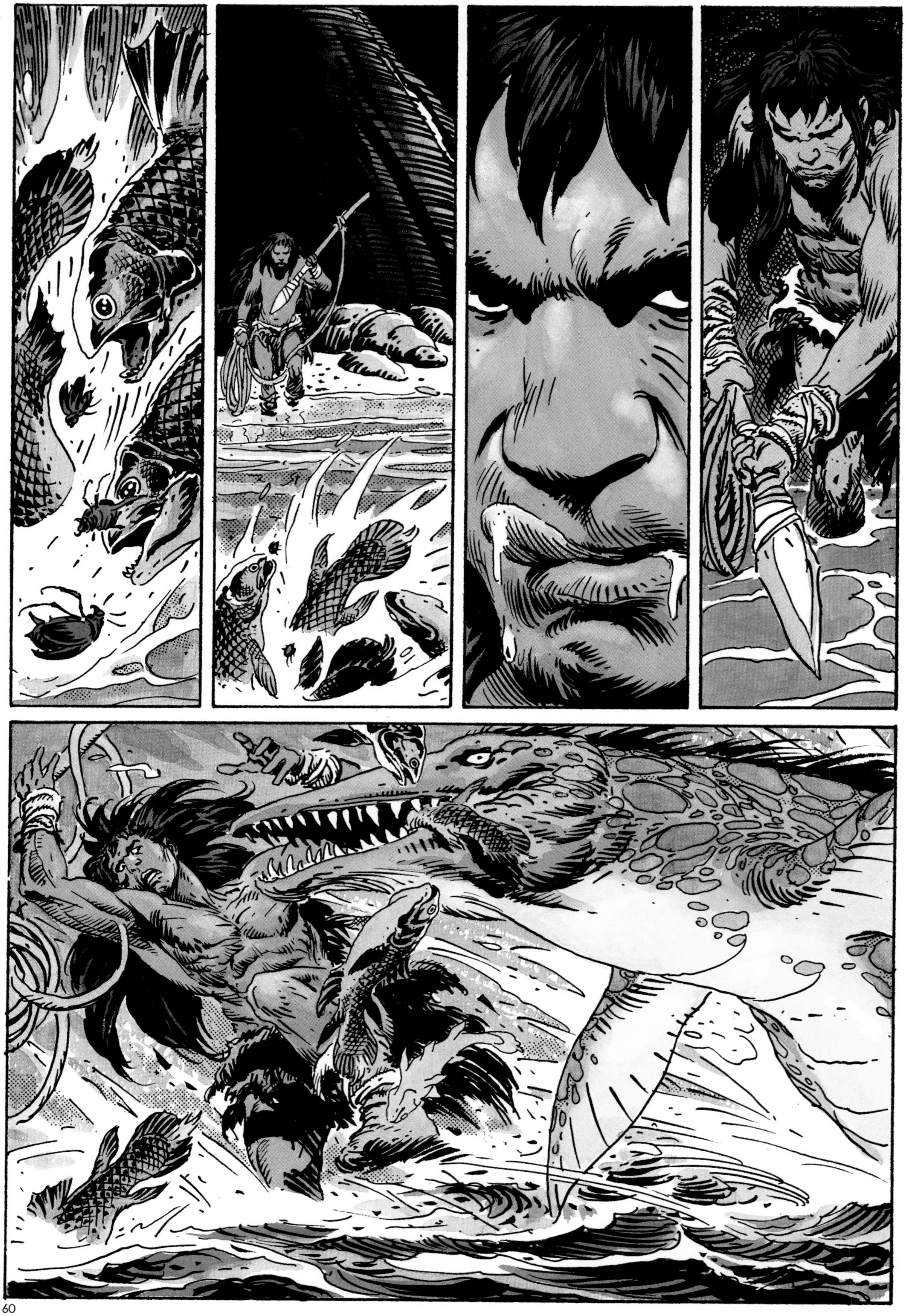

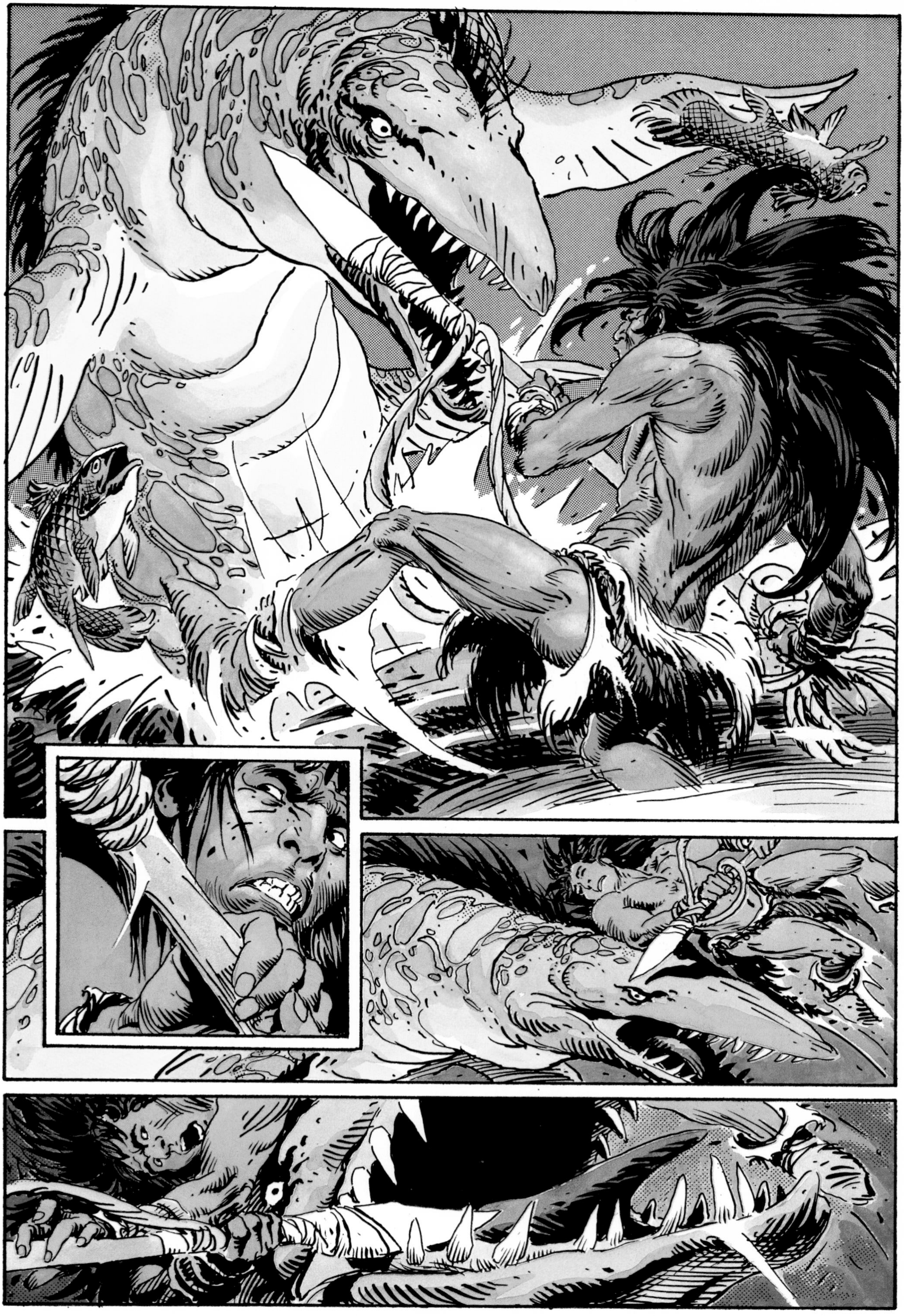

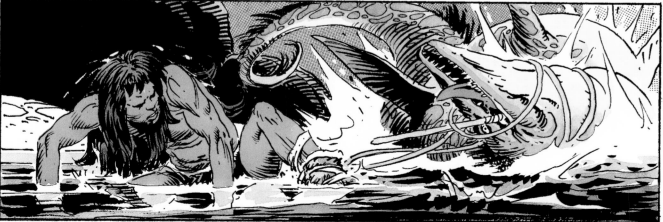

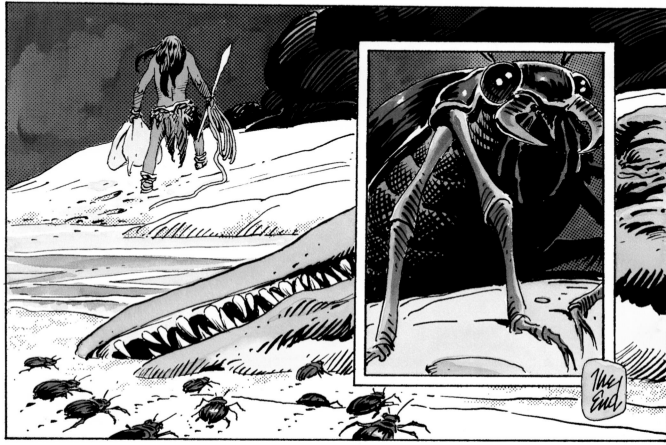

The End

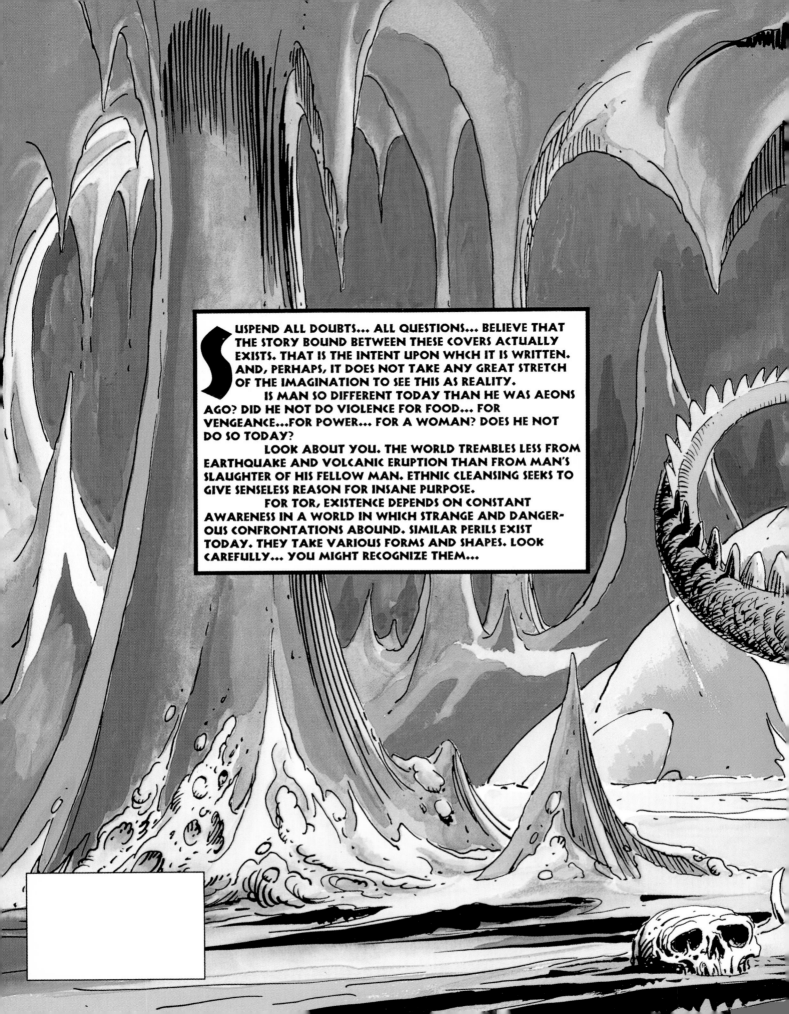

SUSPEND ALL DOUBTS... ALL QUESTIONS... BELIEVE THAT THE STORY BOUND BETWEEN THESE COVERS ACTUALLY EXISTS. THAT IS THE INTENT UPON WHCH IT IS WRITTEN. AND, PERHAPS, IT DOES NOT TAKE ANY GREAT STRETCH OF THE IMAGINATION TO SEE THIS AS REALITY.

IS MAN SO DIFFERENT TODAY THAN HE WAS AEONS AGO? DID HE NOT DO VIOLENCE FOR FOOD... FOR VENGEANCE...FOR POWER... FOR A WOMAN? DOES HE NOT DO SO TODAY?

LOOK ABOUT YOU. THE WORLD TREMBLES LESS FROM EARTHQUAKE AND VOLCANIC ERUPTION THAN FROM MAN'S SLAUGHTER OF HIS FELLOW MAN. ETHNIC CLEANSING SEEKS TO GIVE SENSELESS REASON FOR INSANE PURPOSE.

FOR TOR, EXISTENCE DEPENDS ON CONSTANT AWARENESS IN A WORLD IN WHICH STRANGE AND DANGEROUS CONFRONTATIONS ABOUND. SIMILAR PERILS EXIST TODAY. THEY TAKE VARIOUS FORMS AND SHAPES. LOOK CAREFULLY... YOU MIGHT RECOGNIZE THEM...

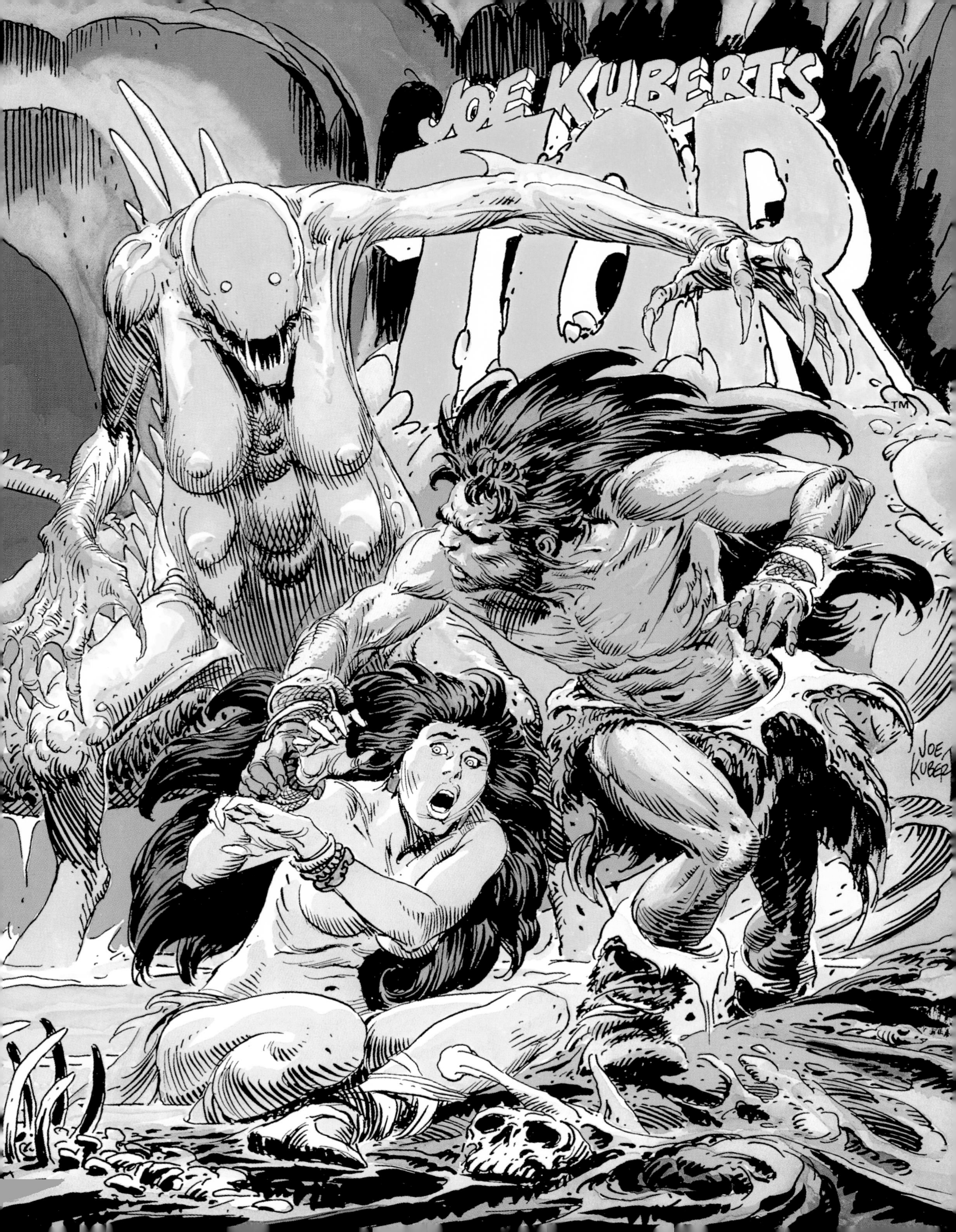
JOE KUBERT'S
TOR
TM
JOE KUBERT

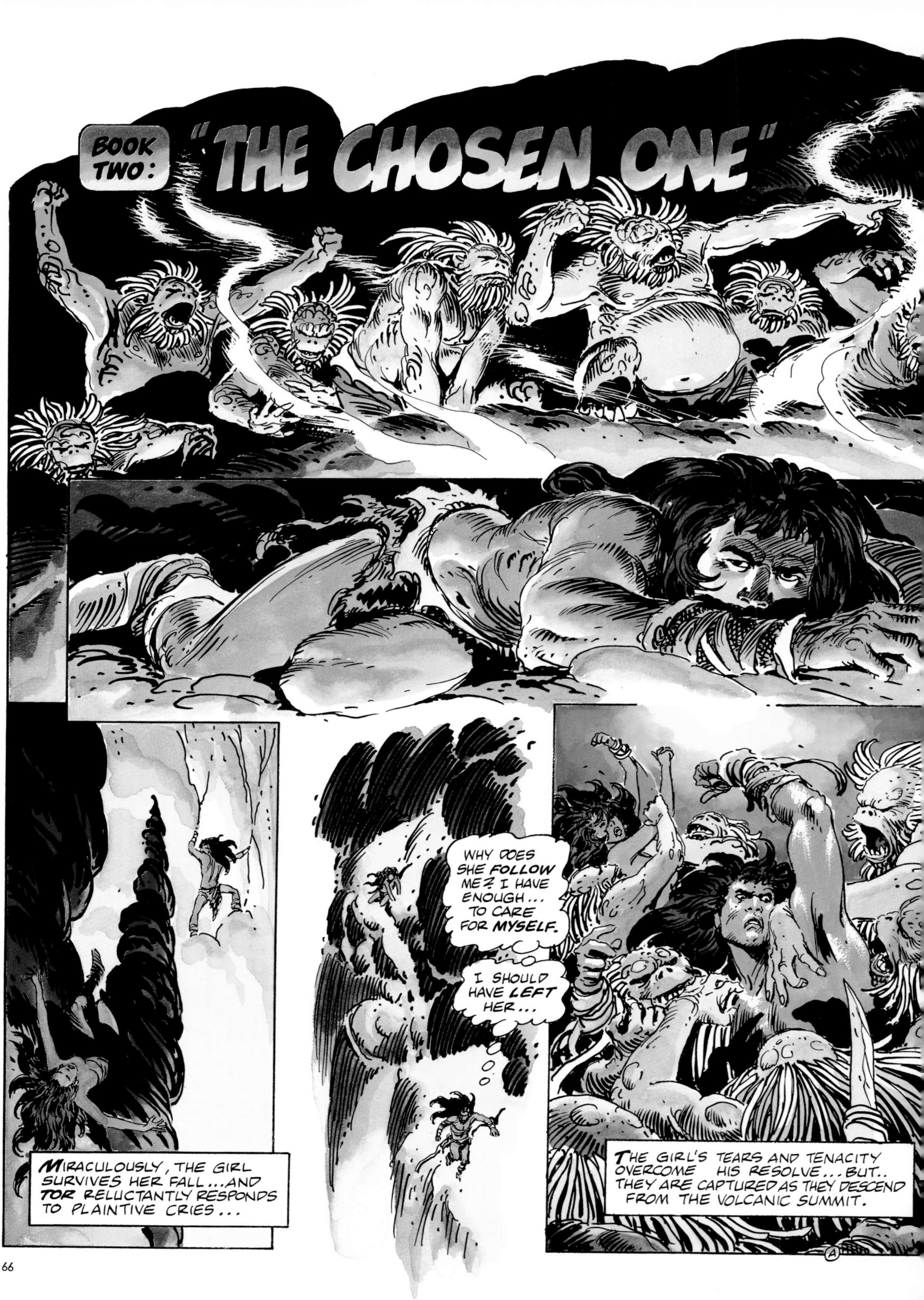
BOOK TWO: "THE CHOSEN ONE"
MIRACULOUSLY, THE GIRL SURVIVES HER FALL...AND TOR RELUCTANTLY RESPONDS TO PLAINTIVE CRIES...
WHY DOES SHE FOLLOW ME? I HAVE ENOUGH... TO CARE FOR MYSELF.
I SHOULD HAVE LEFT HER...
THE GIRL'S TEARS AND TENACITY OVERCOME HIS RESOLVE... BUT.. THEY ARE CAPTURED AS THEY DESCEND FROM THE VOLCANIC SUMMIT.

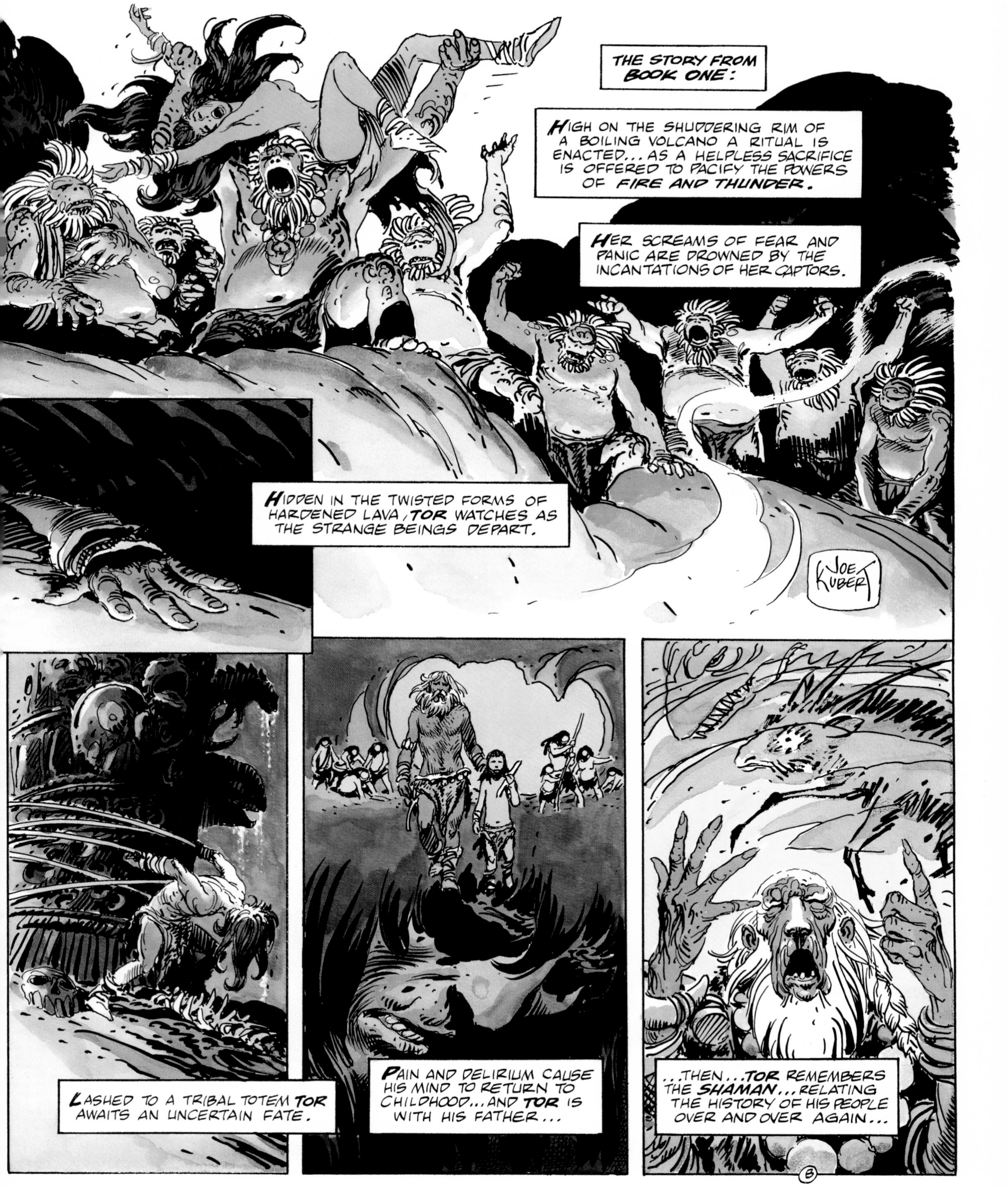
THE STORY FROM BOOK ONE:
HIGH ON THE SHUDDERING RIM OF A BOILING VOLCANO A RITUAL IS ENACTED... AS A HELPLESS SACRIFICE IS OFFERED TO PACIFY THE POWERS OF FIRE AND THUNDER.
HER SCREAMS OF FEAR AND PANIC ARE DROWNED BY THE INCANTATIONS OF HER CAPTORS.
HIDDEN IN THE TWISTED FORMS OF HARDENED LAVA, TOR WATCHES AS THE STRANGE BEINGS DEPART.
JOE KUBERT
LASHED TO A TRIBAL TOTEM TOR AWAITS AN UNCERTAIN FATE.
PAIN AND DELIRIUM CAUSE HIS MIND TO RETURN TO CHILDHOOD... AND TOR IS WITH HIS FATHER...
...THEN...TOR REMEMBERS THE SHAMAN...RELATING THE HISTORY OF HIS PEOPLE OVER AND OVER AGAIN...
B

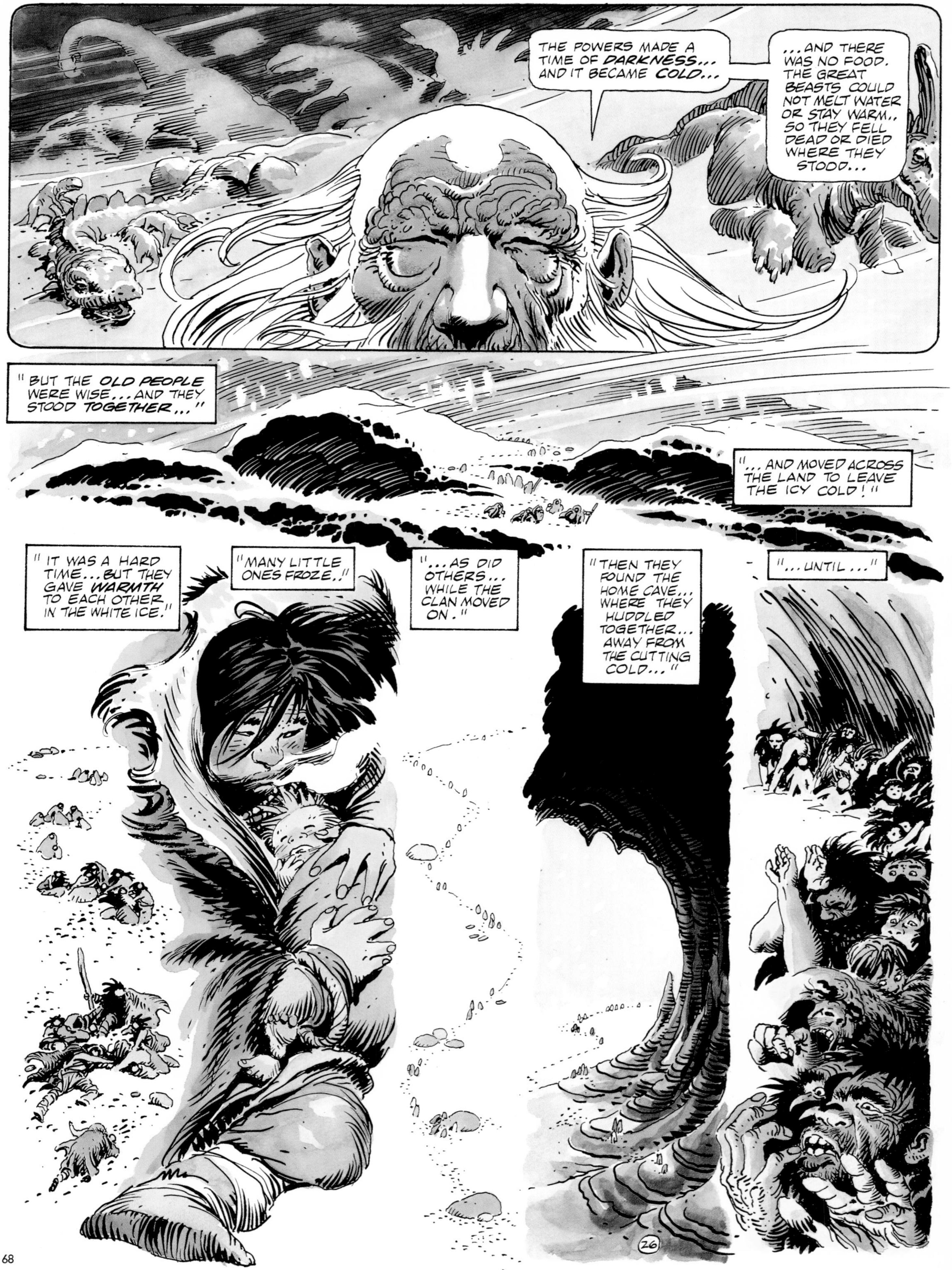
THE POWERS MADE A TIME OF DARKNESS... AND IT BECAME COLD...
...AND THERE WAS NO FOOD. THE GREAT BEASTS COULD NOT MELT WATER OR STAY WARM.. SO THEY FELL DEAD OR DIED WHERE THEY STOOD...
"BUT THE OLD PEOPLE WERE WISE... AND THEY STOOD TOGETHER..."
"...AND MOVED ACROSS THE LAND TO LEAVE THE ICY COLD!"
"IT WAS A HARD TIME... BUT THEY GAVE WARMTH TO EACH OTHER IN THE WHITE ICE."
"MANY LITTLE ONES FROZE.."
"...AS DID OTHERS... WHILE THE CLAN MOVED ON."
"THEN THEY FOUND THE HOME CAVE... WHERE THEY HUDDLED TOGETHER... AWAY FROM THE CUTTING COLD..."
"...UNTIL..."
26

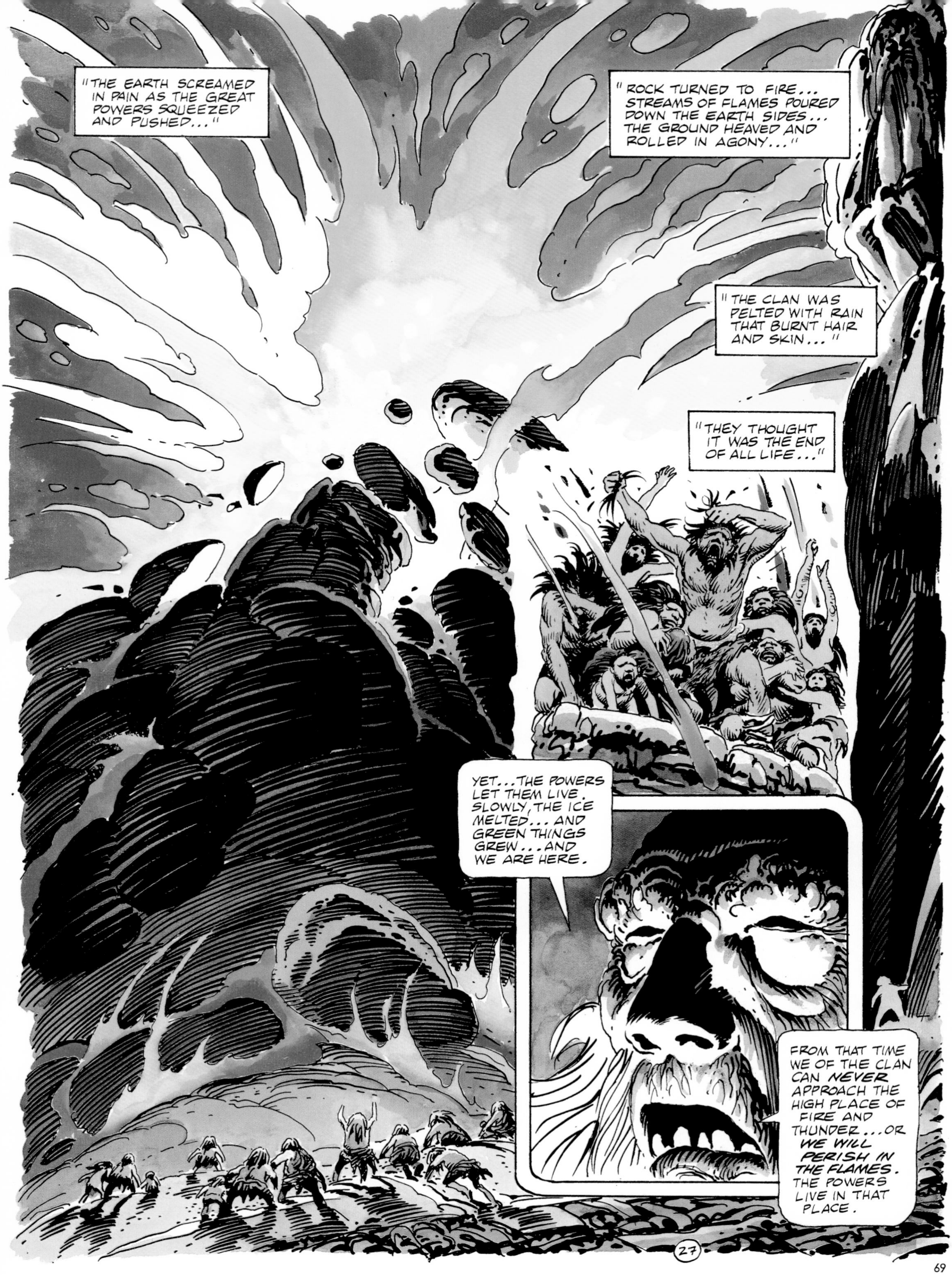
"THE EARTH SCREAMED IN PAIN AS THE GREAT POWERS SQUEEZED AND PUSHED..."
"ROCK TURNED TO FIRE... STREAMS OF FLAMES POURED DOWN THE EARTH SIDES... THE GROUND HEAVED AND ROLLED IN AGONY..."
"THE CLAN WAS PELTED WITH RAIN THAT BURNT HAIR AND SKIN..."
"THEY THOUGHT IT WAS THE END OF ALL LIFE..."
YET... THE POWERS LET THEM LIVE. SLOWLY, THE ICE MELTED... AND GREEN THINGS GREW... AND WE ARE HERE.
FROM THAT TIME WE OF THE CLAN CAN NEVER APPROACH THE HIGH PLACE OF FIRE AND THUNDER... OR WE WILL PERISH IN THE FLAMES. THE POWERS LIVE IN THAT PLACE.
27

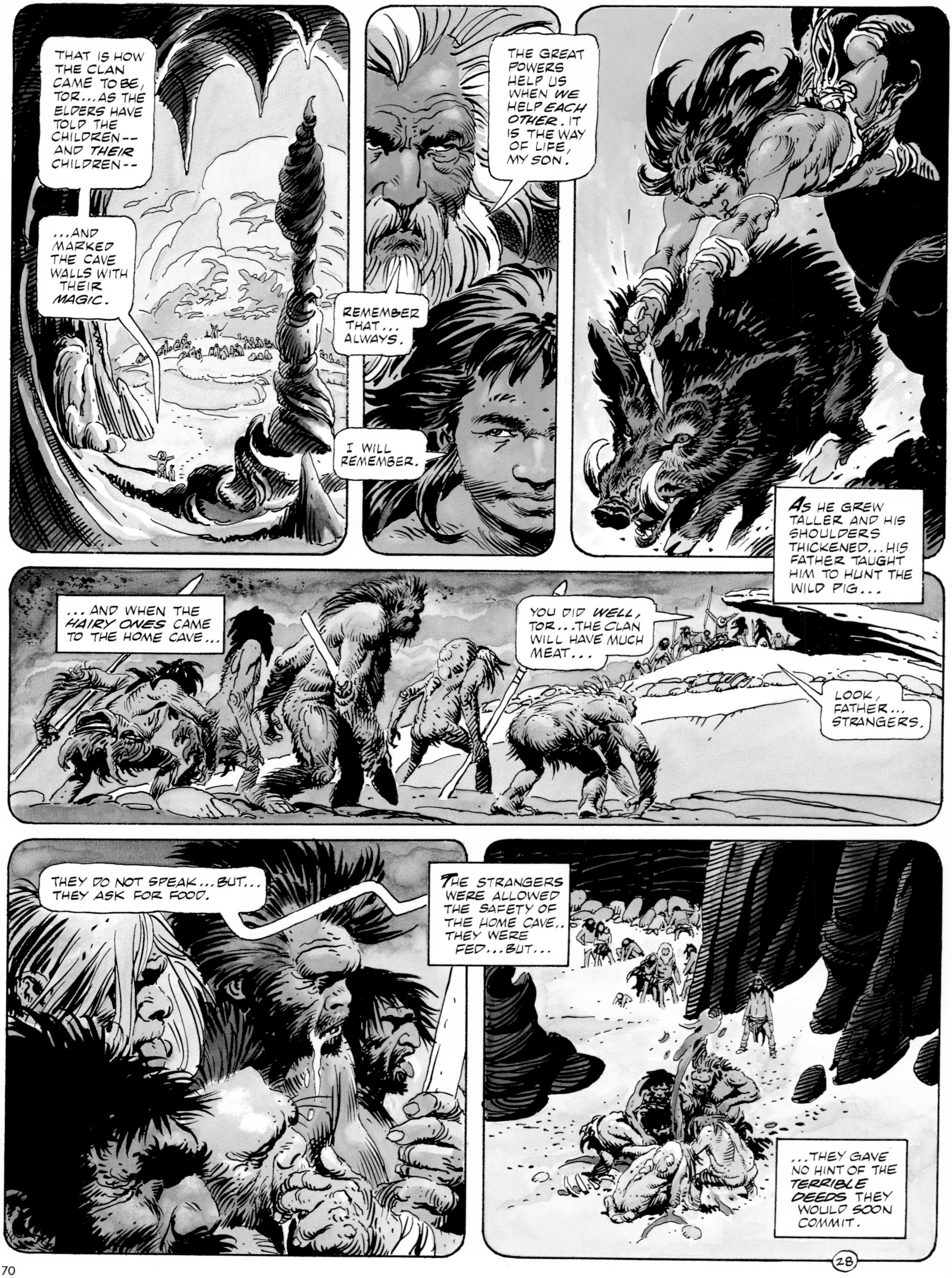
THAT IS HOW THE CLAN CAME TO BE, TOR... AS THE ELDERS HAVE TOLD THE CHILDREN-- AND THEIR CHILDREN--
...AND MARKED THE CAVE WALLS WITH THEIR MAGIC.
THE GREAT POWERS HELP US WHEN WE HELP EACH OTHER. IT IS THE WAY OF LIFE, MY SON.
REMEMBER THAT... ALWAYS.
I WILL REMEMBER.
AS HE GREW TALLER AND HIS SHOULDERS THICKENED... HIS FATHER TAUGHT HIM TO HUNT THE WILD PIG...
YOU DID WELL, TOR... THE CLAN WILL HAVE MUCH MEAT...
...AND WHEN THE HAIRY ONES CAME TO THE HOME CAVE...
LOOK, FATHER... STRANGERS.
THEY DO NOT SPEAK... BUT... THEY ASK FOR FOOD.
THE STRANGERS WERE ALLOWED THE SAFETY OF THE HOME CAVE.. THEY WERE FED... BUT...
...THEY GAVE NO HINT OF THE TERRIBLE DEEDS THEY WOULD SOON COMMIT.
28

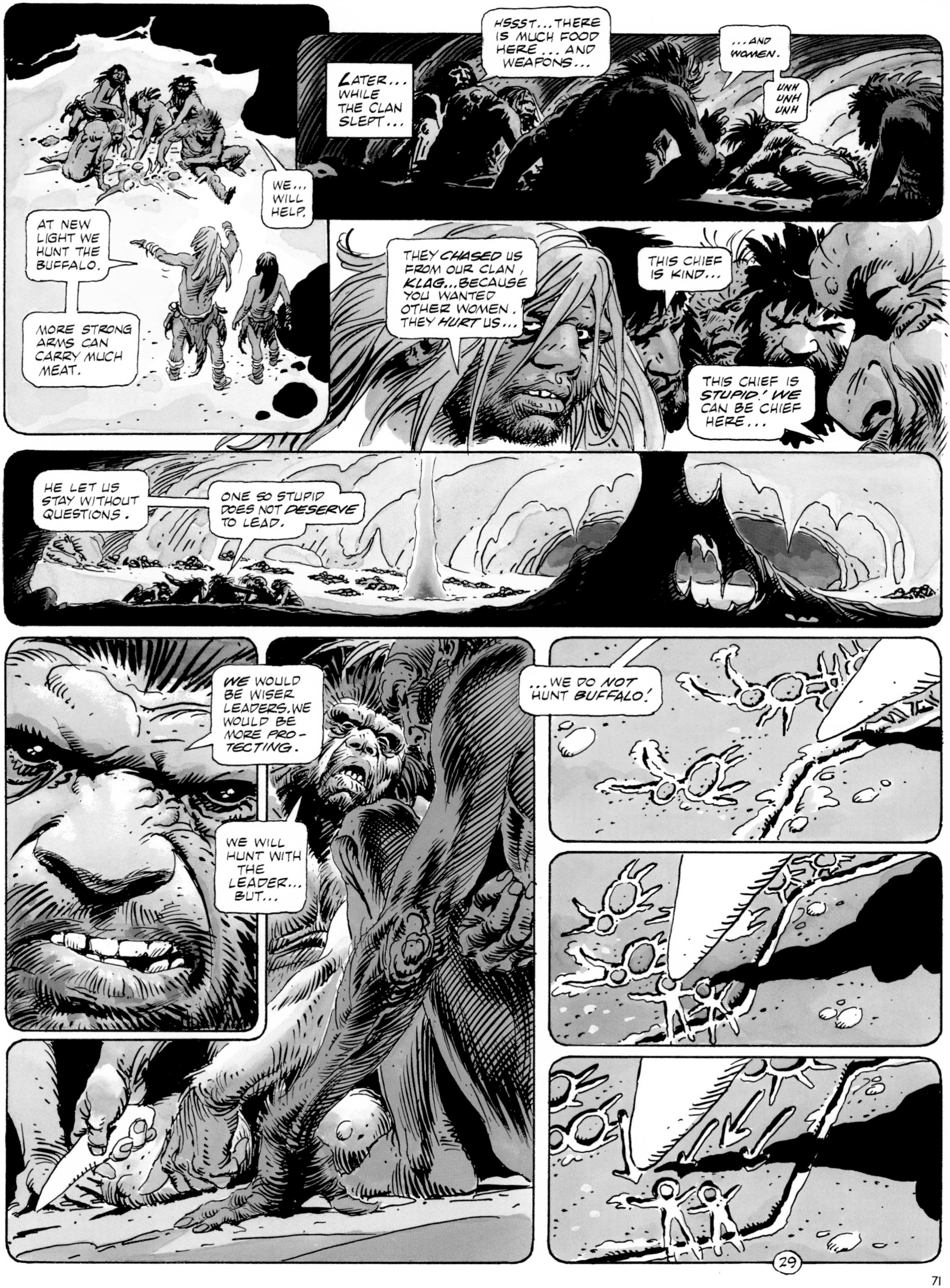
WE... WILL HELP.
AT NEW LIGHT WE HUNT THE BUFFALO.
MORE STRONG ARMS CAN CARRY MUCH MEAT.
LATER... WHILE THE CLAN SLEPT...
HSSST... THERE IS MUCH FOOD HERE ... AND WEAPONS...
...AND WOMEN.
UNH UNH UNH
THEY CHASED US FROM OUR CLAN, KLAG...BECAUSE YOU WANTED OTHER WOMEN. THEY HURT US...
THIS CHIEF IS KIND...
THIS CHIEF IS STUPID! WE CAN BE CHIEF HERE...
HE LET US STAY WITHOUT QUESTIONS.
ONE SO STUPID DOES NOT DESERVE TO LEAD.
WE WOULD BE WISER LEADERS. WE WOULD BE MORE PRO-TECTING.
WE WILL HUNT WITH THE LEADER... BUT...
...WE DO NOT HUNT BUFFALO!
29

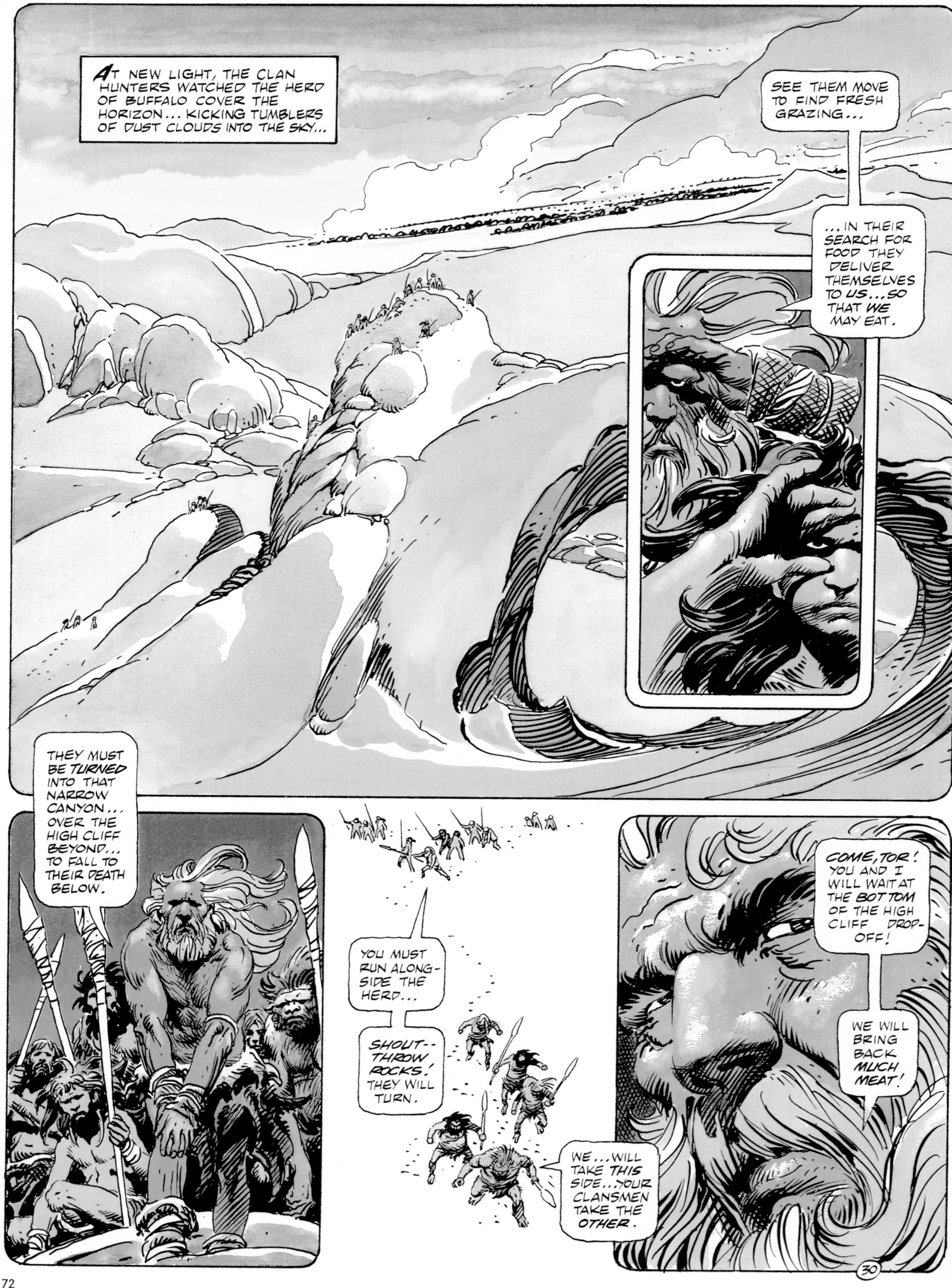
At new light, the clan hunters watched the herd of buffalo cover the horizon... kicking tumblers of dust clouds into the sky...
See them move to find fresh grazing...
...in their search for food they deliver themselves to us... so that we may eat.
They must be turned into that narrow canyon... over the high cliff beyond... to fall to their death below.
You must run alongside the herd...
Shout--throw rocks! They will turn.
We... will take this side... your clansmen take the other.
Come, Tor! You and I will wait at the bottom of the high cliff drop-off!
We will bring back much meat!
30

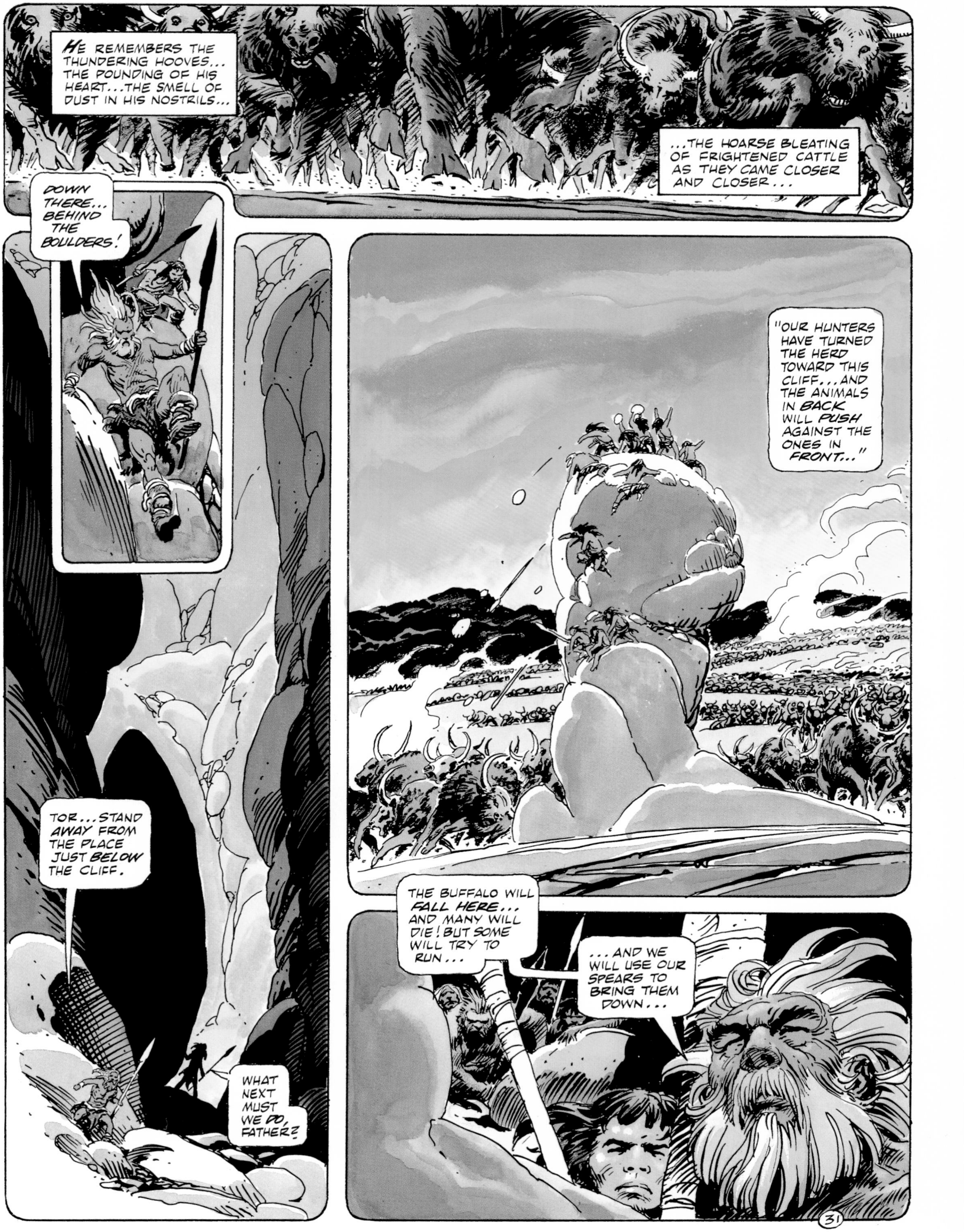
HE REMEMBERS THE THUNDERING HOOVES... THE POUNDING OF HIS HEART...THE SMELL OF DUST IN HIS NOSTRILS...
...THE HOARSE BLEATING OF FRIGHTENED CATTLE AS THEY CAME CLOSER AND CLOSER...
DOWN THERE... BEHIND THE BOULDERS!
"OUR HUNTERS HAVE TURNED THE HERD TOWARD THIS CLIFF...AND THE ANIMALS IN BACK WILL PUSH AGAINST THE ONES IN FRONT..."
TOR...STAND AWAY FROM THE PLACE JUST BELOW THE CLIFF.
WHAT NEXT MUST WE DO, FATHER?
THE BUFFALO WILL FALL HERE... AND MANY WILL DIE! BUT SOME WILL TRY TO RUN...
...AND WE WILL USE OUR SPEARS TO BRING THEM DOWN...
31

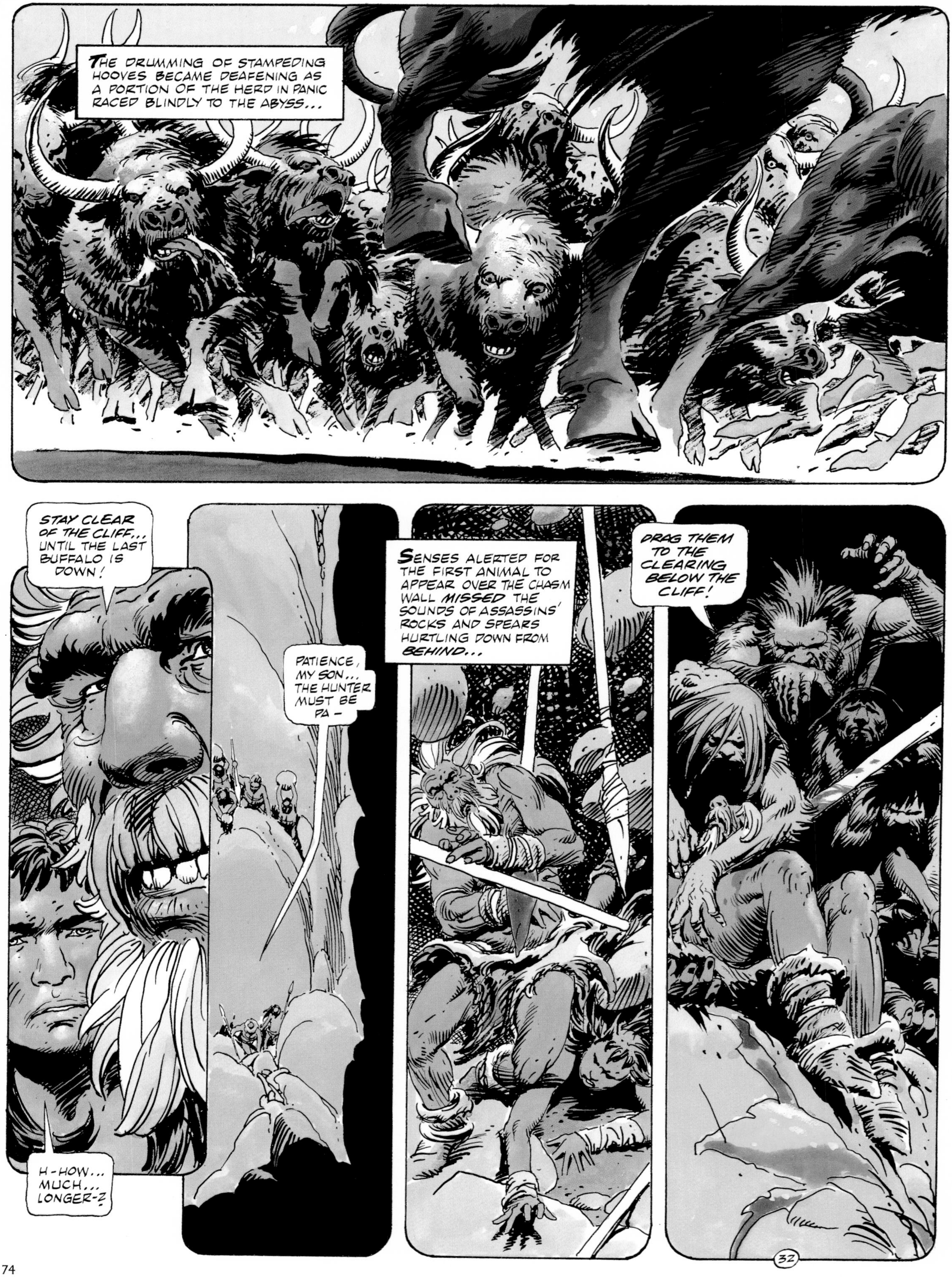
THE DRUMMING OF STAMPEDING HOOVES BECAME DEAFENING AS A PORTION OF THE HERD IN PANIC RACED BLINDLY TO THE ABYSS...
STAY CLEAR OF THE CLIFF... UNTIL THE LAST BUFFALO IS DOWN!
H-HOW... MUCH... LONGER-?
PATIENCE, MY SON... THE HUNTER MUST BE PA–
SENSES ALERTED FOR THE FIRST ANIMAL TO APPEAR OVER THE CHASM WALL MISSED THE SOUNDS OF ASSASSINS' ROCKS AND SPEARS HURTLING DOWN FROM BEHIND...
DRAG THEM TO THE CLEARING BELOW THE CLIFF!
32

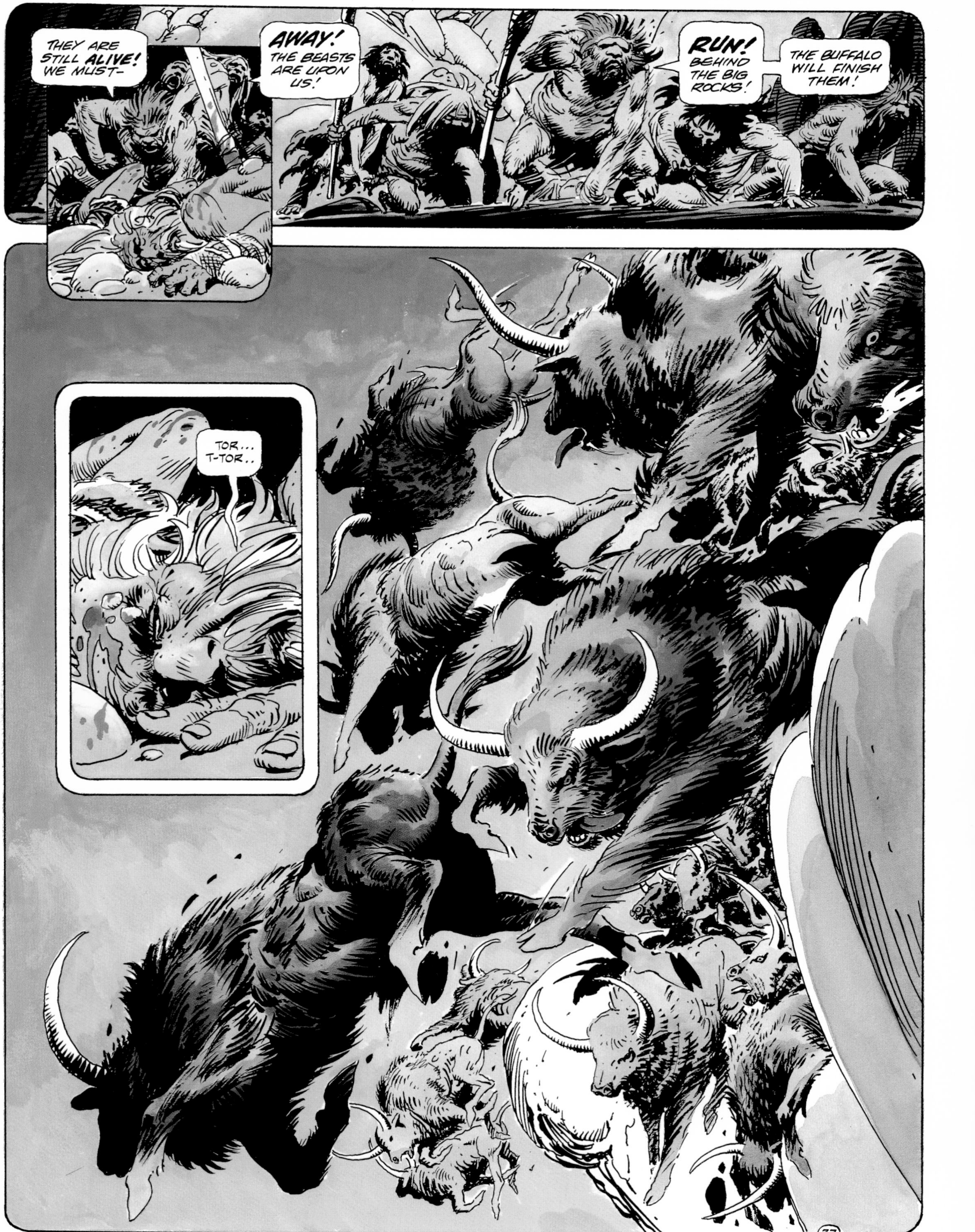
THEY ARE STILL ALIVE! WE MUST-
AWAY! THE BEASTS ARE UPON US!
RUN! BEHIND THE BIG ROCKS!
THE BUFFALO WILL FINISH THEM!
TOR... T-TOR..
33

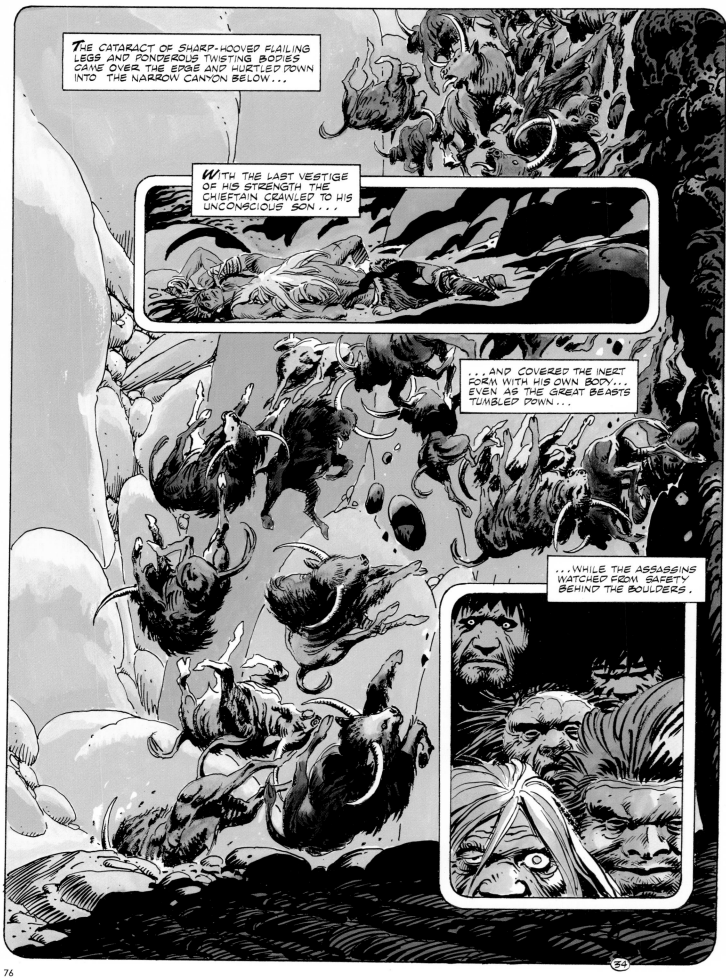

THE CATARACT OF SHARP-HOOVED FLAILING LEGS AND PONDEROUS TWISTING BODIES CAME OVER THE EDGE AND HURTLED DOWN INTO THE NARROW CANYON BELOW...

WITH THE LAST VESTIGE OF HIS STRENGTH THE CHIEFTAIN CRAWLED TO HIS UNCONSCIOUS SON...

...AND COVERED THE INERT FORM WITH HIS OWN BODY... EVEN AS THE GREAT BEASTS TUMBLED DOWN...

...WHILE THE ASSASSINS WATCHED FROM SAFETY BEHIND THE BOULDERS.

34

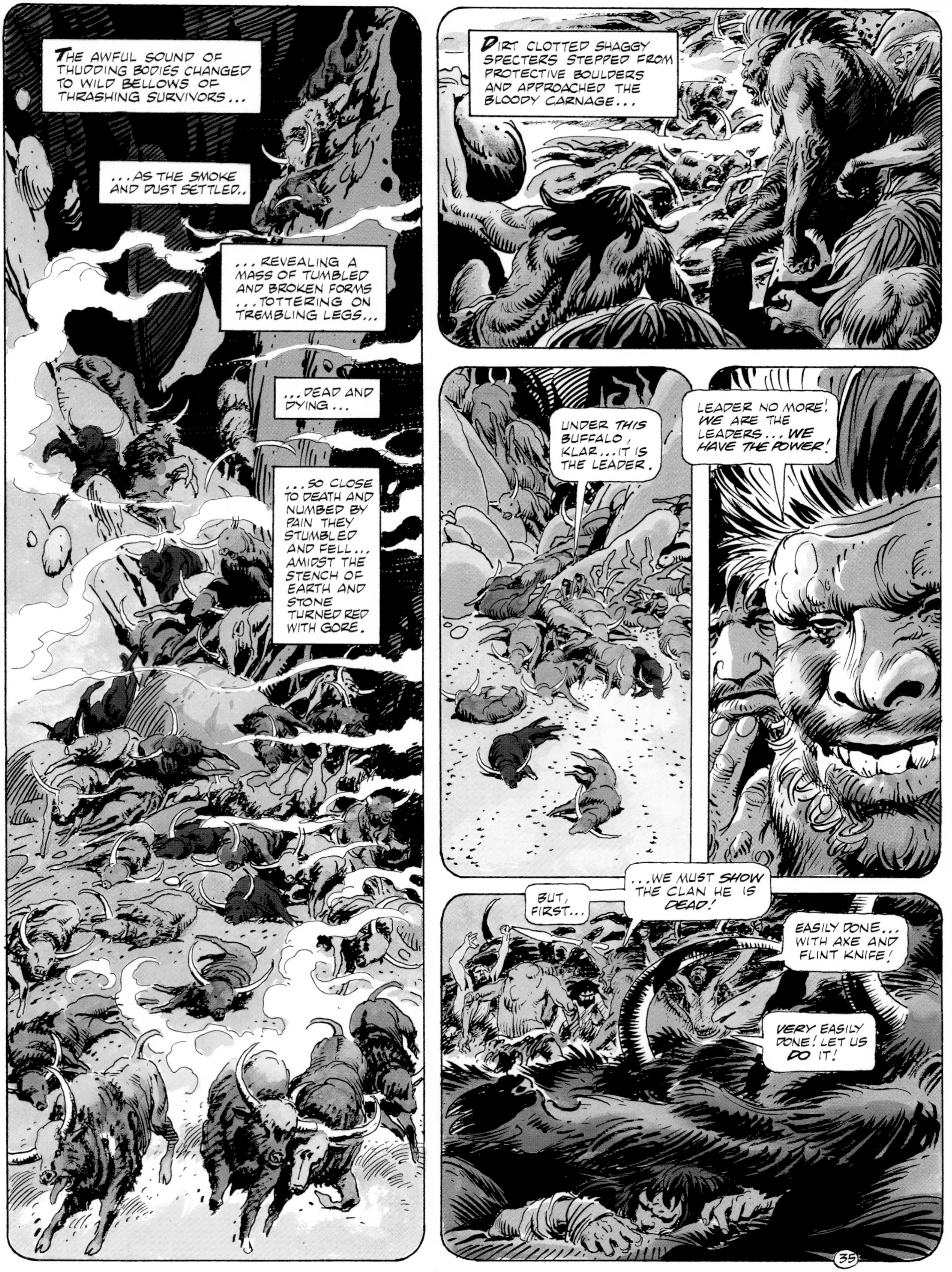
THE AWFUL SOUND OF THUDDING BODIES CHANGED TO WILD BELLOWS OF THRASHING SURVIVORS...
...AS THE SMOKE AND DUST SETTLED..
...REVEALING A MASS OF TUMBLED AND BROKEN FORMS ...TOTTERING ON TREMBLING LEGS...
...DEAD AND DYING...
...SO CLOSE TO DEATH AND NUMBED BY PAIN THEY STUMBLED AND FELL... AMIDST THE STENCH OF EARTH AND STONE TURNED RED WITH GORE.
DIRT CLOTTED SHAGGY SPECTERS STEPPED FROM PROTECTIVE BOULDERS AND APPROACHED THE BLOODY CARNAGE...
UNDER THIS BUFFALO, KLAR... IT IS THE LEADER.
LEADER NO MORE! WE ARE THE LEADERS... WE HAVE THE POWER!
BUT, FIRST...
...WE MUST SHOW THE CLAN HE IS DEAD!
EASILY DONE... WITH AXE AND FLINT KNIFE!
VERY EASILY DONE! LET US DO IT!
35

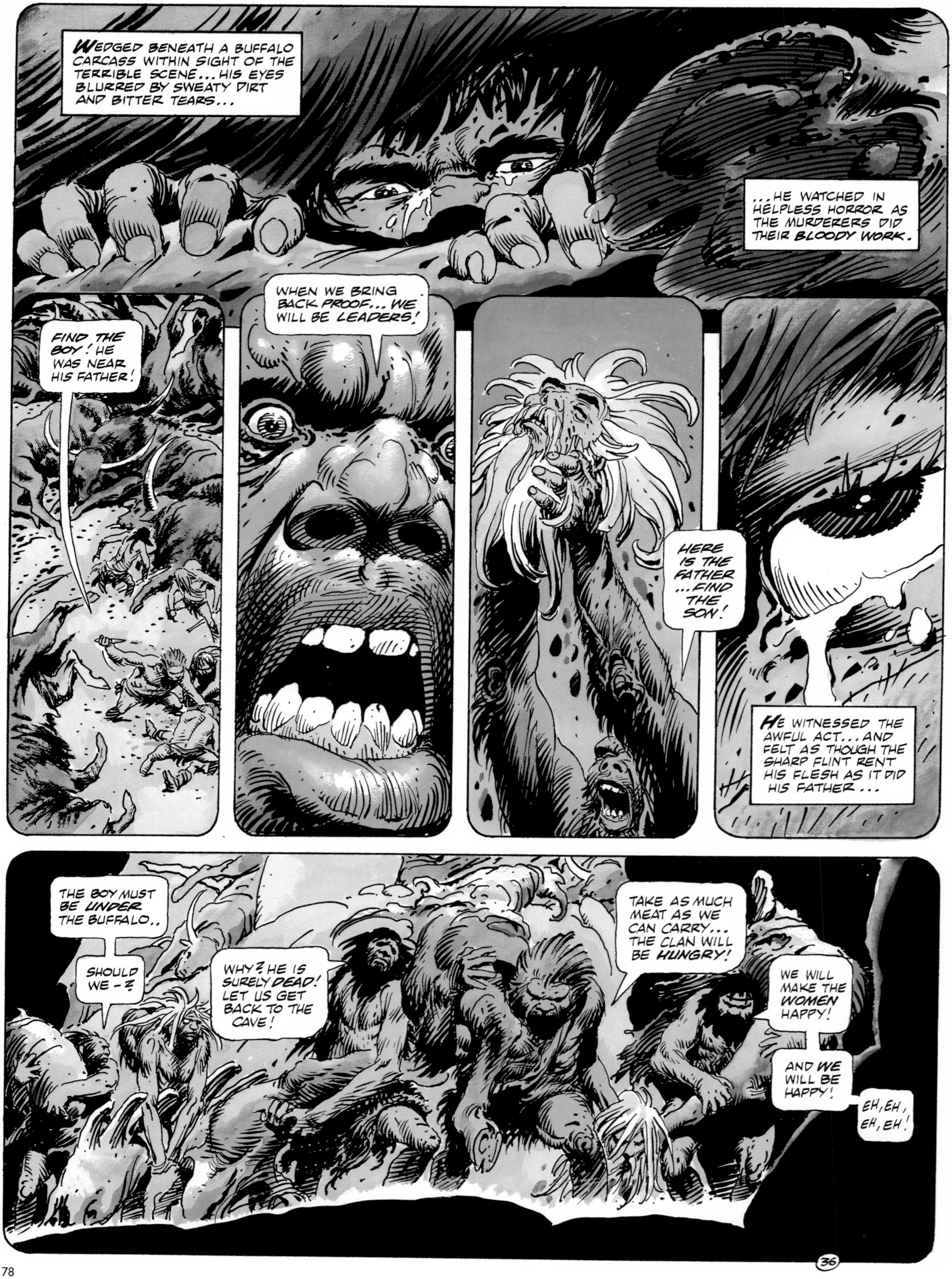
WEDGED BENEATH A BUFFALO CARCASS WITHIN SIGHT OF THE TERRIBLE SCENE... HIS EYES BLURRED BY SWEATY DIRT AND BITTER TEARS...
...HE WATCHED IN HELPLESS HORROR AS THE MURDERERS DID THEIR BLOODY WORK.
FIND THE BOY! HE WAS NEAR HIS FATHER!
WHEN WE BRING BACK PROOF... WE WILL BE LEADERS!
HERE IS THE FATHER ...FIND THE SON!
HE WITNESSED THE AWFUL ACT... AND FELT AS THOUGH THE SHARP FLINT RENT HIS FLESH AS IT DID HIS FATHER...
THE BOY MUST BE UNDER THE BUFFALO..
SHOULD WE -?
WHY? HE IS SURELY DEAD! LET US GET BACK TO THE CAVE!
TAKE AS MUCH MEAT AS WE CAN CARRY... THE CLAN WILL BE HUNGRY!
WE WILL MAKE THE WOMEN HAPPY!
AND WE WILL BE HAPPY!
EH, EH, EH, EH!
36

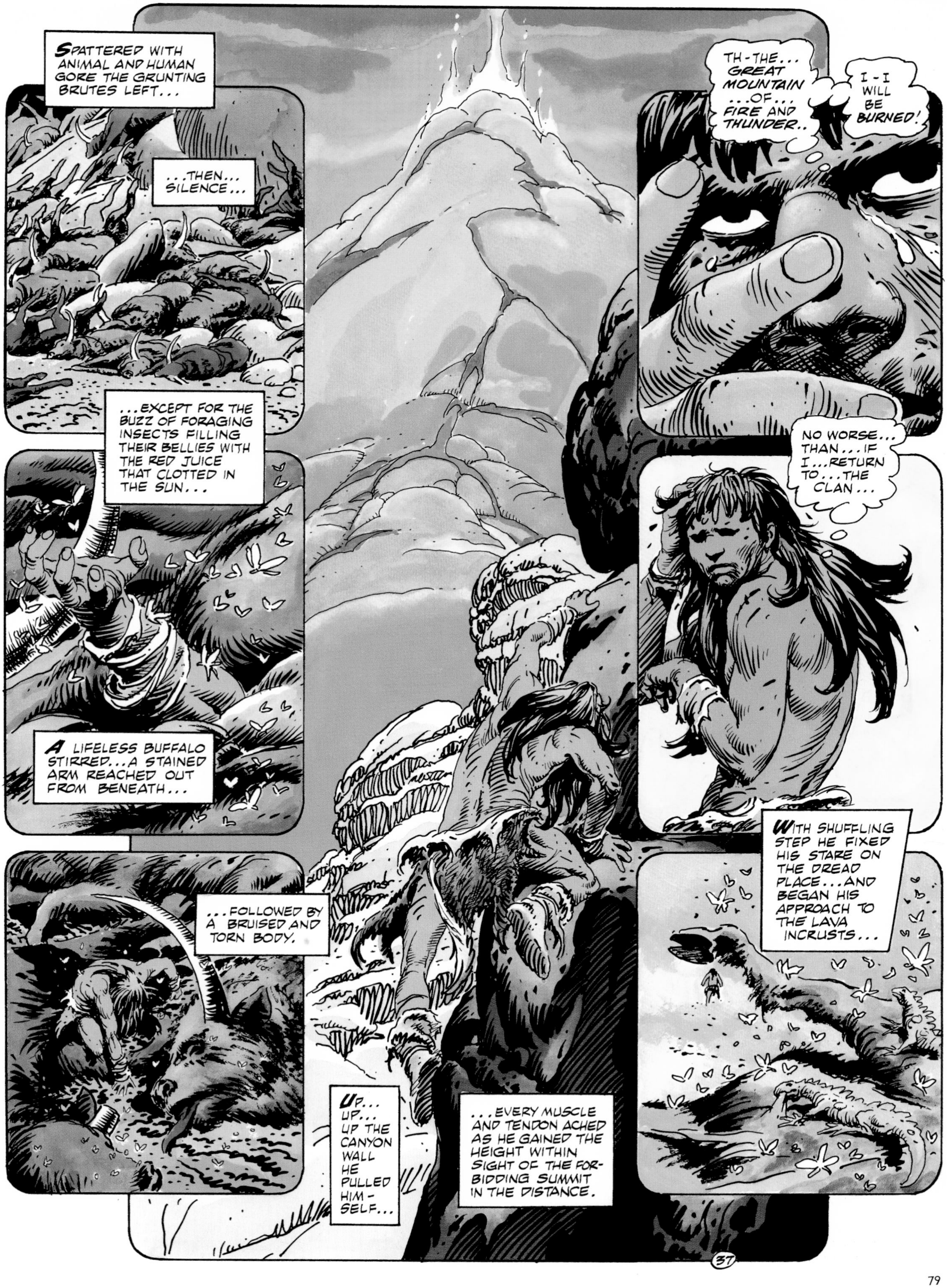

SPATTERED WITH ANIMAL AND HUMAN GORE THE GRUNTING BRUTES LEFT...
...THEN... SILENCE...
...EXCEPT FOR THE BUZZ OF FORAGING INSECTS FILLING THEIR BELLIES WITH THE RED JUICE THAT CLOTTED IN THE SUN...
A LIFELESS BUFFALO STIRRED...A STAINED ARM REACHED OUT FROM BENEATH...
...FOLLOWED BY A BRUISED AND TORN BODY.
UP... UP... UP THE CANYON WALL HE PULLED HIM-SELF...
...EVERY MUSCLE AND TENDON ACHED AS HE GAINED THE HEIGHT WITHIN SIGHT OF THE FOR-BIDDING SUMMIT IN THE DISTANCE.
TH-THE... GREAT MOUNTAIN ...OF... FIRE AND THUNDER..
I-I WILL BE BURNED!
NO WORSE... THAN... IF I...RETURN TO...THE CLAN...
WITH SHUFFLING STEP HE FIXED HIS STARE ON THE DREAD PLACE...AND BEGAN HIS APPROACH TO THE LAVA INCRUSTS...
37

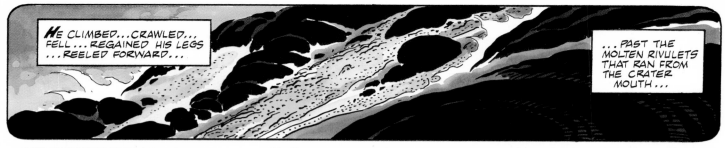

HE CLIMBED...CRAWLED...FELL...REGAINED HIS LEGS...REELED FORWARD...

...PAST THE MOLTEN RIVULETS THAT RAN FROM THE CRATER MOUTH...

UNH...THE G-GROUND...BURNS...

HE SCUTTLED BEHIND AN OUTCROPPING...JUST IN TIME TO AVOID A NEW LAVA FLOW...

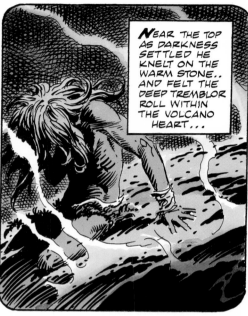

NEAR THE TOP AS DARKNESS SETTLED HE KNELT ON THE WARM STONE...AND FELT THE DEEP TREMBLOR ROLL WITHIN THE VOLCANO HEART...

HE LICKED HIS WOUNDS AND MEWLED FOR THE SOFT ACHE HE FELT INSIDE...FOR HIS FATHER...FOR HIM-SELF...

DARKNESS TURNED TO LIGHT MANY TIMES...SLOWLY THE WOUNDS HEALED INTO HARD SCARS...

MANY TIMES HE WATCHED THE PROCESSION LEADING A SACRIFICE TO THE YAWNING CRATER EDGE...

WHY DID HE HELP THIS GIRL? NOW HE IS TO BE SACRIFICED...LIKE THE STUPID STAMPEDING BUFFALO!

"WE MUST HELP EACH OTHER..."

THE WORDS OF HIS FATHER RANG IN HIS EARS...

38

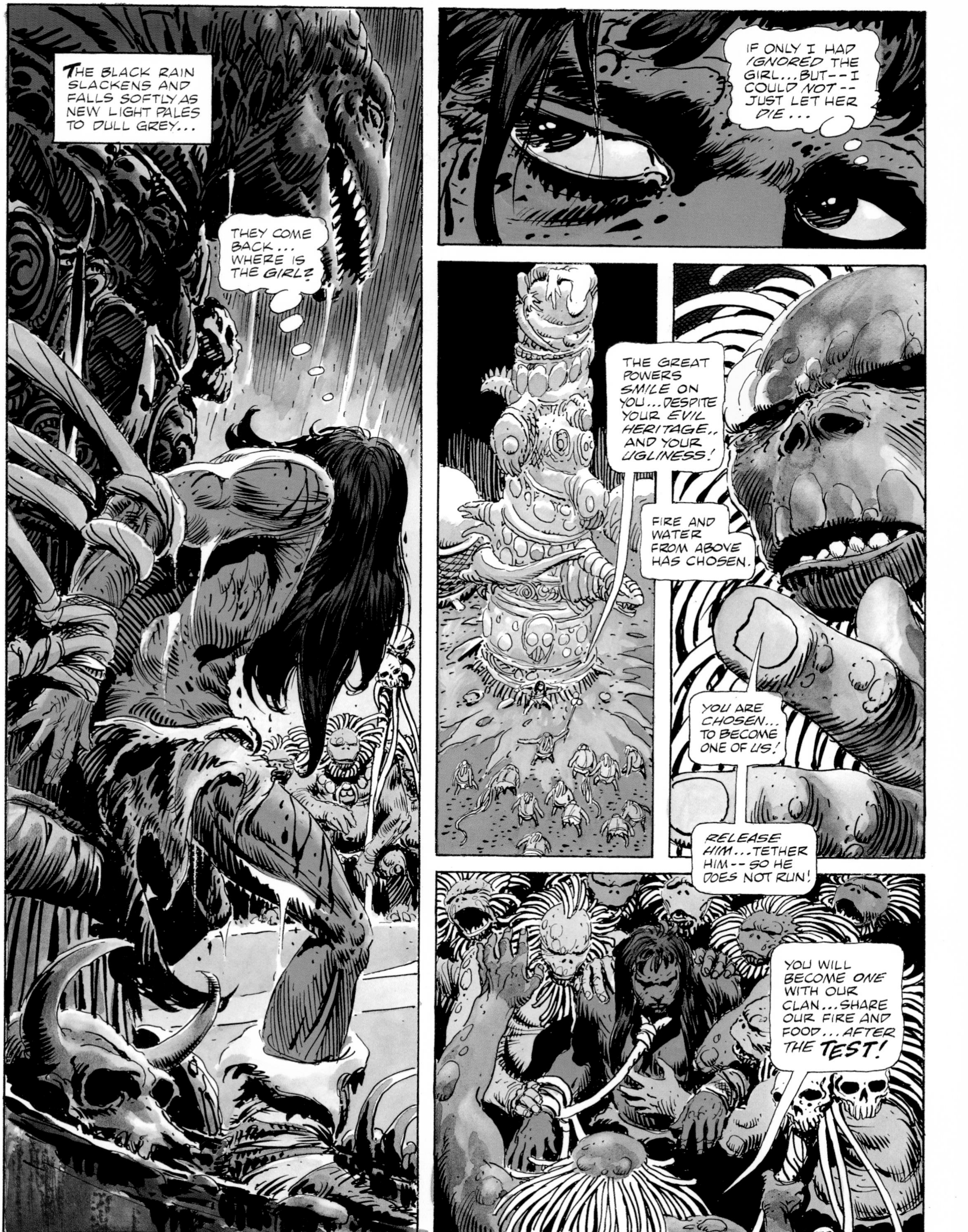
THE BLACK RAIN SLACKENS AND FALLS SOFTLY AS NEW LIGHT PALES TO DULL GREY...
THEY COME BACK... WHERE IS THE GIRL?
IF ONLY I HAD IGNORED THE GIRL...BUT-- I COULD NOT-- JUST LET HER DIE...
THE GREAT POWERS SMILE ON YOU...DESPITE YOUR EVIL HERITAGE.. AND YOUR UGLINESS!
FIRE AND WATER FROM ABOVE HAS CHOSEN.
YOU ARE CHOSEN... TO BECOME ONE OF US!
RELEASE HIM...TETHER HIM-- SO HE DOES NOT RUN!
YOU WILL BECOME ONE WITH OUR CLAN...SHARE OUR FIRE AND FOOD...AFTER THE TEST!
39

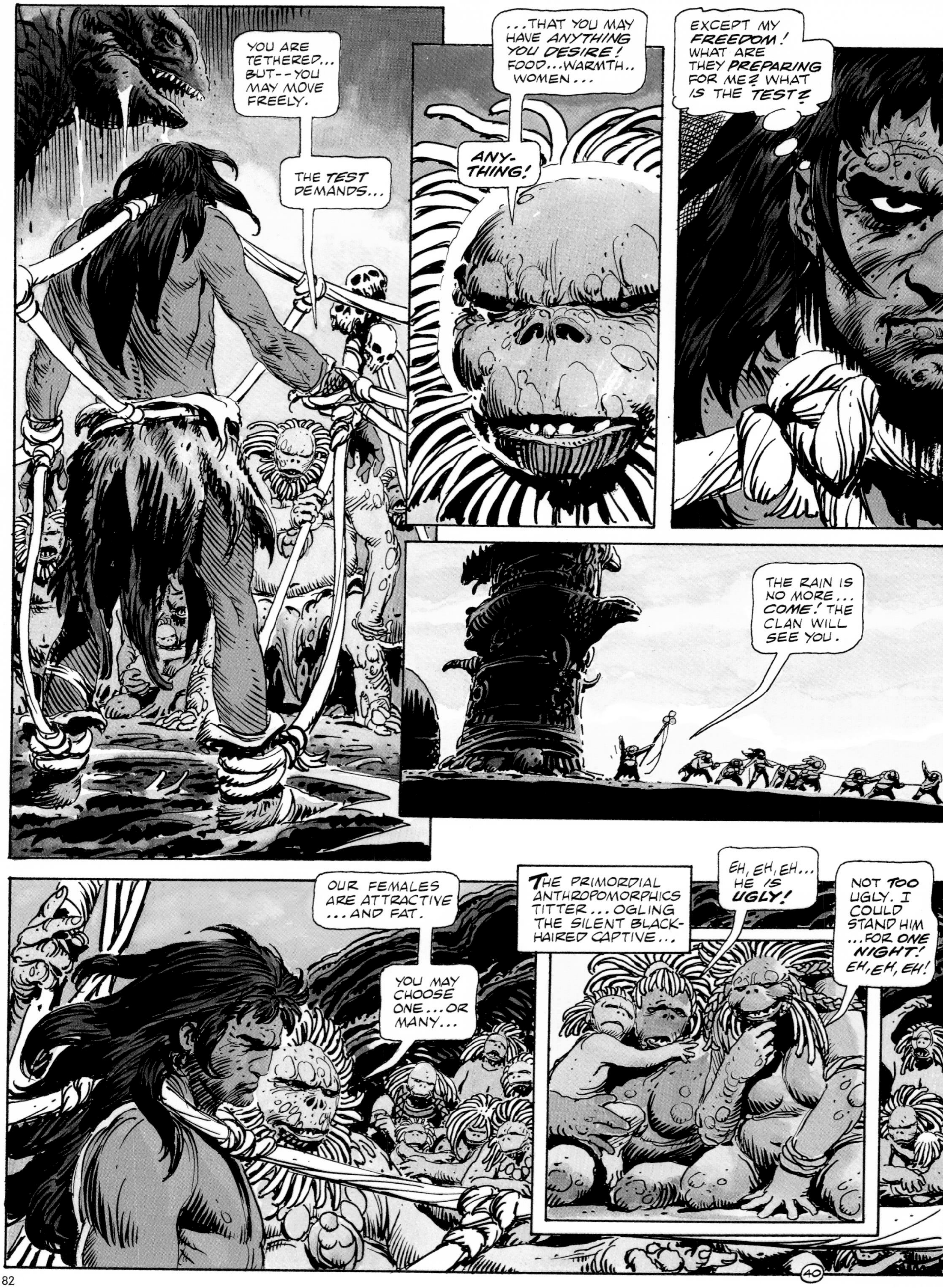
YOU ARE TETHERED... BUT--YOU MAY MOVE FREELY.
THE TEST DEMANDS...
...THAT YOU MAY HAVE ANYTHING YOU DESIRE! FOOD...WARMTH.. WOMEN...
ANY-THING!
EXCEPT MY FREEDOM! WHAT ARE THEY PREPARING FOR ME? WHAT IS THE TEST?
THE RAIN IS NO MORE... COME! THE CLAN WILL SEE YOU.
OUR FEMALES ARE ATTRACTIVE ...AND FAT.
YOU MAY CHOOSE ONE...OR MANY...
THE PRIMORDIAL ANTHROPOMORPHICS TITTER...OGLING THE SILENT BLACK-HAIRED CAPTIVE...
EH, EH, EH... HE IS UGLY!
NOT TOO UGLY. I COULD STAND HIM ...FOR ONE NIGHT! EH, EH, EH!
40

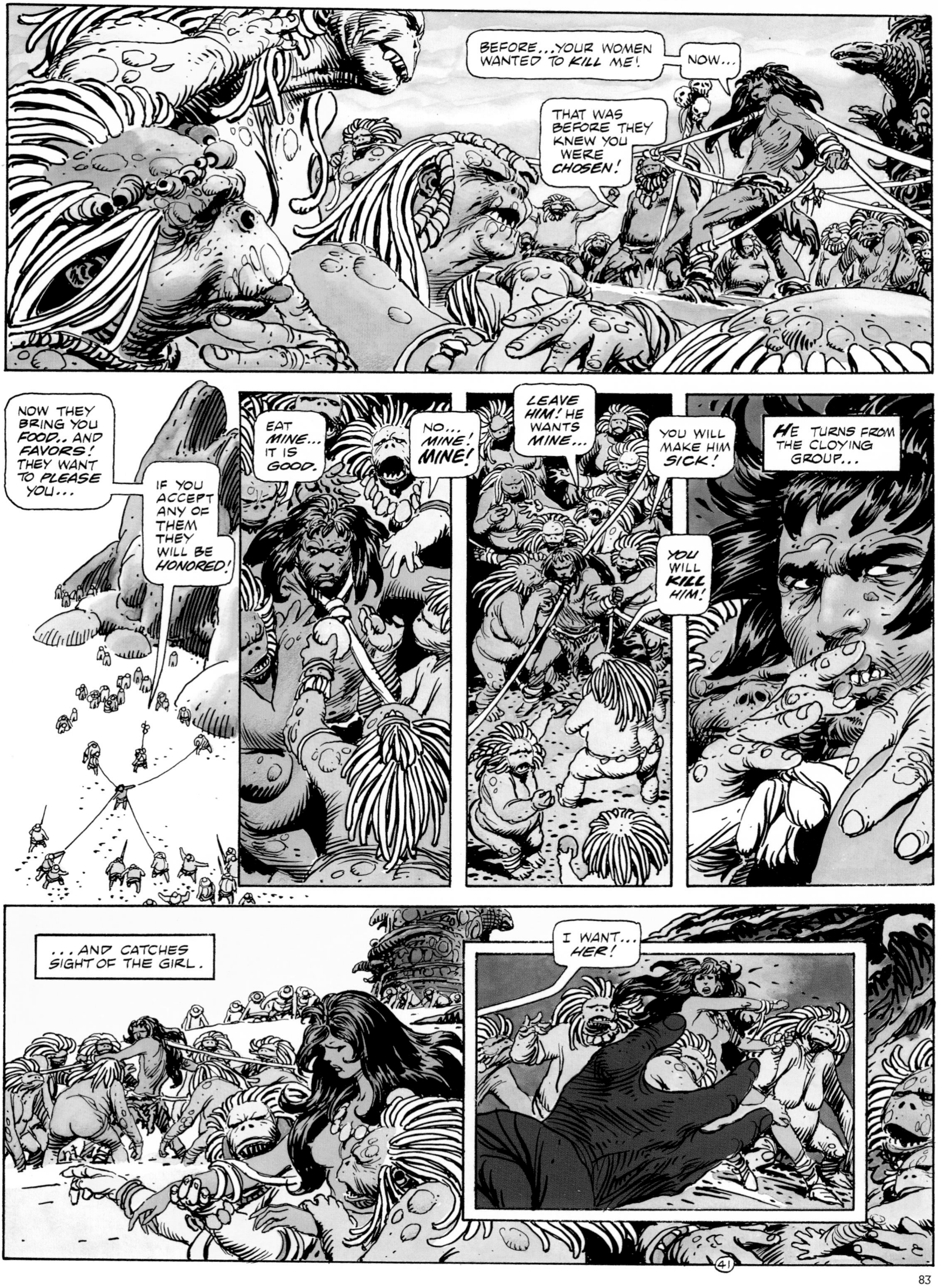
BEFORE...YOUR WOMEN WANTED TO KILL ME!
NOW...
THAT WAS BEFORE THEY KNEW YOU WERE CHOSEN!
NOW THEY BRING YOU FOOD.. AND FAVORS! THEY WANT TO PLEASE YOU...
IF YOU ACCEPT ANY OF THEM THEY WILL BE HONORED!
EAT MINE... IT IS GOOD.
NO... MINE! MINE!
LEAVE HIM! HE WANTS MINE...
YOU WILL MAKE HIM SICK!
YOU WILL KILL HIM!
HE TURNS FROM THE CLOYING GROUP...
...AND CATCHES SIGHT OF THE GIRL.
I WANT... HER!
41

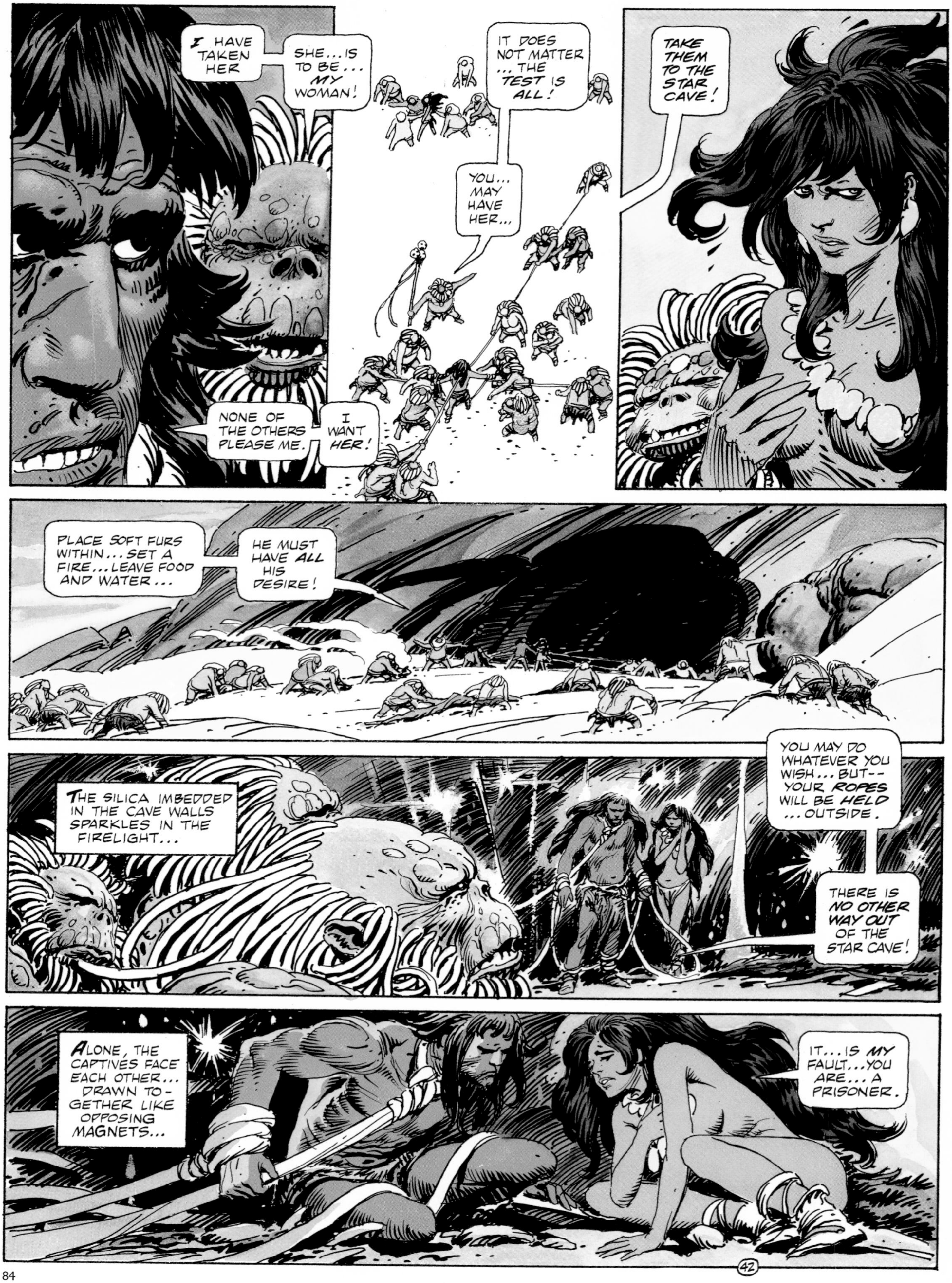
I HAVE TAKEN HER
SHE... IS TO BE... MY WOMAN!
NONE OF THE OTHERS PLEASE ME.
I WANT HER!
IT DOES NOT MATTER ... THE TEST IS ALL!
YOU... MAY HAVE HER...
TAKE THEM TO THE STAR CAVE!
PLACE SOFT FURS WITHIN... SET A FIRE... LEAVE FOOD AND WATER...
HE MUST HAVE ALL HIS DESIRE!
THE SILICA IMBEDDED IN THE CAVE WALLS SPARKLES IN THE FIRELIGHT...
YOU MAY DO WHATEVER YOU WISH... BUT-- YOUR ROPES WILL BE HELD ... OUTSIDE.
THERE IS NO OTHER WAY OUT OF THE STAR CAVE!
ALONE, THE CAPTIVES FACE EACH OTHER... DRAWN TO-GETHER LIKE OPPOSING MAGNETS...
IT... IS MY FAULT... YOU ARE... A PRISONER.
42

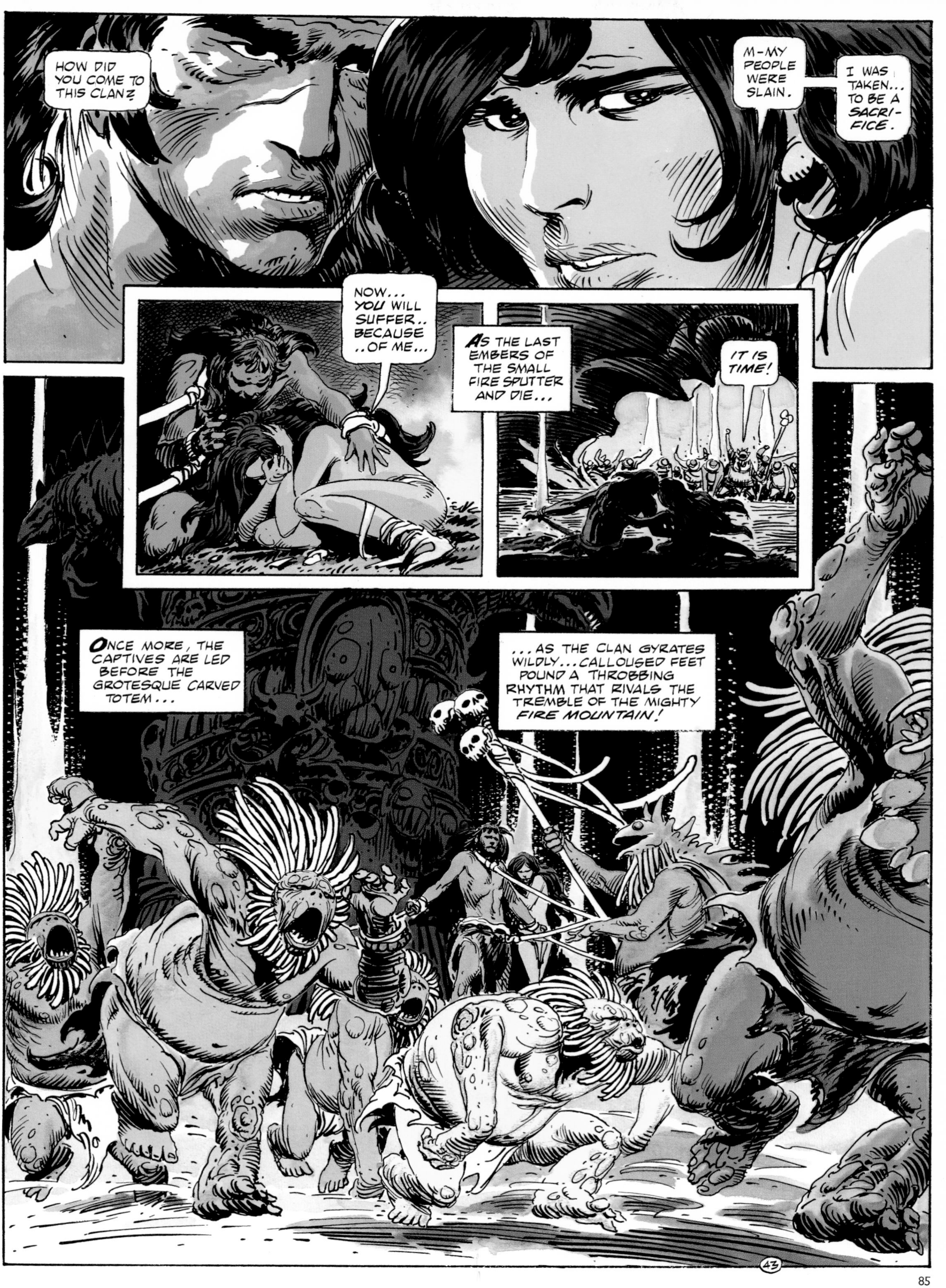
HOW DID YOU COME TO THIS CLAN?
M-MY PEOPLE WERE SLAIN.
I WAS TAKEN... TO BE A SACRIFICE.
NOW... YOU WILL SUFFER.. BECAUSE ..OF ME...
AS THE LAST EMBERS OF THE SMALL FIRE SPUTTER AND DIE...
IT IS TIME!
ONCE MORE, THE CAPTIVES ARE LED BEFORE THE GROTESQUE CARVED TOTEM...
...AS THE CLAN GYRATES WILDLY...CALLOUSED FEET POUND A THROBBING RHYTHM THAT RIVALS THE TREMBLE OF THE MIGHTY FIRE MOUNTAIN!
43

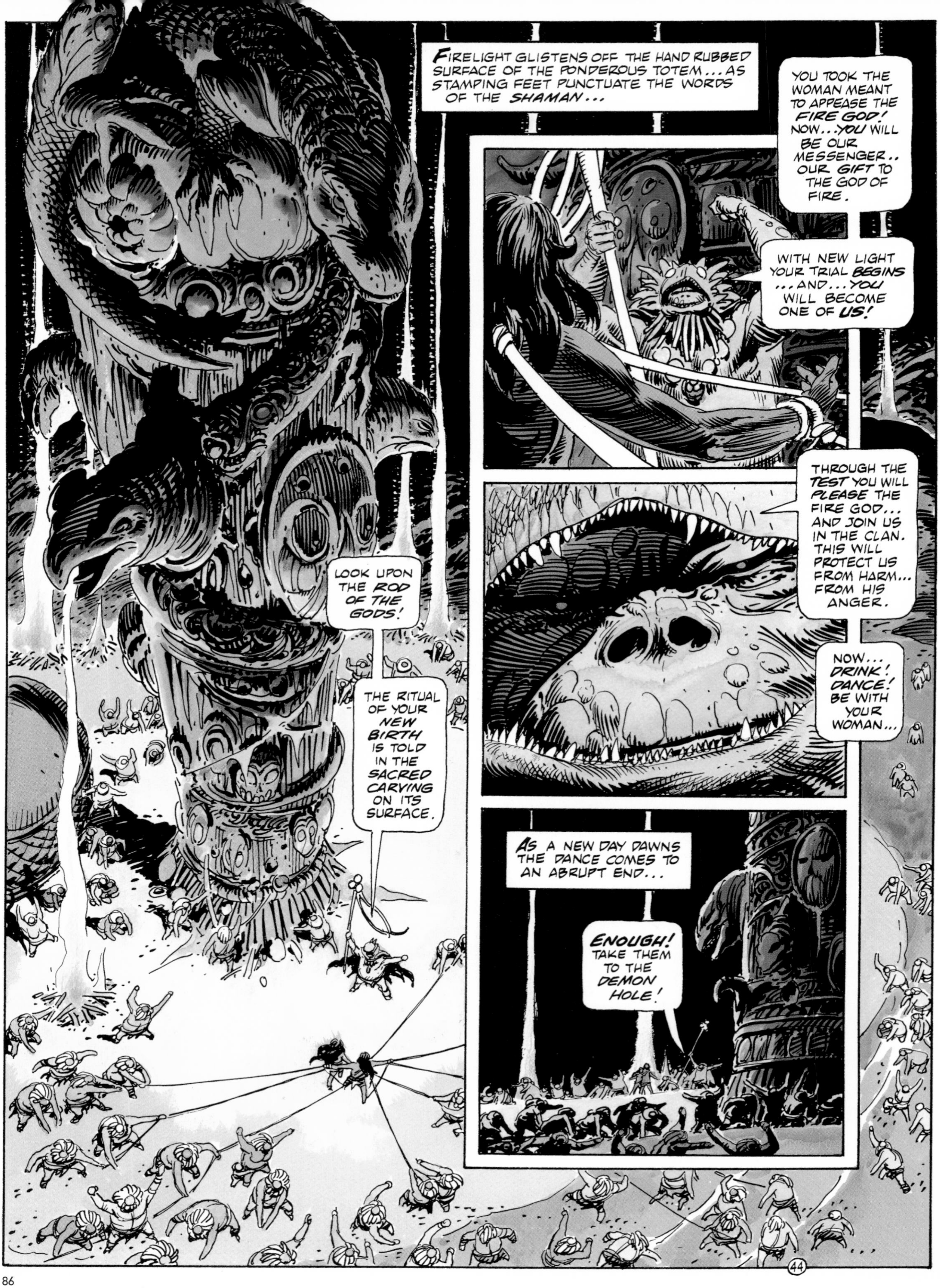
FIRELIGHT GLISTENS OFF THE HAND RUBBED SURFACE OF THE PONDEROUS TOTEM... AS STAMPING FEET PUNCTUATE THE WORDS OF THE SHAMAN...
LOOK UPON THE ROD OF THE GODS!
THE RITUAL OF YOUR NEW BIRTH IS TOLD IN THE SACRED CARVING ON ITS SURFACE.
YOU TOOK THE WOMAN MEANT TO APPEASE THE FIRE GOD! NOW... YOU WILL BE OUR MESSENGER.. OUR GIFT TO THE GOD OF FIRE.
WITH NEW LIGHT YOUR TRIAL BEGINS ... AND... YOU WILL BECOME ONE OF US!
THROUGH THE TEST YOU WILL PLEASE THE FIRE GOD... AND JOIN US IN THE CLAN. THIS WILL PROTECT US FROM HARM... FROM HIS ANGER.
NOW... DRINK! DANCE! BE WITH YOUR WOMAN...
AS A NEW DAY DAWNS THE DANCE COMES TO AN ABRUPT END...
ENOUGH! TAKE THEM TO THE DEMON HOLE!
44

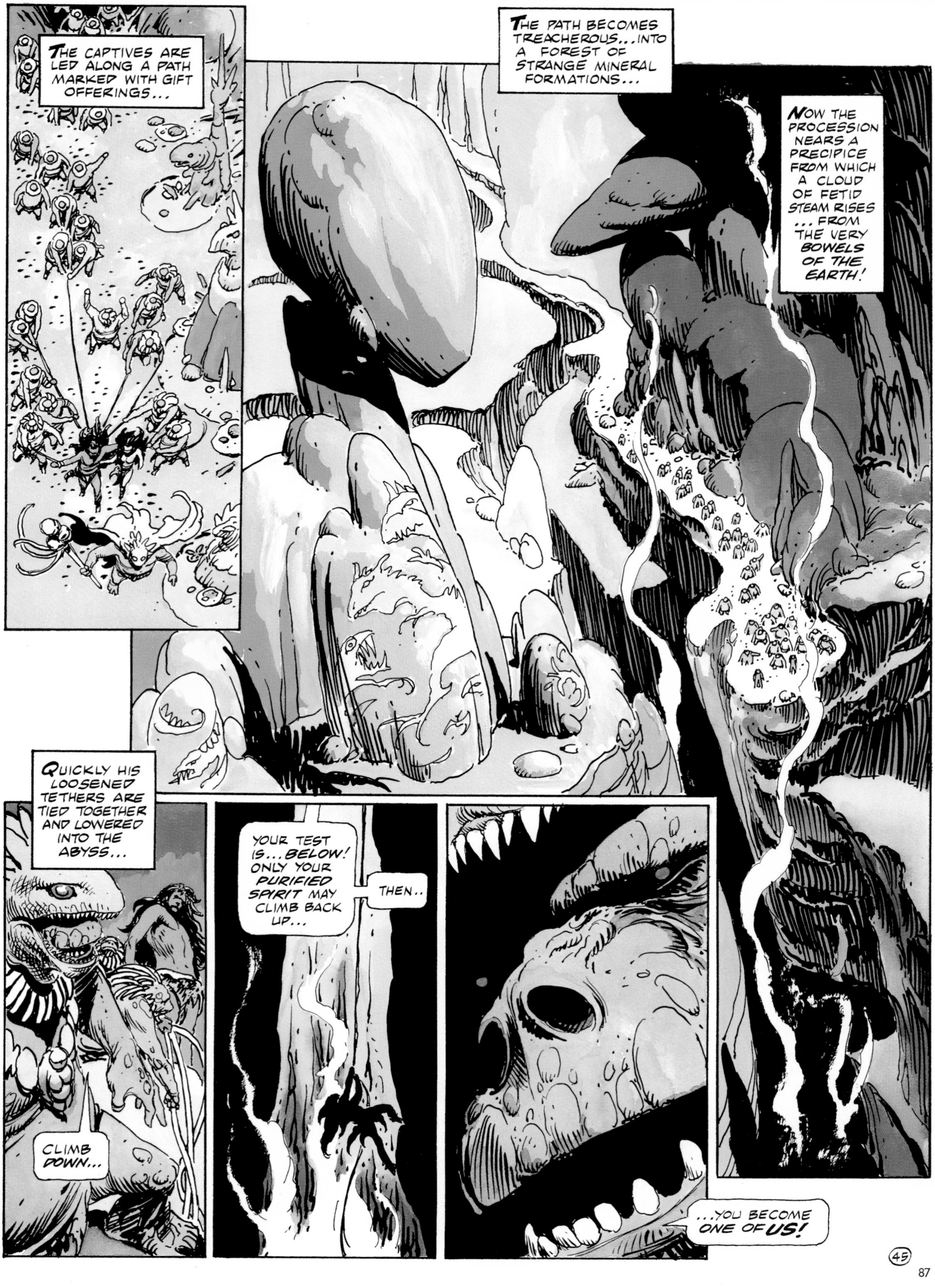
THE CAPTIVES ARE LED ALONG A PATH MARKED WITH GIFT OFFERINGS...
THE PATH BECOMES TREACHEROUS...INTO A FOREST OF STRANGE MINERAL FORMATIONS...
NOW THE PROCESSION NEARS A PRECIPICE FROM WHICH A CLOUD OF FETID STEAM RISES ...FROM THE VERY BOWELS OF THE EARTH!
QUICKLY HIS LOOSENED TETHERS ARE TIED TOGETHER AND LOWERED INTO THE ABYSS...
CLIMB DOWN...
YOUR TEST IS...BELOW! ONLY YOUR PURIFIED SPIRIT MAY CLIMB BACK UP...
THEN..
...YOU BECOME ONE OF US!
45

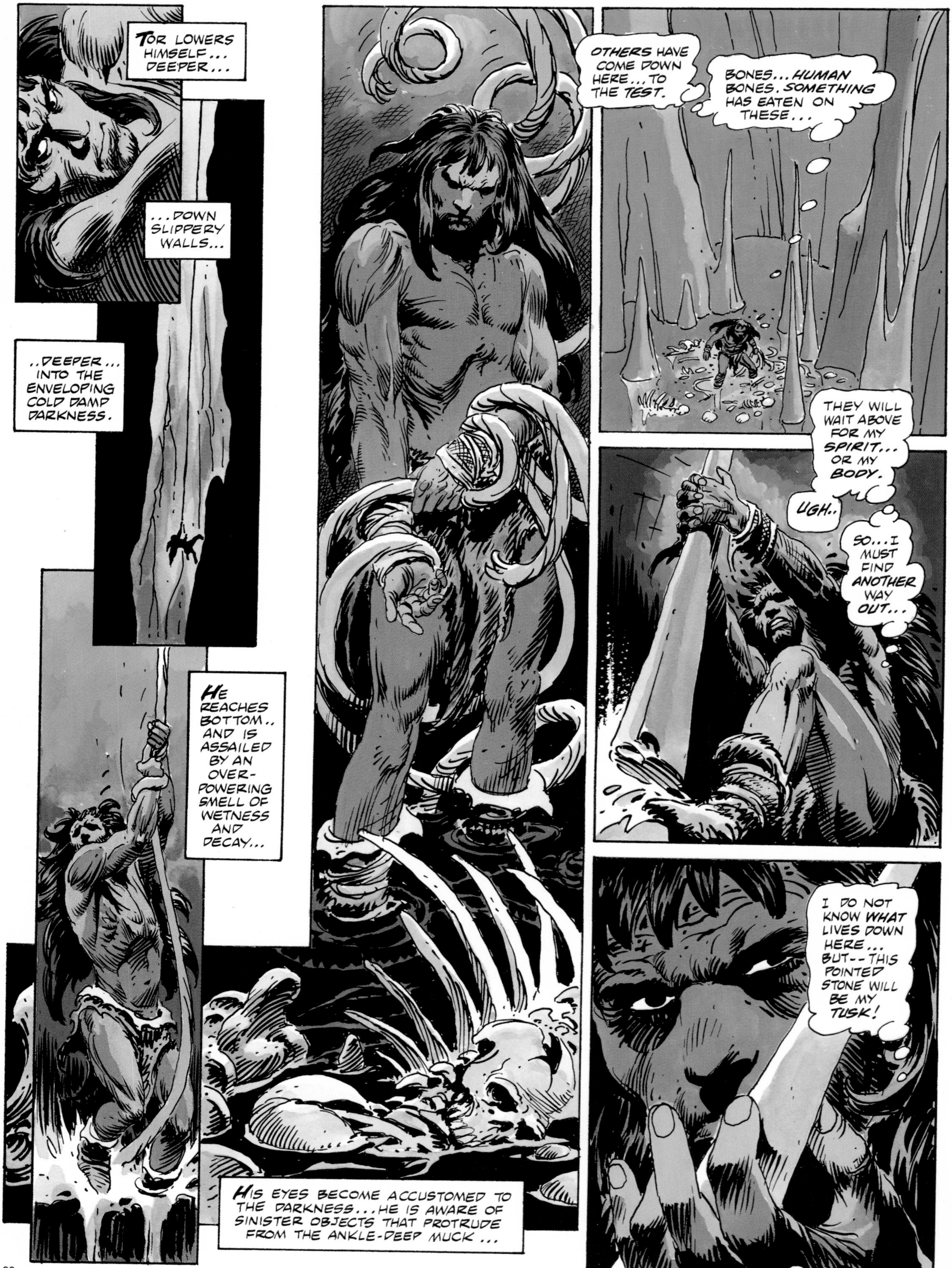
TOR LOWERS HIMSELF... DEEPER...
...DOWN SLIPPERY WALLS...
..DEEPER... INTO THE ENVELOPING COLD DAMP DARKNESS.
HE REACHES BOTTOM.. AND IS ASSAILED BY AN OVER-POWERING SMELL OF WETNESS AND DECAY...
HIS EYES BECOME ACCUSTOMED TO THE DARKNESS...HE IS AWARE OF SINISTER OBJECTS THAT PROTRUDE FROM THE ANKLE-DEEP MUCK ...
OTHERS HAVE COME DOWN HERE...TO THE TEST.
BONES...HUMAN BONES. SOMETHING HAS EATEN ON THESE...
THEY WILL WAIT ABOVE FOR MY SPIRIT... OR MY BODY.
UGH..
SO...I MUST FIND ANOTHER WAY OUT...
I DO NOT KNOW WHAT LIVES DOWN HERE... BUT--THIS POINTED STONE WILL BE MY TUSK!

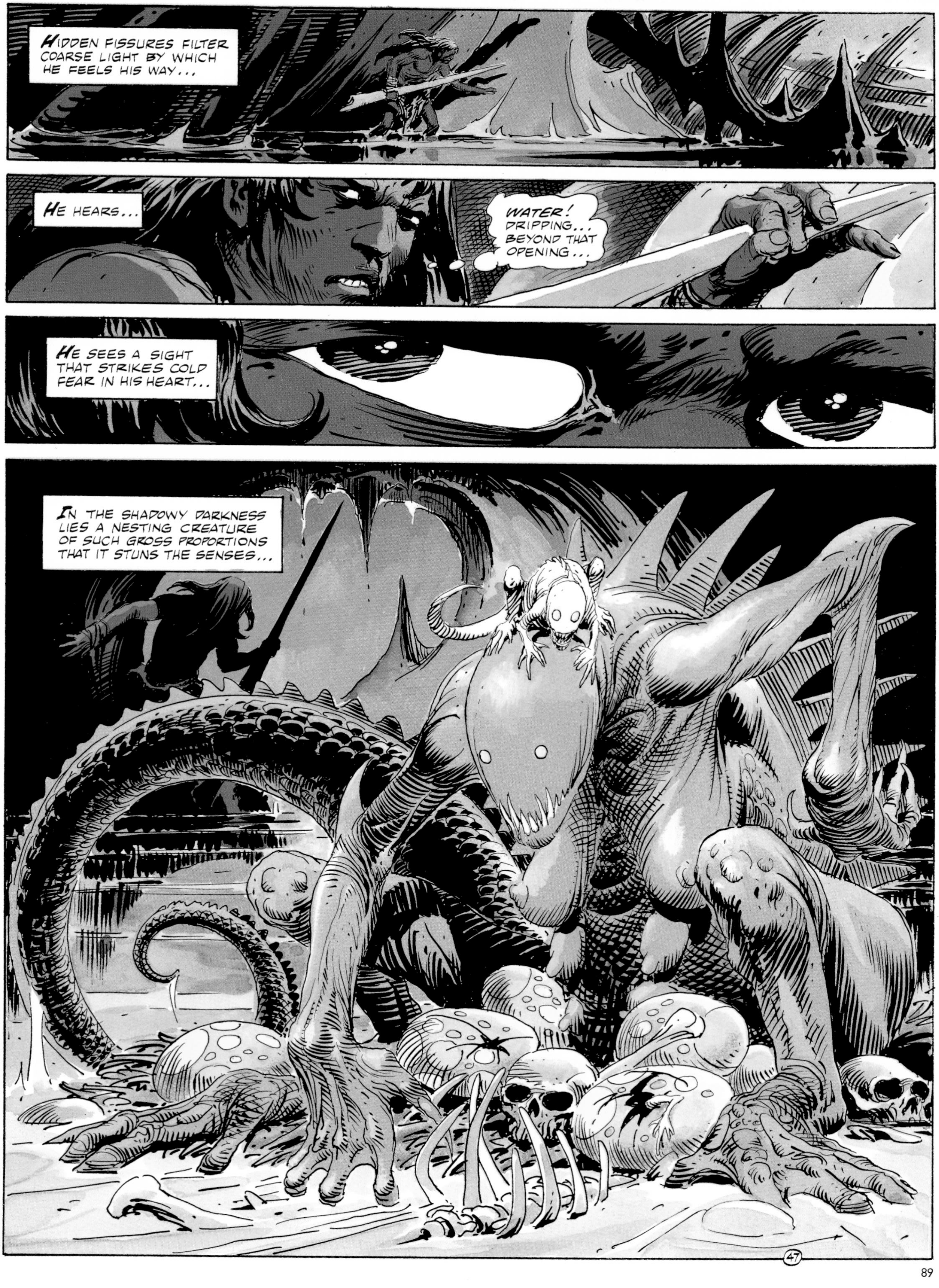
HIDDEN FISSURES FILTER COARSE LIGHT BY WHICH HE FEELS HIS WAY...
HE HEARS...
WATER! DRIPPING... BEYOND THAT OPENING...
HE SEES A SIGHT THAT STRIKES COLD FEAR IN HIS HEART...
IN THE SHADOWY DARKNESS LIES A NESTING CREATURE OF SUCH GROSS PROPORTIONS THAT IT STUNS THE SENSES...
47

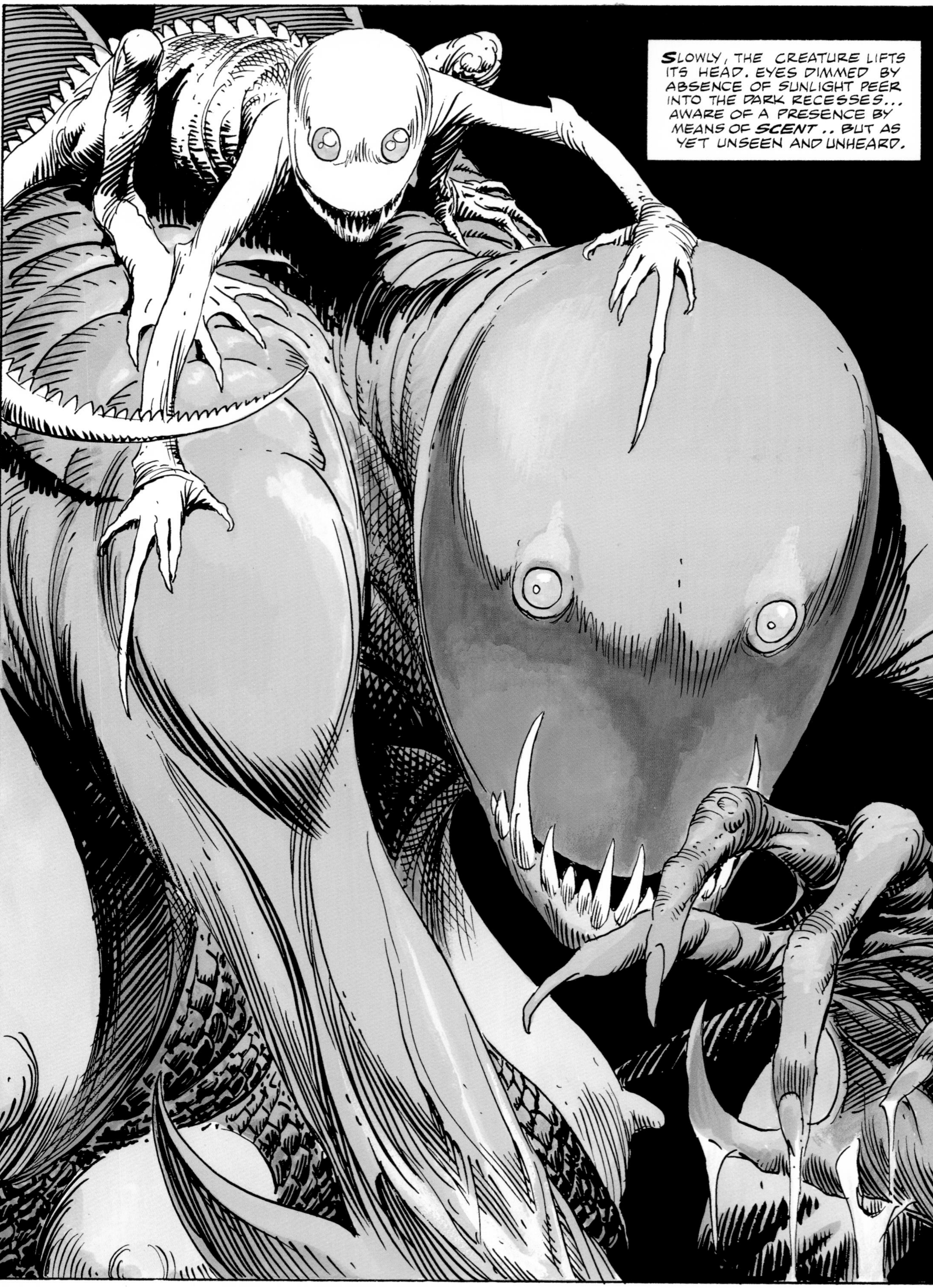
SLOWLY, THE CREATURE LIFTS ITS HEAD. EYES DIMMED BY ABSENCE OF SUNLIGHT PEER INTO THE DARK RECESSES... AWARE OF A PRESENCE BY MEANS OF SCENT.. BUT AS YET UNSEEN AND UNHEARD.

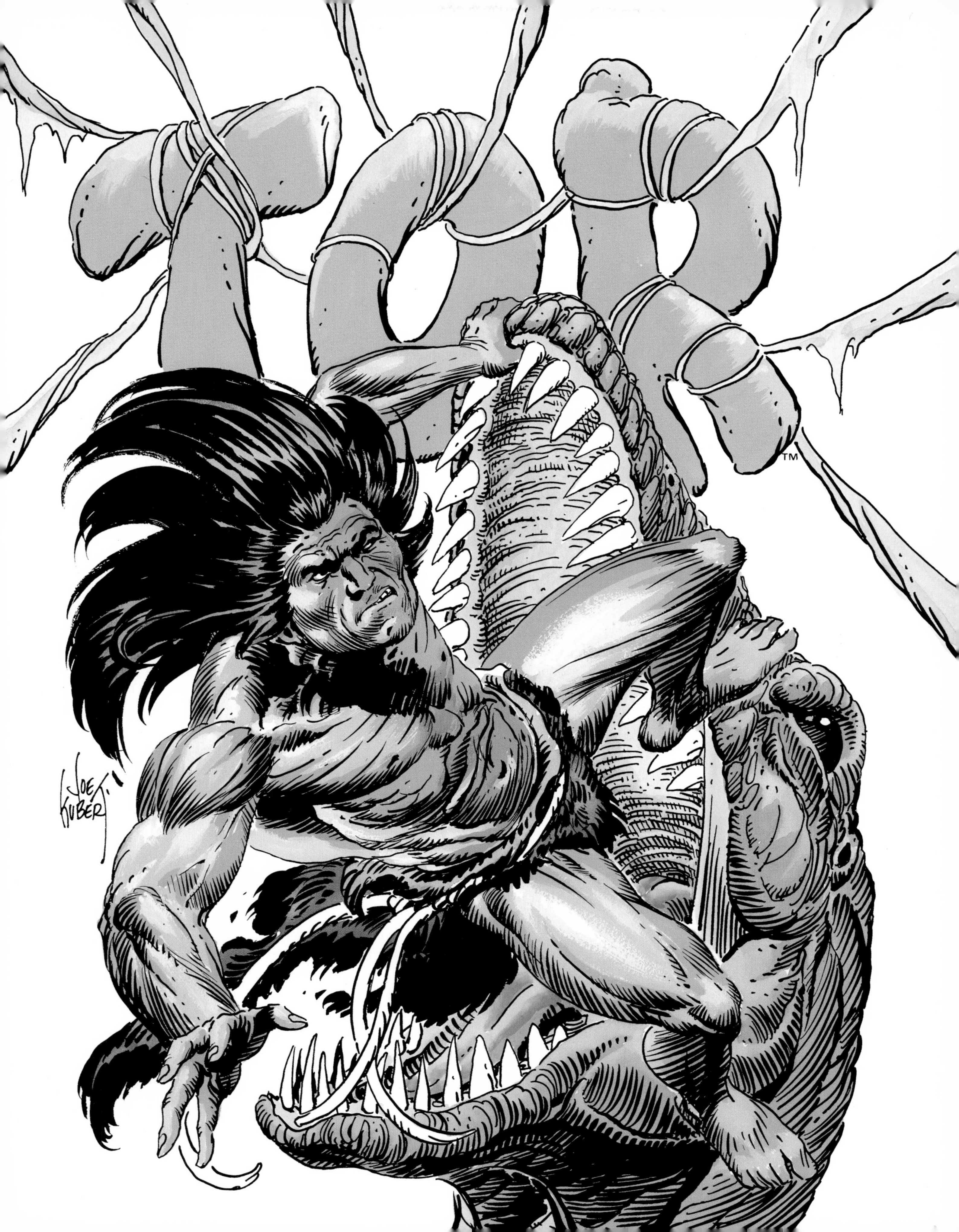
TOR™
JOE KUBERT

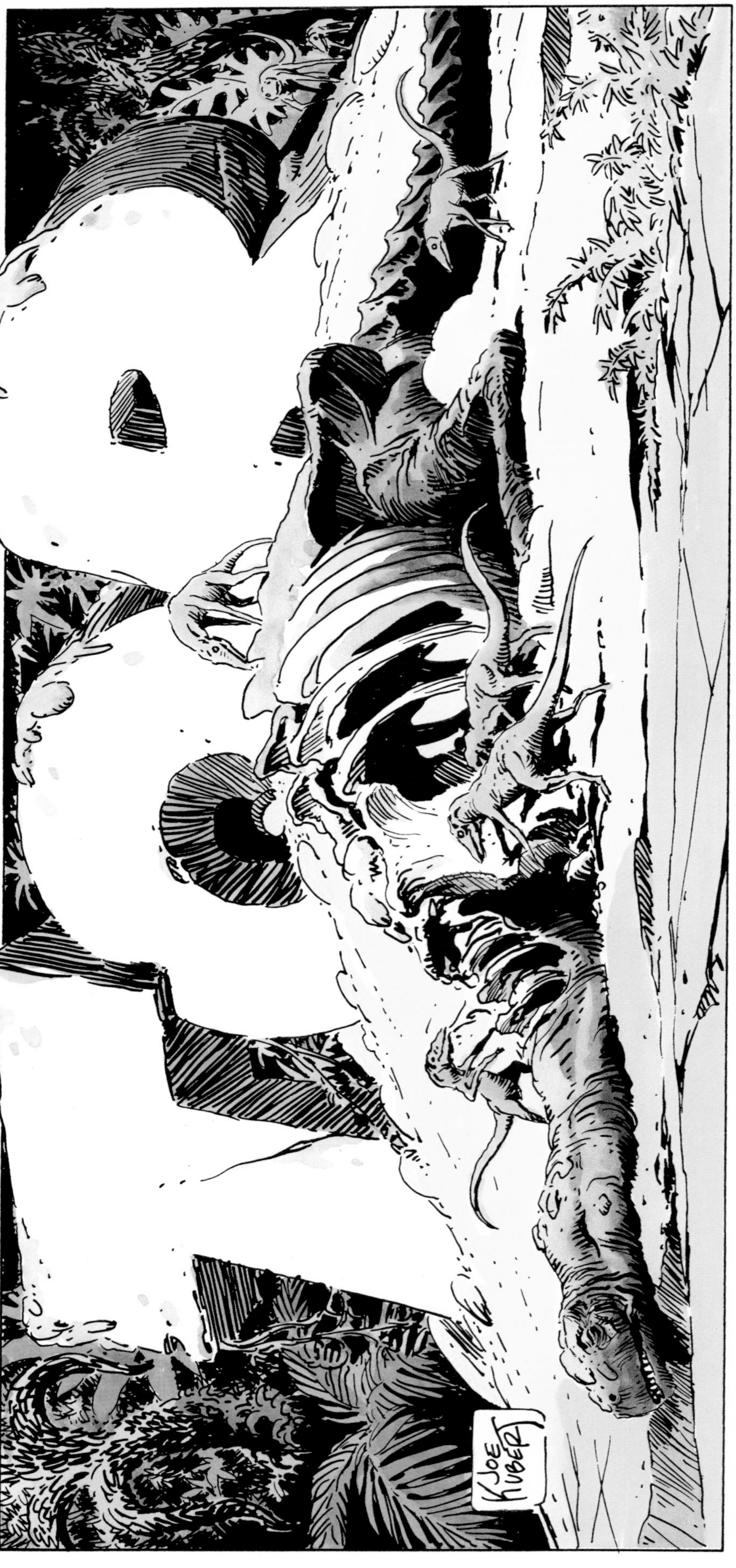
TOR
JOE KUBERT

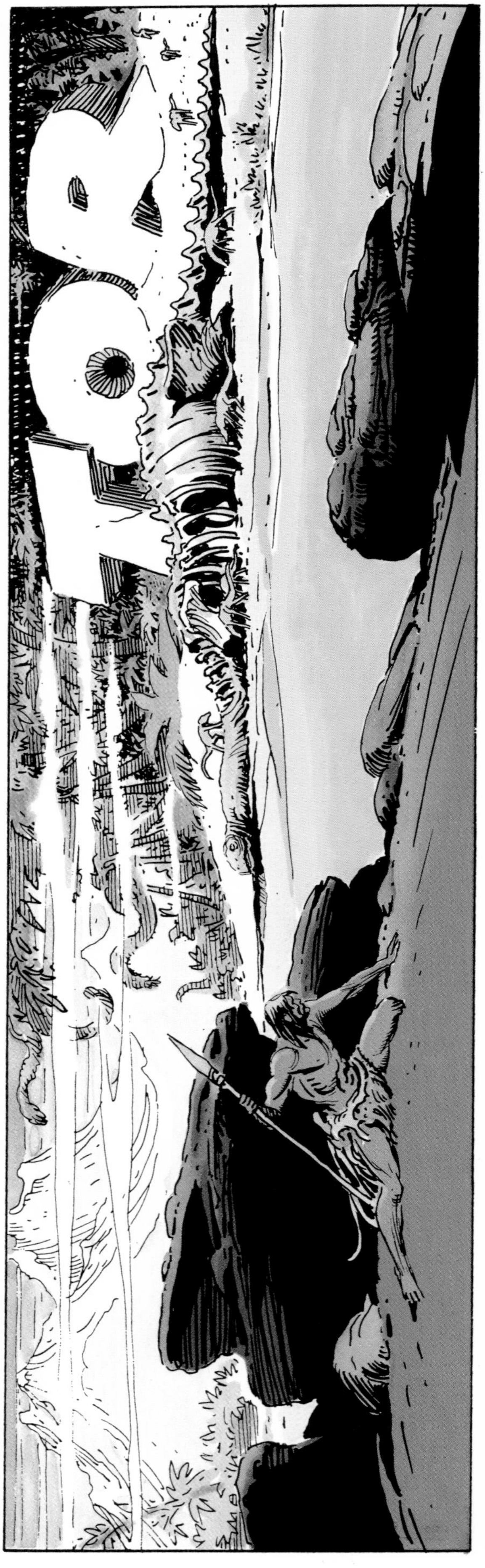
TOR

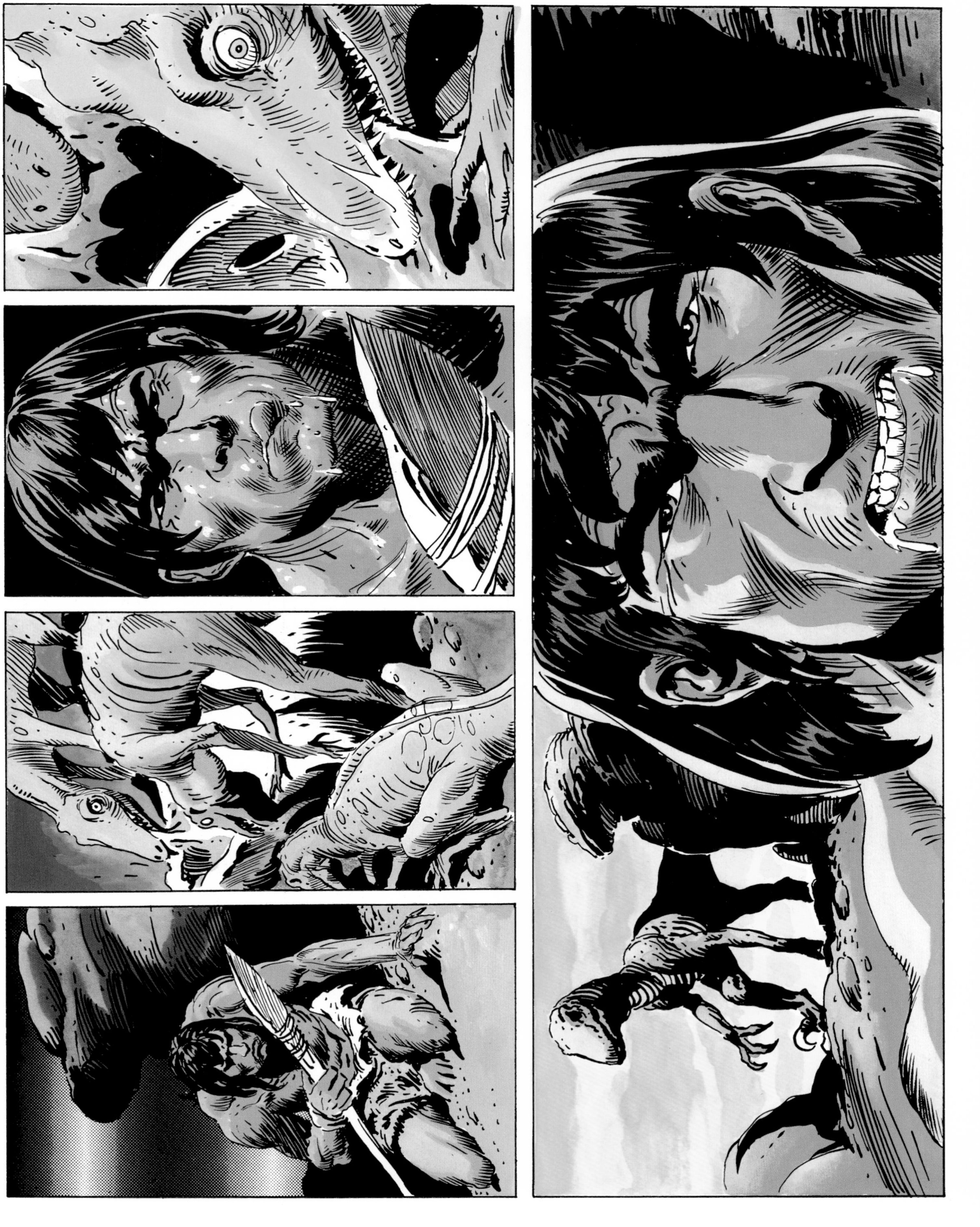

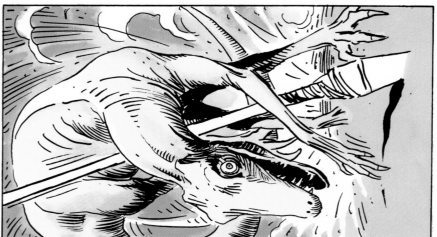

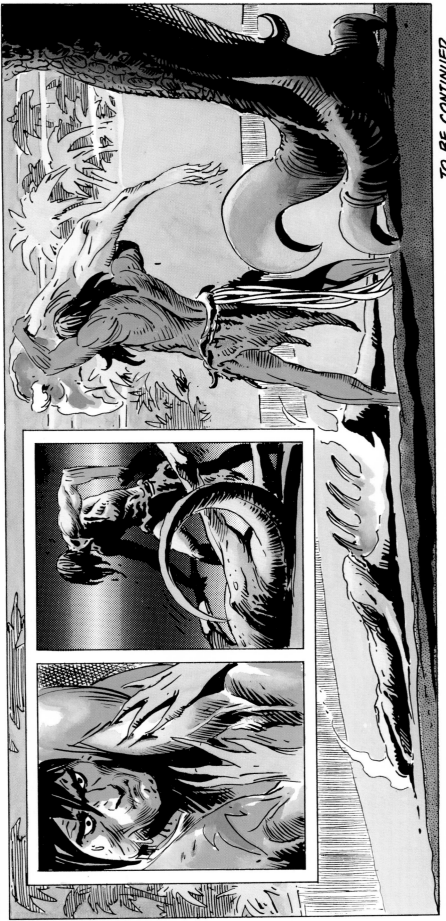

TO BE CONTINUED...

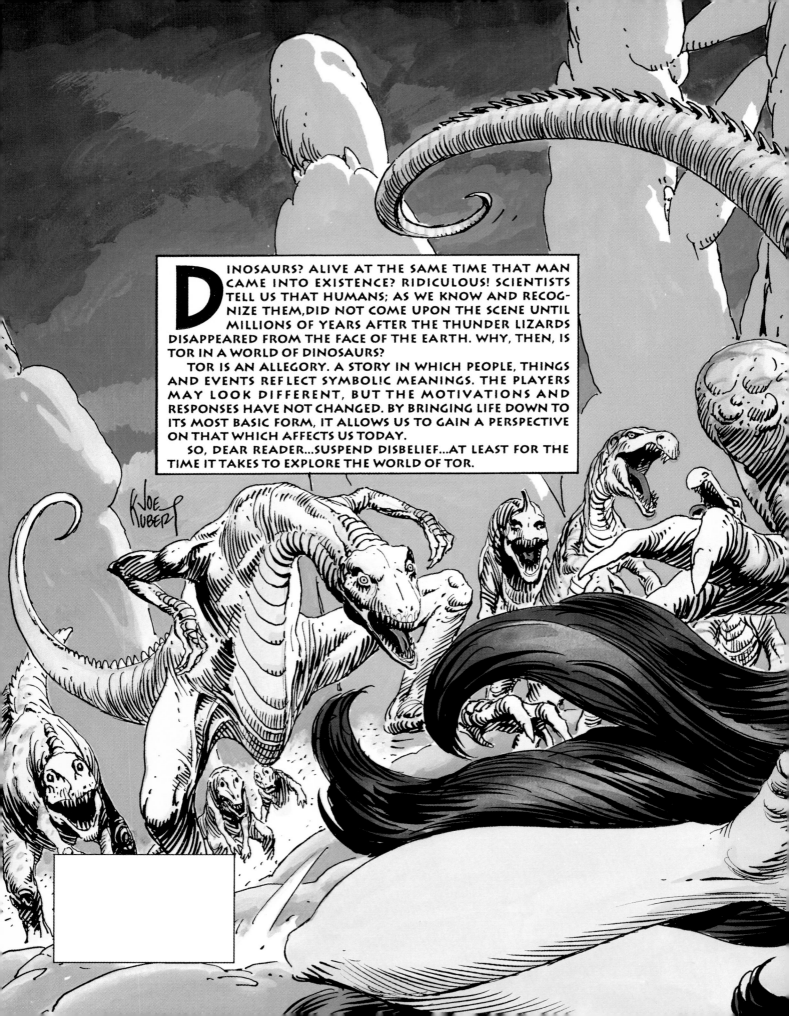

DINOSAURS? ALIVE AT THE SAME TIME THAT MAN CAME INTO EXISTENCE? RIDICULOUS! SCIENTISTS TELL US THAT HUMANS; AS WE KNOW AND RECOGNIZE THEM, DID NOT COME UPON THE SCENE UNTIL MILLIONS OF YEARS AFTER THE THUNDER LIZARDS DISAPPEARED FROM THE FACE OF THE EARTH. WHY, THEN, IS TOR IN A WORLD OF DINOSAURS?

TOR IS AN ALLEGORY. A STORY IN WHICH PEOPLE, THINGS AND EVENTS REFLECT SYMBOLIC MEANINGS. THE PLAYERS MAY LOOK DIFFERENT, BUT THE MOTIVATIONS AND RESPONSES HAVE NOT CHANGED. BY BRINGING LIFE DOWN TO ITS MOST BASIC FORM, IT ALLOWS US TO GAIN A PERSPECTIVE ON THAT WHICH AFFECTS US TODAY.

SO, DEAR READER...SUSPEND DISBELIEF...AT LEAST FOR THE TIME IT TAKES TO EXPLORE THE WORLD OF TOR.

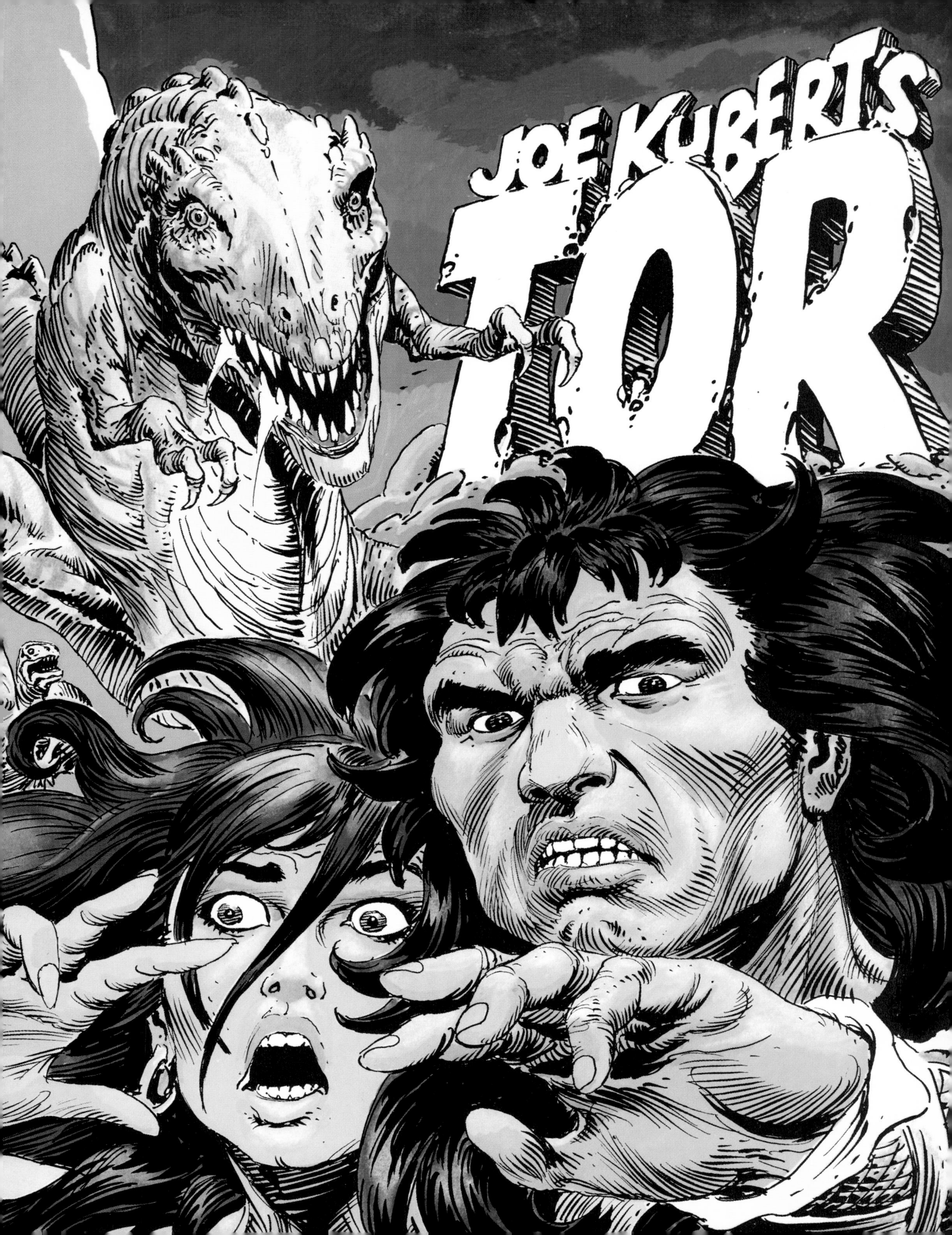
JOE KUBERT'S
TOR

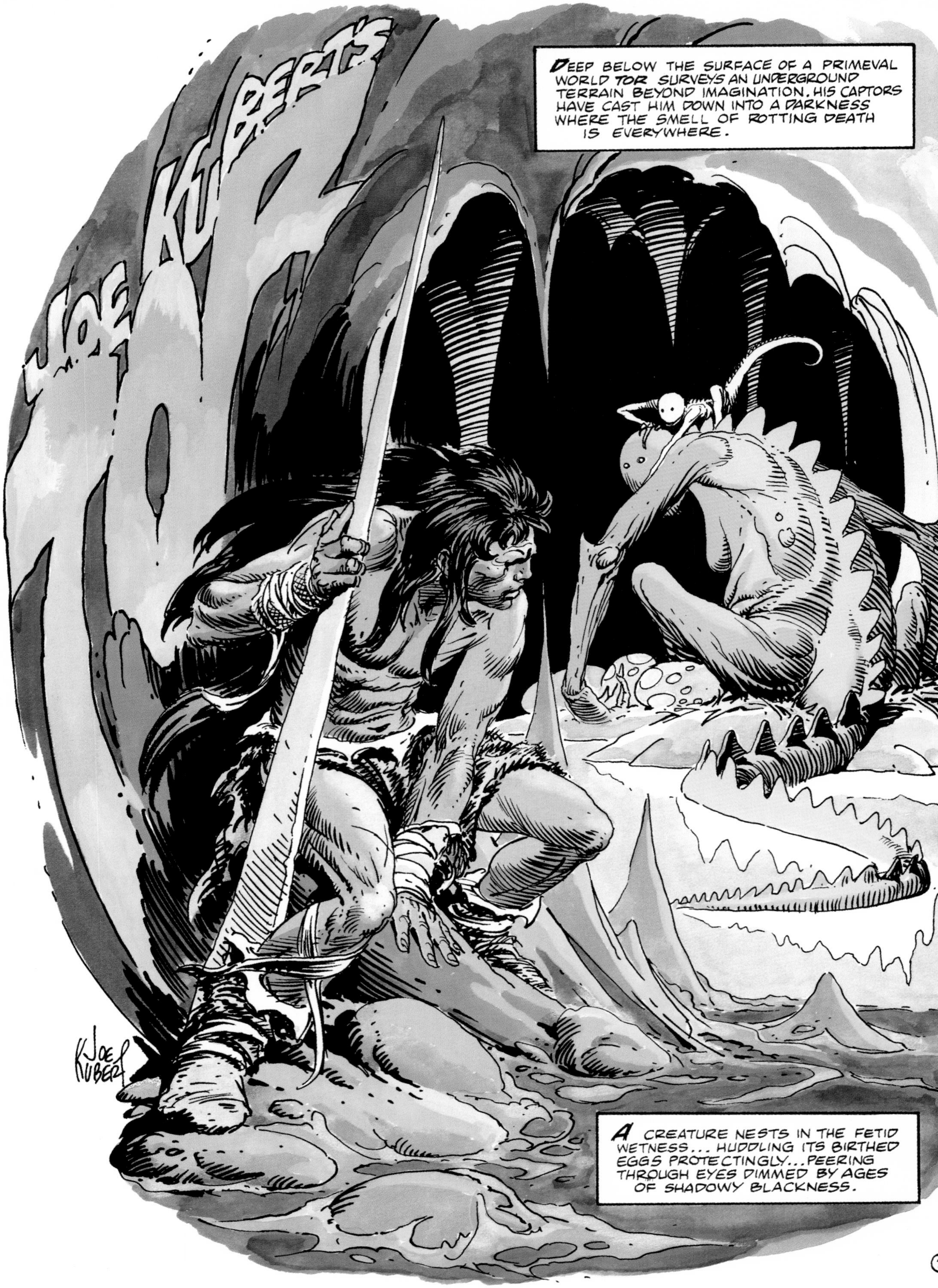
JOE KUBERT'S TOR
DEEP BELOW THE SURFACE OF A PRIMEVAL WORLD TOR SURVEYS AN UNDERGROUND TERRAIN BEYOND IMAGINATION. HIS CAPTORS HAVE CAST HIM DOWN INTO A DARKNESS WHERE THE SMELL OF ROTTING DEATH IS EVERYWHERE.
JOE KUBERT
A CREATURE NESTS IN THE FETID WETNESS... HUDDLING ITS BIRTHED EGGS PROTECTINGLY...PEERING THROUGH EYES DIMMED BY AGES OF SHADOWY BLACKNESS.
1

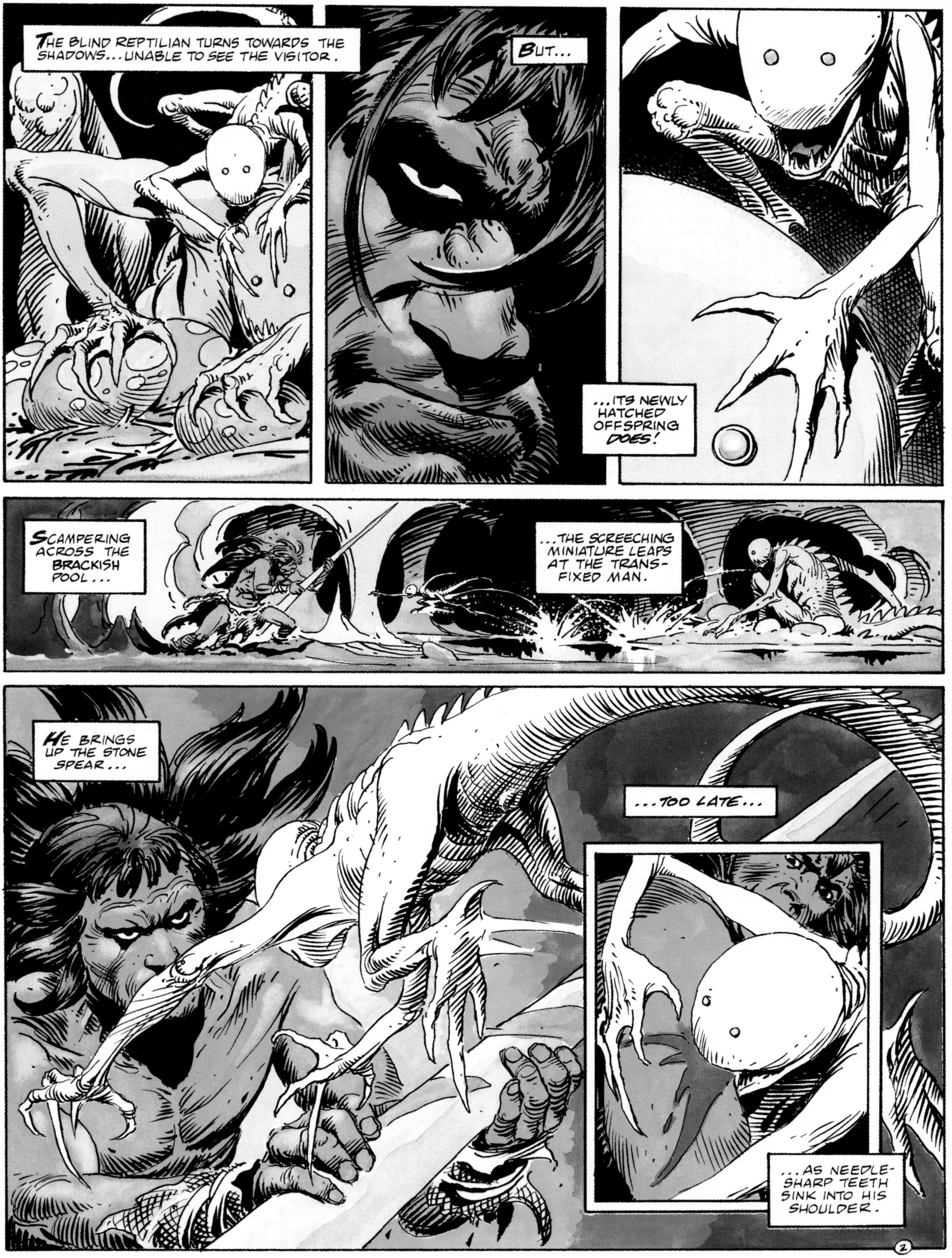
THE BLIND REPTILIAN TURNS TOWARDS THE SHADOWS... UNABLE TO SEE THE VISITOR.
BUT...
...ITS NEWLY HATCHED OFFSPRING DOES!
SCAMPERING ACROSS THE BRACKISH POOL...
...THE SCREECHING MINIATURE LEAPS AT THE TRANS-FIXED MAN.
HE BRINGS UP THE STONE SPEAR...
...TOO LATE...
...AS NEEDLE-SHARP TEETH SINK INTO HIS SHOULDER.
2

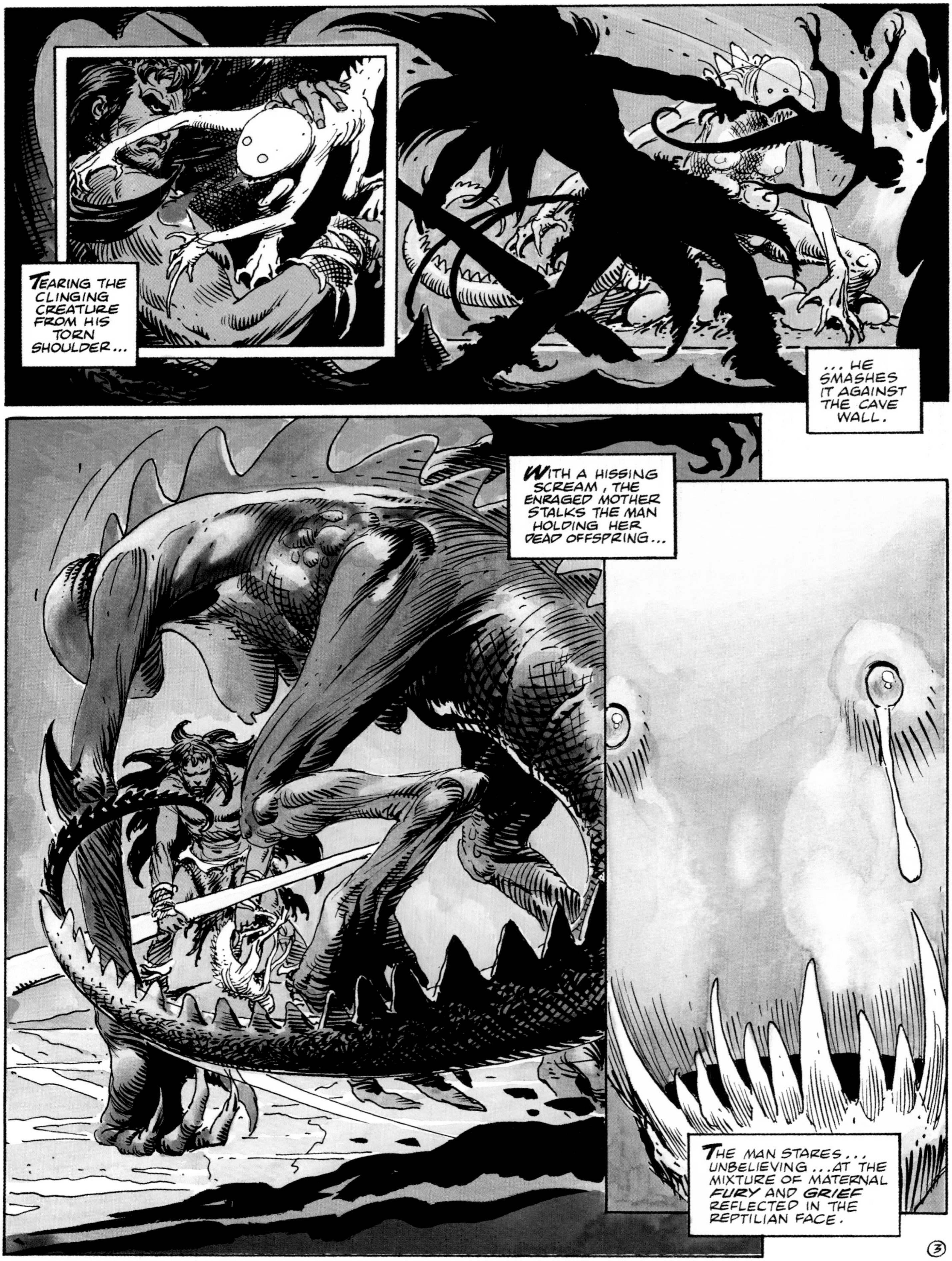
TEARING THE CLINGING CREATURE FROM HIS TORN SHOULDER...
... HE SMASHES IT AGAINST THE CAVE WALL.
WITH A HISSING SCREAM, THE ENRAGED MOTHER STALKS THE MAN HOLDING HER DEAD OFFSPRING...
THE MAN STARES... UNBELIEVING... AT THE MIXTURE OF MATERNAL FURY AND GRIEF REFLECTED IN THE REPTILIAN FACE.
3

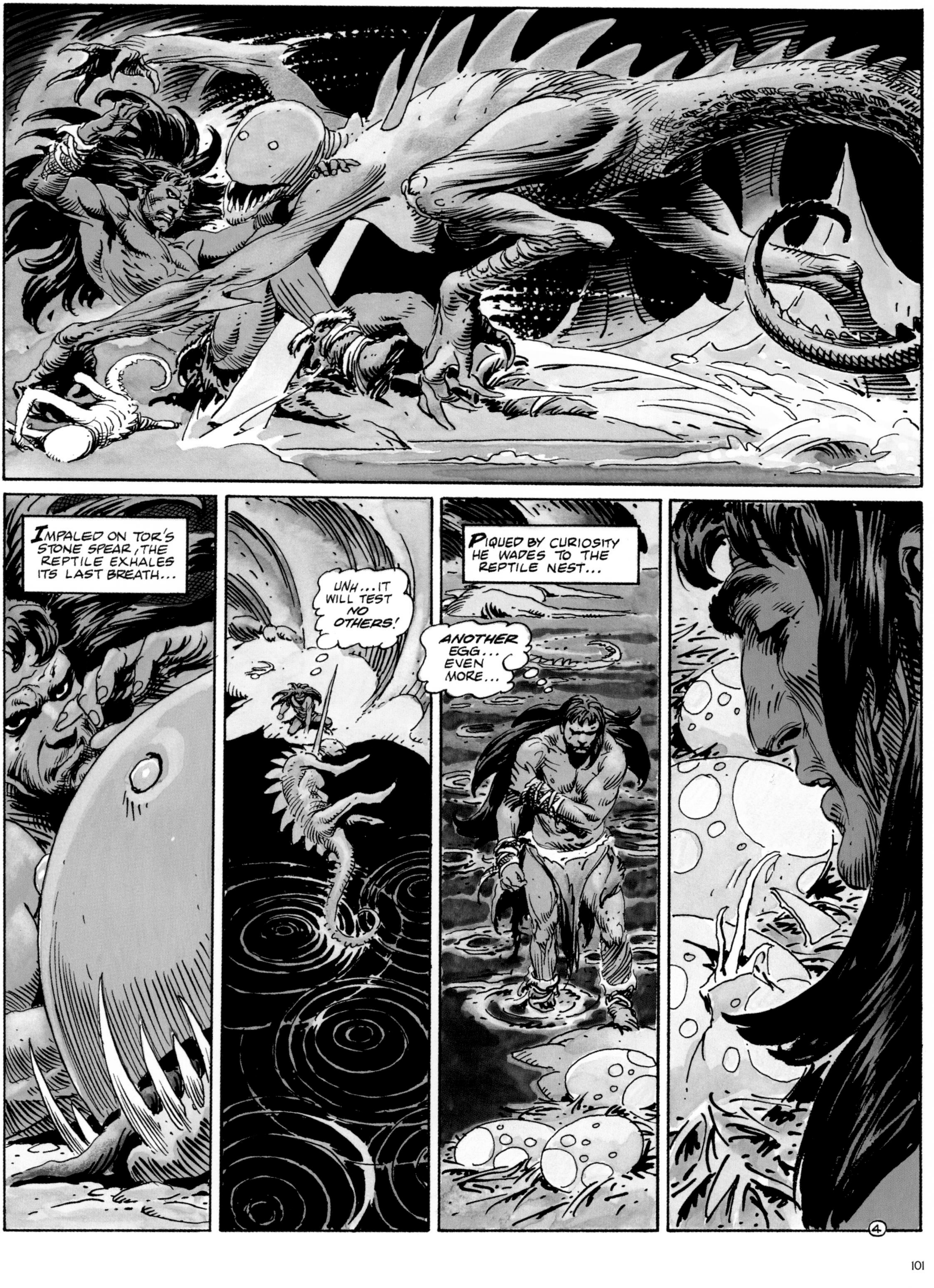
IMPALED ON TOR'S STONE SPEAR, THE REPTILE EXHALES ITS LAST BREATH...
UNH... IT WILL TEST NO OTHERS!
PIQUED BY CURIOSITY HE WADES TO THE REPTILE NEST...
ANOTHER EGG... EVEN MORE...
4

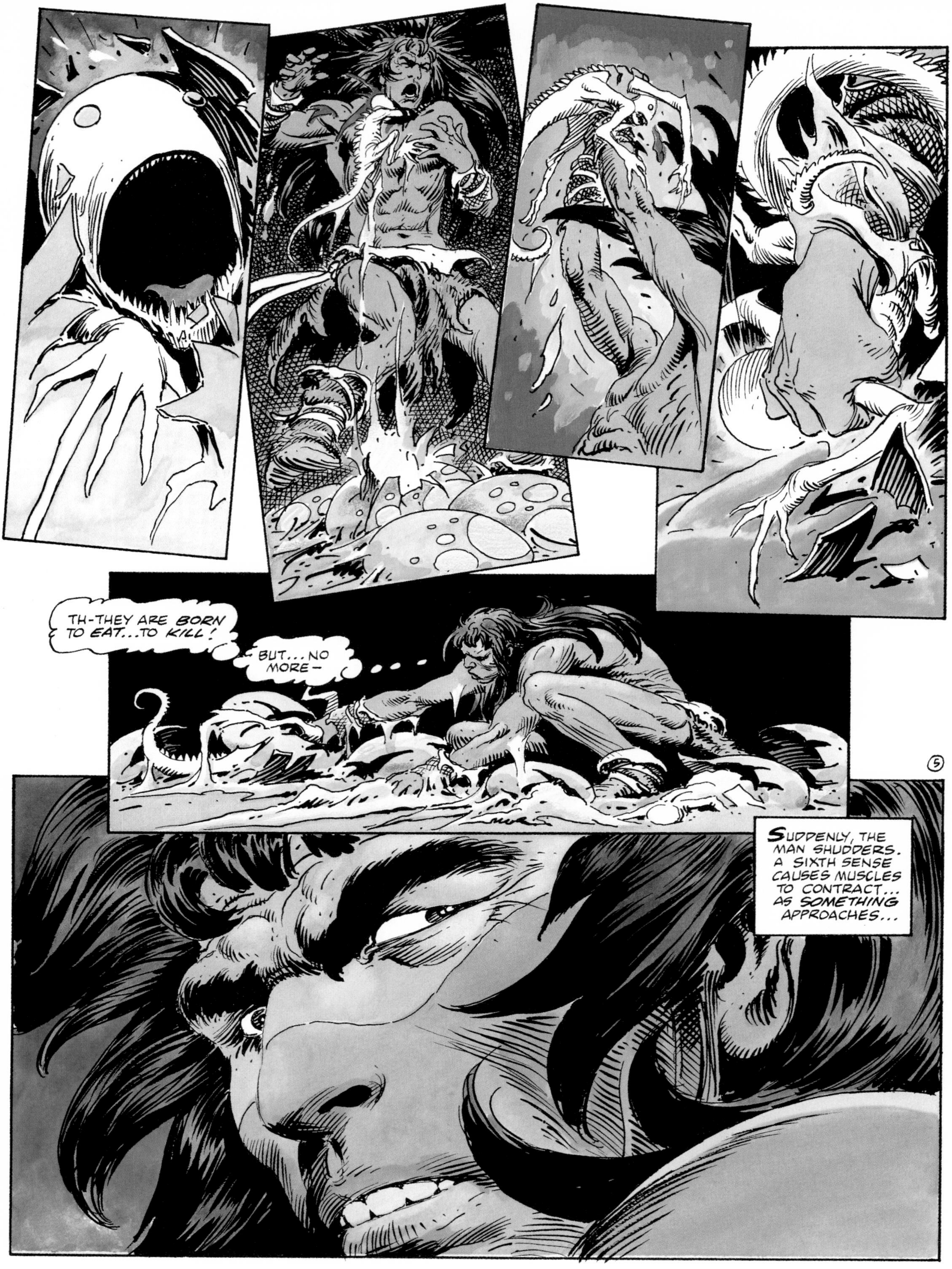
TH-THEY ARE BORN TO EAT...TO KILL!
BUT...NO MORE-
5
SUDDENLY, THE MAN SHUDDERS. A SIXTH SENSE CAUSES MUSCLES TO CONTRACT... AS SOMETHING APPROACHES...

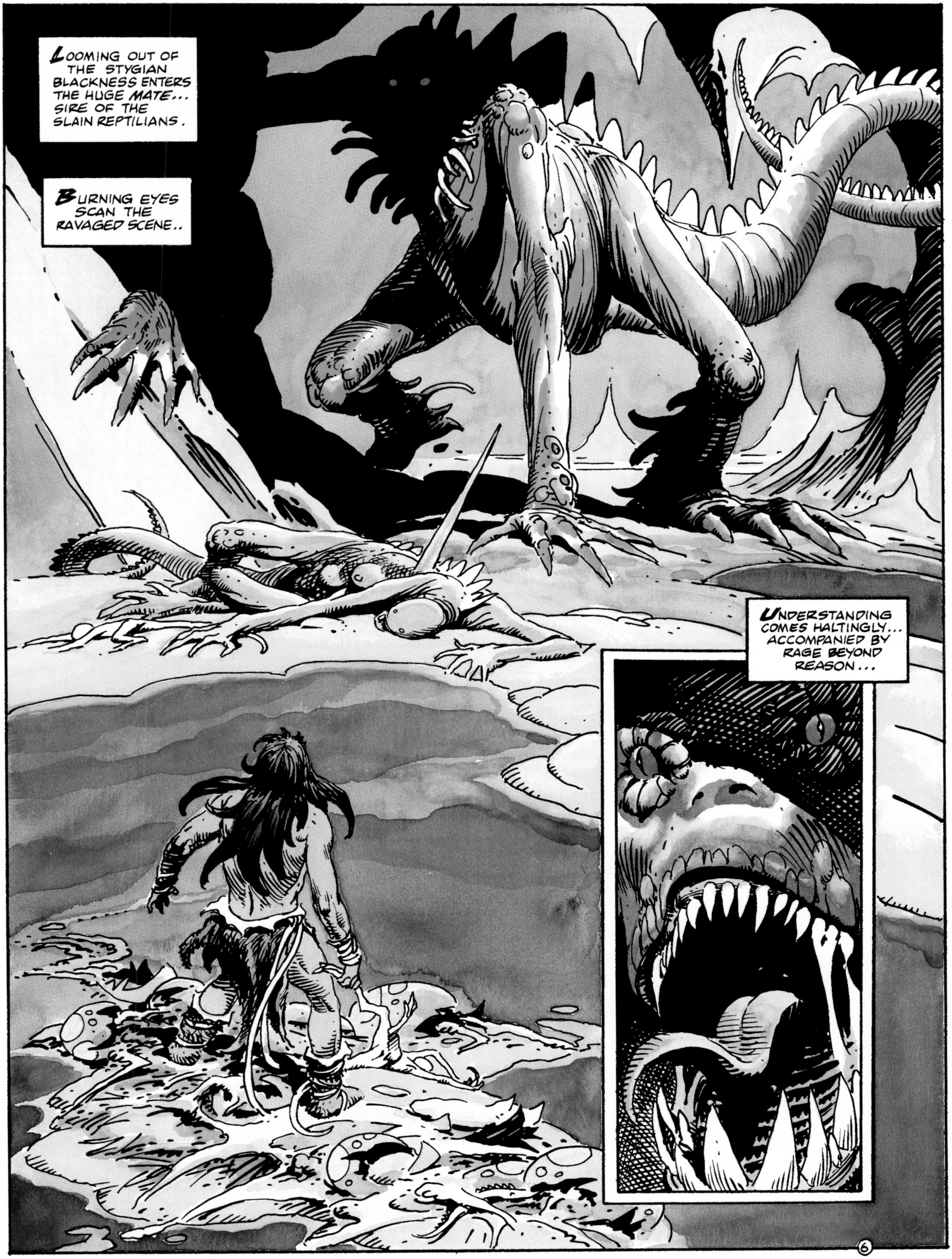
LOOMING OUT OF THE STYGIAN BLACKNESS ENTERS THE HUGE MATE... SIRE OF THE SLAIN REPTILIANS.
BURNING EYES SCAN THE RAVAGED SCENE..
UNDERSTANDING COMES HALTINGLY... ACCOMPANIED BY RAGE BEYOND REASON...
6

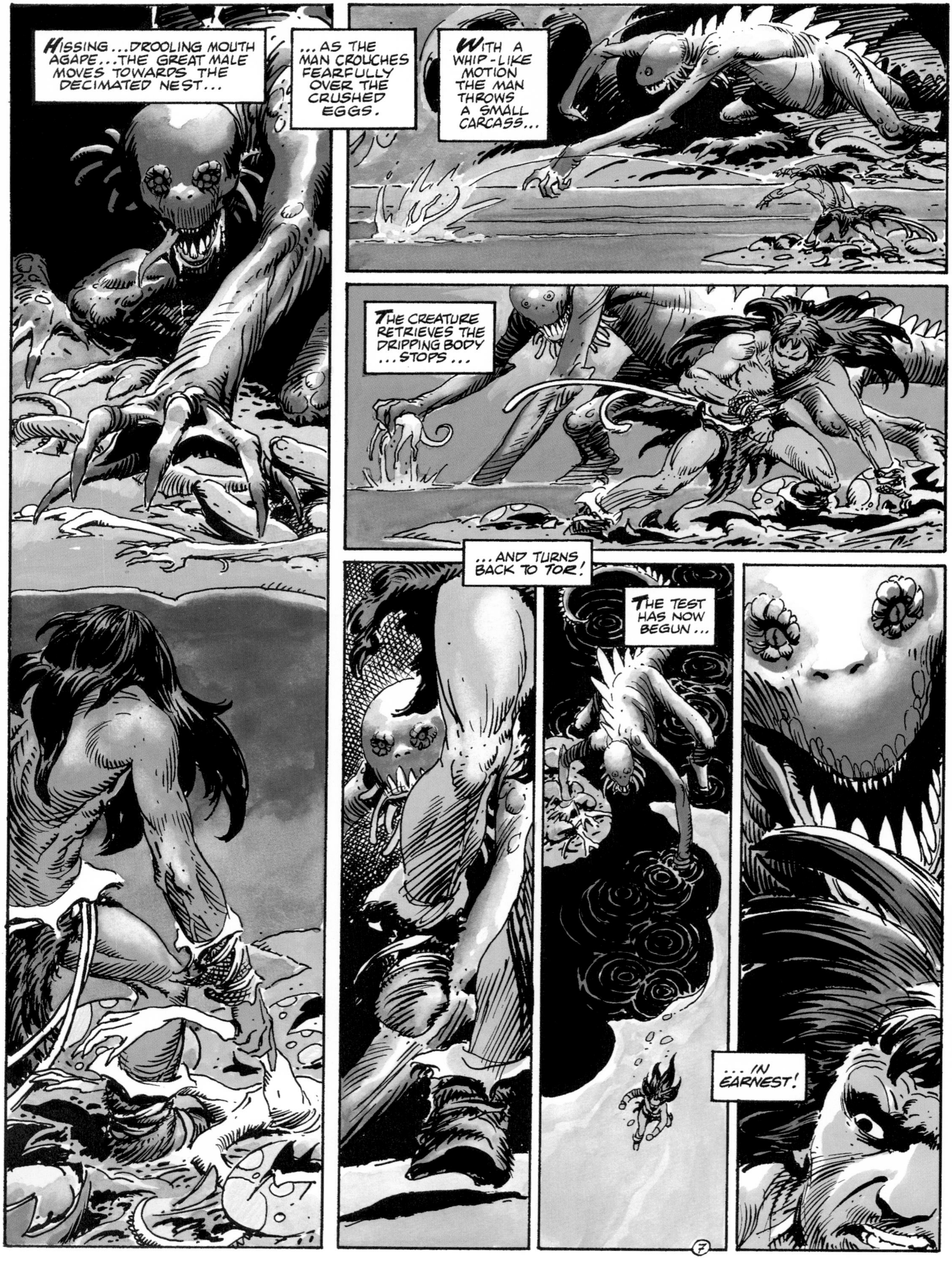
HISSING...DROOLING MOUTH AGAPE...THE GREAT MALE MOVES TOWARDS THE DECIMATED NEST...
...AS THE MAN CROUCHES FEARFULLY OVER THE CRUSHED EGGS.
WITH A WHIP-LIKE MOTION THE MAN THROWS A SMALL CARCASS...
THE CREATURE RETRIEVES THE DRIPPING BODY ...STOPS...
...AND TURNS BACK TO TOR!
THE TEST HAS NOW BEGUN...
...IN EARNEST!
7

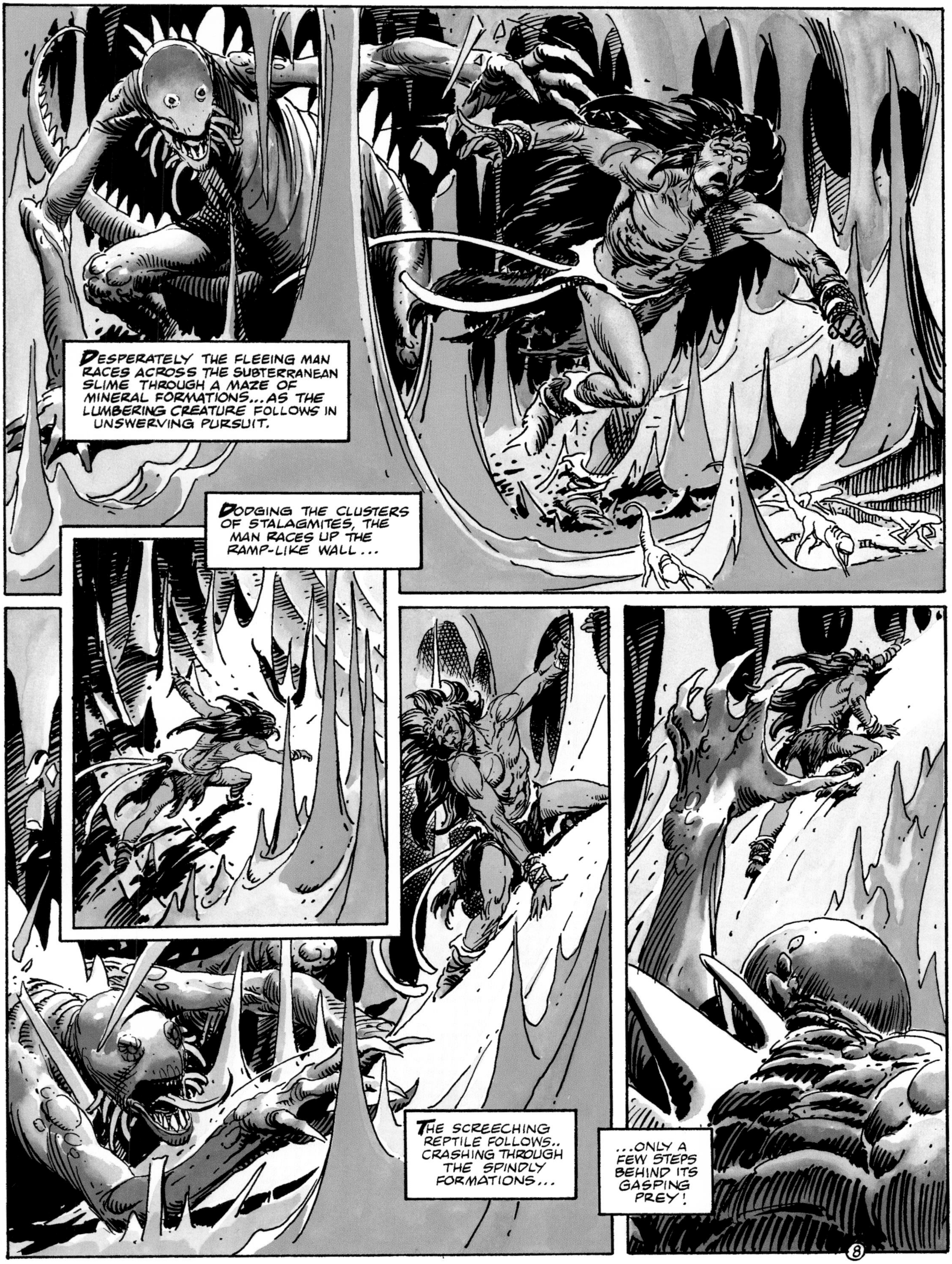
DESPERATELY THE FLEEING MAN RACES ACROSS THE SUBTERRANEAN SLIME THROUGH A MAZE OF MINERAL FORMATIONS... AS THE LUMBERING CREATURE FOLLOWS IN UNSWERVING PURSUIT.
DODGING THE CLUSTERS OF STALAGMITES, THE MAN RACES UP THE RAMP-LIKE WALL...
THE SCREECHING REPTILE FOLLOWS.. CRASHING THROUGH THE SPINDLY FORMATIONS...
...ONLY A FEW STEPS BEHIND ITS GASPING PREY!
8

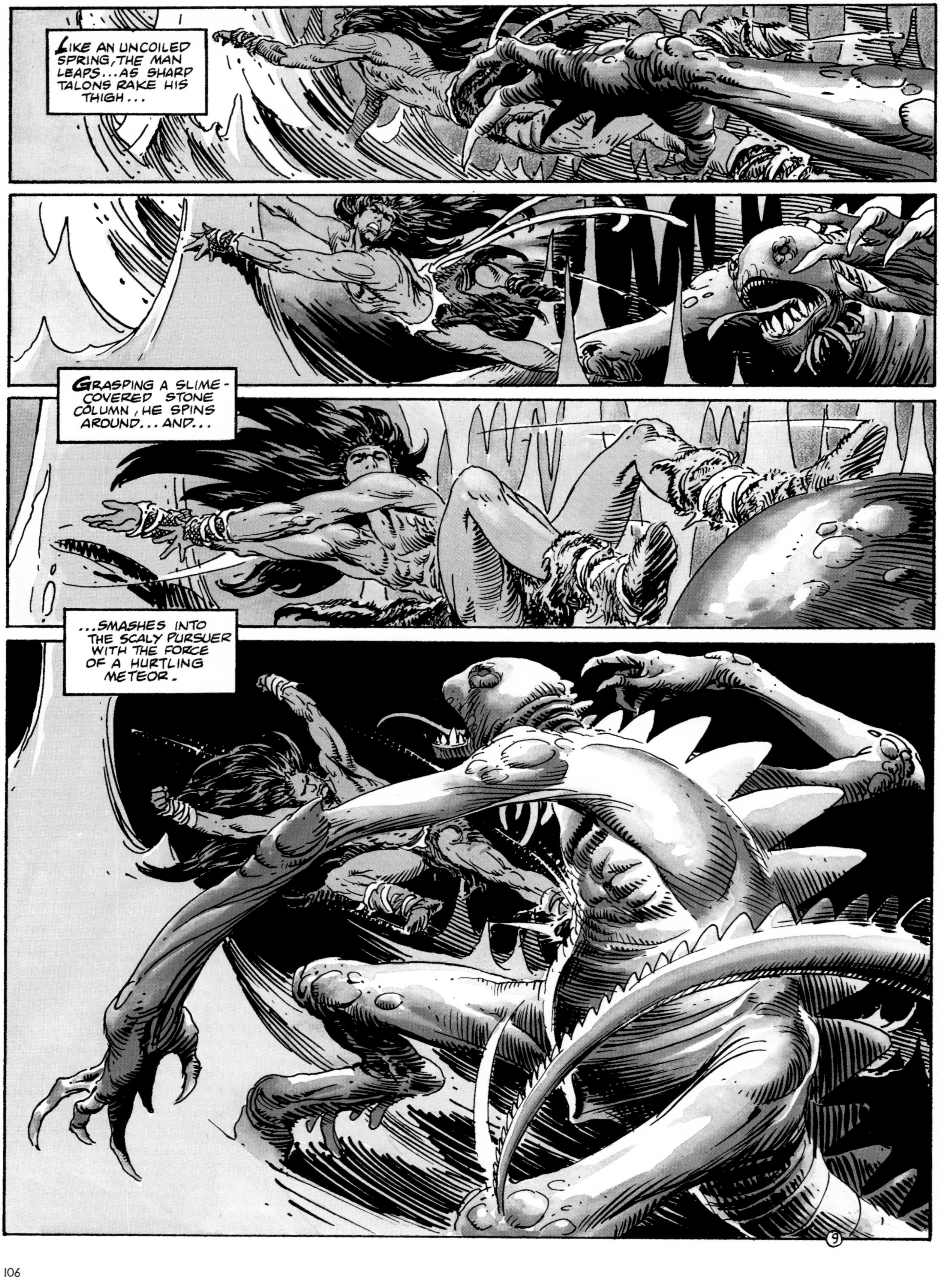
LIKE AN UNCOILED SPRING, THE MAN LEAPS...AS SHARP TALONS RAKE HIS THIGH...
GRASPING A SLIME-COVERED STONE COLUMN, HE SPINS AROUND...AND...
...SMASHES INTO THE SCALY PURSUER WITH THE FORCE OF A HURTLING METEOR.
9

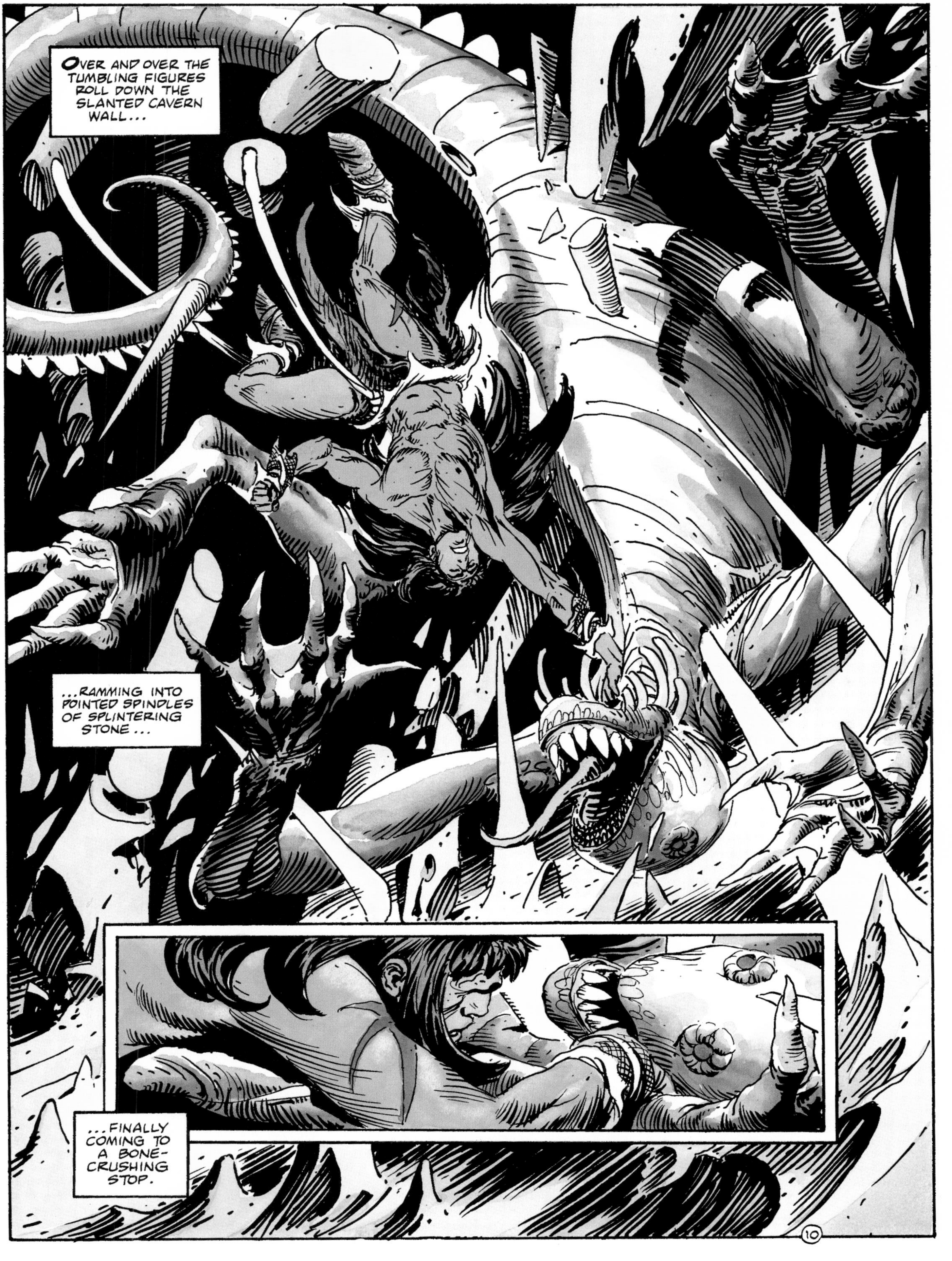
OVER AND OVER THE TUMBLING FIGURES ROLL DOWN THE SLANTED CAVERN WALL...
...RAMMING INTO POINTED SPINDLES OF SPLINTERING STONE...
...FINALLY COMING TO A BONE-CRUSHING STOP.
10

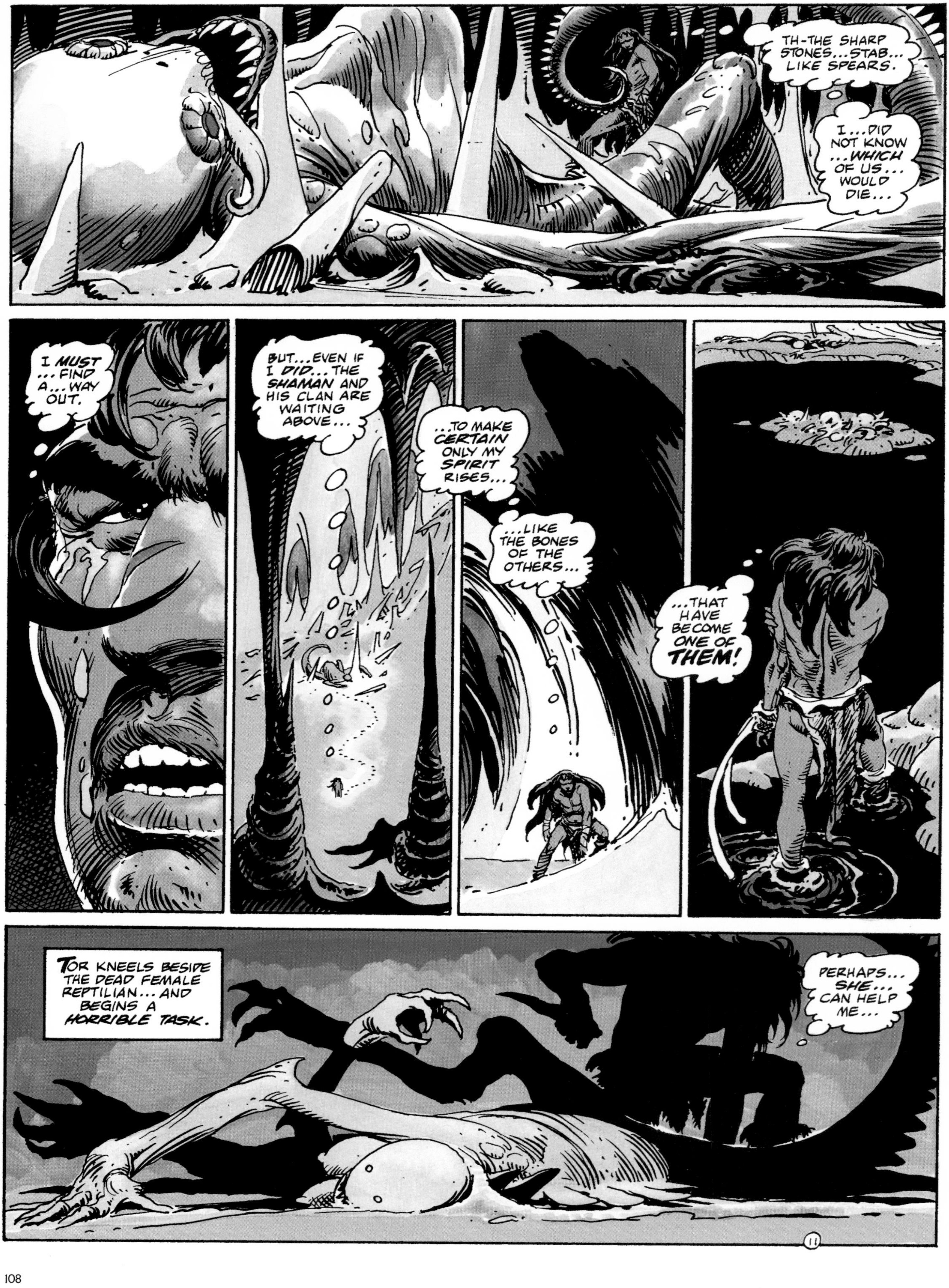
TH-THE SHARP STONES... STAB... LIKE SPEARS.
I... DID NOT KNOW ...WHICH OF US... WOULD DIE...
I MUST ... FIND A... WAY OUT.
BUT... EVEN IF I DID... THE SHAMAN AND HIS CLAN ARE WAITING ABOVE...
...TO MAKE CERTAIN ONLY MY SPIRIT RISES...
...LIKE THE BONES OF THE OTHERS...
...THAT HAVE BECOME ONE OF THEM!
TOR KNEELS BESIDE THE DEAD FEMALE REPTILIAN... AND BEGINS A HORRIBLE TASK.
PERHAPS... SHE... CAN HELP ME...
11

GRIMLY...METHODICALLY HE HACKS WITH BROKEN STONE SHARDS AT THE CARCASS...HIS BODY STREAKED WITH GREEN FLUORESCENT GORE...

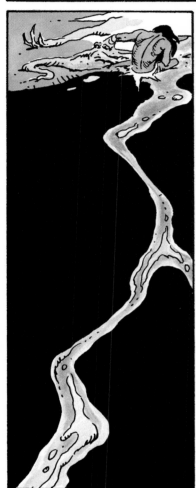

A SIGHTLESS EYE WATCHES ITS OWN EVISCERATION...

GUT IS RUBBED CLEAN TO BE USED AS CORDAGE...

A WEIRD SHADOW STIRS ON THE CAVE WALL... AS IF RISING FROM ITS OWN TORN REMAINS.

12

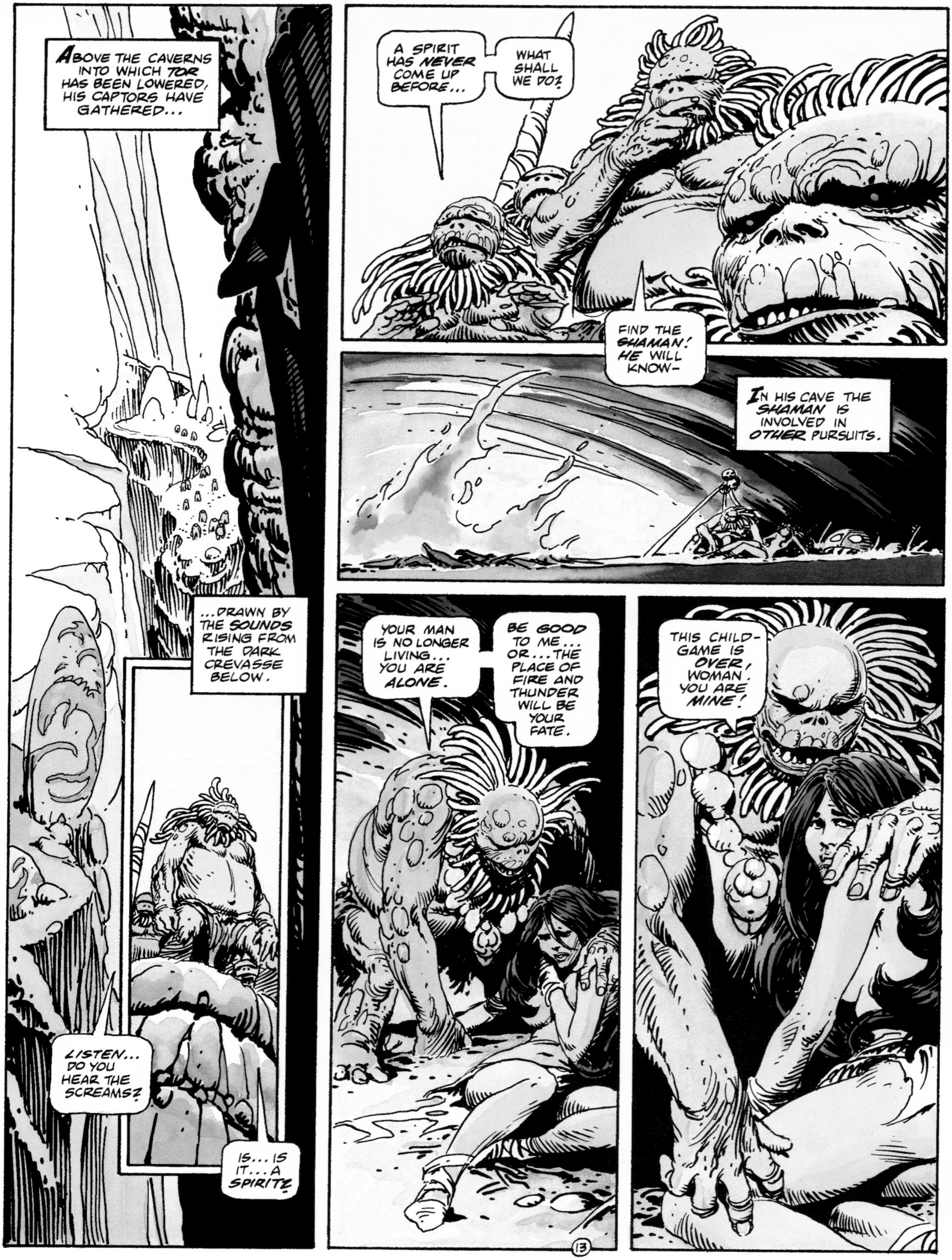
ABOVE THE CAVERNS INTO WHICH TOR HAS BEEN LOWERED, HIS CAPTORS HAVE GATHERED...
...DRAWN BY THE SOUNDS RISING FROM THE DARK CREVASSE BELOW.
LISTEN... DO YOU HEAR THE SCREAMS?
IS... IS IT... A SPIRIT?
A SPIRIT HAS NEVER COME UP BEFORE...
WHAT SHALL WE DO?
FIND THE SHAMAN! HE WILL KNOW-
IN HIS CAVE THE SHAMAN IS INVOLVED IN OTHER PURSUITS.
YOUR MAN IS NO LONGER LIVING... YOU ARE ALONE.
BE GOOD TO ME... OR... THE PLACE OF FIRE AND THUNDER WILL BE YOUR FATE.
THIS CHILD-GAME IS OVER, WOMAN, YOU ARE MINE!
13

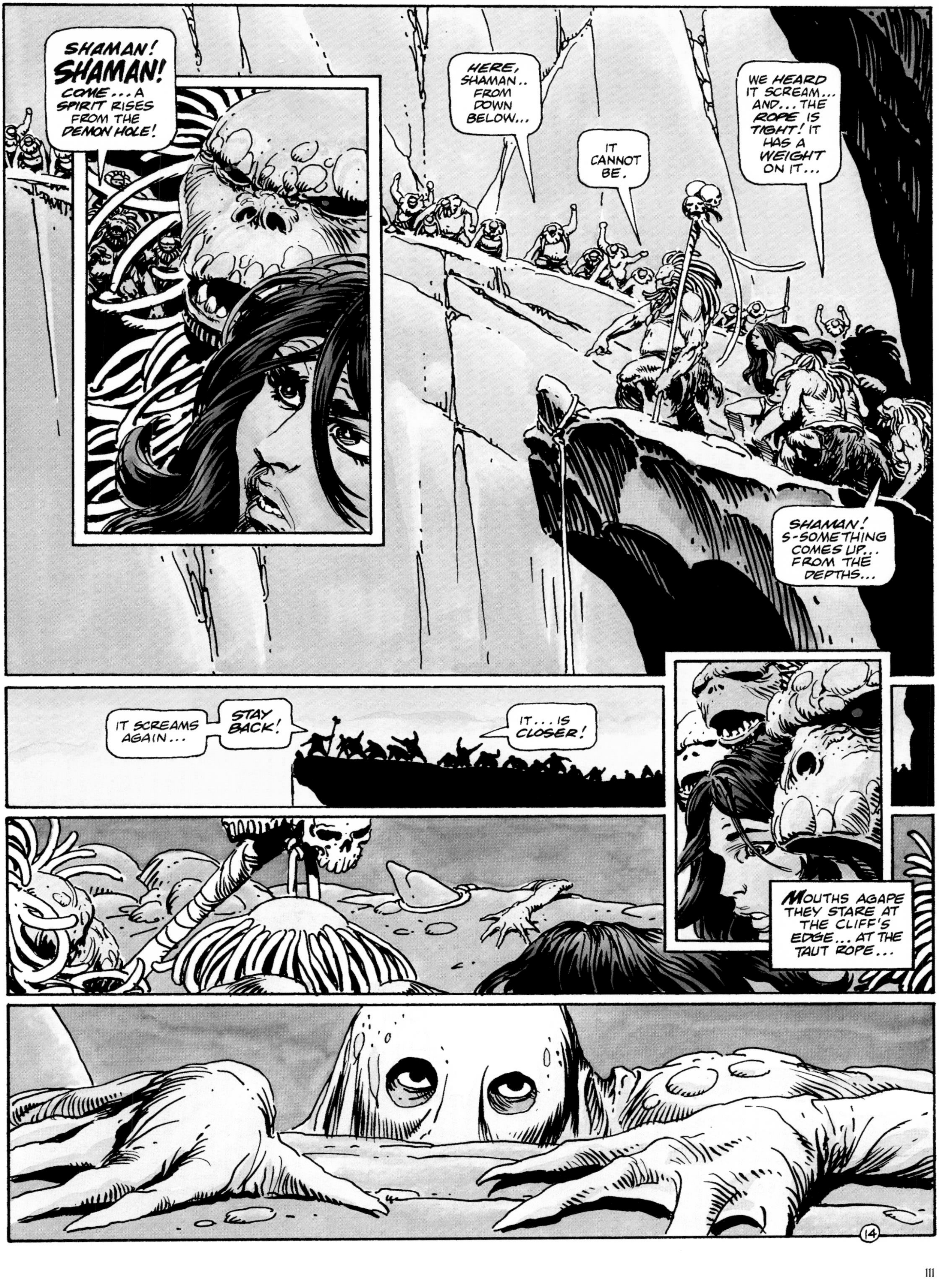
SHAMAN! SHAMAN! COME... A SPIRIT RISES FROM THE DEMON HOLE!
HERE, SHAMAN.. FROM DOWN BELOW...
IT CANNOT BE.
WE HEARD IT SCREAM... AND... THE ROPE IS TIGHT! IT HAS A WEIGHT ON IT...
SHAMAN! S-SOMETHING COMES UP... FROM THE DEPTHS...
IT SCREAMS AGAIN...
STAY BACK!
IT... IS CLOSER!
MOUTHS AGAPE THEY STARE AT THE CLIFF'S EDGE... AT THE TAUT ROPE...
14

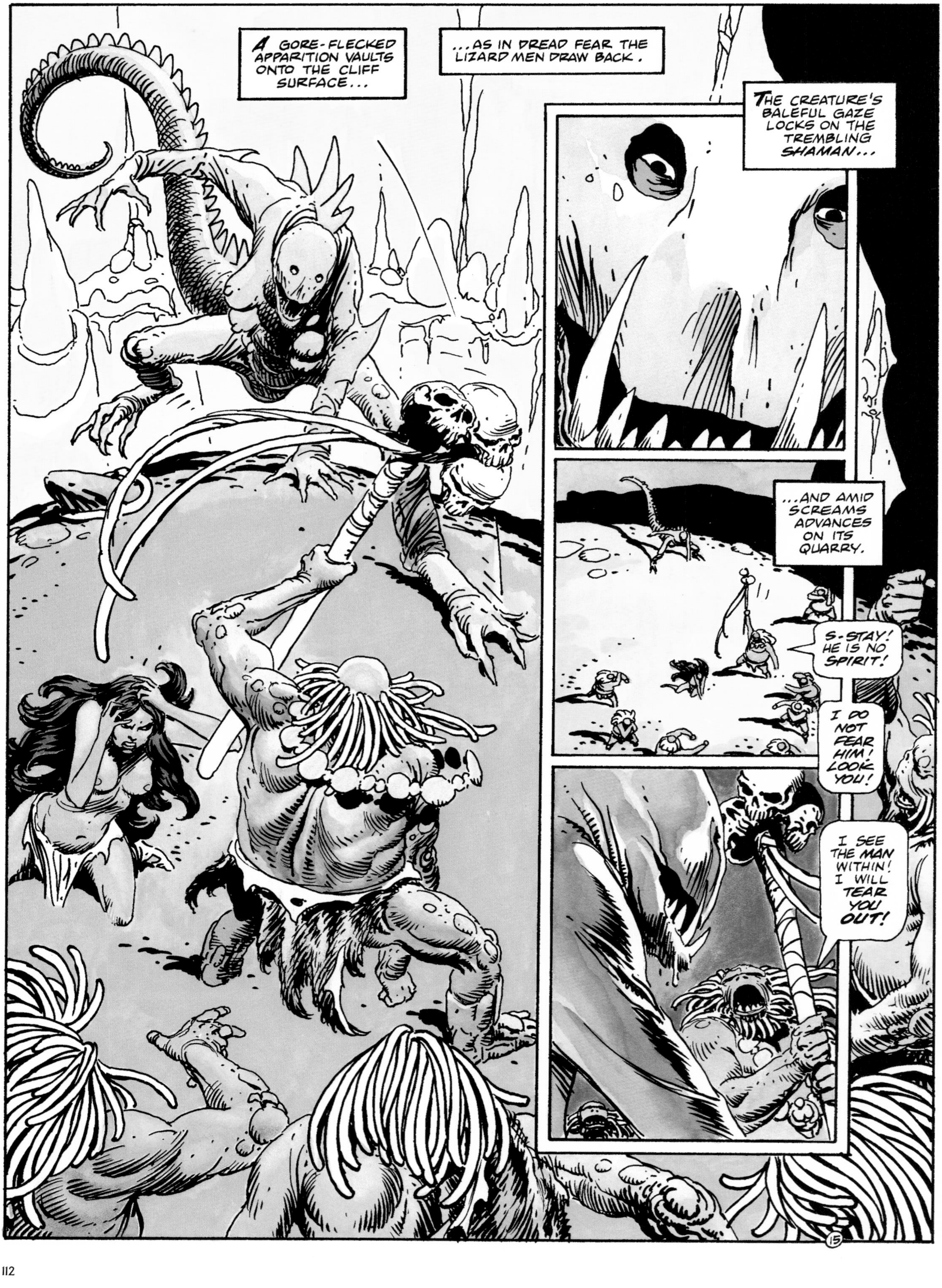
A GORE-FLECKED APPARITION VAULTS ONTO THE CLIFF SURFACE...
...AS IN DREAD FEAR THE LIZARD MEN DRAW BACK.
THE CREATURE'S BALEFUL GAZE LOCKS ON THE TREMBLING SHAMAN...
...AND AMID SCREAMS ADVANCES ON ITS QUARRY.
S-STAY! HE IS NO SPIRIT!
I DO NOT FEAR HIM! LOOK YOU!
I SEE THE MAN WITHIN! I WILL TEAR YOU OUT!
15

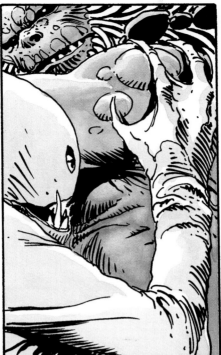

I WILL SEND YOU *BACK* TO THE BOTTOM OF THE *DEVIL HOLE!*

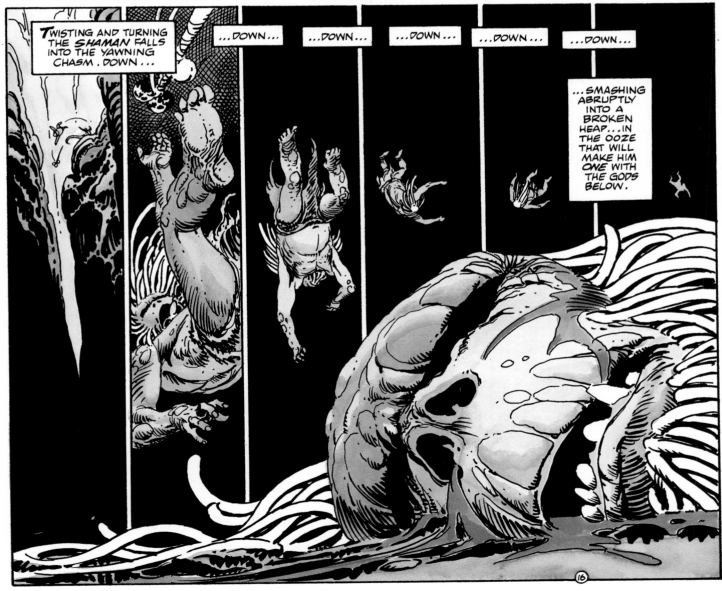

*T*WISTING AND TURNING THE *SHAMAN* FALLS INTO THE YAWNING CHASM. DOWN...

...DOWN...

...DOWN...

...DOWN...

...DOWN...

...DOWN...

...SMASHING ABRUPTLY INTO A BROKEN HEAP...IN THE OOZE THAT WILL MAKE HIM *ONE* WITH THE GODS BELOW.

⑯

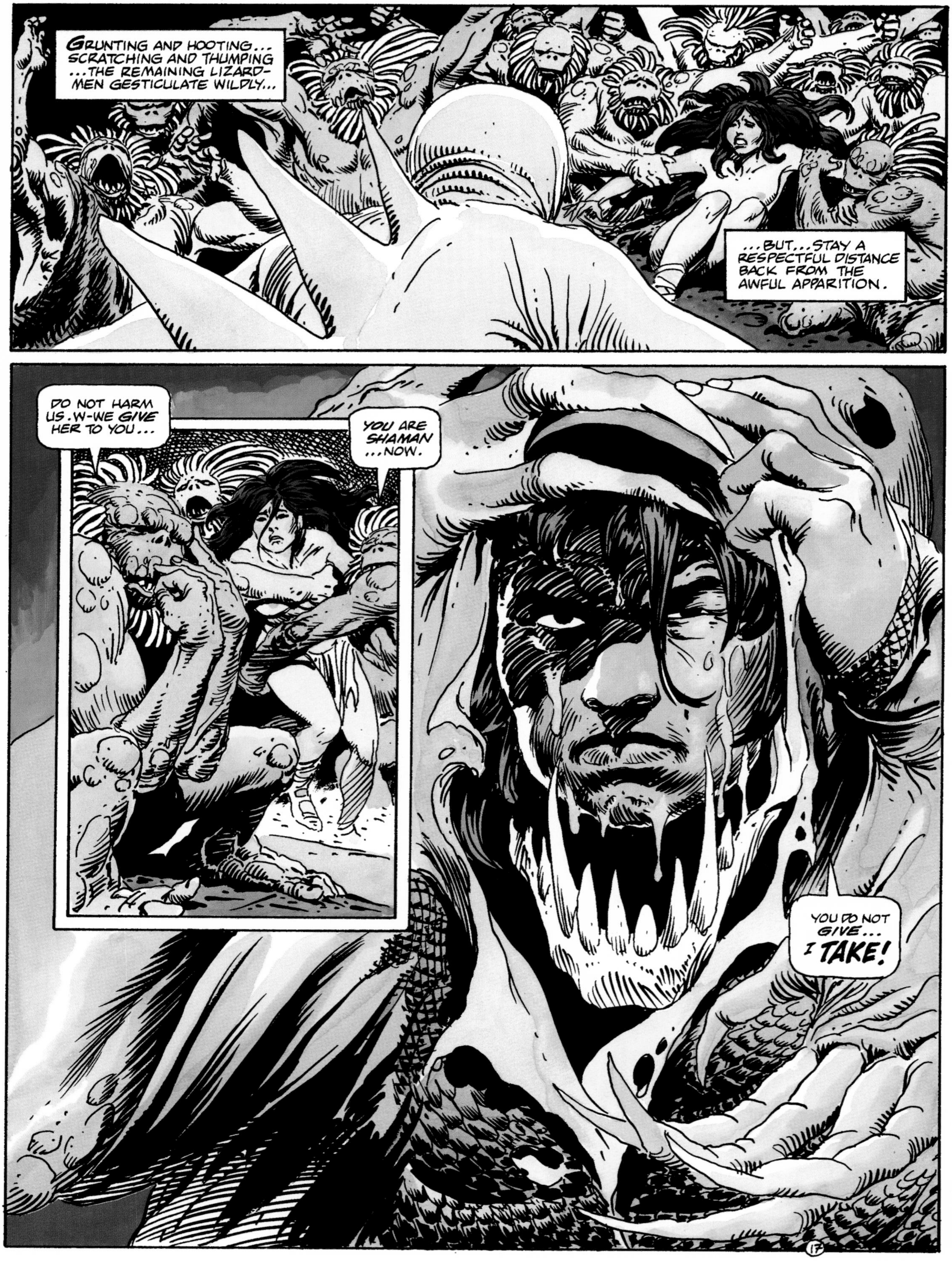
GRUNTING AND HOOTING...
SCRATCHING AND THUMPING
...THE REMAINING LIZARD-
MEN GESTICULATE WILDLY...
...BUT...STAY A RESPECTFUL DISTANCE BACK FROM THE AWFUL APPARITION.
DO NOT HARM US. W-WE GIVE HER TO YOU...
YOU ARE SHAMAN ...NOW.
YOU DO NOT GIVE... I TAKE!
17

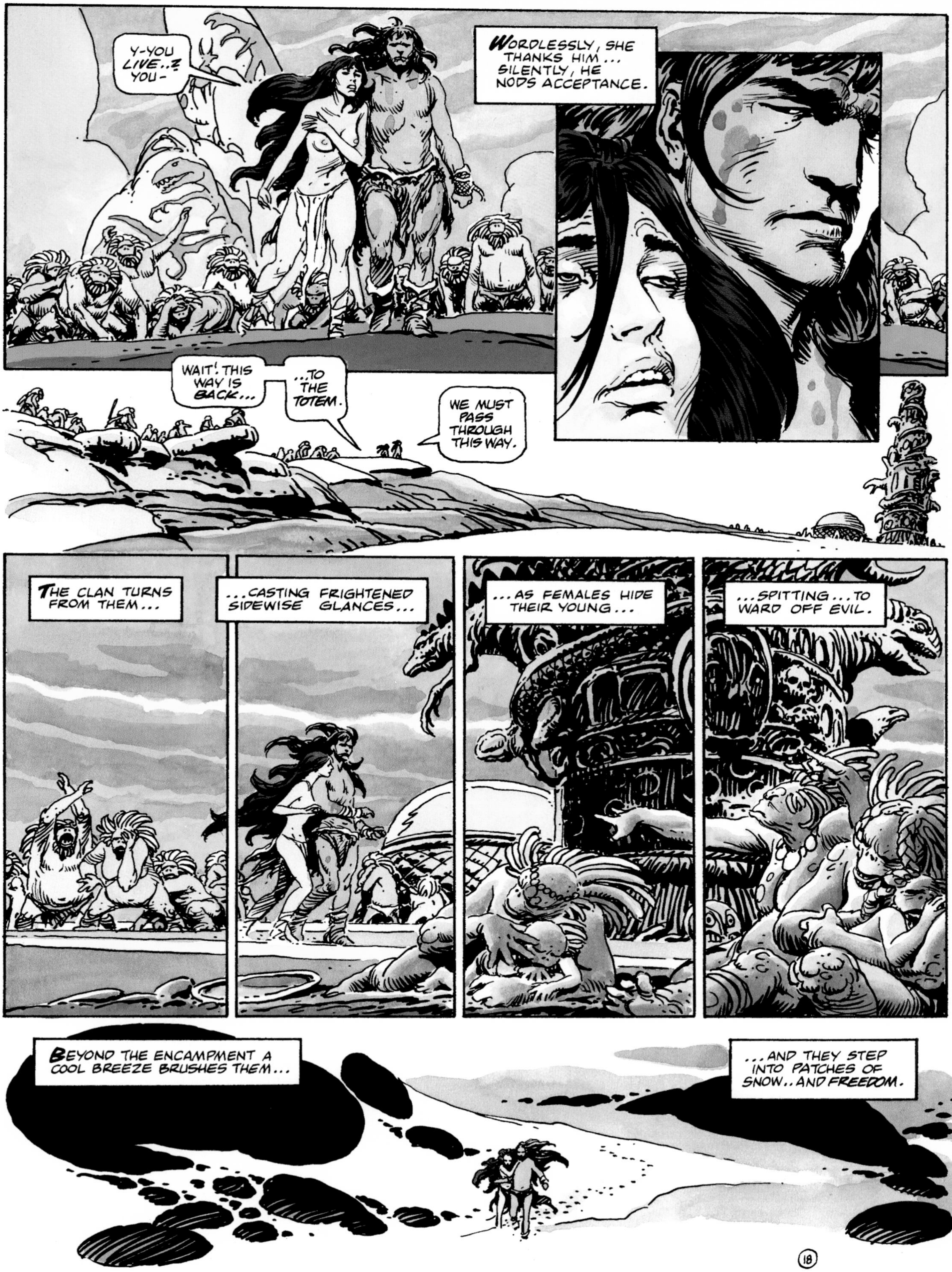
Y-YOU LIVE..?! YOU-
WORDLESSLY, SHE THANKS HIM... SILENTLY, HE NODS ACCEPTANCE.
WAIT! THIS WAY IS BACK...
...TO THE TOTEM.
WE MUST PASS THROUGH THIS WAY.
THE CLAN TURNS FROM THEM...
...CASTING FRIGHTENED SIDEWISE GLANCES...
...AS FEMALES HIDE THEIR YOUNG...
...SPITTING...TO WARD OFF EVIL.
BEYOND THE ENCAMPMENT A COOL BREEZE BRUSHES THEM...
...AND THEY STEP INTO PATCHES OF SNOW...AND FREEDOM.
18

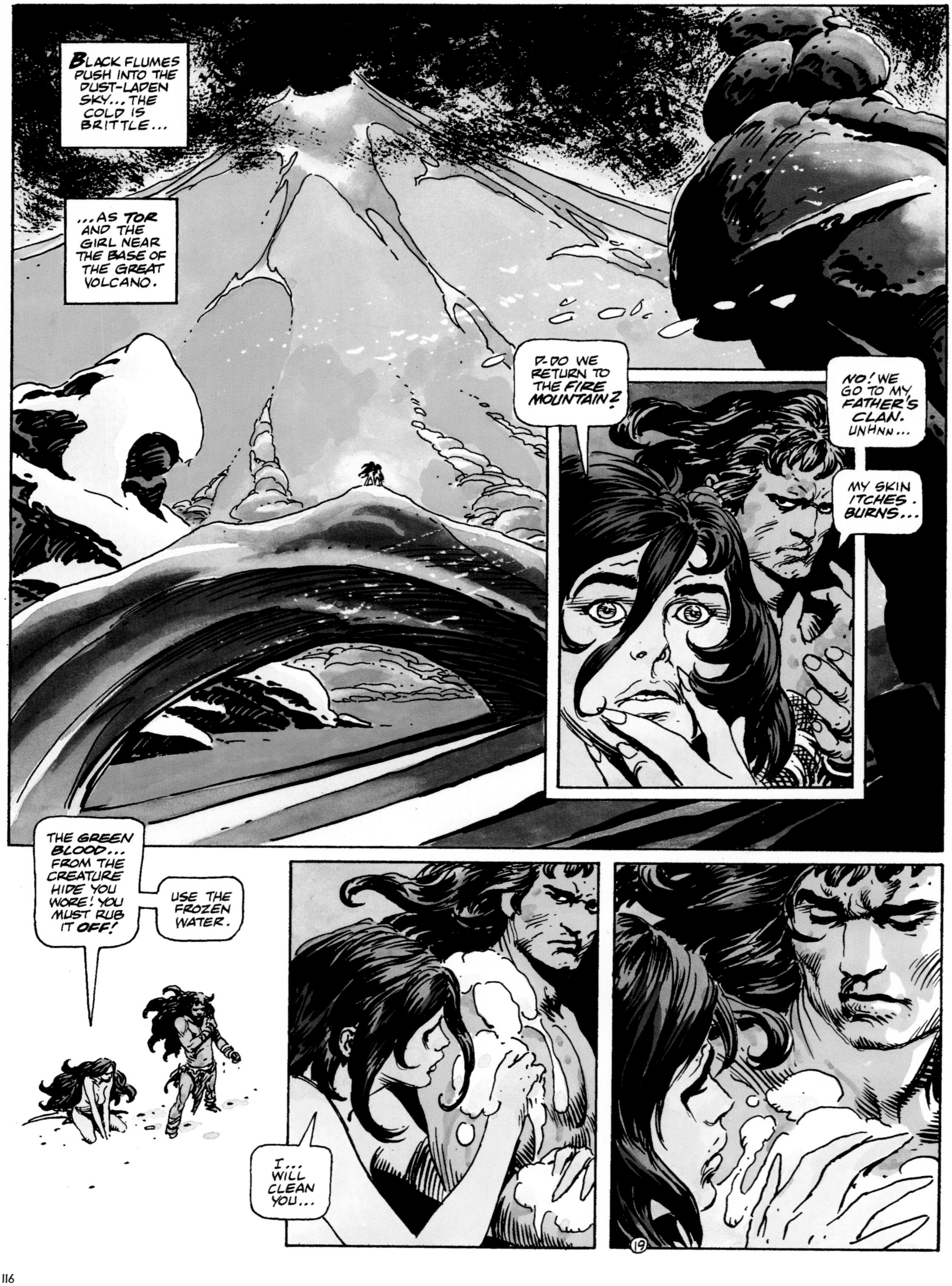
BLACK FLUMES PUSH INTO THE DUST-LADEN SKY... THE COLD IS BRITTLE...
...AS TOR AND THE GIRL NEAR THE BASE OF THE GREAT VOLCANO.
D-DO WE RETURN TO THE FIRE MOUNTAIN?
NO! WE GO TO MY FATHER'S CLAN. UNHNN...
MY SKIN ITCHES. BURNS...
THE GREEN BLOOD... FROM THE CREATURE HIDE YOU WORE! YOU MUST RUB IT OFF!
USE THE FROZEN WATER.
I... WILL CLEAN YOU...
19

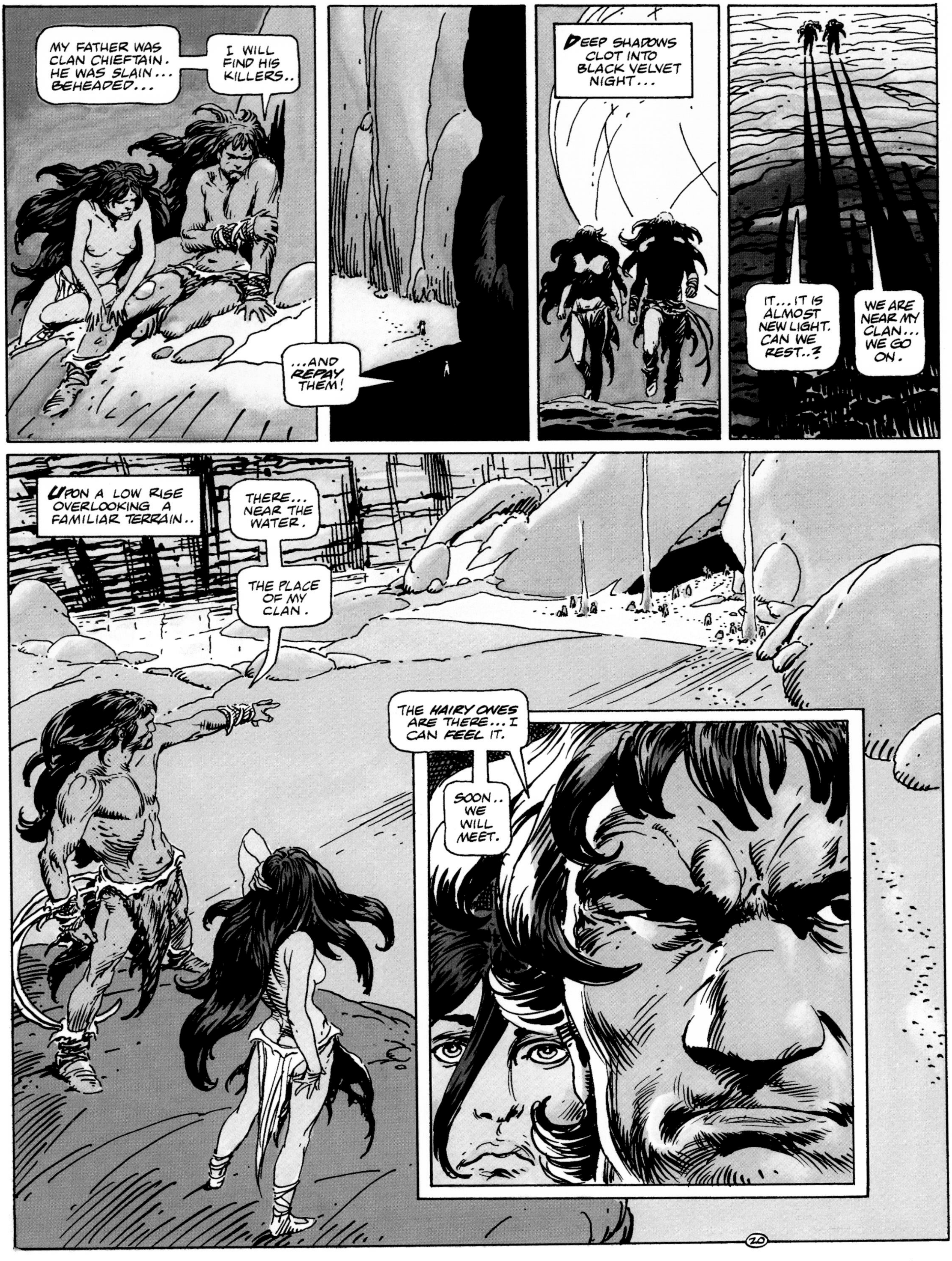
MY FATHER WAS CLAN CHIEFTAIN. HE WAS SLAIN... BEHEADED...
I WILL FIND HIS KILLERS..
...AND REPAY THEM!
DEEP SHADOWS CLOT INTO BLACK VELVET NIGHT...
IT... IT IS ALMOST NEW LIGHT. CAN WE REST..?
WE ARE NEAR MY CLAN... WE GO ON.
UPON A LOW RISE OVERLOOKING A FAMILIAR TERRAIN..
THERE... NEAR THE WATER.
THE PLACE OF MY CLAN.
THE HAIRY ONES ARE THERE... I CAN FEEL IT.
SOON.. WE WILL MEET.
20

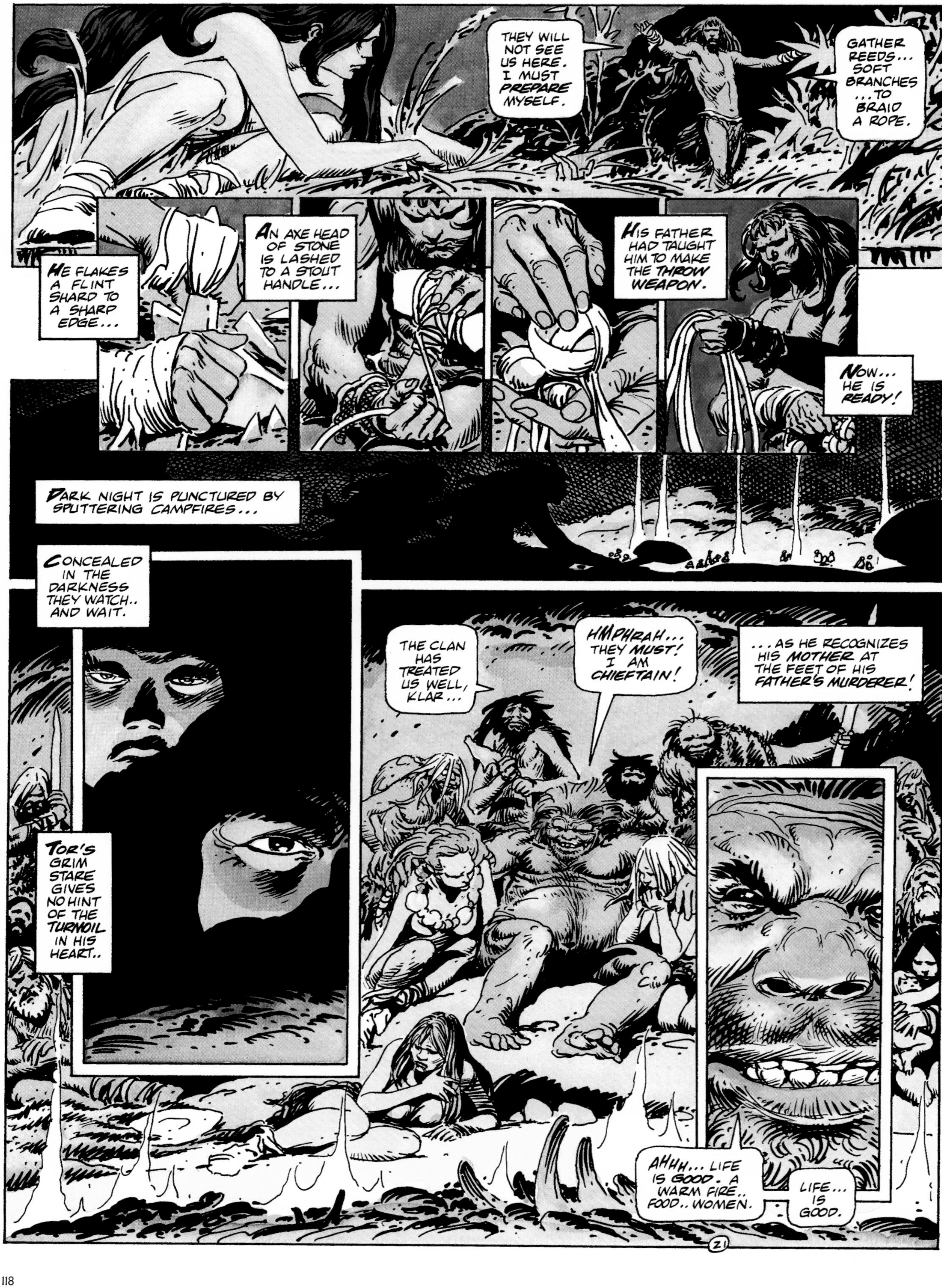
THEY WILL NOT SEE US HERE. I MUST PREPARE MYSELF.
GATHER REEDS... SOFT BRANCHES ...TO BRAID A ROPE.
HE FLAKES A FLINT SHARD TO A SHARP EDGE...
AN AXE HEAD OF STONE IS LASHED TO A STOUT HANDLE...
HIS FATHER HAD TAUGHT HIM TO MAKE THE THROW WEAPON.
NOW... HE IS READY!
DARK NIGHT IS PUNCTURED BY SPUTTERING CAMPFIRES...
CONCEALED IN THE DARKNESS THEY WATCH.. AND WAIT.
TOR'S GRIM STARE GIVES NO HINT OF THE TURMOIL IN HIS HEART..
THE CLAN HAS TREATED US WELL, KLAR...
HMPHRAH... THEY MUST! I AM CHIEFTAIN!
...AS HE RECOGNIZES HIS MOTHER AT THE FEET OF HIS FATHER'S MURDERER!
AHHH... LIFE IS GOOD. A WARM FIRE.. FOOD.. WOMEN.
LIFE... IS GOOD.
21

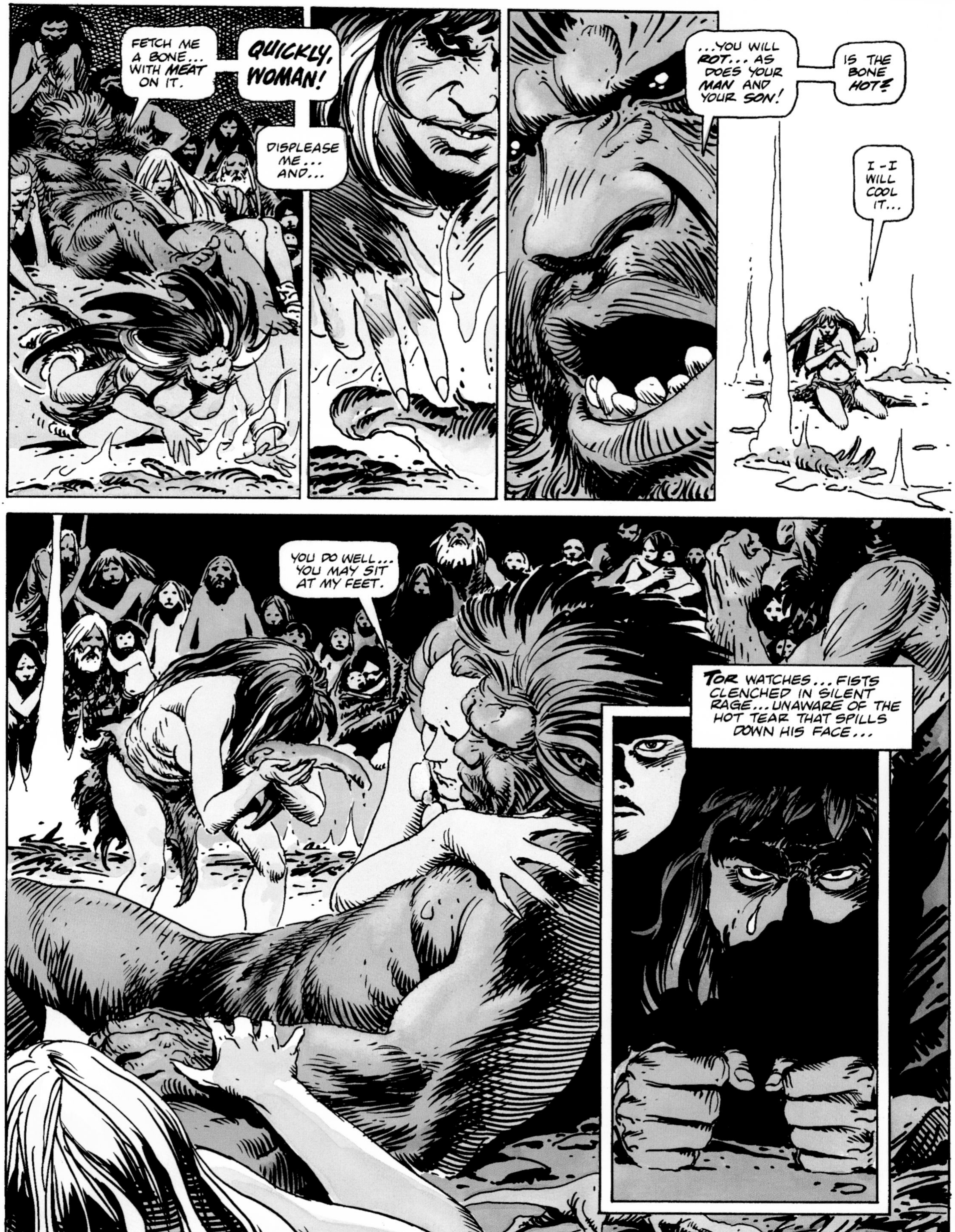
FETCH ME A BONE... WITH MEAT ON IT.
QUICKLY, WOMAN!
DISPLEASE ME... AND...
...YOU WILL ROT... AS DOES YOUR MAN AND YOUR SON!
IS THE BONE HOT?
I-I WILL COOL IT...
YOU DO WELL... YOU MAY SIT AT MY FEET.
TOR WATCHES... FISTS CLENCHED IN SILENT RAGE... UNAWARE OF THE HOT TEAR THAT SPILLS DOWN HIS FACE...
22

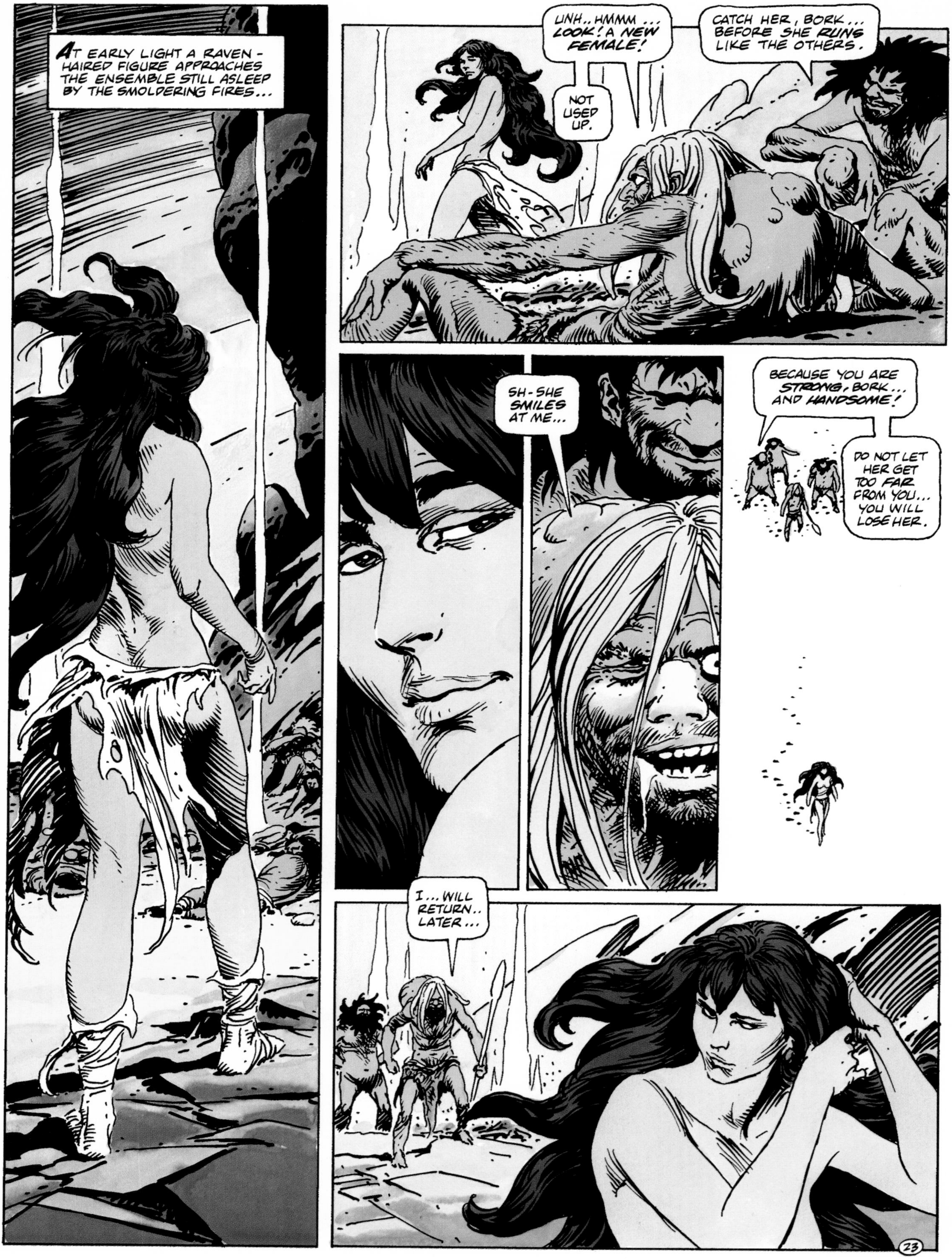
AT EARLY LIGHT A RAVEN-HAIRED FIGURE APPROACHES THE ENSEMBLE STILL ASLEEP BY THE SMOLDERING FIRES...
UNH.. HMMM ... LOOK! A NEW FEMALE!
NOT USED UP.
CATCH HER, BORK... BEFORE SHE RUNS LIKE THE OTHERS.
SH-SHE SMILES AT ME...
BECAUSE YOU ARE STRONG, BORK... AND HANDSOME!
DO NOT LET HER GET TOO FAR FROM YOU... YOU WILL LOSE HER.
I... WILL RETURN.. LATER...
23

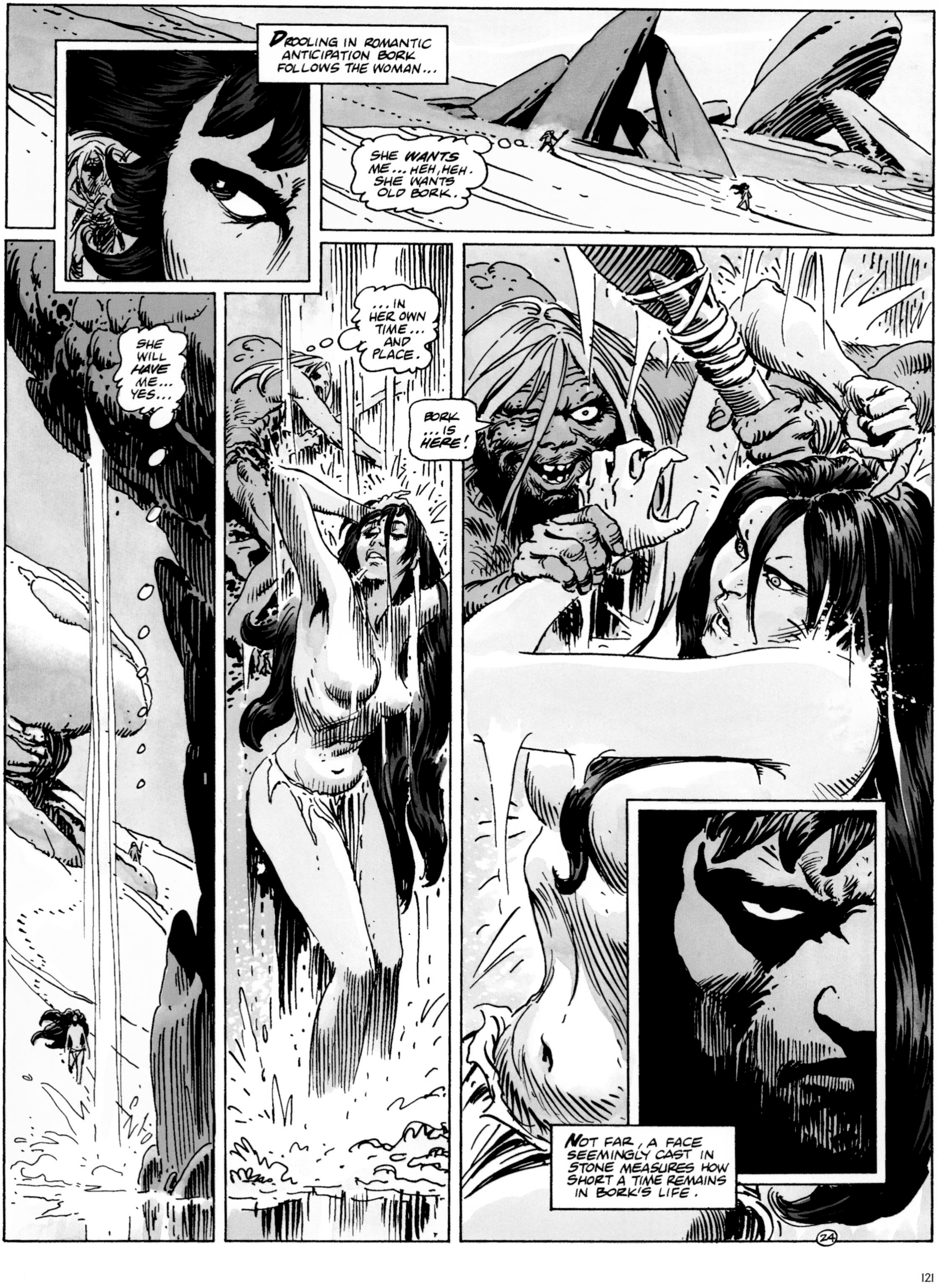
DROOLING IN ROMANTIC ANTICIPATION BORK FOLLOWS THE WOMAN...
SHE WANTS ME... HEH, HEH. SHE WANTS OLD BORK.
SHE WILL HAVE ME... YES...
...IN HER OWN TIME... AND PLACE.
BORK ...IS HERE!
NOT FAR, A FACE SEEMINGLY CAST IN STONE MEASURES HOW SHORT A TIME REMAINS IN BORK'S LIFE.
24

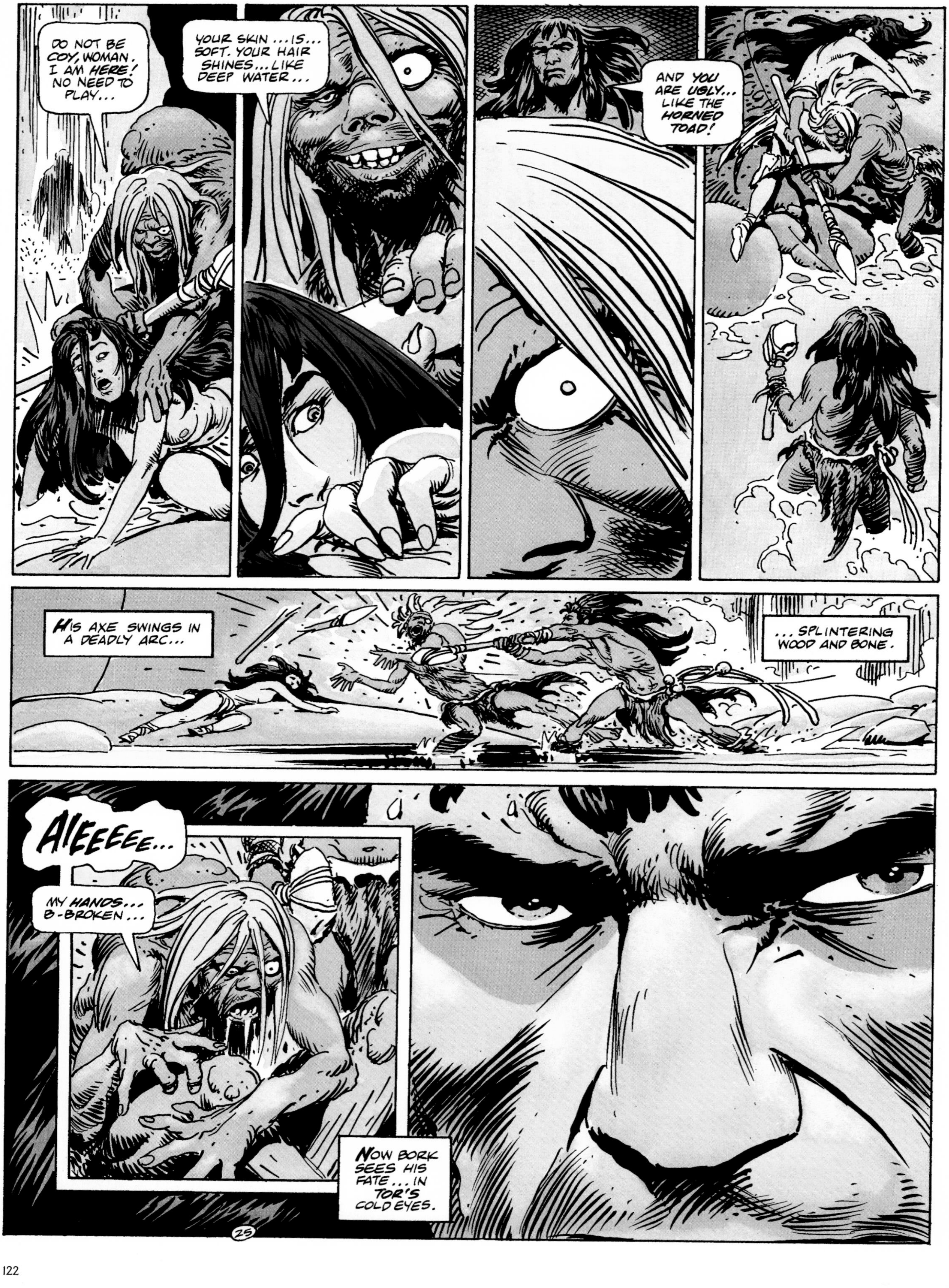
DO NOT BE COY, WOMAN. I AM HERE! NO NEED TO PLAY...
YOUR SKIN... IS... SOFT. YOUR HAIR SHINES... LIKE DEEP WATER...
AND YOU ARE UGLY... LIKE THE HORNED TOAD!
HIS AXE SWINGS IN A DEADLY ARC...
...SPLINTERING WOOD AND BONE.
AIEEEEE...
MY HANDS... B-BROKEN...
NOW BORK SEES HIS FATE... IN TOR'S COLD EYES.
25

AND NOW, TOR'S STRUGGLE FOR SURVIVAL CONTINUES...

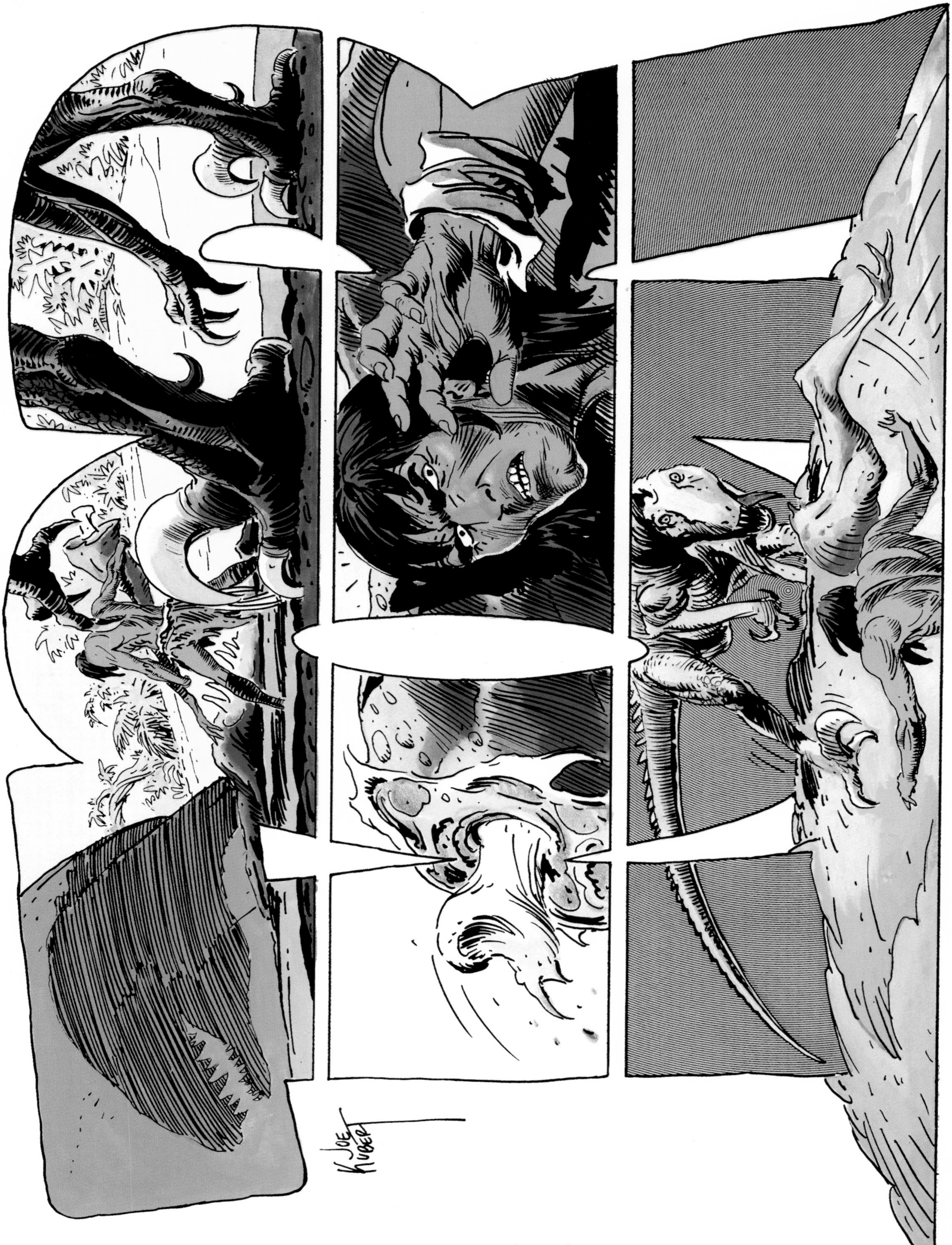
JOE KUBERT

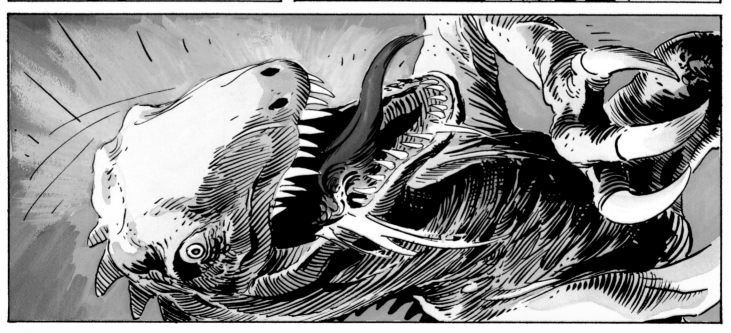

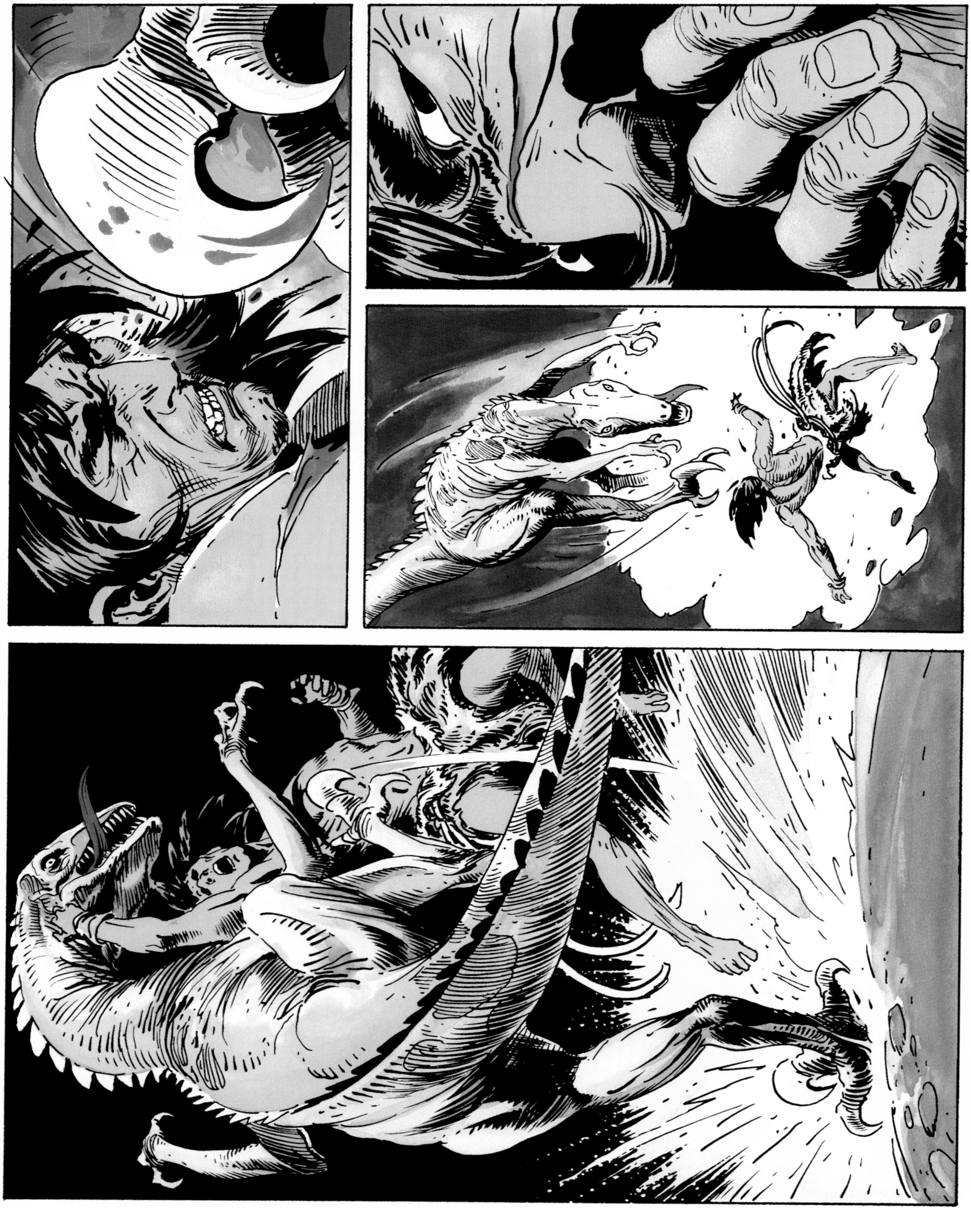

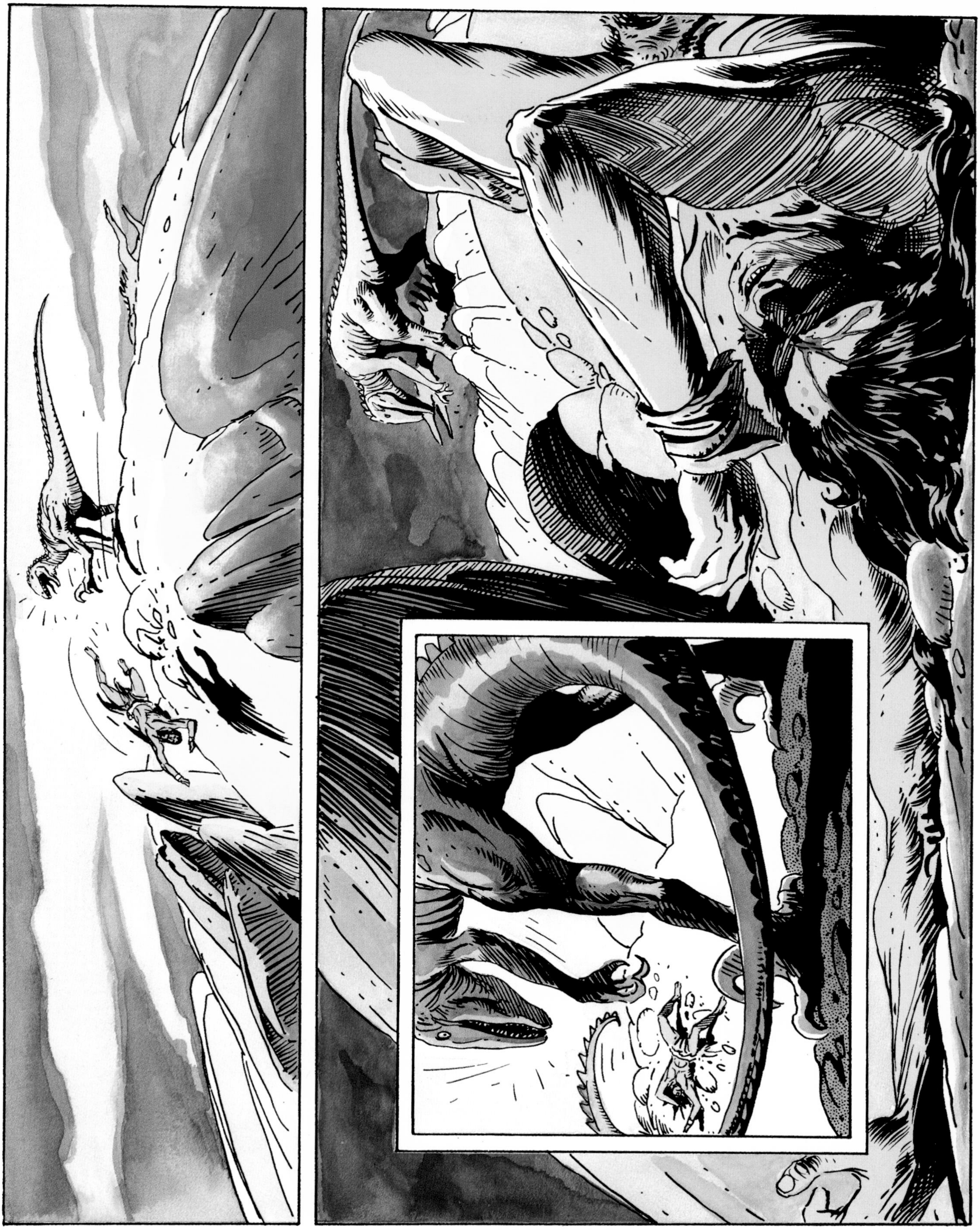

TO BE CONTINUED...

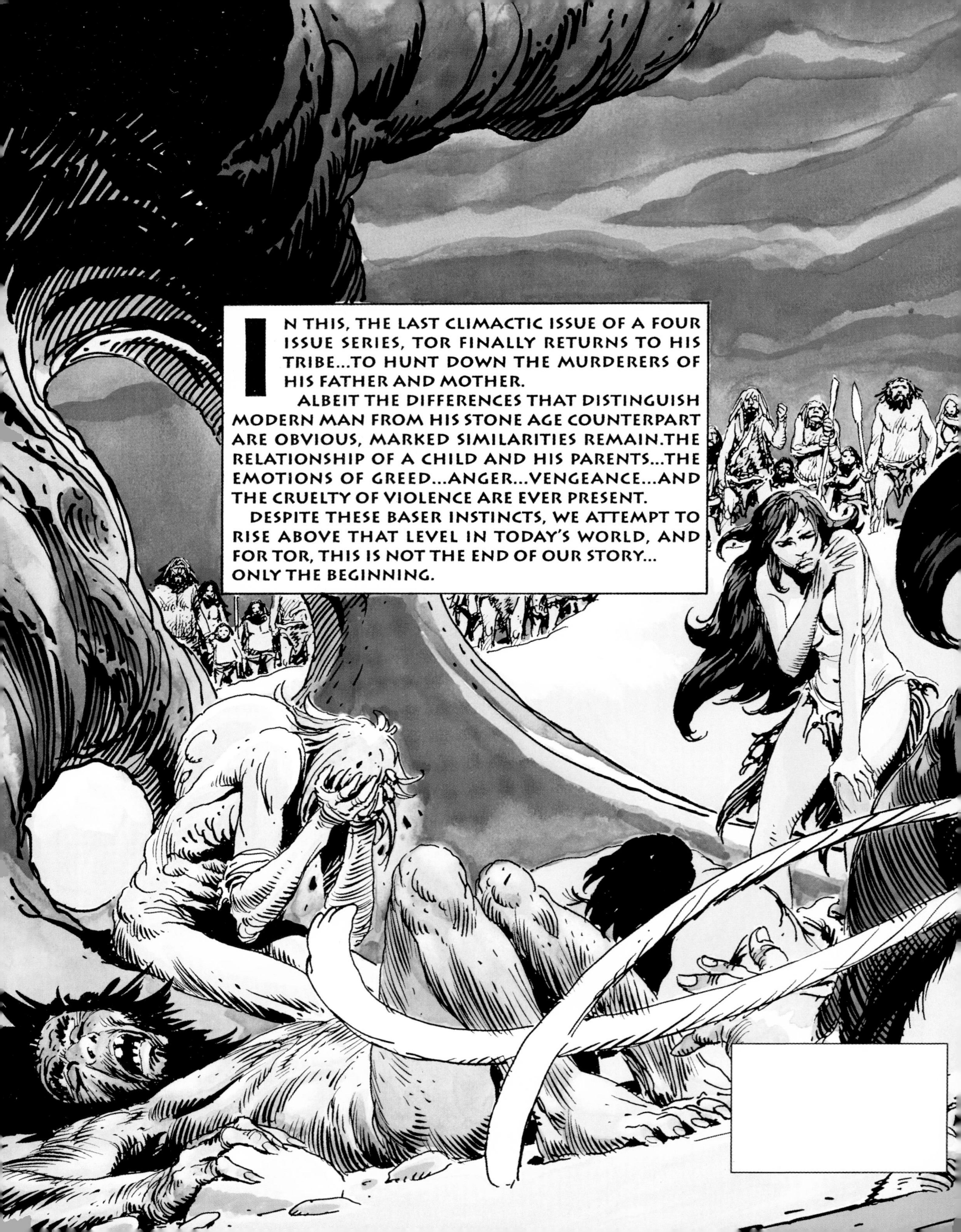
IN THIS, THE LAST CLIMACTIC ISSUE OF A FOUR ISSUE SERIES, TOR FINALLY RETURNS TO HIS TRIBE...TO HUNT DOWN THE MURDERERS OF HIS FATHER AND MOTHER.
ALBEIT THE DIFFERENCES THAT DISTINGUISH MODERN MAN FROM HIS STONE AGE COUNTERPART ARE OBVIOUS, MARKED SIMILARITIES REMAIN.THE RELATIONSHIP OF A CHILD AND HIS PARENTS...THE EMOTIONS OF GREED...ANGER...VENGEANCE...AND THE CRUELTY OF VIOLENCE ARE EVER PRESENT.
DESPITE THESE BASER INSTINCTS, WE ATTEMPT TO RISE ABOVE THAT LEVEL IN TODAY'S WORLD, AND FOR TOR, THIS IS NOT THE END OF OUR STORY... ONLY THE BEGINNING.

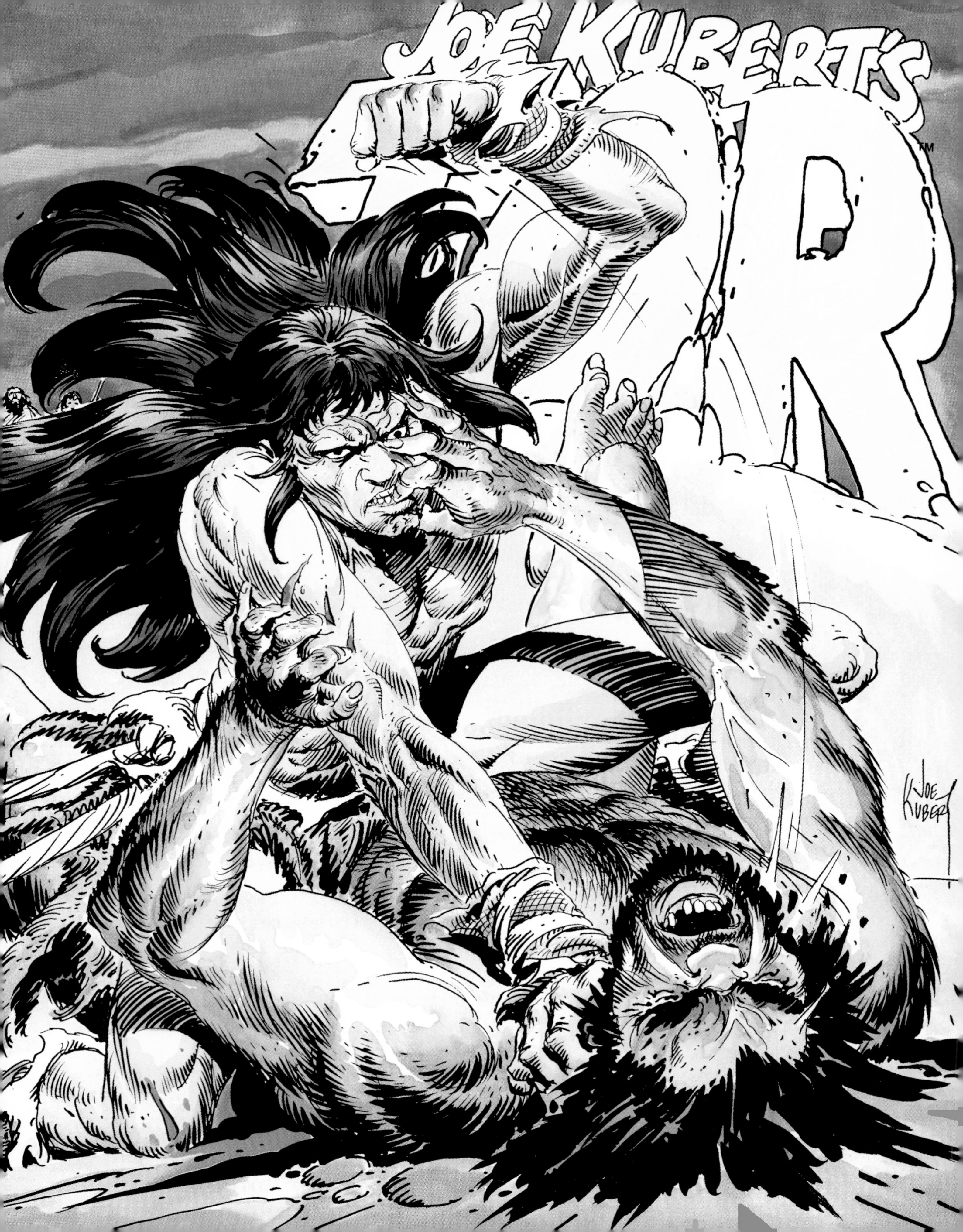
JOE KUBERT'S
JOE KUBERT

CONTINUED FROM BOOK 3:

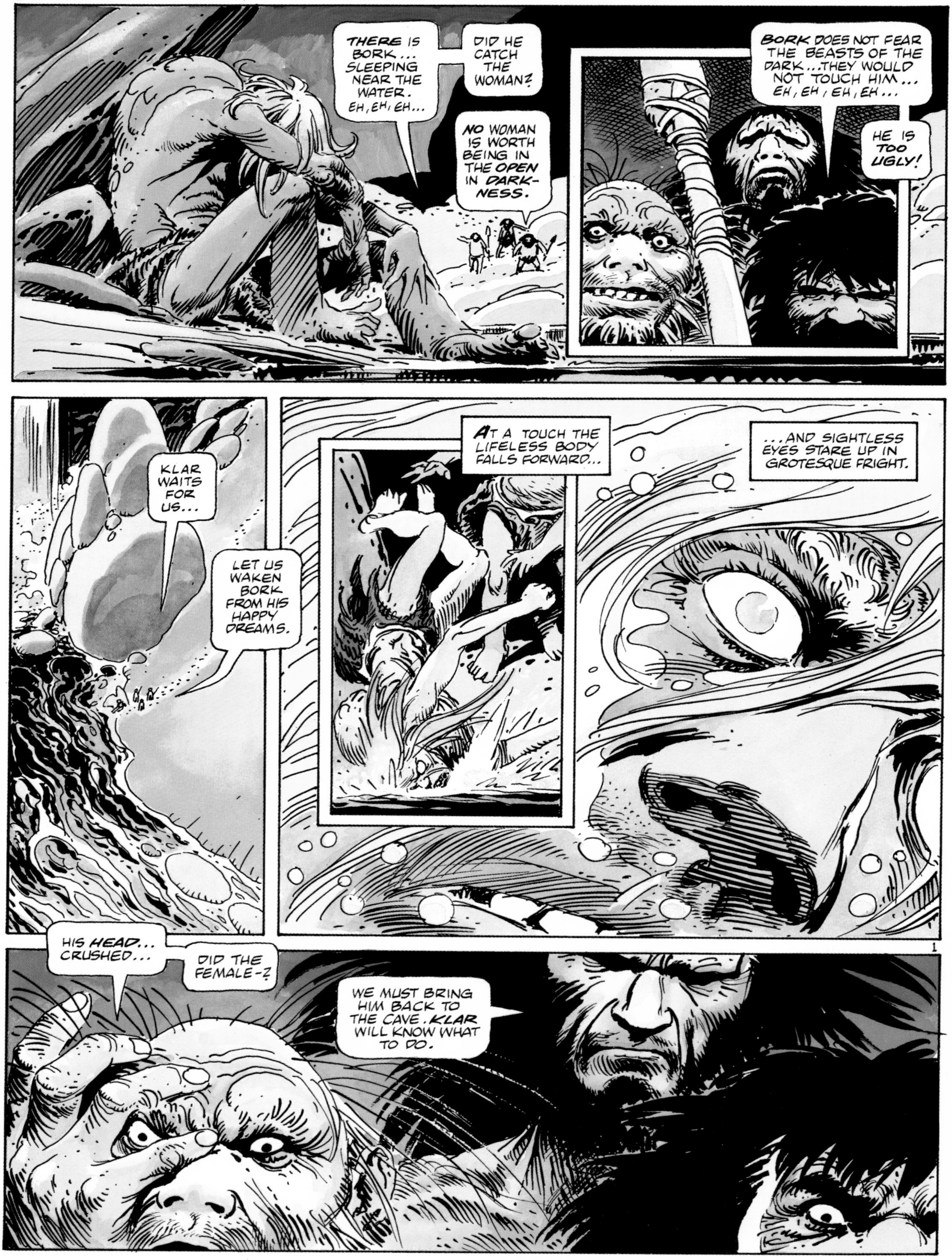
THERE IS BORK... SLEEPING NEAR THE WATER. EH, EH, EH...
DID HE CATCH THE WOMAN?
NO WOMAN IS WORTH BEING IN THE OPEN IN DARKNESS.
BORK DOES NOT FEAR THE BEASTS OF THE DARK...THEY WOULD NOT TOUCH HIM... EH, EH, EH, EH...
HE IS TOO UGLY!
KLAR WAITS FOR US...
LET US WAKEN BORK FROM HIS HAPPY DREAMS.
AT A TOUCH THE LIFELESS BODY FALLS FORWARD...
...AND SIGHTLESS EYES STARE UP IN GROTESQUE FRIGHT.
HIS HEAD... CRUSHED...
DID THE FEMALE-?
WE MUST BRING HIM BACK TO THE CAVE. KLAR WILL KNOW WHAT TO DO.

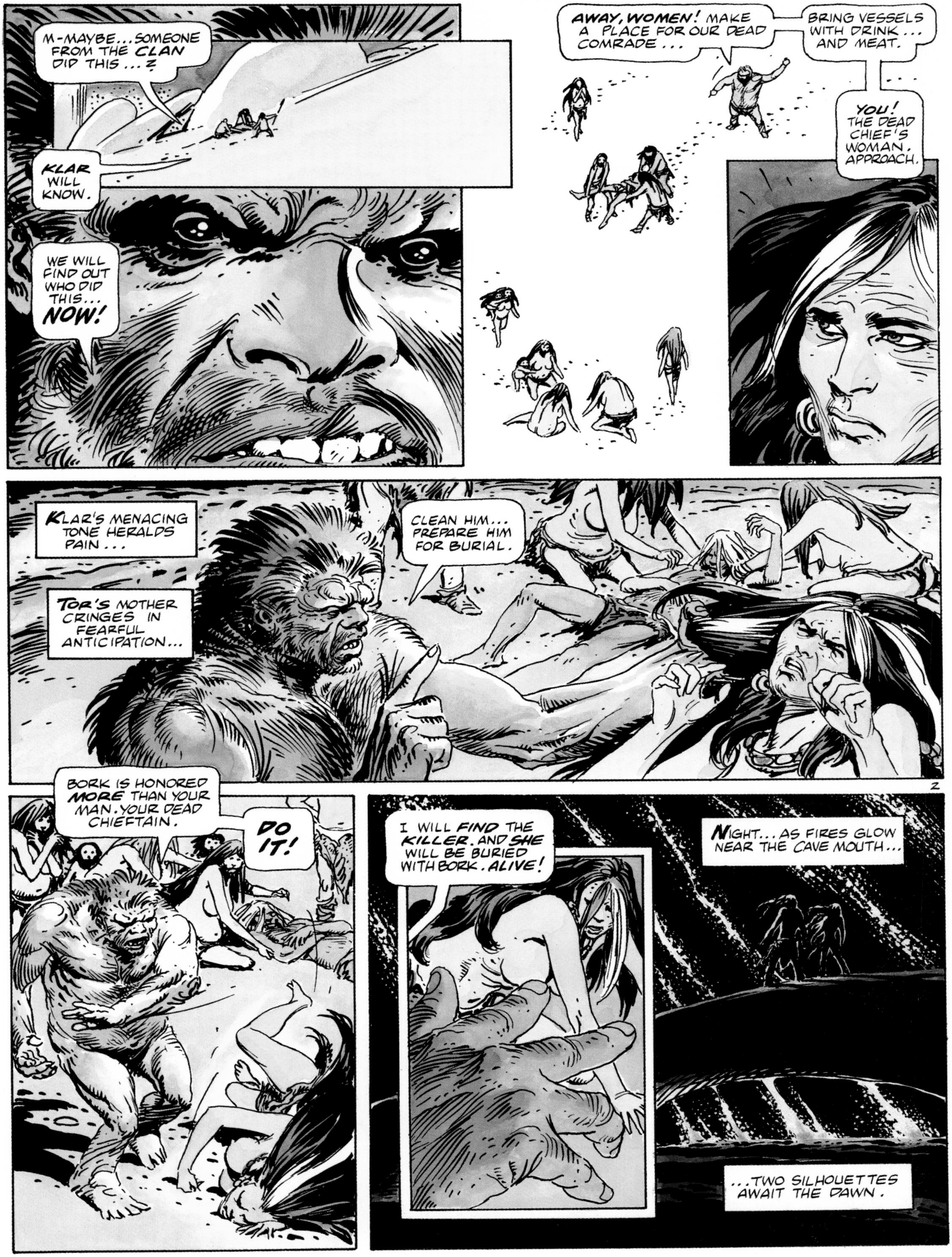

M-MAYBE... SOMEONE FROM THE CLAN DID THIS ... ?
KLAR WILL KNOW.
WE WILL FIND OUT WHO DID THIS... NOW!
AWAY, WOMEN! MAKE A PLACE FOR OUR DEAD COMRADE ...
BRING VESSELS WITH DRINK ... AND MEAT.
YOU! THE DEAD CHIEF'S WOMAN. APPROACH.
KLAR'S MENACING TONE HERALDS PAIN ...
TOR'S MOTHER CRINGES IN FEARFUL ANTICIPATION...
CLEAN HIM... PREPARE HIM FOR BURIAL.
2
BORK IS HONORED MORE THAN YOUR MAN. YOUR DEAD CHIEFTAIN.
DO IT!
I WILL FIND THE KILLER. AND SHE WILL BE BURIED WITH BORK. ALIVE!
NIGHT... AS FIRES GLOW NEAR THE CAVE MOUTH...
...TWO SILHOUETTES AWAIT THE DAWN.

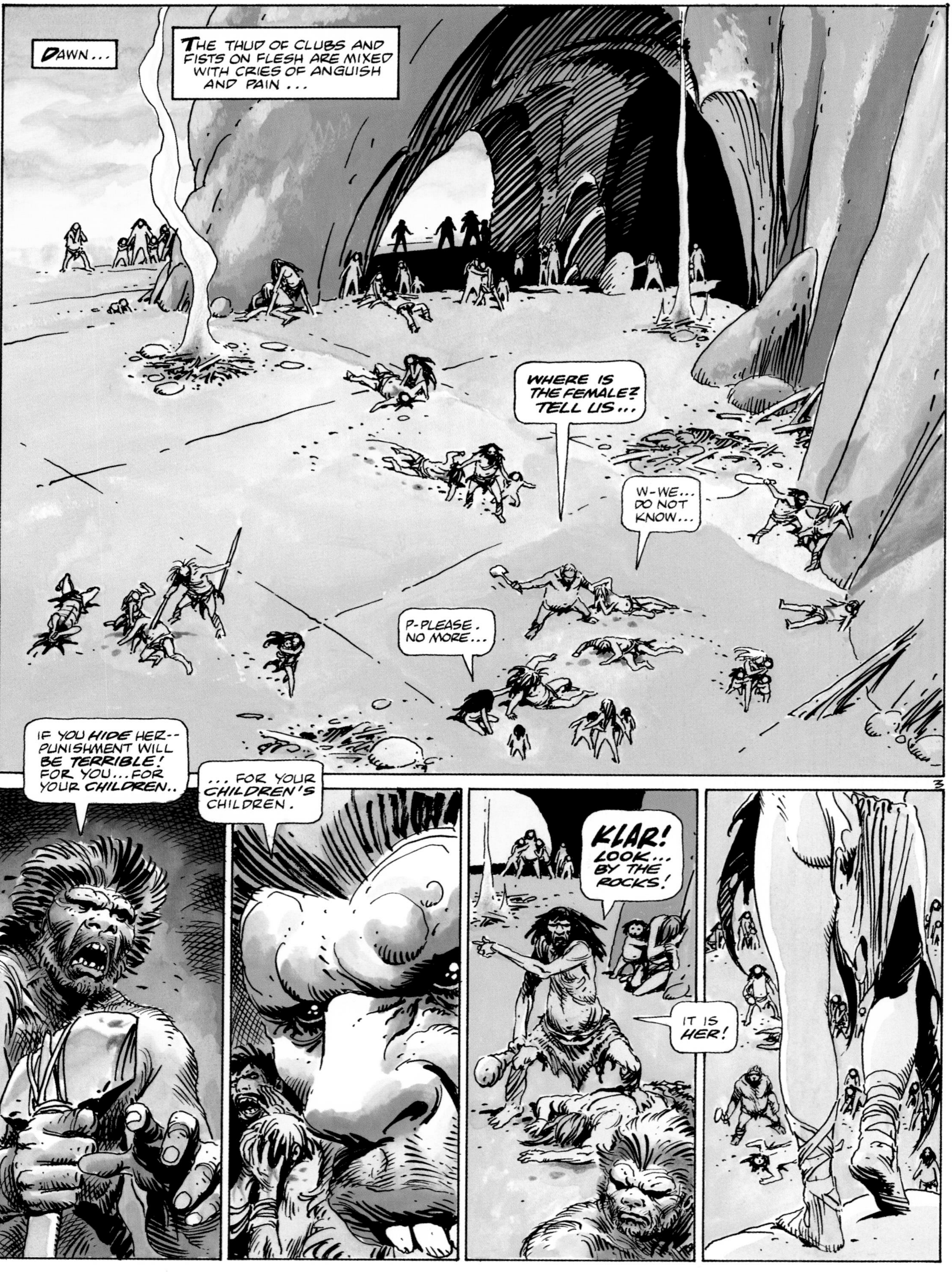
DAWN...
THE THUD OF CLUBS AND FISTS ON FLESH ARE MIXED WITH CRIES OF ANGUISH AND PAIN...
WHERE IS THE FEMALE? TELL US...
W-WE... DO NOT KNOW...
P-PLEASE. NO MORE...
3
IF YOU HIDE HER-- PUNISHMENT WILL BE TERRIBLE! FOR YOU... FOR YOUR CHILDREN..
...FOR YOUR CHILDREN'S CHILDREN.
KLAR! LOOK... BY THE ROCKS!
IT IS HER!

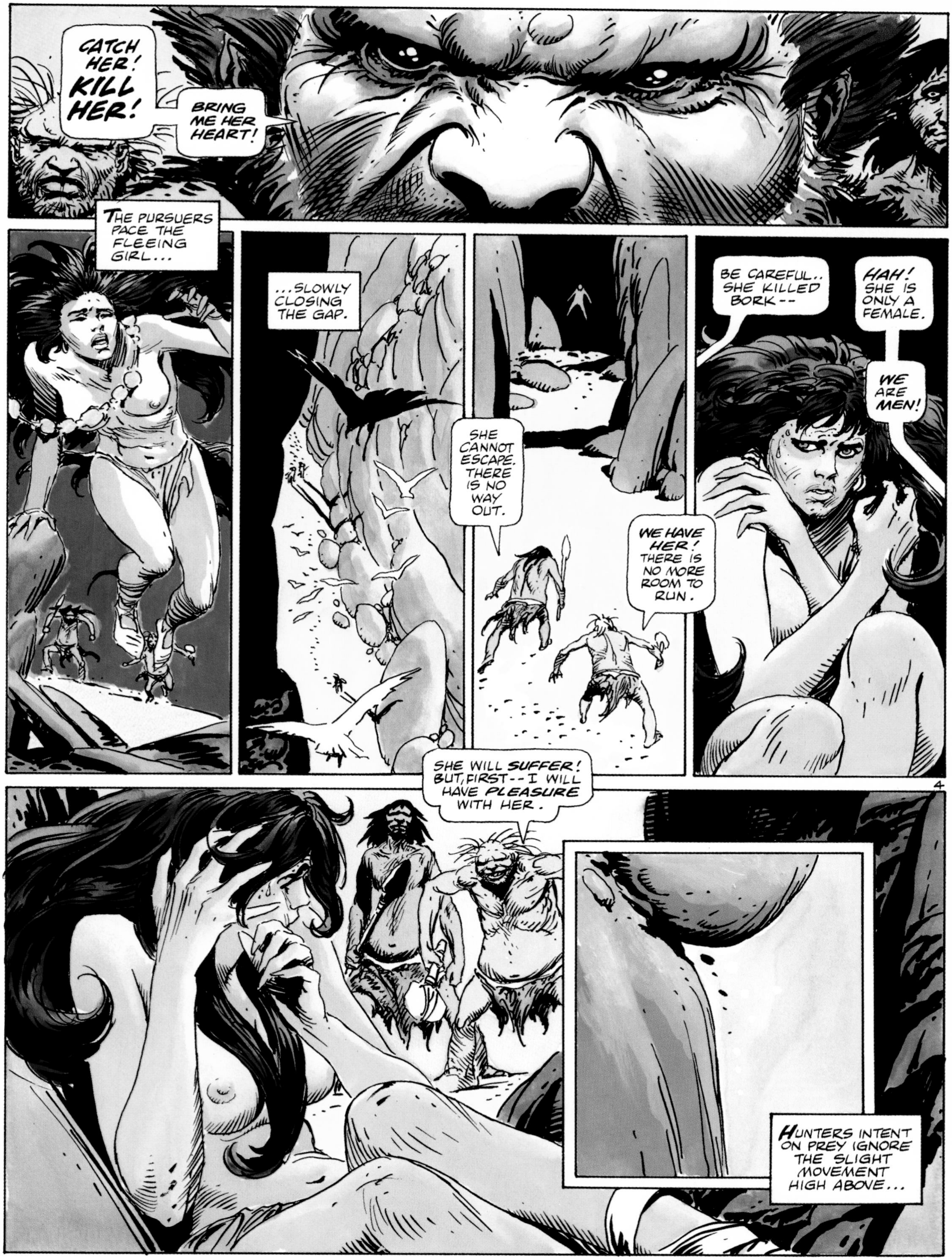
CATCH HER! KILL HER!
BRING ME HER HEART!
THE PURSUERS PACE THE FLEEING GIRL...
...SLOWLY CLOSING THE GAP.
SHE CANNOT ESCAPE. THERE IS NO WAY OUT.
WE HAVE HER! THERE IS NO MORE ROOM TO RUN.
BE CAREFUL.. SHE KILLED BORK--
HAH! SHE IS ONLY A FEMALE.
WE ARE MEN!
SHE WILL SUFFER! BUT, FIRST-- I WILL HAVE PLEASURE WITH HER.
4
HUNTERS INTENT ON PREY IGNORE THE SLIGHT MOVEMENT HIGH ABOVE...

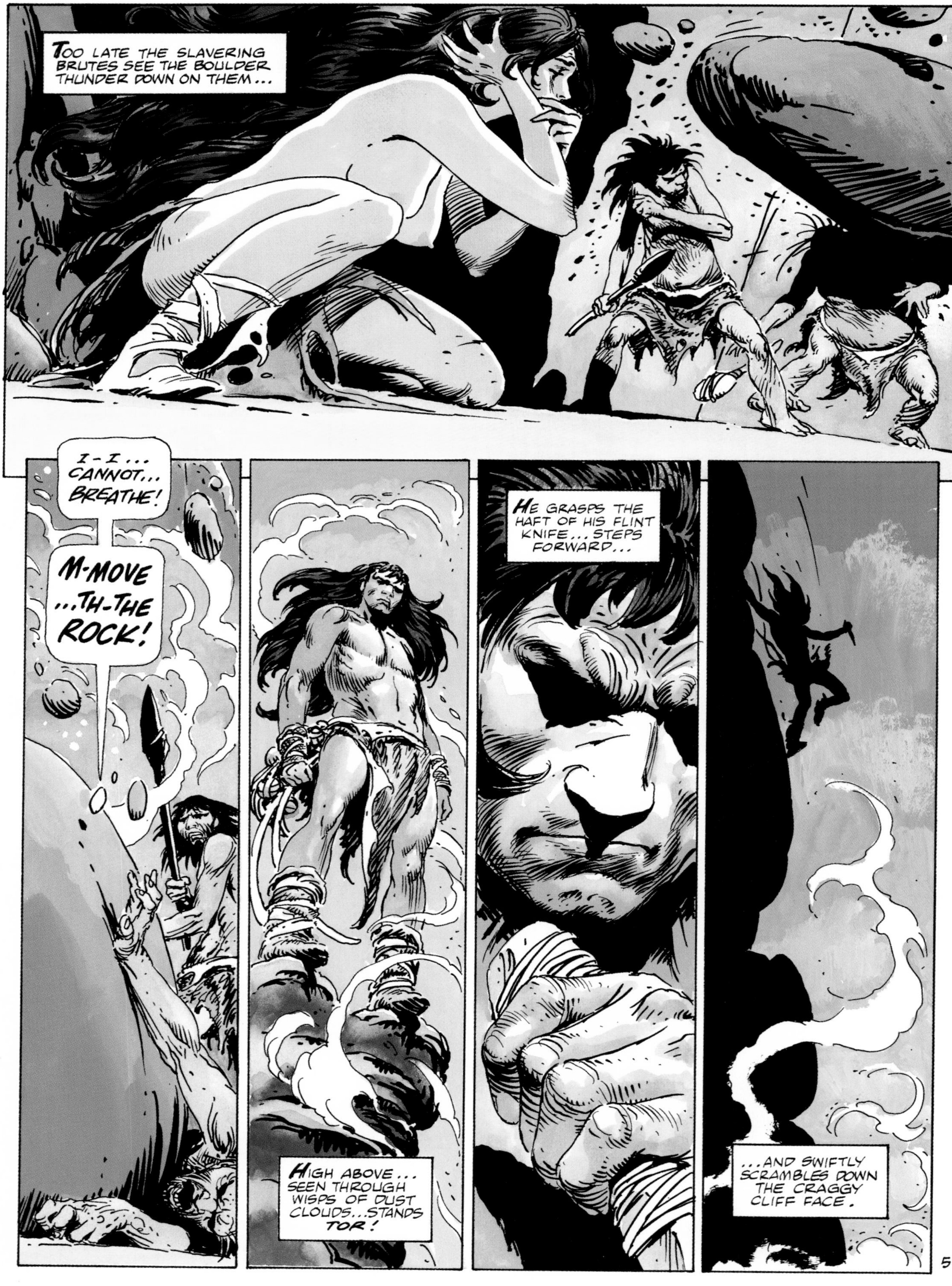
TOO LATE THE SLAVERING BRUTES SEE THE BOULDER THUNDER DOWN ON THEM...
I-I... CANNOT... BREATHE!
M-MOVE ...TH-THE ROCK!
HIGH ABOVE... SEEN THROUGH WISPS OF DUST CLOUDS... STANDS TOR!
HE GRASPS THE HAFT OF HIS FLINT KNIFE... STEPS FORWARD...
...AND SWIFTLY SCRAMBLES DOWN THE CRAGGY CLIFF FACE.
5

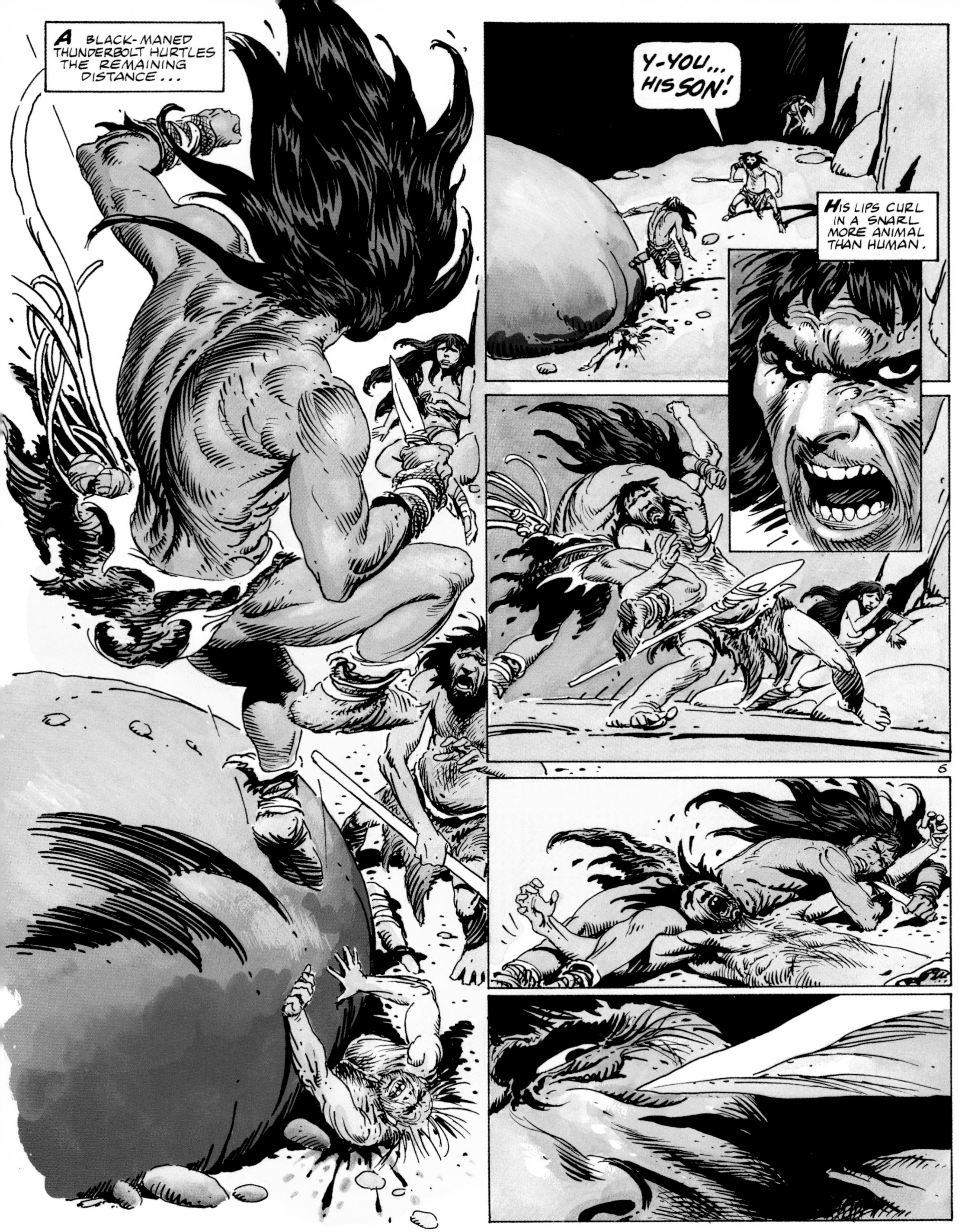
A BLACK-MANED THUNDERBOLT HURTLES THE REMAINING DISTANCE...
Y-YOU... HIS SON!
HIS LIPS CURL IN A SNARL MORE ANIMAL THAN HUMAN.
6

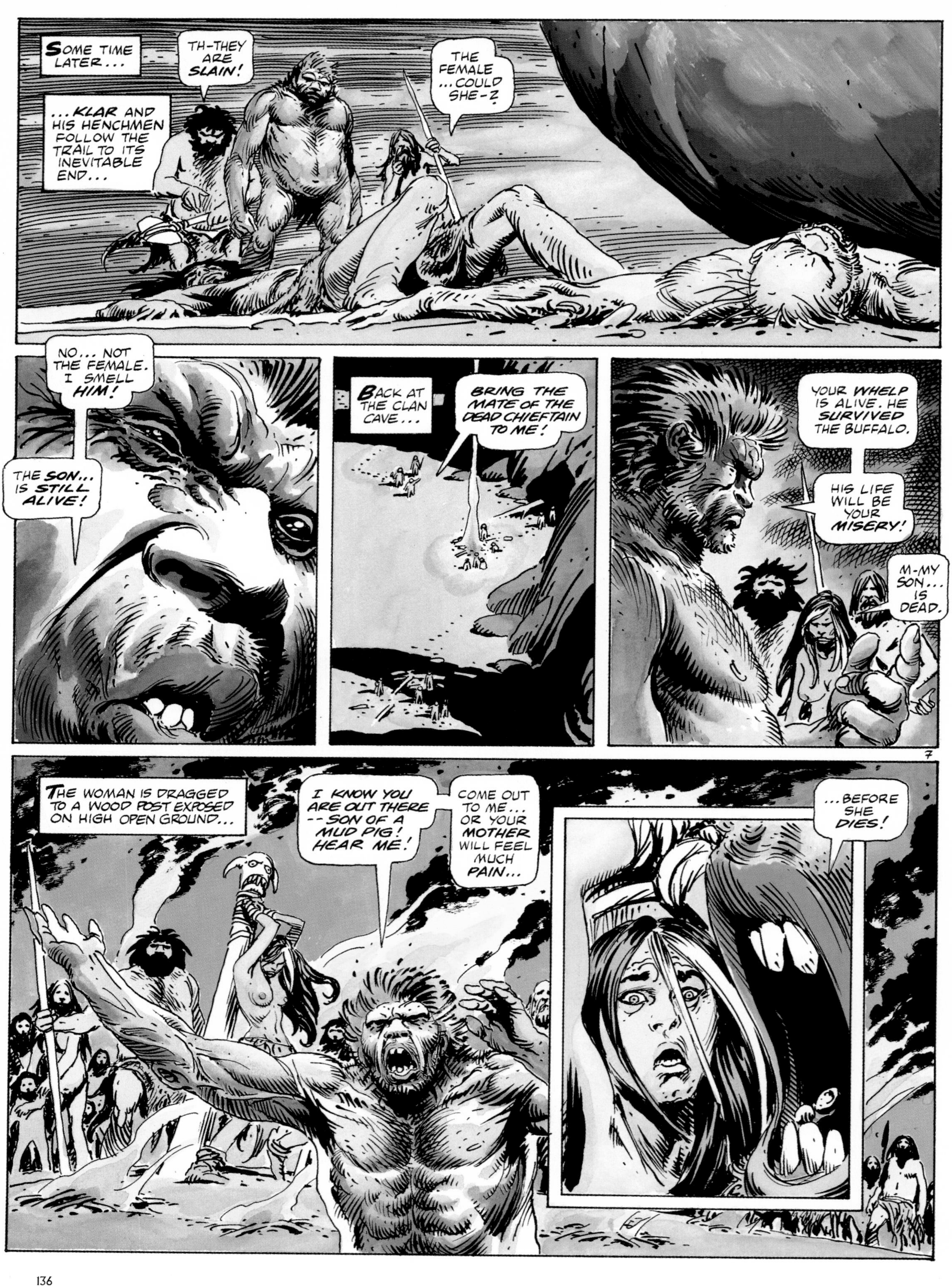
SOME TIME LATER...
TH-THEY ARE SLAIN!
...KLAR AND HIS HENCHMEN FOLLOW THE TRAIL TO ITS INEVITABLE END...
THE FEMALE ...COULD SHE-?
NO... NOT THE FEMALE. I SMELL HIM!
THE SON... IS STILL ALIVE!
BACK AT THE CLAN CAVE...
BRING THE MATE OF THE DEAD CHIEFTAIN TO ME!
YOUR WHELP IS ALIVE. HE SURVIVED THE BUFFALO.
HIS LIFE WILL BE YOUR MISERY!
M-MY SON... IS DEAD.
7
THE WOMAN IS DRAGGED TO A WOOD POST EXPOSED ON HIGH OPEN GROUND...
I KNOW YOU ARE OUT THERE --SON OF A MUD PIG! HEAR ME!
COME OUT TO ME... OR YOUR MOTHER WILL FEEL MUCH PAIN...
...BEFORE SHE DIES!

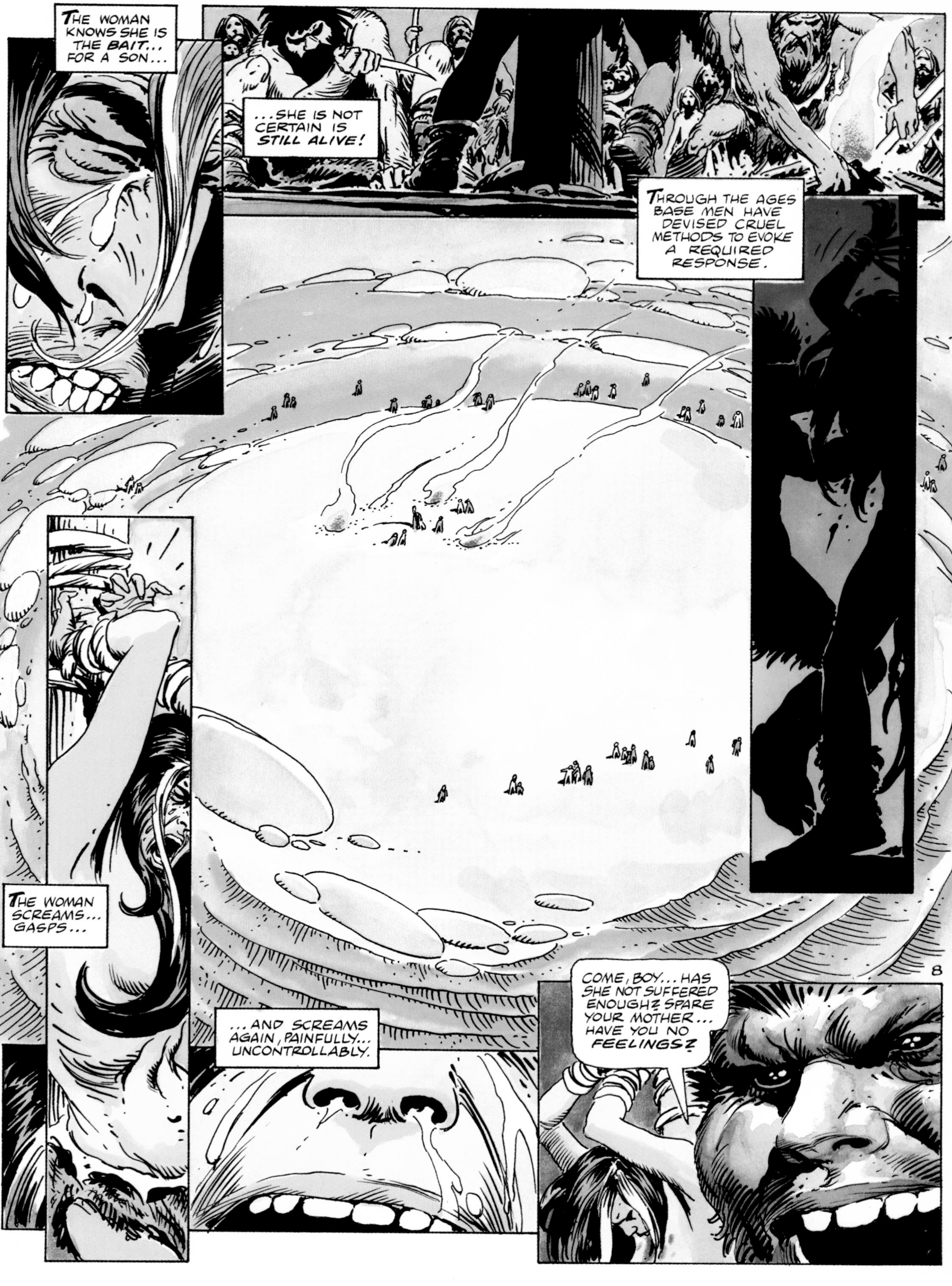
THE WOMAN KNOWS SHE IS THE BAIT... FOR A SON...
...SHE IS NOT CERTAIN IS STILL ALIVE!
THROUGH THE AGES BASE MEN HAVE DEVISED CRUEL METHODS TO EVOKE A REQUIRED RESPONSE.
THE WOMAN SCREAMS... GASPS...
...AND SCREAMS AGAIN, PAINFULLY... UNCONTROLLABLY.
COME, BOY... HAS SHE NOT SUFFERED ENOUGH? SPARE YOUR MOTHER... HAVE YOU NO FEELINGS?
8

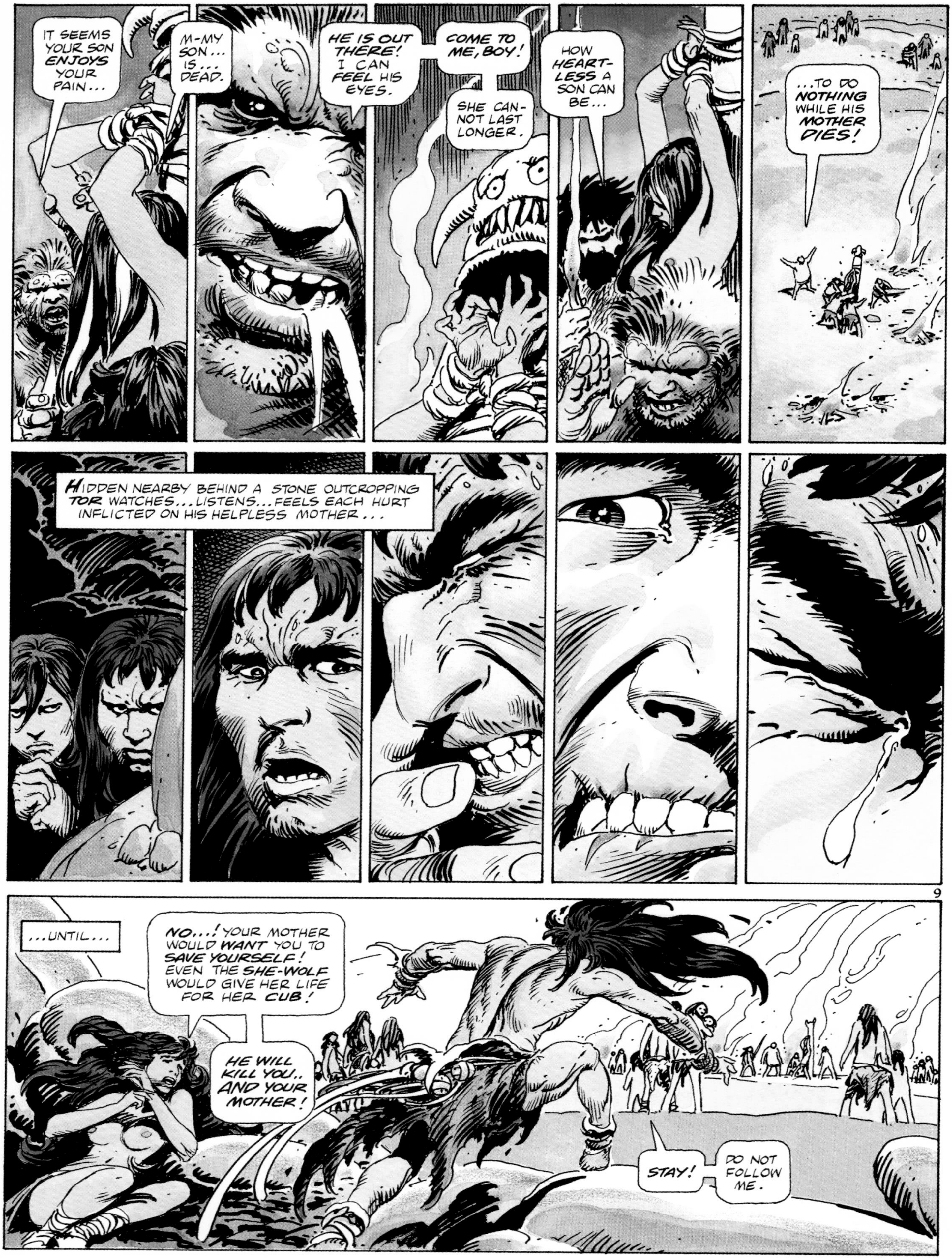
IT SEEMS YOUR SON ENJOYS YOUR PAIN...
M-MY SON... IS... DEAD.
HE IS OUT THERE! I CAN FEEL HIS EYES.
COME TO ME, BOY!
SHE CANNOT LAST LONGER.
HOW HEARTLESS A SON CAN BE...
...TO DO NOTHING WHILE HIS MOTHER DIES!
HIDDEN NEARBY BEHIND A STONE OUTCROPPING TOR WATCHES... LISTENS... FEELS EACH HURT INFLICTED ON HIS HELPLESS MOTHER...
9
...UNTIL...
NO...! YOUR MOTHER WOULD WANT YOU TO SAVE YOURSELF! EVEN THE SHE-WOLF WOULD GIVE HER LIFE FOR HER CUB!
HE WILL KILL YOU.. AND YOUR MOTHER!
STAY!
DO NOT FOLLOW ME.

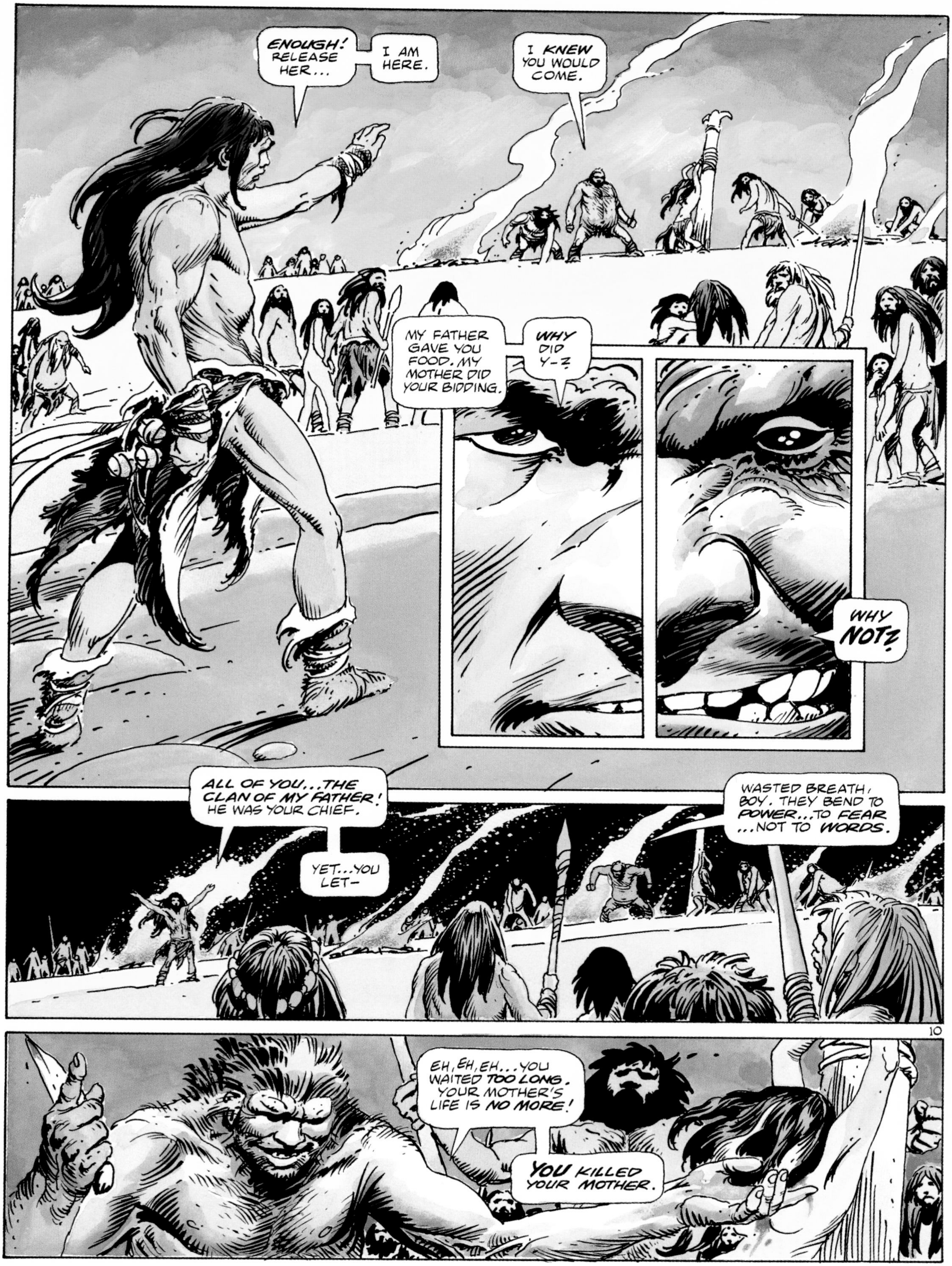
ENOUGH! RELEASE HER...
I AM HERE.
I KNEW YOU WOULD COME.
MY FATHER GAVE YOU FOOD. MY MOTHER DID YOUR BIDDING.
WHY DID Y-?
WHY NOT?
ALL OF YOU...THE CLAN OF MY FATHER! HE WAS YOUR CHIEF.
YET...YOU LET-
WASTED BREATH, BOY. THEY BEND TO POWER...TO FEAR ...NOT TO WORDS.
10
EH, EH, EH...YOU WAITED TOO LONG. YOUR MOTHER'S LIFE IS NO MORE!
YOU KILLED YOUR MOTHER.

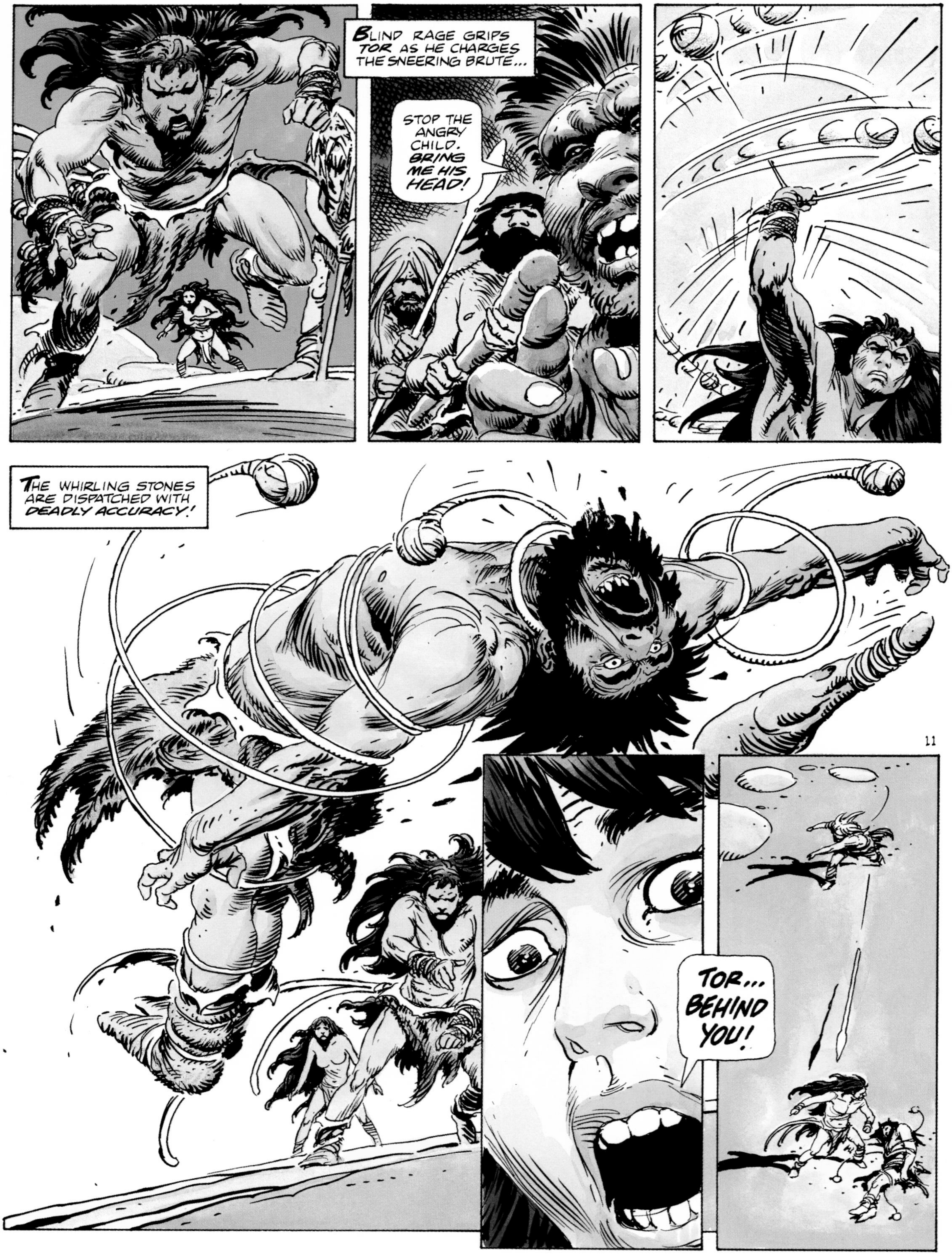
BLIND RAGE GRIPS TOR AS HE CHARGES THE SNEERING BRUTE...
STOP THE ANGRY CHILD. BRING ME HIS HEAD!
THE WHIRLING STONES ARE DISPATCHED WITH DEADLY ACCURACY!
11
TOR... BEHIND YOU!

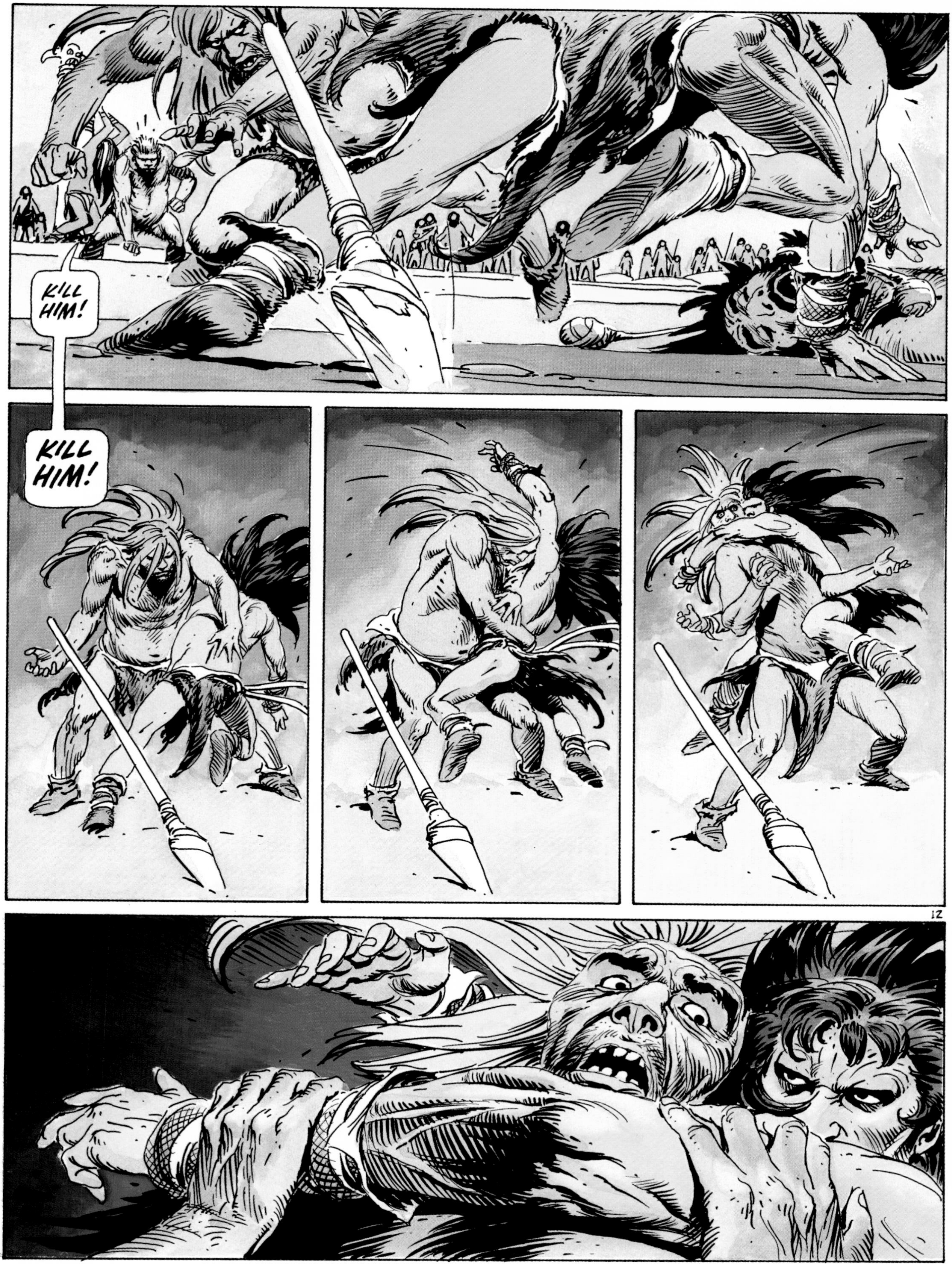
KILL HIM!
KILL HIM!
12

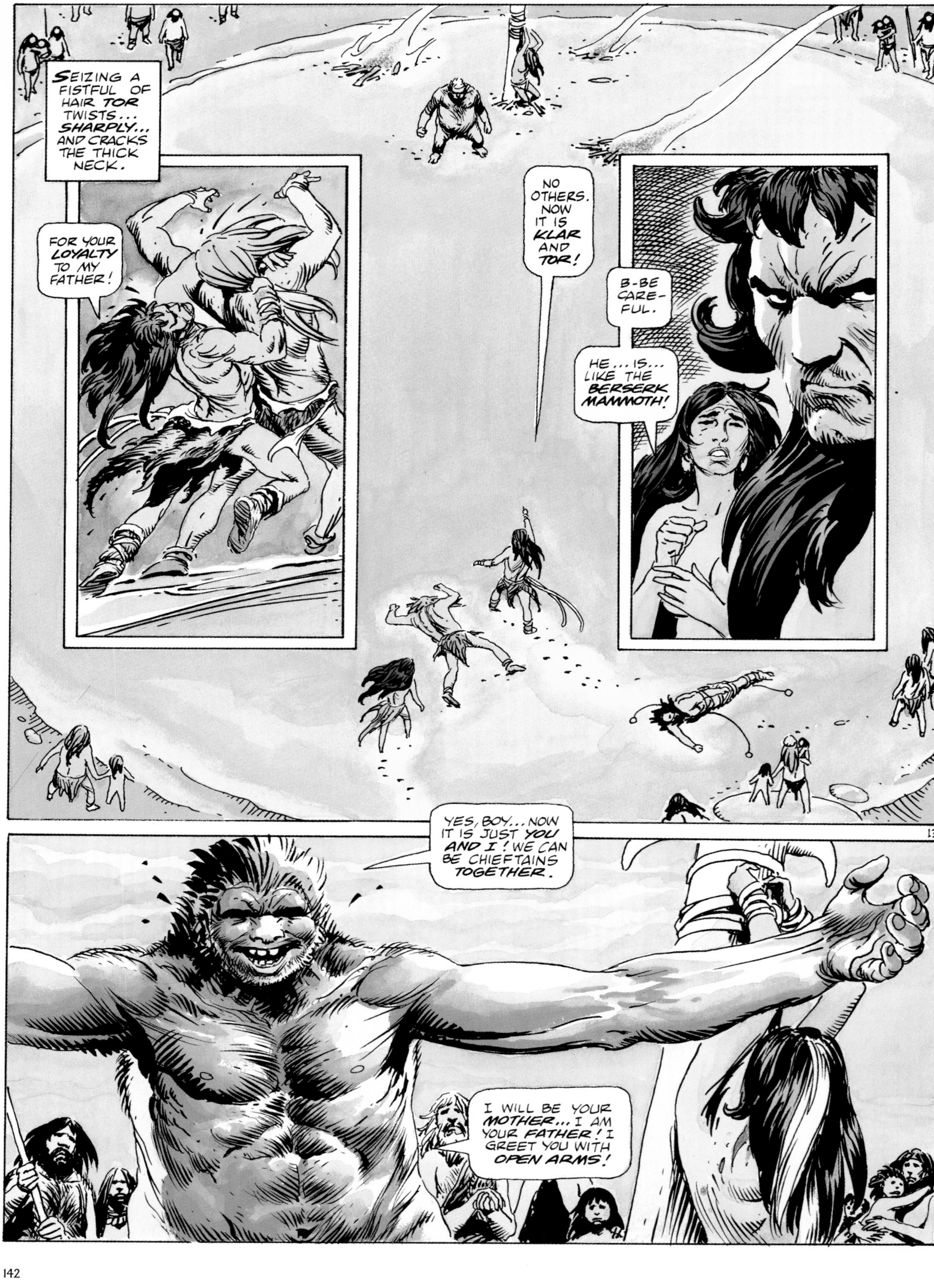
SEIZING A FISTFUL OF HAIR TOR TWISTS... SHARPLY... AND CRACKS THE THICK NECK.
FOR YOUR LOYALTY TO MY FATHER!
NO OTHERS. NOW IT IS KLAR AND TOR!
B-BE CARE-FUL.
HE... IS... LIKE THE BERSERK MAMMOTH!
13
YES, BOY... NOW IT IS JUST YOU AND I! WE CAN BE CHIEFTAINS TOGETHER.
I WILL BE YOUR MOTHER... I AM YOUR FATHER! I GREET YOU WITH OPEN ARMS!

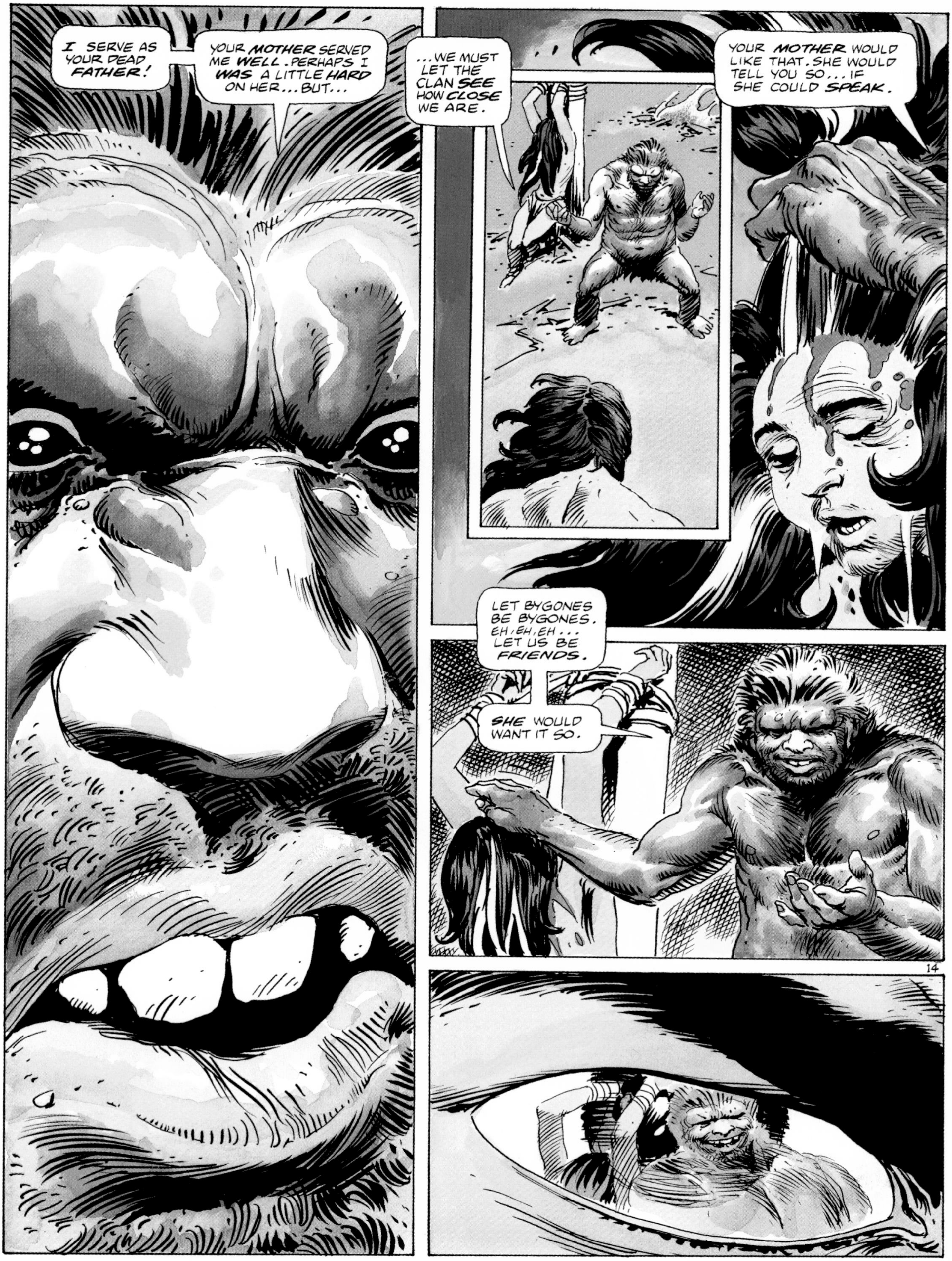
I SERVE AS YOUR DEAD FATHER!
YOUR MOTHER SERVED ME WELL. PERHAPS I WAS A LITTLE HARD ON HER... BUT...
...WE MUST LET THE CLAN SEE HOW CLOSE WE ARE.
YOUR MOTHER WOULD LIKE THAT. SHE WOULD TELL YOU SO... IF SHE COULD SPEAK.
LET BYGONES BE BYGONES. EH, EH, EH... LET US BE FRIENDS.
SHE WOULD WANT IT SO.
14

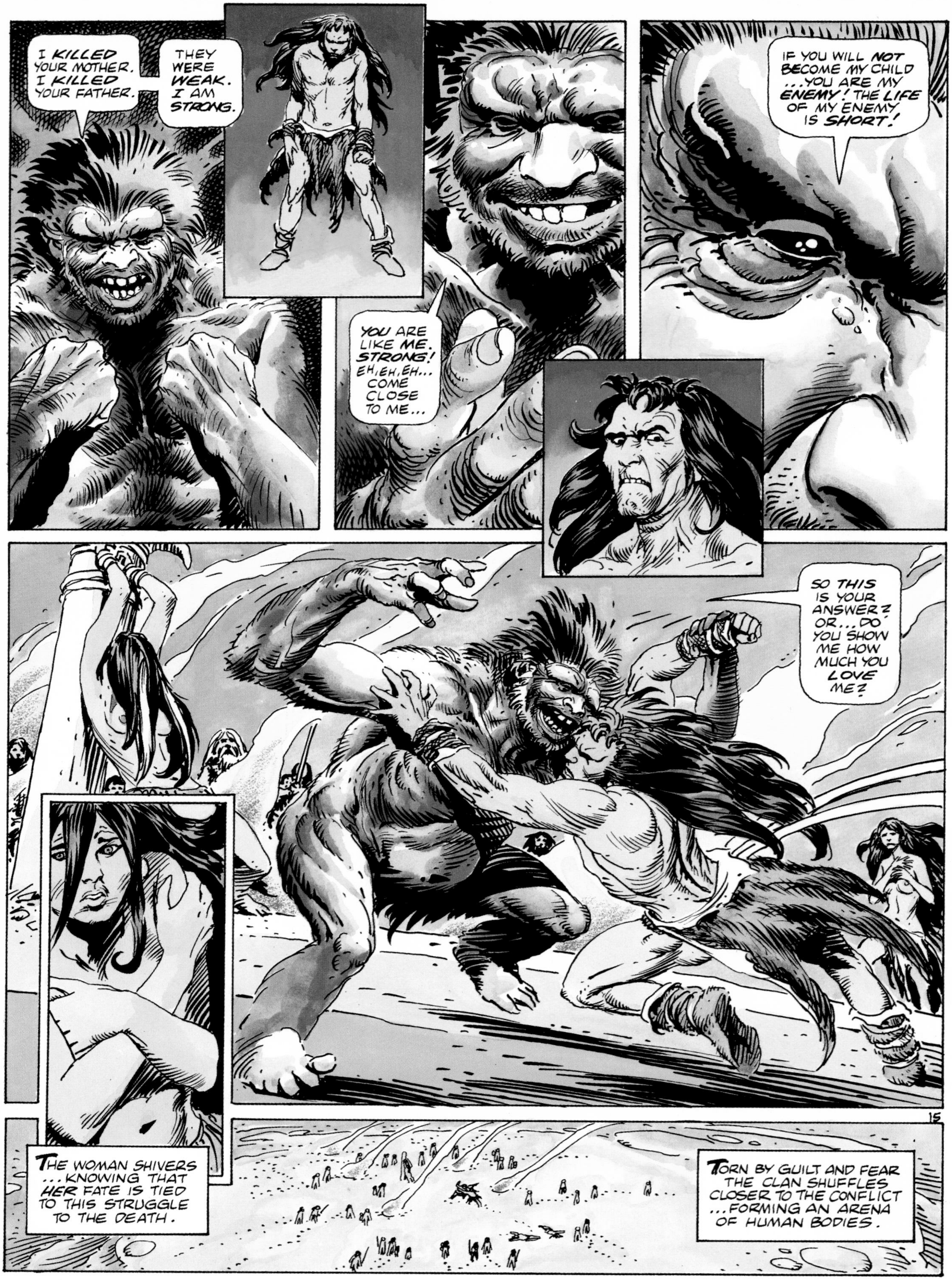

I KILLED YOUR MOTHER. I KILLED YOUR FATHER.
THEY WERE WEAK. I AM STRONG.
YOU ARE LIKE ME. STRONG! EH, EH, EH... COME CLOSE TO ME...
IF YOU WILL NOT BECOME MY CHILD ...YOU ARE MY ENEMY! THE LIFE OF MY ENEMY IS SHORT!
SO THIS IS YOUR ANSWER? OR... DO YOU SHOW ME HOW MUCH YOU LOVE ME?
15
THE WOMAN SHIVERS ...KNOWING THAT HER FATE IS TIED TO THIS STRUGGLE TO THE DEATH.
TORN BY GUILT AND FEAR THE CLAN SHUFFLES CLOSER TO THE CONFLICT ...FORMING AN ARENA OF HUMAN BODIES.

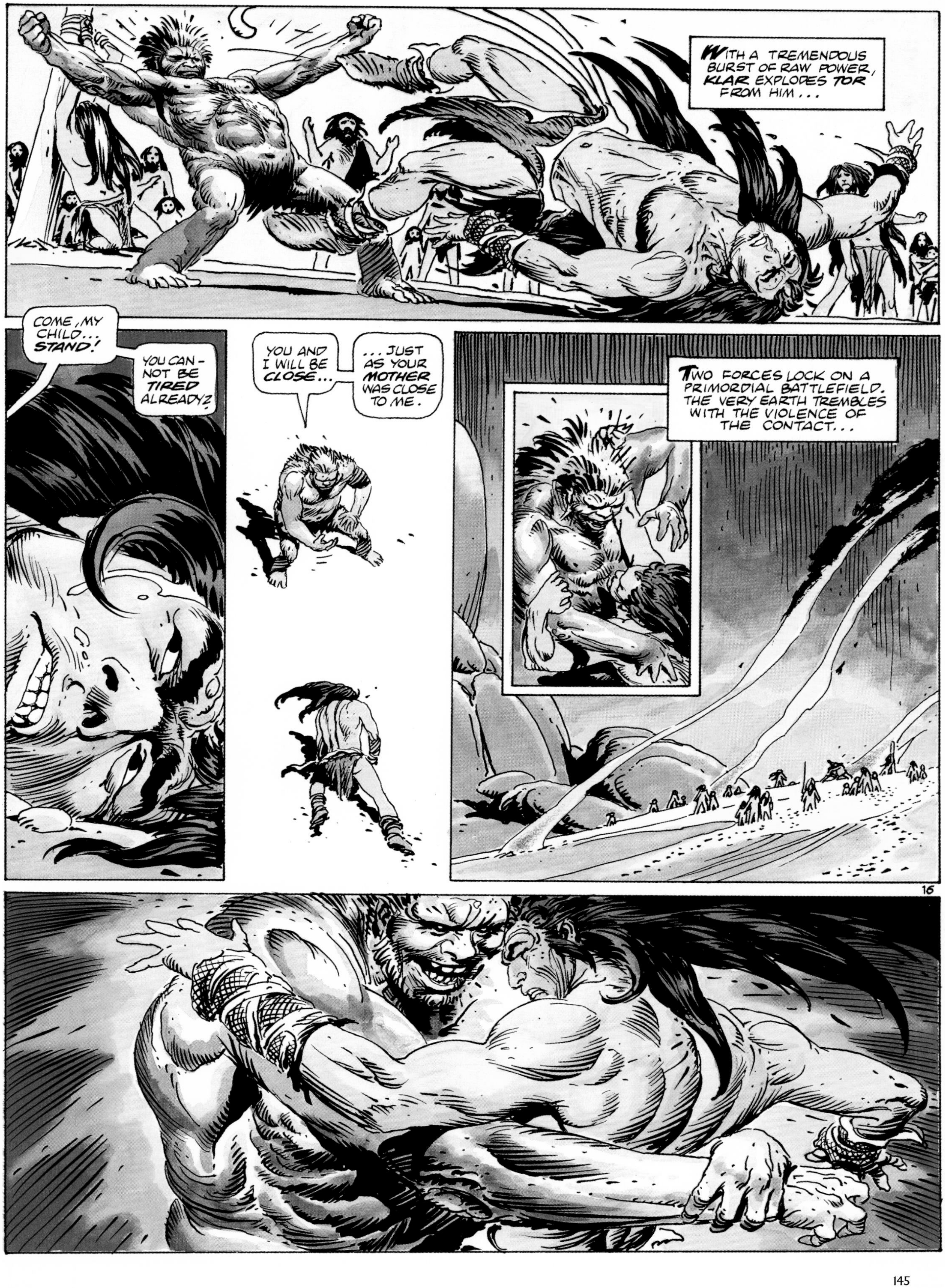

WITH A TREMENDOUS BURST OF RAW POWER, KLAR EXPLODES TOR FROM HIM...
COME, MY CHILD... STAND!
YOU CAN-NOT BE TIRED ALREADY?
YOU AND I WILL BE CLOSE...
...JUST AS YOUR MOTHER WAS CLOSE TO ME.
TWO FORCES LOCK ON A PRIMORDIAL BATTLEFIELD. THE VERY EARTH TREMBLES WITH THE VIOLENCE OF THE CONTACT...
16

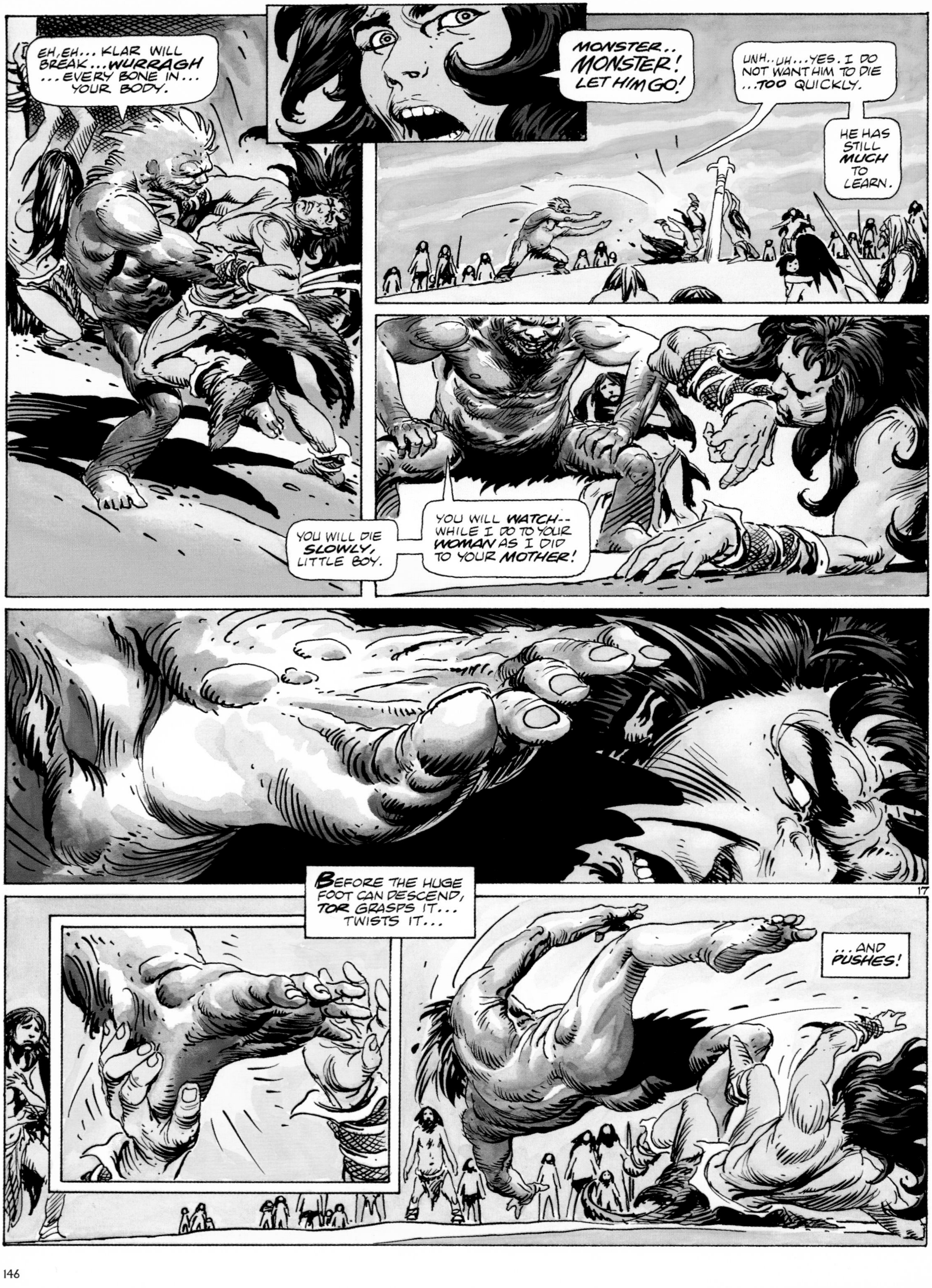
EH, EH... KLAR WILL BREAK... WURRAGH ...EVERY BONE IN... YOUR BODY.
MONSTER.. MONSTER! LET HIM GO!
UNH.. UH... YES. I DO NOT WANT HIM TO DIE ...TOO QUICKLY.
HE HAS STILL MUCH TO LEARN.
YOU WILL DIE SLOWLY, LITTLE BOY.
YOU WILL WATCH-- WHILE I DO TO YOUR WOMAN AS I DID TO YOUR MOTHER!
17
BEFORE THE HUGE FOOT CAN DESCEND, TOR GRASPS IT... TWISTS IT...
...AND PUSHES!

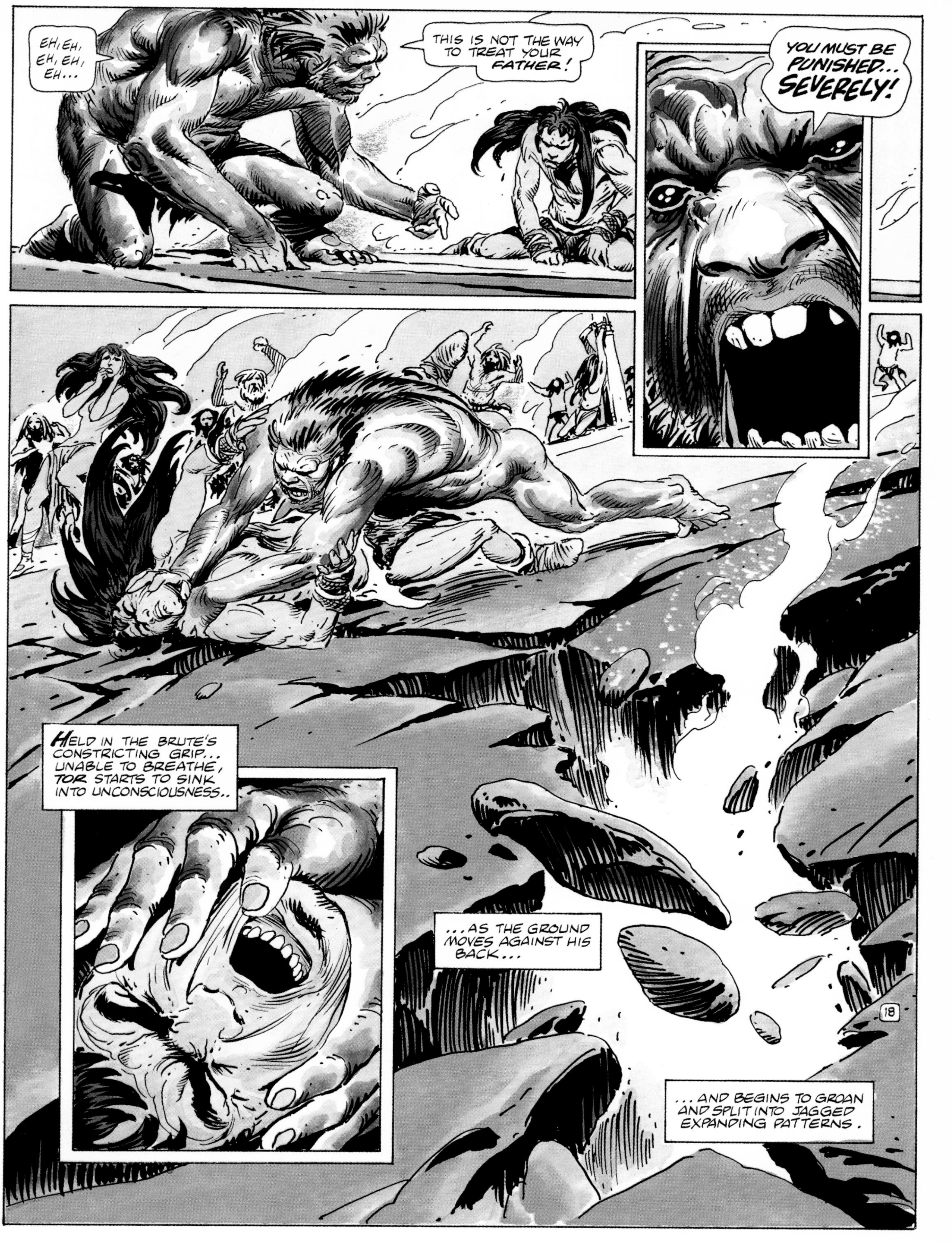
EH, EH, EH, EH, EH, EH...
THIS IS NOT THE WAY TO TREAT YOUR FATHER!
YOU MUST BE PUNISHED... SEVERELY!
HELD IN THE BRUTE'S CONSTRICTING GRIP... UNABLE TO BREATHE, TOR STARTS TO SINK INTO UNCONSCIOUSNESS..
...AS THE GROUND MOVES AGAINST HIS BACK...
...AND BEGINS TO GROAN AND SPLIT INTO JAGGED EXPANDING PATTERNS.
18

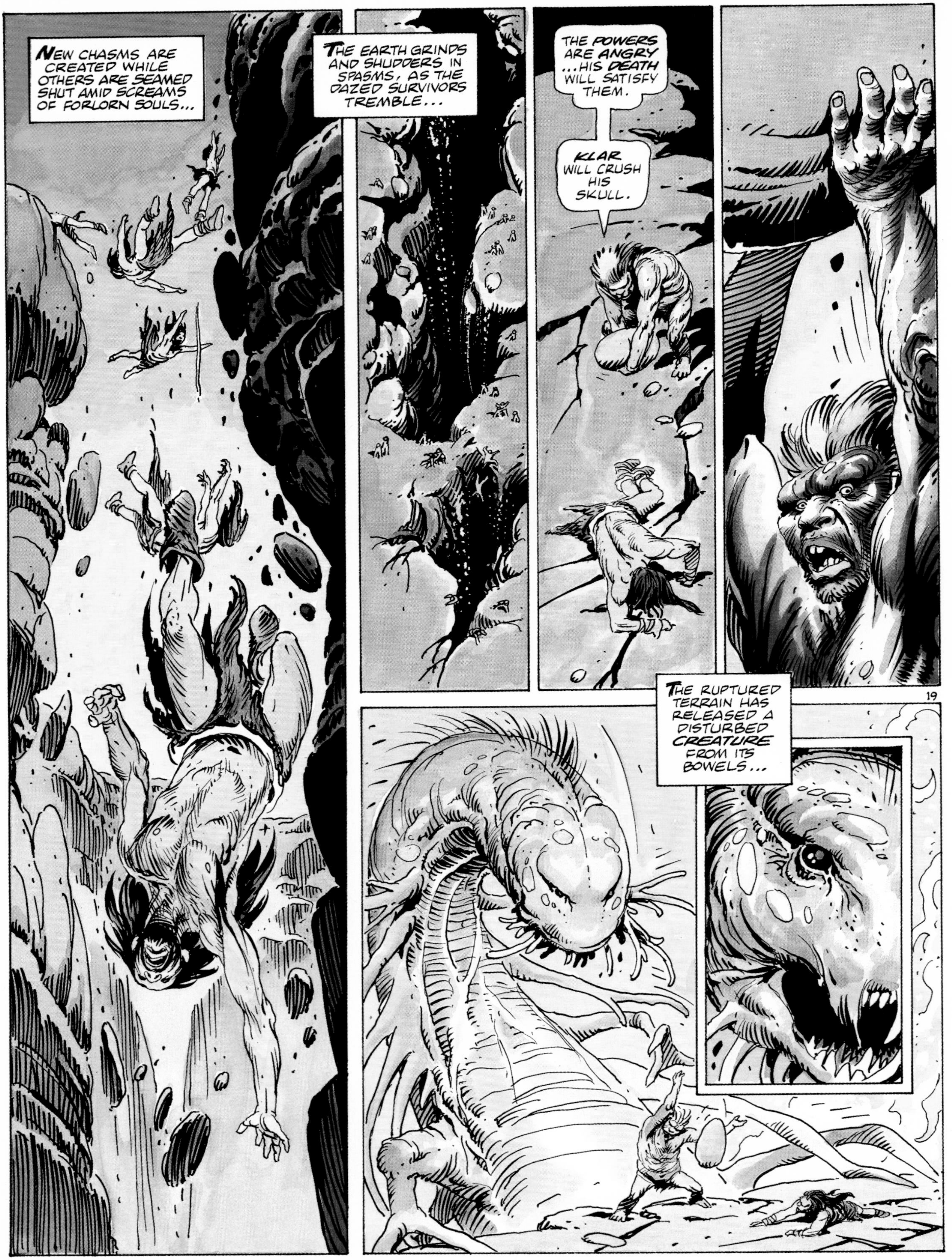
NEW CHASMS ARE CREATED WHILE OTHERS ARE SEAMED SHUT AMID SCREAMS OF FORLORN SOULS...
THE EARTH GRINDS AND SHUDDERS IN SPASMS, AS THE DAZED SURVIVORS TREMBLE...
THE POWERS ARE ANGRY ...HIS DEATH WILL SATISFY THEM.
KLAR WILL CRUSH HIS SKULL.
19
THE RUPTURED TERRAIN HAS RELEASED A DISTURBED CREATURE FROM ITS BOWELS...

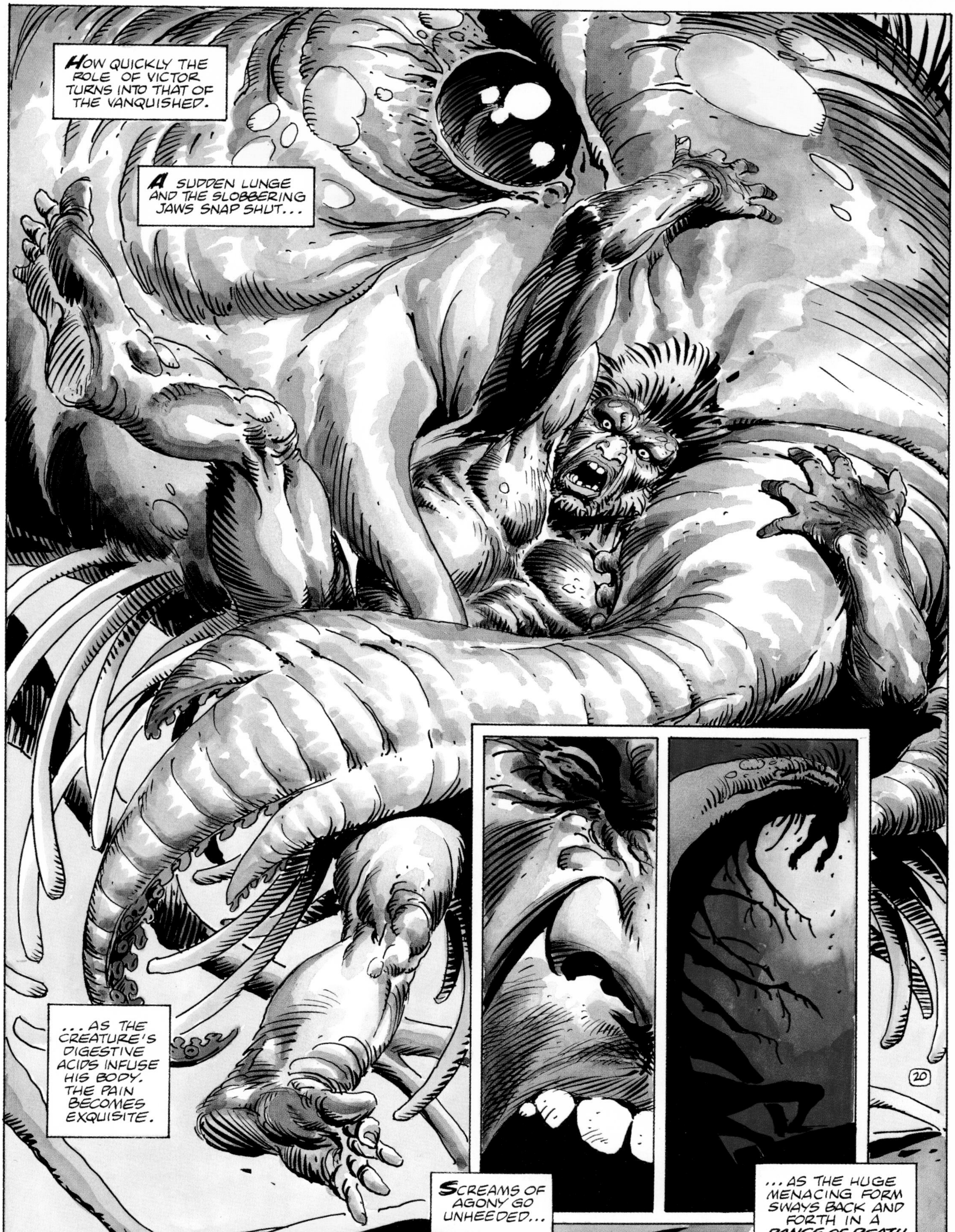
HOW QUICKLY THE ROLE OF VICTOR TURNS INTO THAT OF THE VANQUISHED.
A SUDDEN LUNGE AND THE SLOBBERING JAWS SNAP SHUT...
...AS THE CREATURE'S DIGESTIVE ACIDS INFUSE HIS BODY. THE PAIN BECOMES EXQUISITE.
20
SCREAMS OF AGONY GO UNHEEDED...
...AS THE HUGE MENACING FORM SWAYS BACK AND FORTH IN A DANCE OF DEATH.

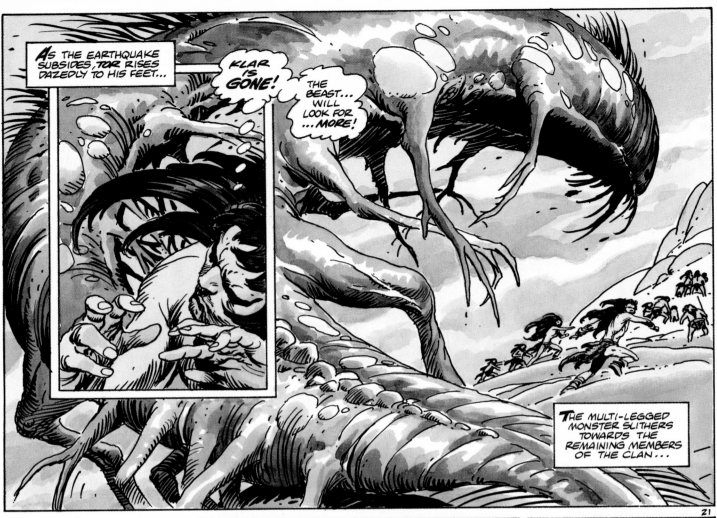

As the earthquake subsides, *Tor* rises dazedly to his feet...

KLAR IS **GONE!**

THE BEAST... WILL LOOK FOR ...MORE!

The multi-legged monster slithers towards the remaining members of the clan...

21

Moving close to the ascending creature...

...Tor scurries under the veined belly...

*...and **throws** himself at the scraping legs.*

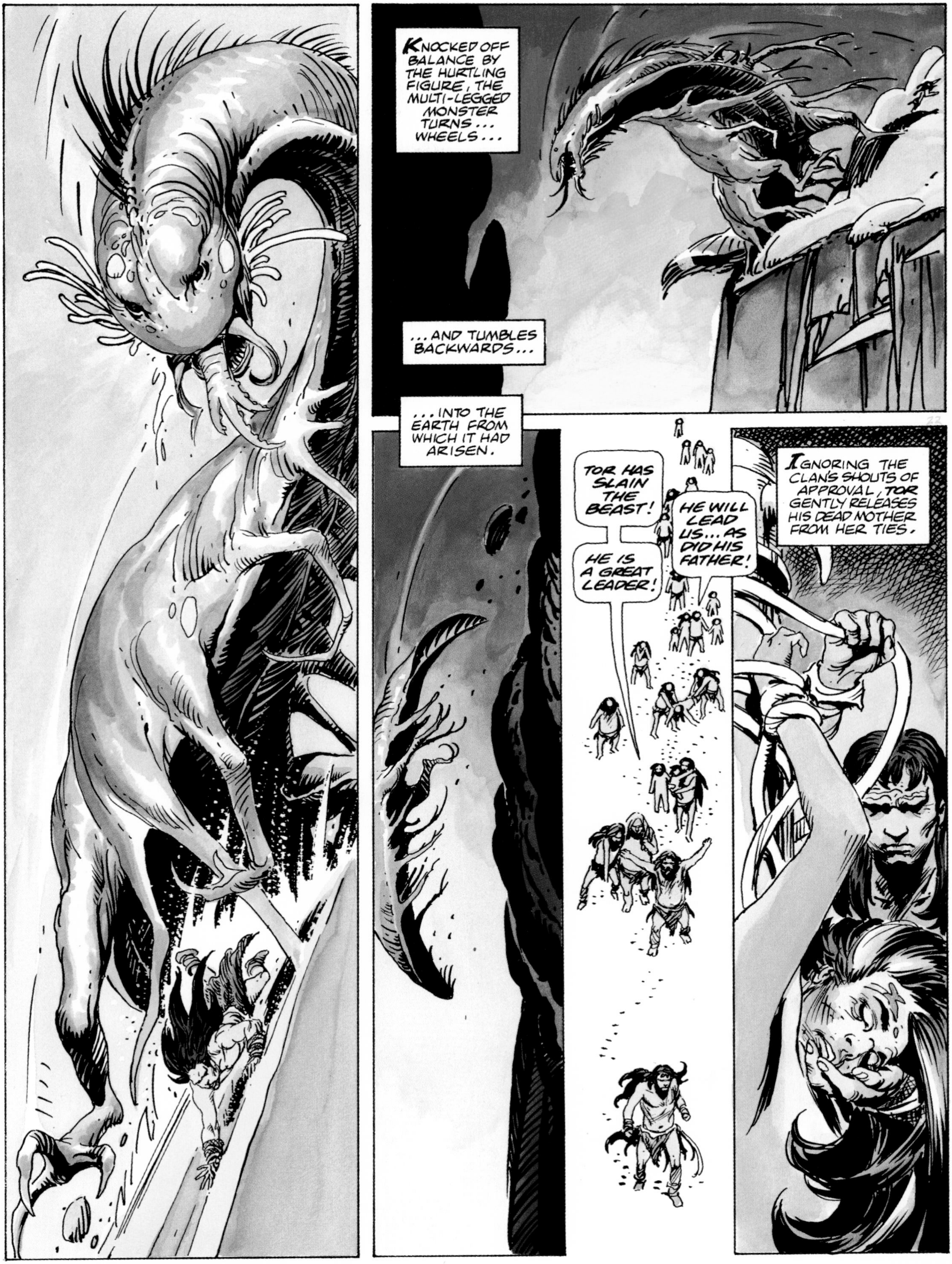
KNOCKED OFF BALANCE BY THE HURTLING FIGURE, THE MULTI-LEGGED MONSTER TURNS... WHEELS...
...AND TUMBLES BACKWARDS...
...INTO THE EARTH FROM WHICH IT HAD ARISEN.
TOR HAS SLAIN THE BEAST!
HE IS A GREAT LEADER!
HE WILL LEAD US... AS DID HIS FATHER!
IGNORING THE CLAN'S SHOUTS OF APPROVAL, TOR GENTLY RELEASES HIS DEAD MOTHER FROM HER TIES.

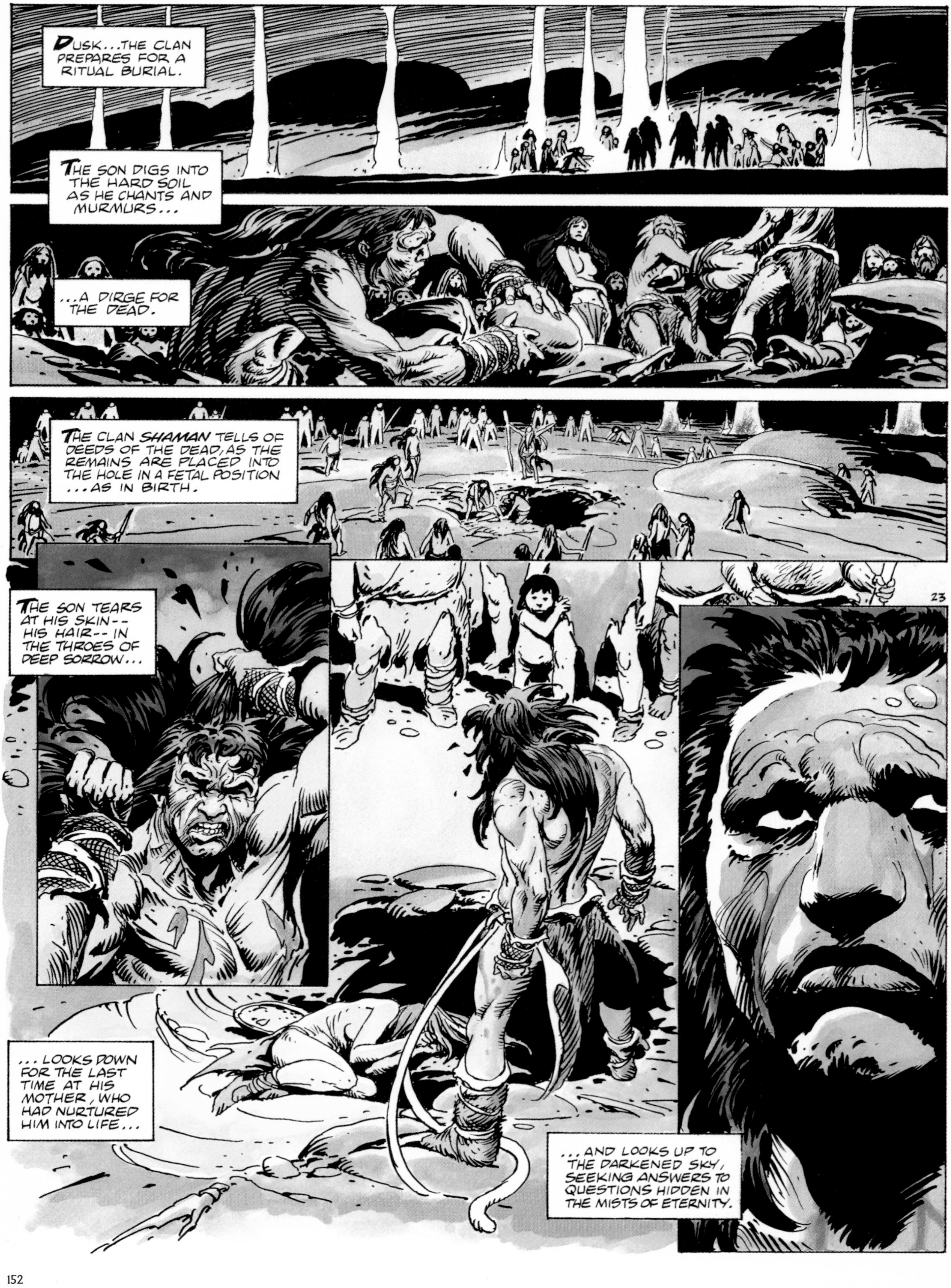
DUSK...THE CLAN PREPARES FOR A RITUAL BURIAL.
THE SON DIGS INTO THE HARD SOIL AS HE CHANTS AND MURMURS...
...A DIRGE FOR THE DEAD.
THE CLAN SHAMAN TELLS OF DEEDS OF THE DEAD, AS THE REMAINS ARE PLACED INTO THE HOLE IN A FETAL POSITION ...AS IN BIRTH.
THE SON TEARS AT HIS SKIN-- HIS HAIR-- IN THE THROES OF DEEP SORROW...
23
...LOOKS DOWN FOR THE LAST TIME AT HIS MOTHER, WHO HAD NURTURED HIM INTO LIFE...
...AND LOOKS UP TO THE DARKENED SKY, SEEKING ANSWERS TO QUESTIONS HIDDEN IN THE MISTS OF ETERNITY.

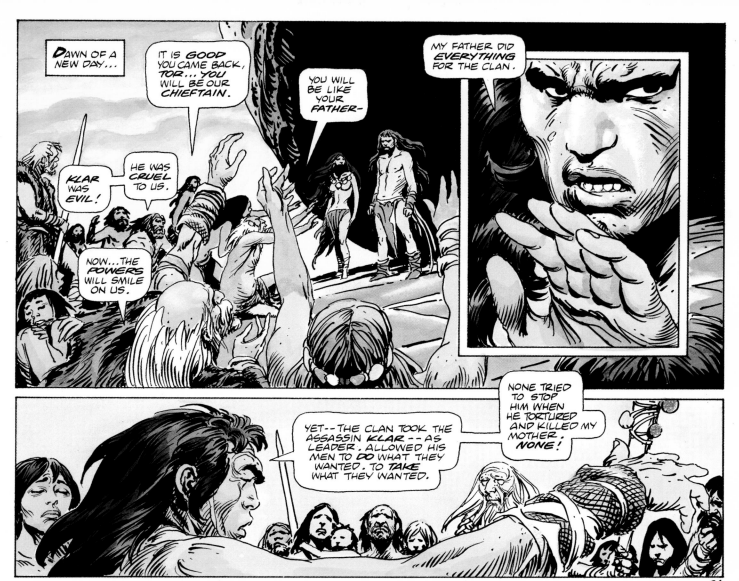

DAWN OF A NEW DAY...

IT IS *GOOD* YOU CAME BACK, TOR... *YOU* WILL BE OUR CHIEFTAIN.

KLAR WAS *EVIL!*

HE WAS *CRUEL* TO US.

NOW...THE *POWERS* WILL SMILE ON US.

YOU WILL BE LIKE YOUR *FATHER*—

MY FATHER DID *EVERYTHING* FOR THE CLAN.

YET--THE CLAN TOOK THE ASSASSIN *KLAR*--AS LEADER. ALLOWED HIS MEN TO *DO* WHAT THEY WANTED. TO *TAKE* WHAT THEY WANTED.

NONE TRIED TO STOP HIM WHEN HE TORTURED AND KILLED MY MOTHER. *NONE!*

24

SHE LIES *THERE*...BENEATH YOUR FEET. IN THE GROUND.

I CAN NO LONGER LIVE WITH THE CLAN.

*A*S TOR GATHERS THE FEW FRAGMENTS LEFT BY HIS MOTHER AND FATHER...

I WANT TO GO WITH YOU.

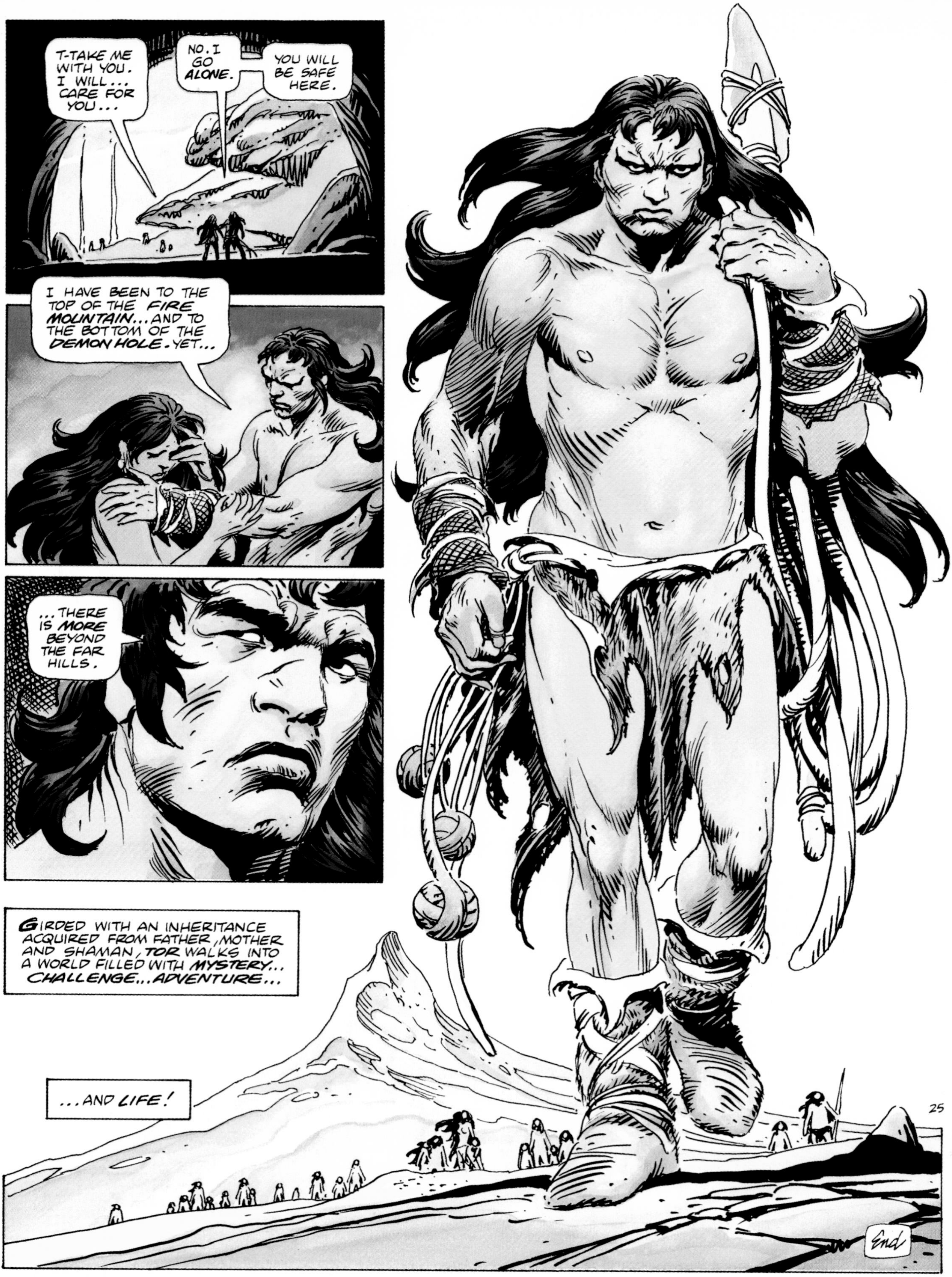
T-TAKE ME WITH YOU. I WILL... CARE FOR YOU...
NO. I GO ALONE.
YOU WILL BE SAFE HERE.
I HAVE BEEN TO THE TOP OF THE FIRE MOUNTAIN... AND TO THE BOTTOM OF THE DEMON HOLE. YET...
...THERE IS MORE BEYOND THE FAR HILLS.
GIRDED WITH AN INHERITANCE ACQUIRED FROM FATHER, MOTHER AND SHAMAN, TOR WALKS INTO A WORLD FILLED WITH MYSTERY... CHALLENGE... ADVENTURE...
...AND LIFE!
25
End

THE DEVELOPMENT OF TOR ...THE COMIC BOOK

The story you have just finished reading completes this four issue series. I first envisioned this character, Tor, while enroute to Europe via troopship in 1950, during the Korean War. That was, let's see... 43 years ago.

Since that time, the ubiquitous caveman has appeared in several varieties of comic book publications. Including 3-D!

In answer to questions re: my work procedures, I have included the following pages containing sketches, explanations & descriptions of the "project in progress".

17
88
TOR'S ARM HOOKED UNDER BADDIE'S CHIN
GIRL CRIES OUT
1
2
3
4
5
6
7
TOR'S RIBS STRAIN
TOR HITS POST HOLDING MOM.. TRIBE WATCHES
• BEAR HUG
• THROWS TOR
• ABOUT TO STOMP HIM
• TOR GRABS FOOT
• TWISTS
BADDIE LAUGHING! "I WILL DO WITH YOUR WOMAN AS I DID WITH YOUR MOTHER!!"
TRIBE
GIRL WATCHING

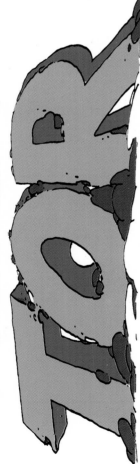

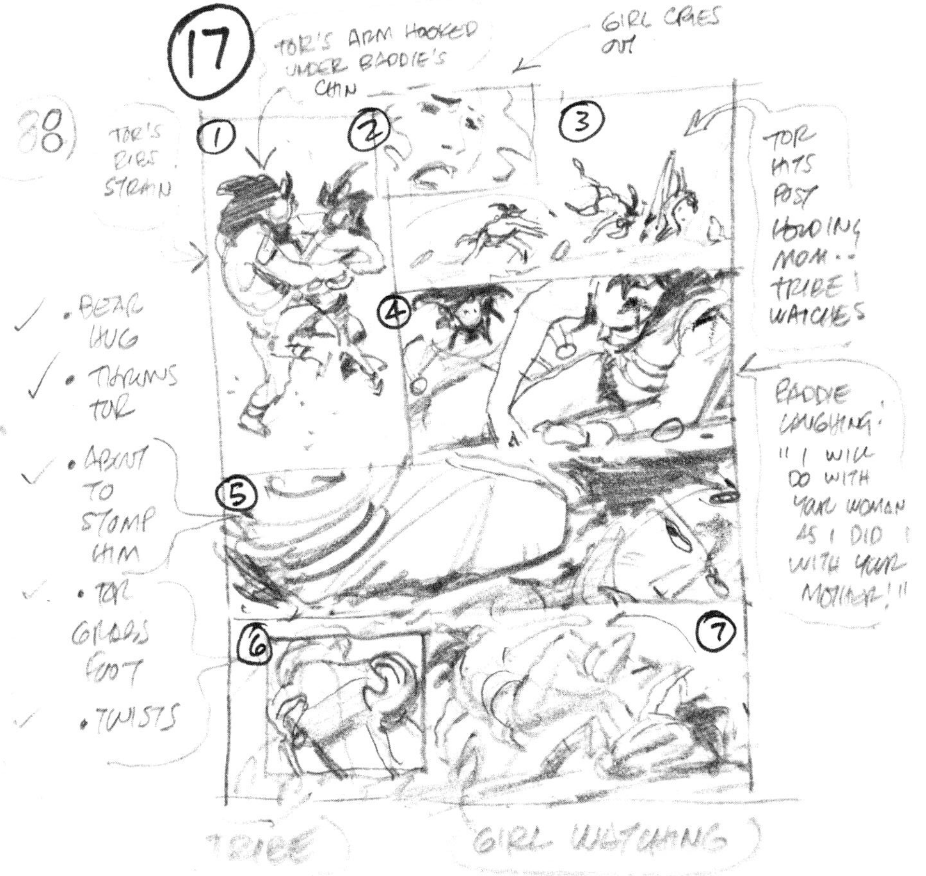

Artists and writers apply different means by which they produce works. Quite different.

The forgoing is my way of achieving the desired results.

The following pages contain my original layouts/roughs -- actual size -- of some of the finished pages in this current book. They were done in pencil, along with notes and thoughts to be incorporated in the finished work.

HUNCHBACK

Preliminary sketch of one of the renegades responsible for the murder of Torkan, Tor's father.

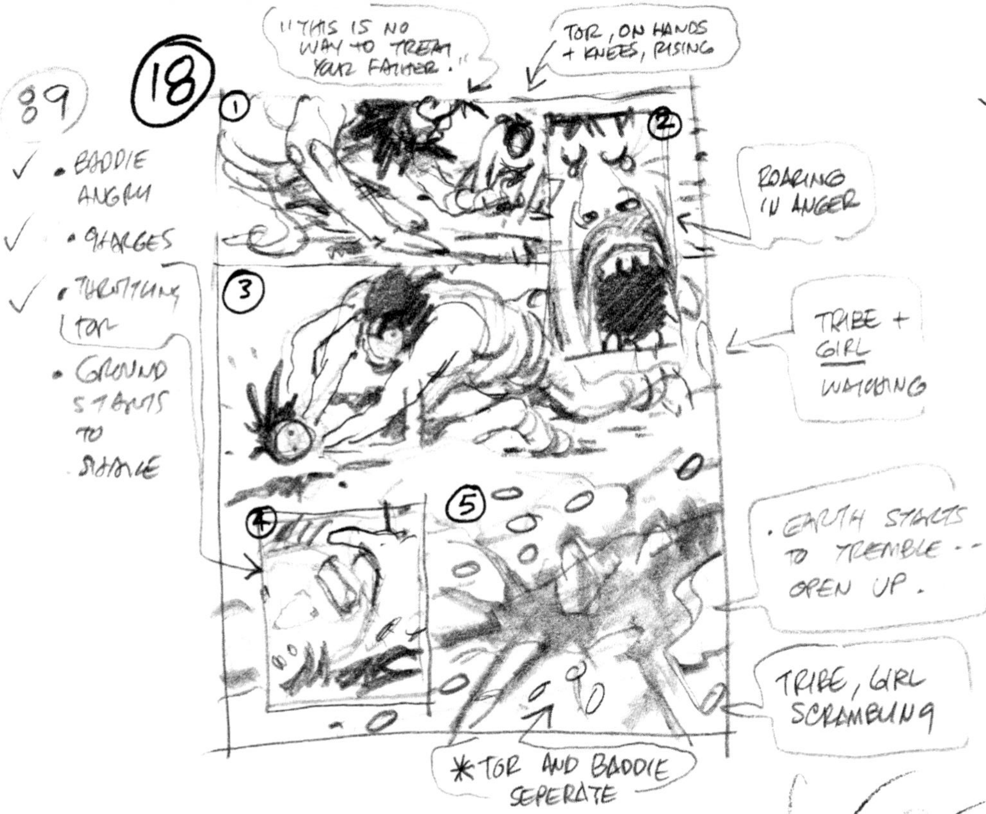
89
18
• BADDIE ANGRY
• CHARGES
• THROTTLING TOR
• GROUND STARTS TO SHAKE
"THIS IS NO WAY TO TREAT YOUR FATHER!"
TOR, ON HANDS + KNEES, RISING
ROARING IN ANGER
TRIBE + GIRL WATCHING
• EARTH STARTS TO TREMBLE - - OPEN UP.
TRIBE, GIRL SCRAMBLING
* TOR AND BADDIE SEPERATE

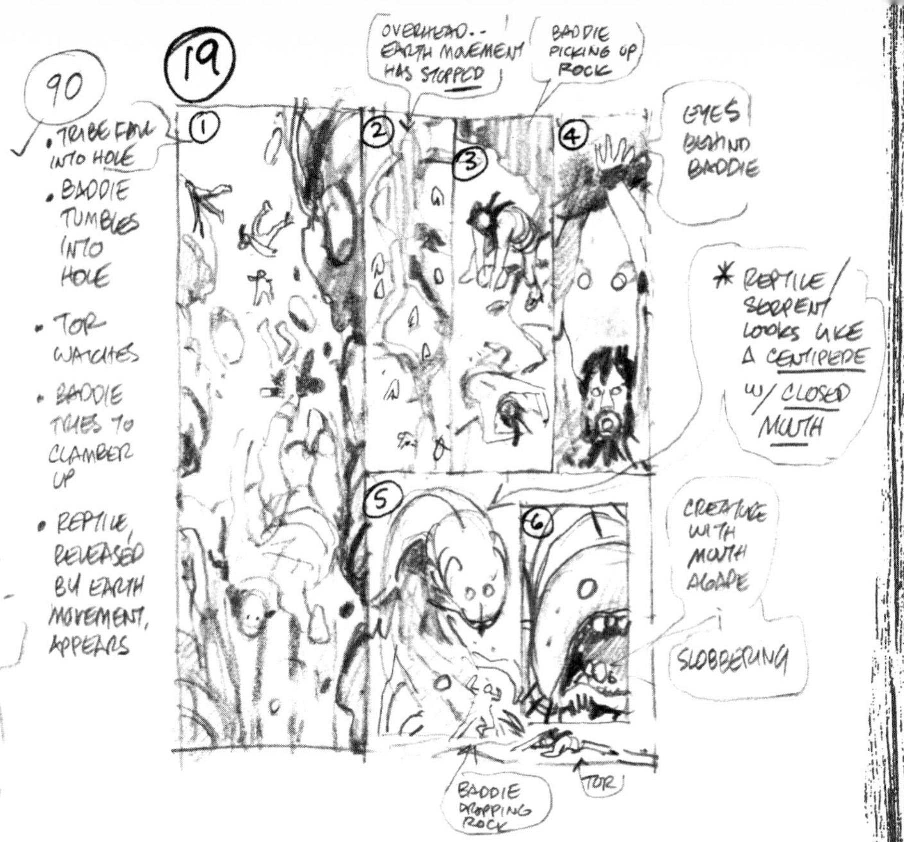
90
19
• TRIBE FALL INTO HOLE
• BADDIE TUMBLES INTO HOLE
• TOR WATCHES
• BADDIE TRIES TO CLAMBER UP
• REPTILE, RELEASED BY EARTH MOVEMENT, APPEARS
OVERHEAD - - EARTH MOVEMENT HAS STOPPED
BADDIE PICKING UP ROCK
EYES BEHIND BADDIE
* REPTILE / SERPENT LOOKS LIKE A CENTIPEDE W/ CLOSED MOUTH
CREATURE WITH MOUTH AGAPE
SLOBBERING
BADDIE DROPPING ROCK
TOR

BEFORE I EVEN ATTEMPTED TO DESIGN ANY OF THE GRAPHICS IN THESE PUBLICATIONS, THE STORY HAD TO BE WRITTEN. CHARACTER SKETCHES AND BACKGROUNDS WERE DONE WHILE THE STORY WAS BEING SCRIPTED. THERE WERE CHANGES (THERE USUALLY ARE!) IN VARIOUS CHARACTERS BY THE TIME THE FINISHED STORY/ART IS DONE

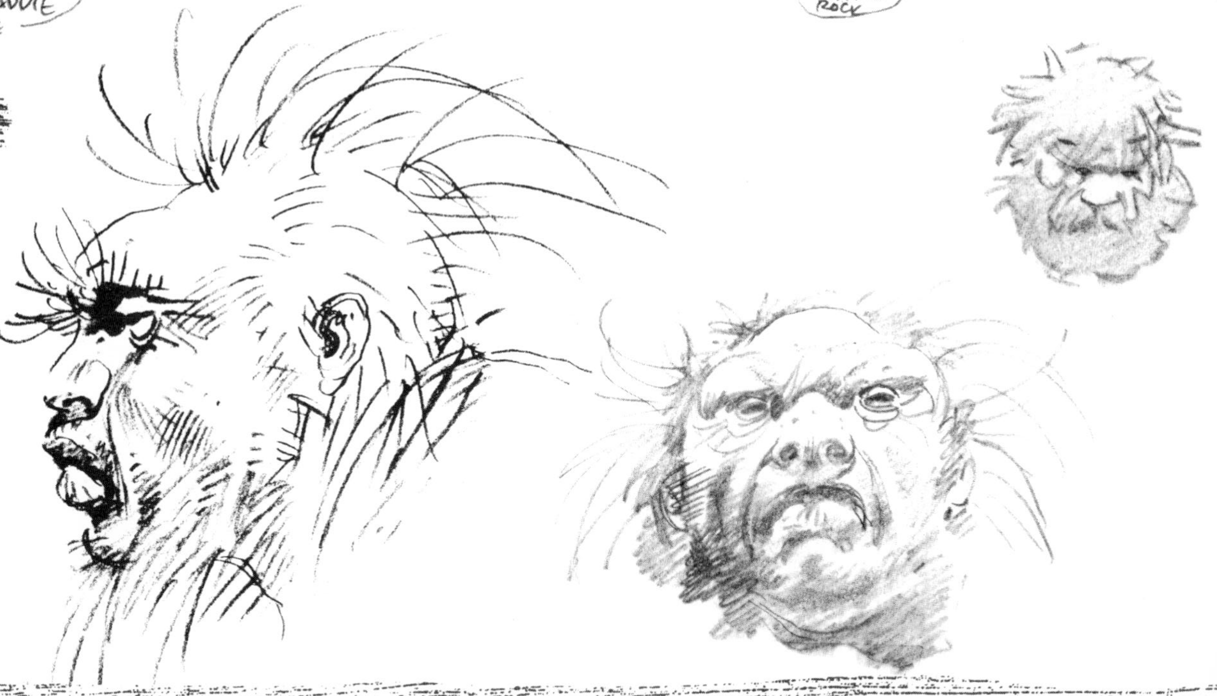

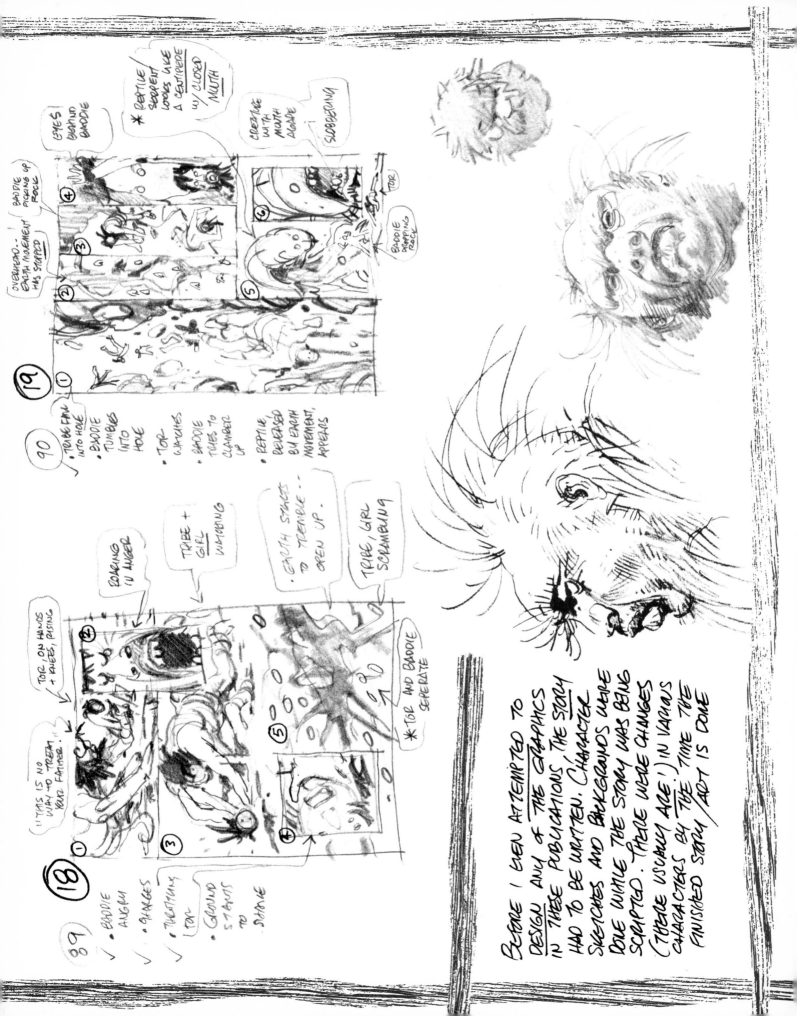

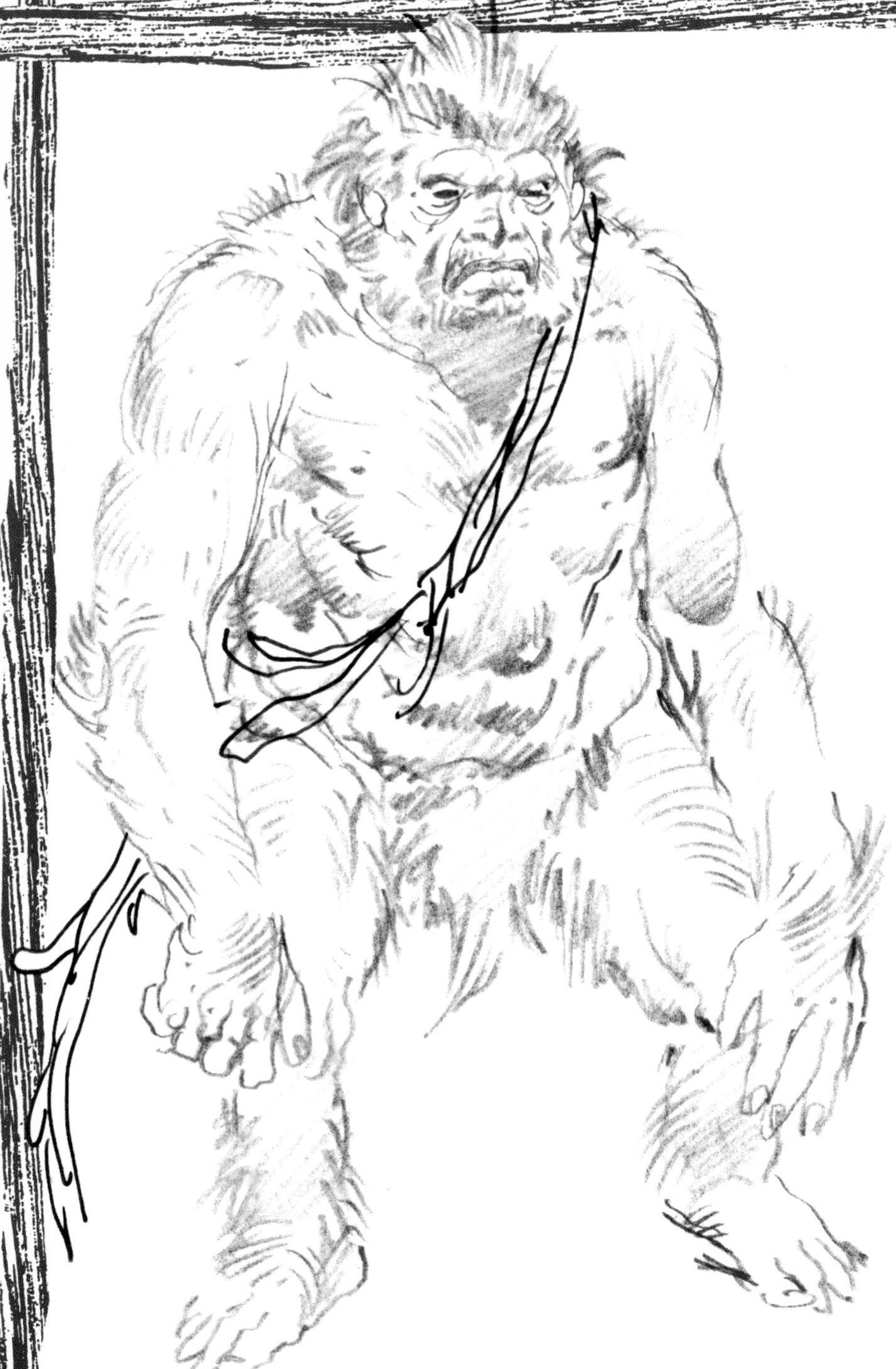

PRELIMINARY SKETCH OF BORK, LEADER OF THE RENEGADES.

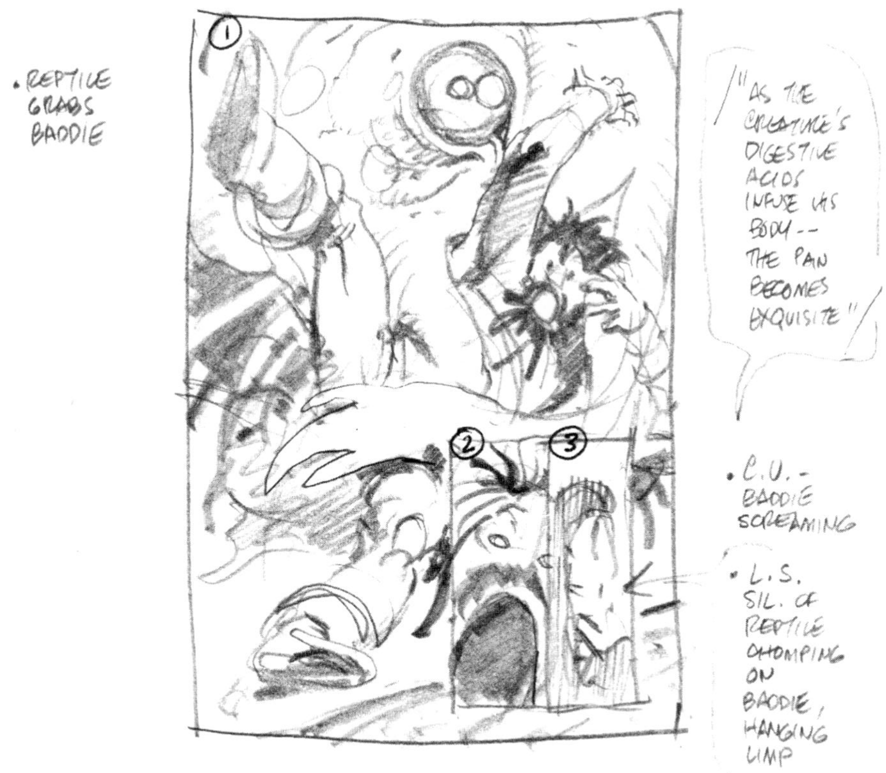

• REPTILE GRABS BADDIE
1
2
3
"AS THE CREATURE'S DIGESTIVE ACIDS INFUSE HIS BODY-- THE PAIN BECOMES EXQUISITE"
• C.U. - BADDIE SCREAMING
• L.S. SIL. OF REPTILE CHOMPING ON BADDIE, HANGING LIMP

MY ATTEMPT IN PAGE DESIGN IS TO CREATE A GRAPHIC IMAGE THAT WILL STIMULATE A RESPONSE IN THE READER TO LOOK AT AND EXAMINE THE DRAWING, AND TO BECOME INVOLVED IN THE STORY. TO EXACT A FEELING OF CREDIBILITY AND BELIEF. SO THAT NO MATTER HOW INCREDIBLE THE SITUATION, IT IS STILL BELIEVEABLE. WITHOUT THIS BELIEF ON THE PART OF THE READER, MY EFFORTS WOULD BE MEANINGLESS.

TOWARDS THAT END, EXPRESSION, ANATOMY, BACKGROUND... ALL MUST HAVE A SENSE OF "RIGHTNESS".

I DEVOTE SPACE TO ENHANCE DRAMATIC EFFECT. THEREFOR, AS SHOWN ON THE PAGE Nº 20 LAYOUT, I DEDICATED THE LARGEST SPACE ON THAT PAGE TO WHAT I DEEMED THE MOST DRAMATIC INSTANCE.

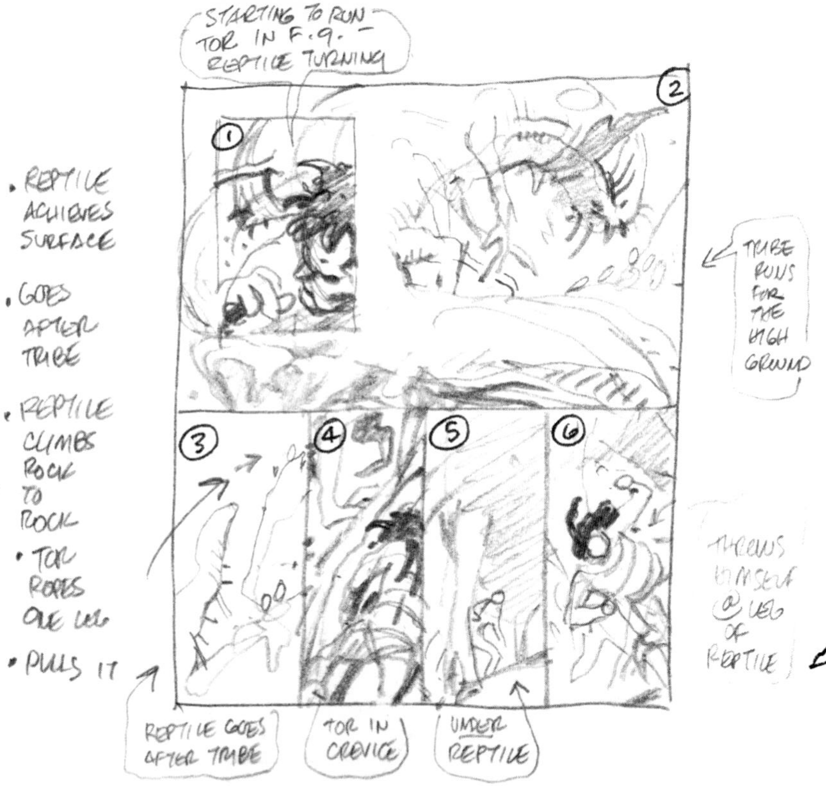
• REPTILE ACHIEVES SURFACE
• GOES AFTER TRIBE
• REPTILE CLIMBS ROCK TO ROCK
• TOR ROPES ONE LEG
• PULLS IT
STARTING TO RUN TOR IN F.G. – REPTILE TURNING
TRIBE RUNS FOR THE HIGH GROUND
THROWS HIMSELF @ LEG OF REPTILE
REPTILE GOES AFTER TRIBE
TOR IN CREVICE
UNDER REPTILE
1
2
3
4
5
6

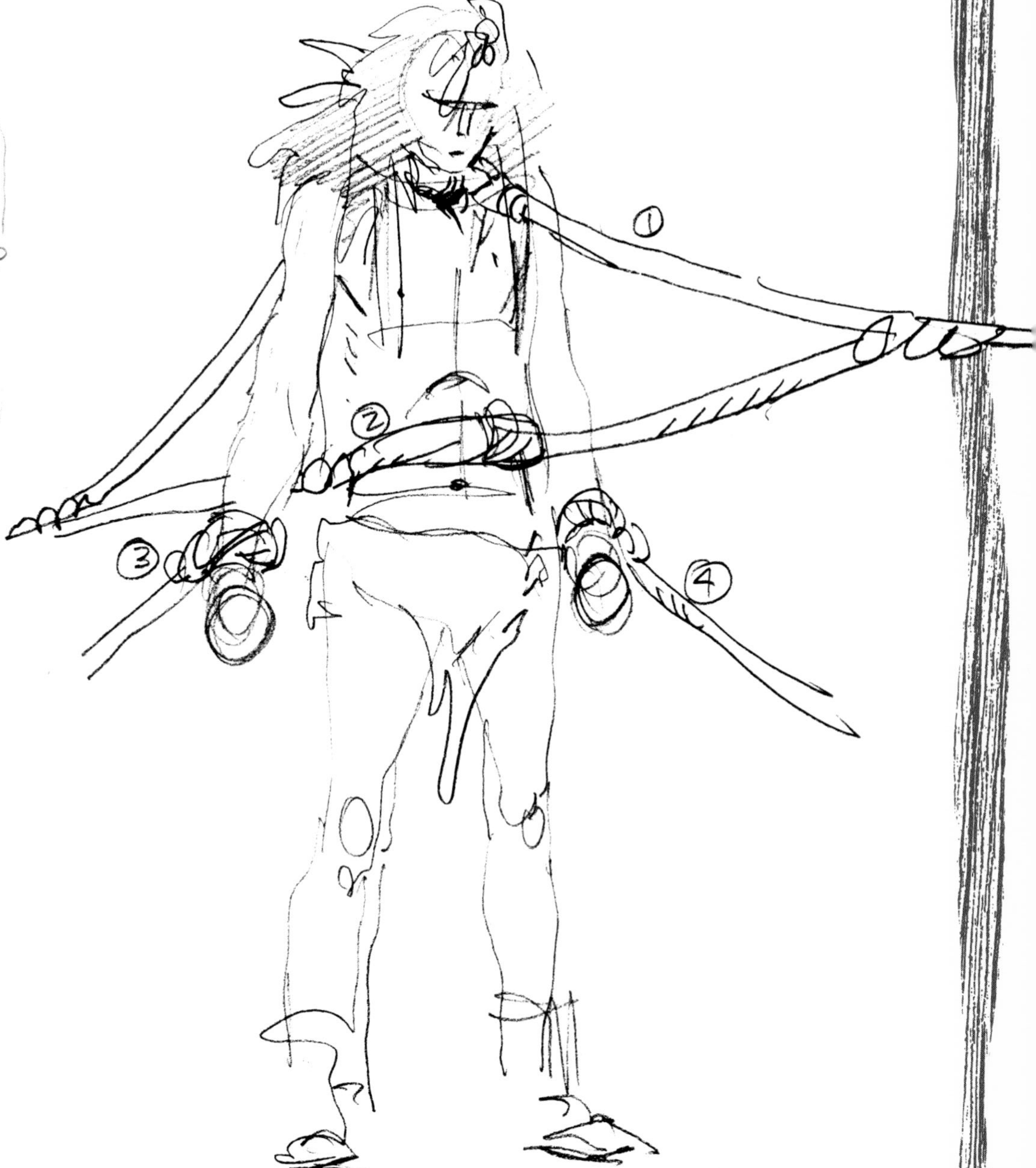
1
2
3
4

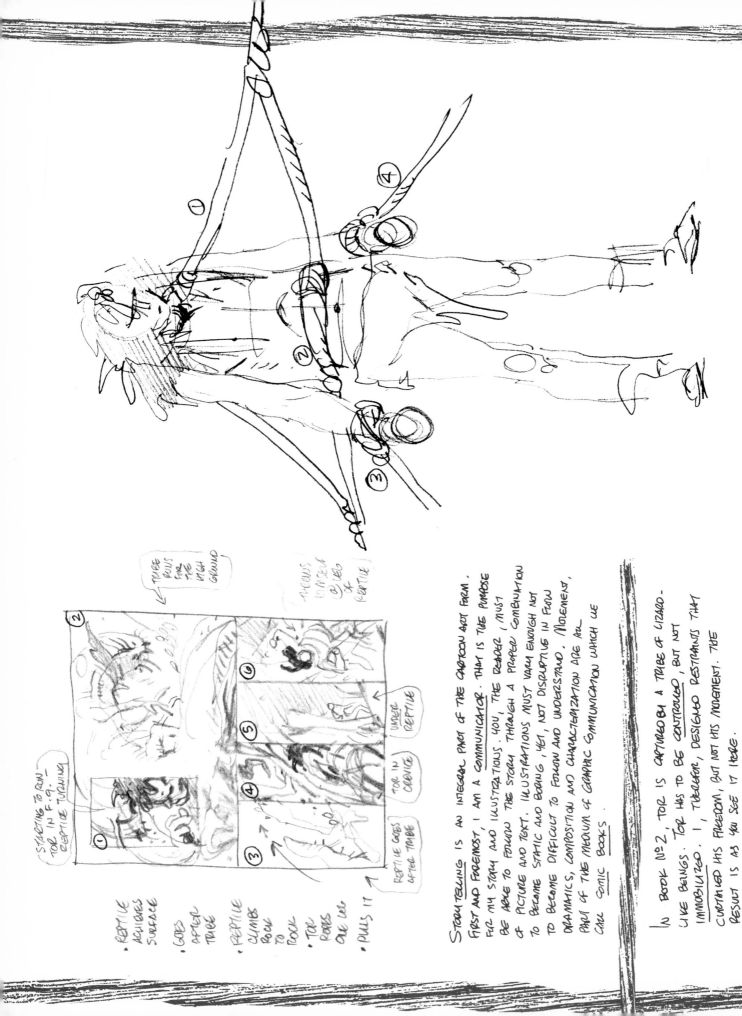

STORYTELLING IS AN INTEGRAL PART OF THE CARTOON ART FORM. FIRST AND FOREMOST, I AM A COMMUNICATOR. THAT IS THE PURPOSE FOR MY STORY AND ILLUSTRATIONS. YOU, THE READER, MUST BE ABLE TO FOLLOW THE STORY THROUGH A PROPER COMBINATION OF PICTURE AND TEXT. ILLUSTRATIONS MUST VARY ENOUGH NOT TO BECOME STATIC AND BORING, YET, NOT DISRUPTIVE IN FLOW TO BECOME DIFFICULT TO FOLLOW AND UNDERSTAND. MOVEMENT, DRAMATICS, COMPOSITION AND CHARACTERIZATION ARE ALL PART OF THE MEDIUM OF GRAPHIC COMMUNICATION WHICH WE CALL COMIC BOOKS.

IN BOOK Nº 2, TOR IS CAPTURED BY A TRIBE OF LIZARD-LIKE BEINGS. TOR HAS TO BE CONTROLLED, BUT NOT IMMOBILIZED. I, THEREFOR, DESIGNED RESTRAINTS THAT CURTAILED HIS FREEDOM, BUT NOT HIS MOVEMENT. THE RESULT IS AS YOU SEE IT HERE.

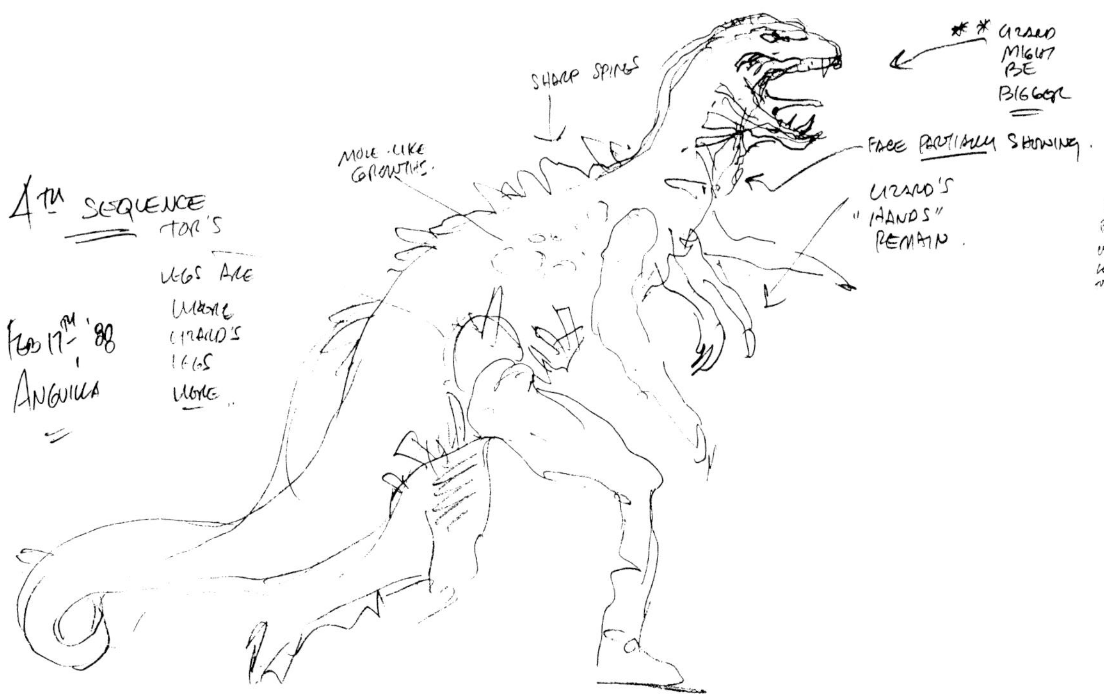
4TH SEQUENCE
TOR'S LEGS ARE WHERE LIZARD'S LEGS WERE.
FEB 17TH, '88
ANGUILLA
HE SKINS
** LIZARD MIGHT BE BIGGER
SHARP SPINES
MOLE-LIKE GROWTHS
FACE PARTIALLY SHOWING.
LIZARD'S "HANDS" REMAIN.

PRELIMINARY SKETCH OF THE "LIZARD SUIT" IN WHICH TOR DISGUISES HIMSELF. *SEE BOOK № 3.

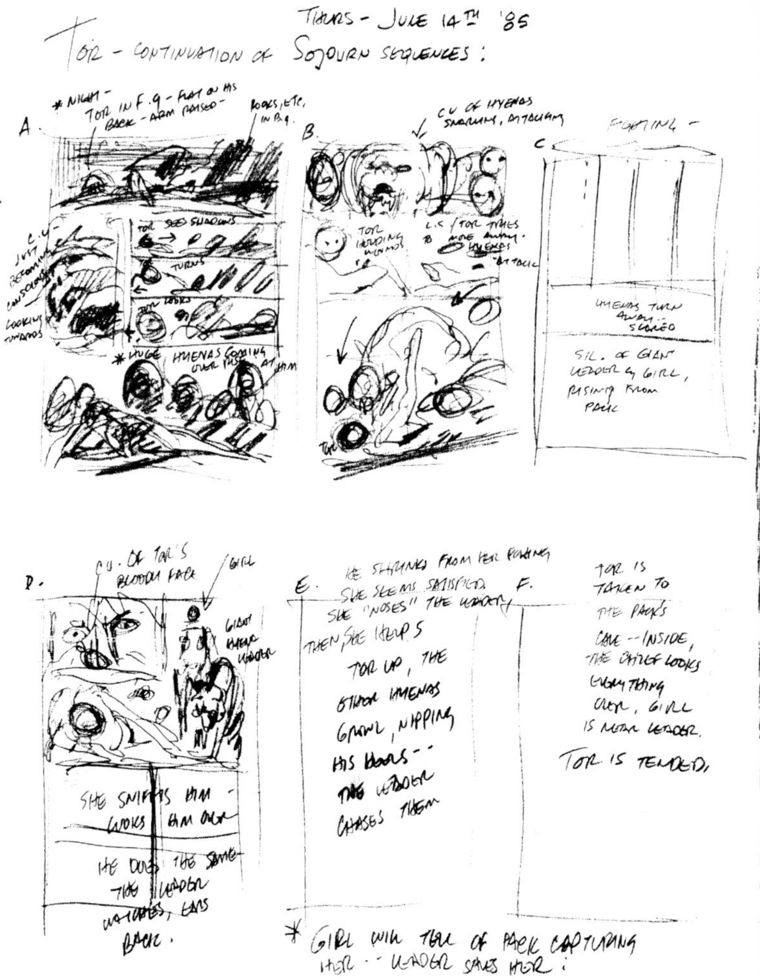
THURS - JUNE 14TH '85
TOR - CONTINUATION OF SOJOURN SEQUENCES:
A.
B.
C.
FIGHTING -
HYENAS TURN AWAY SCARED
SIL. OF GIANT LEADER & GIRL, RISING FROM PACK
D.
E.
F.
GIRL
THEN, SHE HELPS TOR UP, THE OTHER HYENAS GROWL, NIPPING HIS HEELS -- THE LEADER CHASES THEM
TOR IS TAKEN TO THE PACK'S CAVE -- INSIDE, THE CHIEF LOOKS EVERYTHING OVER, GIRL IS NOW LEADER.
TOR IS TENDED.
SHE SNIFFS HIM - WAKES HIM UP
* GIRL WITH TALE OF PACK CAPTURING HER -- LEADER SAVES HER:

ABOVE IS THE LAYOUT / SCRIPT FOR A SIX PAGE STORY TO FOLLOW UP AND COMPLETE THE LAST CHAPTER OF THE BACK-UP STORY WHICH APPEARED IN TOR, ISSUE № 3. PLEASE NOTE THE DATE; JUNE 14TH, '85, AND THE TITLE; "TOR - CONTINUATION OF SOJOURN SEQUENCES". SOJOURN WAS A PUBLICATION THAT APPEARED MORE THAN TEN YEARS AGO, FOR WHICH I WAS CO-PUBLISHER AND EDITOR. IT IS MY INTENTION TO CONTINUE THE STORY OF TOR, AND THIS SIX PAGE STORY WILL BE PART OF THAT EFFORT.

THANKS CARL, MARIE, KEV, AND ALL YOU GOOD PEOPLE AT MARVEL WHO GAVE UNSTINTINGLY OF HELP, ADVICE AND ENCOURAGEMENT. WRITING AND DRAWING THIS FOUR ISSUE SERIES WAS, FOR ME, A PLEASURED EXPERIENCE I LOOK FORWARD TO REPEATING IN THE FUTURE.

Sketchbook

COMMENTARY BY JOE KUBERT

I've had the opportunity to work on many comic book stories featuring a variety of characters. Among them were superheroes, detectives, cowboys, adventurers, sailors, boxers, wrestlers, and list goes on and on. In every case, my attempt was to make the character credible and believable. I designed Tor with this purpose in mind. This sketch is from the early '90s.

Note the lack of an overabundance of muscles. I wanted Tor to look human, with perhaps a well-proportioned body. Athletic, but not a weight lifter. His long black hair protected his vulnerable neck and back, while in front it was cut short for unobstructed vision. His wristlets (lizard skin) prevented bruises, as did the furskin boots he wore. Weighted stones attached to his corded rope enabled him to throw for entrapment of food — or to inhibit an enemy.

49
TOR KILLS BABY
MOTHER ATTACKS
MOM, IN B.9., GETTING OFF HER NEST... ANGRY.
CU OF TEARFUL MOM, ENRAGED.. COMING @ TOR
BABY BITES INTO TOR'S SHOULDER
TOR PULLS BABY FROM HIS THROAT
TOR TURNS - SHADOW IS CAST ACROSS TOR
DEAD MOM

13
IMPISH-LOOKING FACE
* TOTEM IS IN THE FORM OF A GIANT LIZARD CREATURE!
① SPARKS OF PULSING PAIN FLASH BEFORE HIM, GRADUALLY, THE BLACKNESS DISSIPATES... TAKING THE FORM OF PEERING FACES...
② THE SWIRLING VISAGES COMBINE TO BECOME ONE HIDEOUS LEER...
③ ...WORN BY AN IMP-LIKE TORMENTOR!
A): SEE? HE IS AWAKE! THE MONSTER IS AWAKE...
B): HIDE THE BABIES... HE HAS AN EVIL EYE!
④ KID: I AM NOT AFRAID OF HIM...
LEADER: STAND BACK! HE MUST REMAIN UNHARMED...
⑤ OFF: ... FOR NOW!
⑥ FROM BRUISED LIDS, THE MAN ASSESSES HIS SITUATION... WONDERS WHAT FATE WILL BEFALL HIM... AND THE WOMAN WHO CAUSED HIS PREDICAMENT!
ON A RAISED MOUND OF EARTH

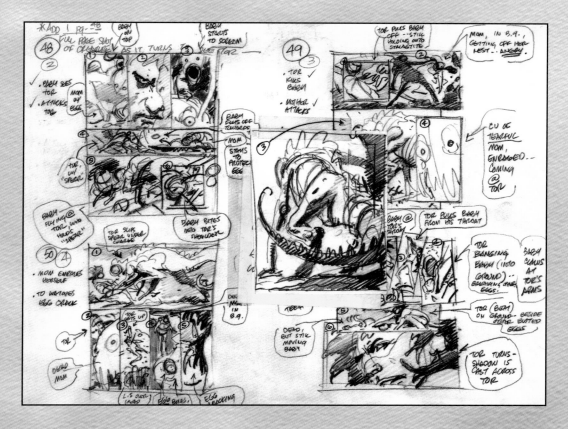

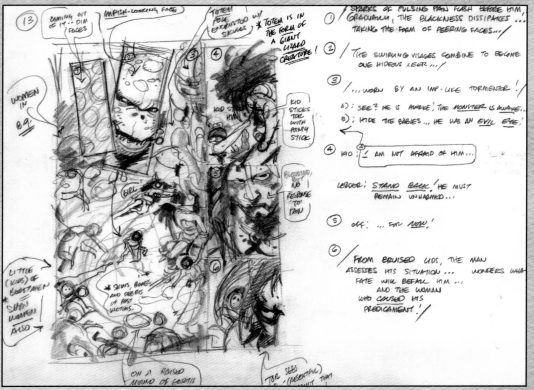

This is the procedure I use for writing my stories and laying out my pages. These sketches were done on 8 1/2" x 11" plain paper.

In addition to the (very) rough sketches, I write many notes to myself so that I won't forget what I had in mind by the time I start to draw on the full-sized boards.

Some dialog can be seen on the bottom right side of the last page. The numbers conform with the numbers on the panels.

The colors on these sketcehs were more for clarification rather than color suggestions.

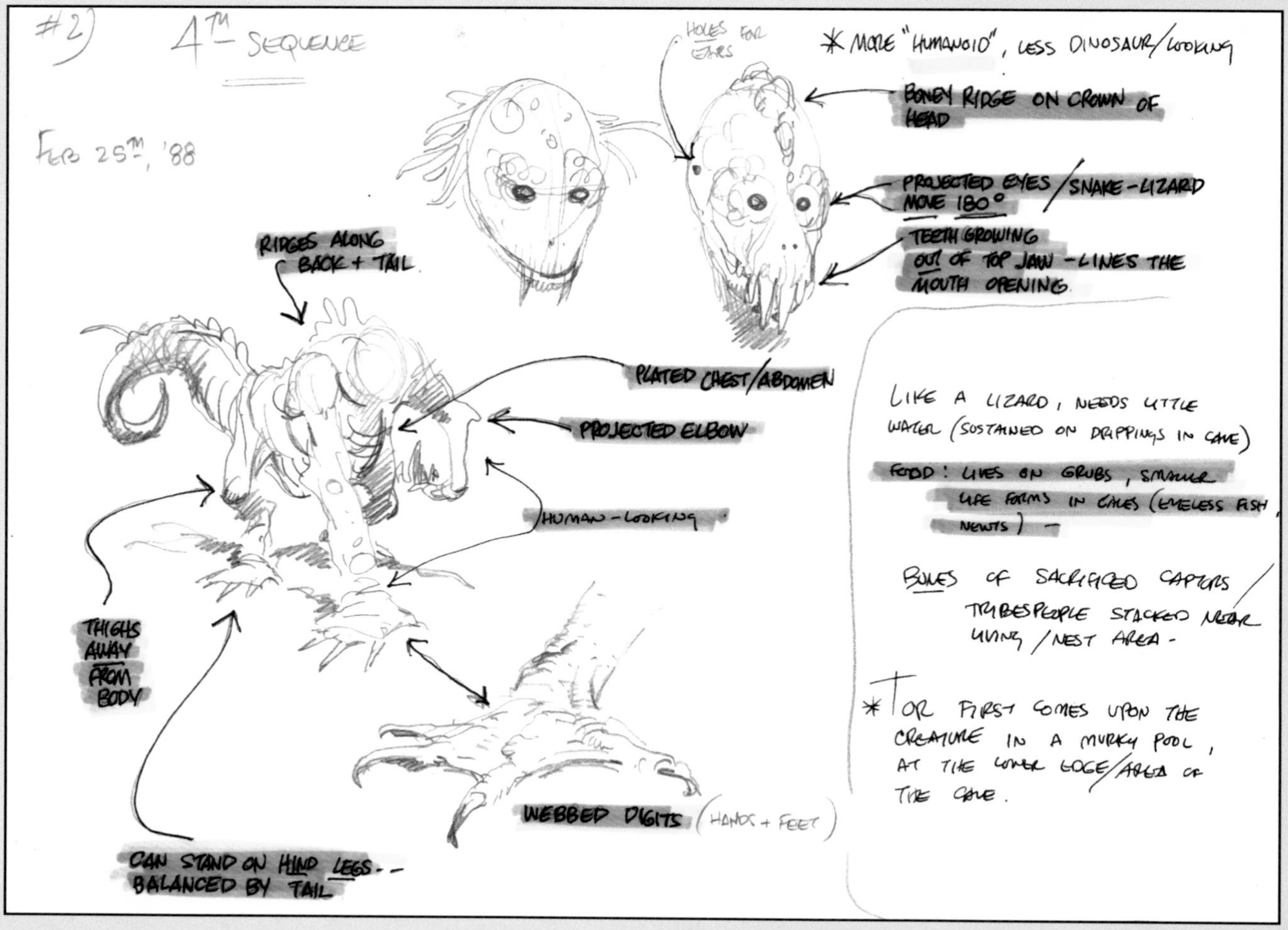
#2)
4TH SEQUENCE
FEB 25TH, '88
HOLES FOR EARS
* MORE "HUMANOID", LESS DINOSAUR/LOOKING
BONEY RIDGE ON CROWN OF HEAD
PROJECTED EYES / SNAKE-LIZARD MOVE 180°
TEETH GROWING OUT OF TOP JAW - LINES THE MOUTH OPENING.
RIDGES ALONG BACK + TAIL
PLATED CHEST/ABDOMEN
PROJECTED ELBOW
HUMAN-LOOKING
THIGHS AWAY FROM BODY
WEBBED DIGITS (HANDS + FEET)
CAN STAND ON HIND LEGS - - BALANCED BY TAIL
LIKE A LIZARD, NEEDS LITTLE WATER (SUSTAINED ON DRIPPINGS IN CAVE)
FOOD: LIVES ON GRUBS, SMALLER LIFE FORMS IN CAVES (EYELESS FISH, NEWTS) -
BONES OF SACRIFICED CAPTURS / TRIBESPEOPLE STACKED NEAR LIVING / NEST AREA -
* TOR FIRST COMES UPON THE CREATURE IN A MURKY POOL, AT THE LOWER EDGE/AREA OF THE CAVE.

JULY 4, '95 / TUESDAY
ROYAL TYRRELL MUSEUM -
DRUMHELLER, ALBERTA, CANADA.

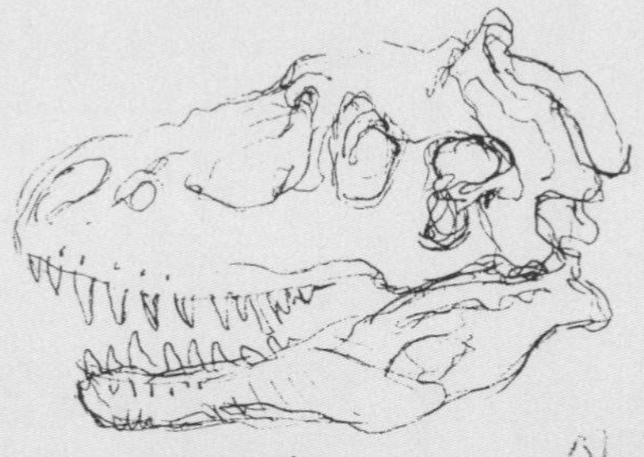
ALBERTOSAURUS

I like to date most of my sketches. It gives me a time line and allows me to consider the sequence in which these drawings were produced. I also make note of the place where the sketches were made.

I try to have a sketch book with me whenever I travel. In this way, I'm able to remember the details of the places I've visited far better than if I'd taken a photograph.

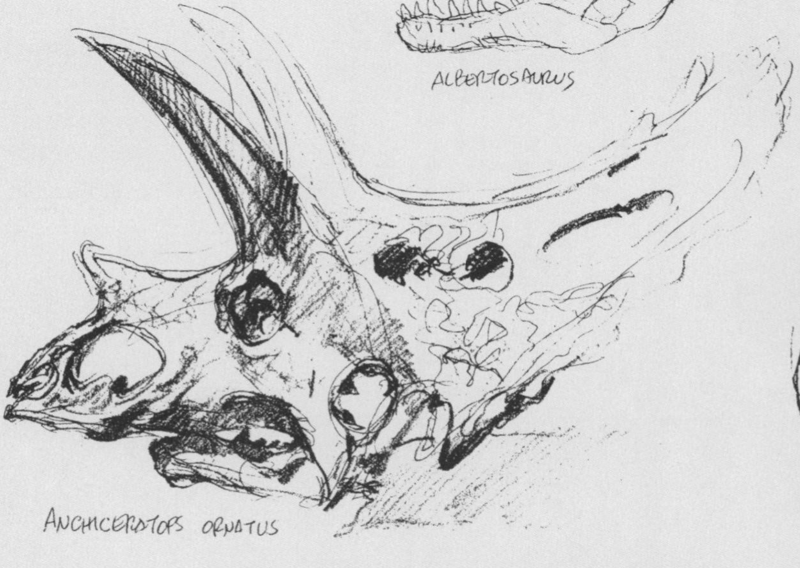
ANCHICERATOPS ORNATUS

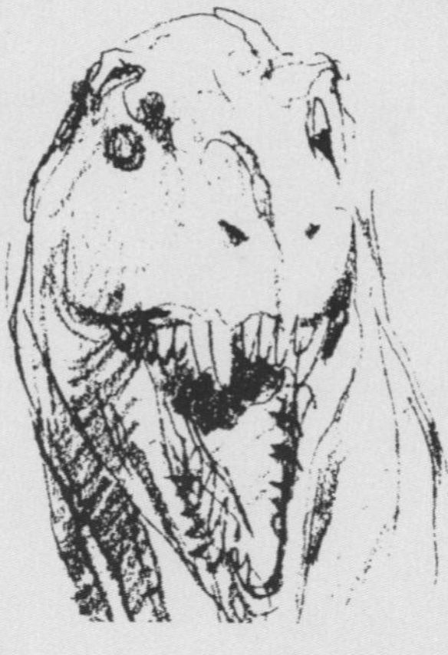
ALBERTOSAURUS

TOR - #2
FOR OCT.
DEAD DINOSAUR IN F. 9
TOR PROTECTS FOOD
TOR SNARLS @ ATTACKING DINOSAUR
TOR TORN BY CLAW, ACROSS CHEST
DINO LOOSENS TOR'S GRIP
TOR VERY SMALL IN ROCKS.

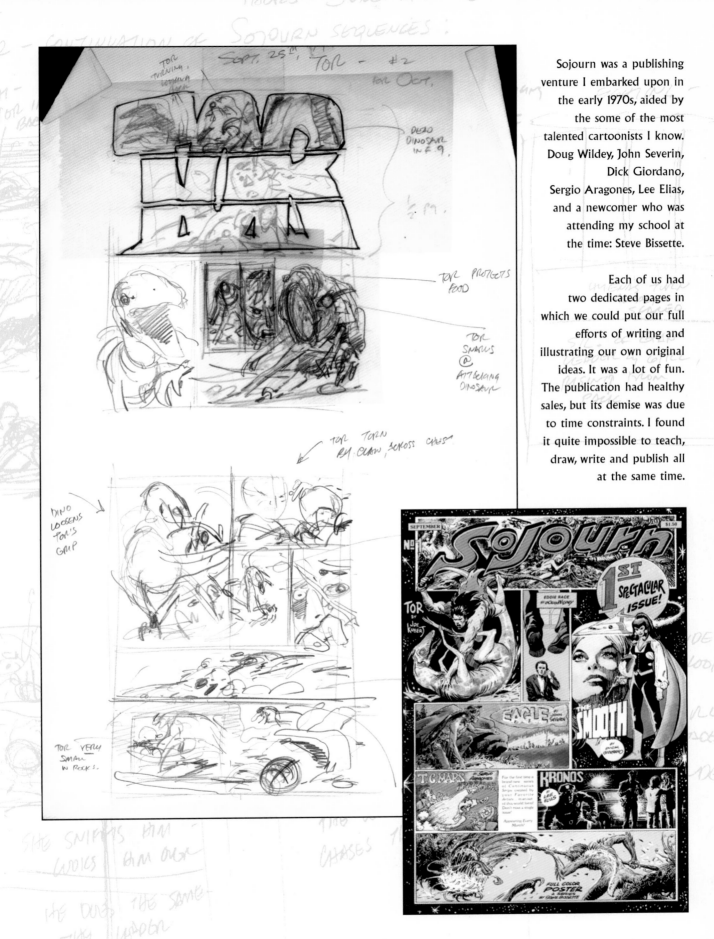

Sojourn was a publishing venture I embarked upon in the early 1970s, aided by the some of the most talented cartoonists I know. Doug Wildey, John Severin, Dick Giordano, Sergio Aragones, Lee Elias, and a newcomer who was attending my school at the time: Steve Bissette.

Each of us had two dedicated pages in which we could put our full efforts of writing and illustrating our own original ideas. It was a lot of fun. The publication had healthy sales, but its demise was due to time constraints. I found it quite impossible to teach, draw, write and publish all at the same time.

SEPTEMBER
$1.50
No 1
Sojourn
1ST SPECTACULAR ISSUE!
TOR BY JOE KUBERT
EDDIE RACE
EAGLE
THE SMOOTH
T.C. MARS
KRONOS
FULL COLOR POSTER

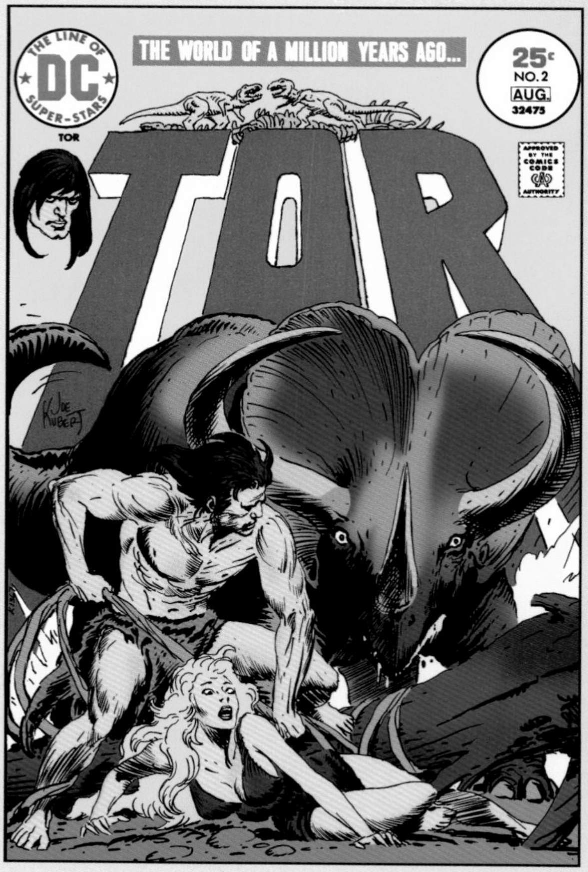
THE LINE OF DC SUPER-STARS
THE WORLD OF A MILLION YEARS AGO...
25¢
NO.2
AUG.
32475
TOR
TOR

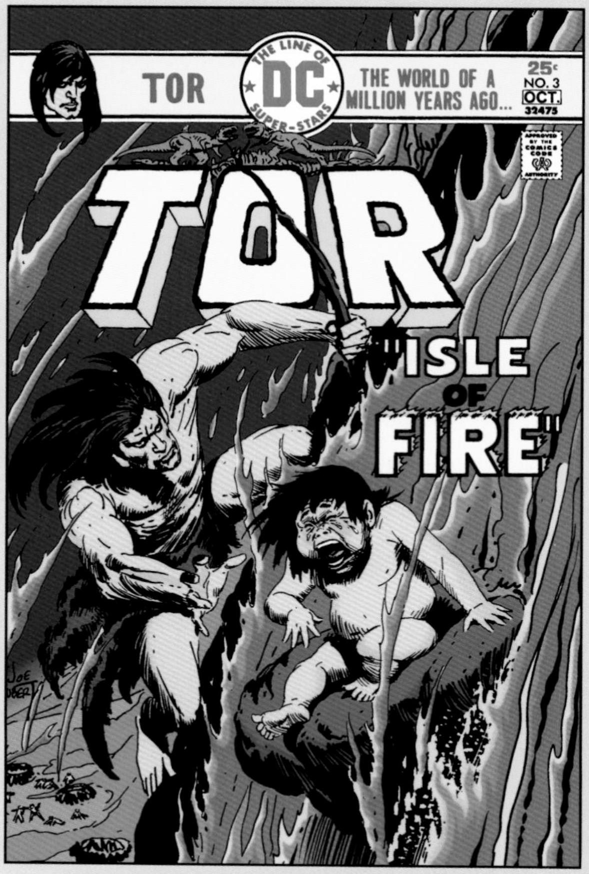
TOR
THE LINE OF DC SUPER-STARS
THE WORLD OF A MILLION YEARS AGO...
25¢
NO. 3
OCT.
32475
TOR
"ISLE OF FIRE"

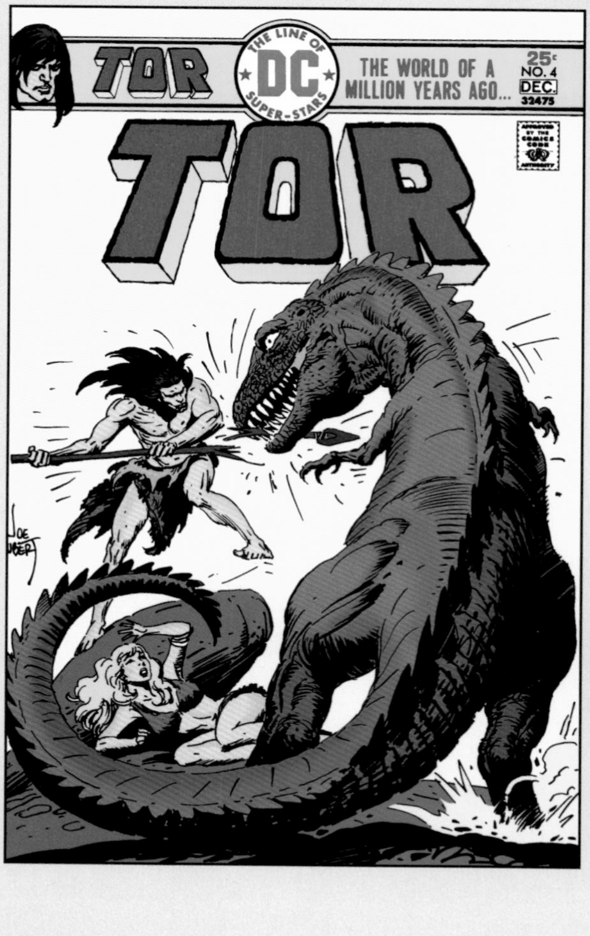
TOR
THE LINE OF DC SUPER-STARS
THE WORLD OF A MILLION YEARS AGO...
25¢
NO. 4
DEC.
32475
TOR

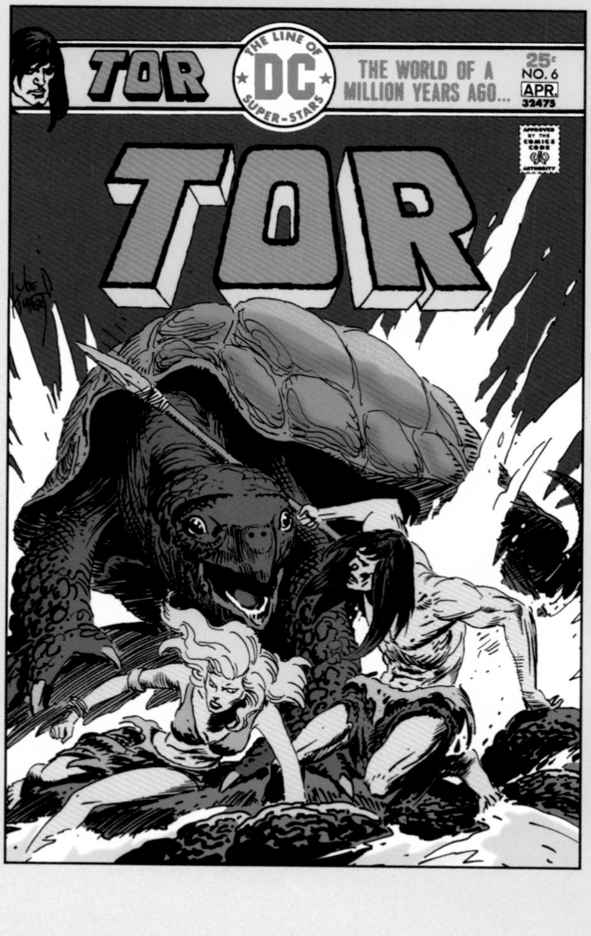
TOR
THE LINE OF DC SUPER-STARS
THE WORLD OF A MILLION YEARS AGO...
25¢
NO. 6
APR.
32475
TOR

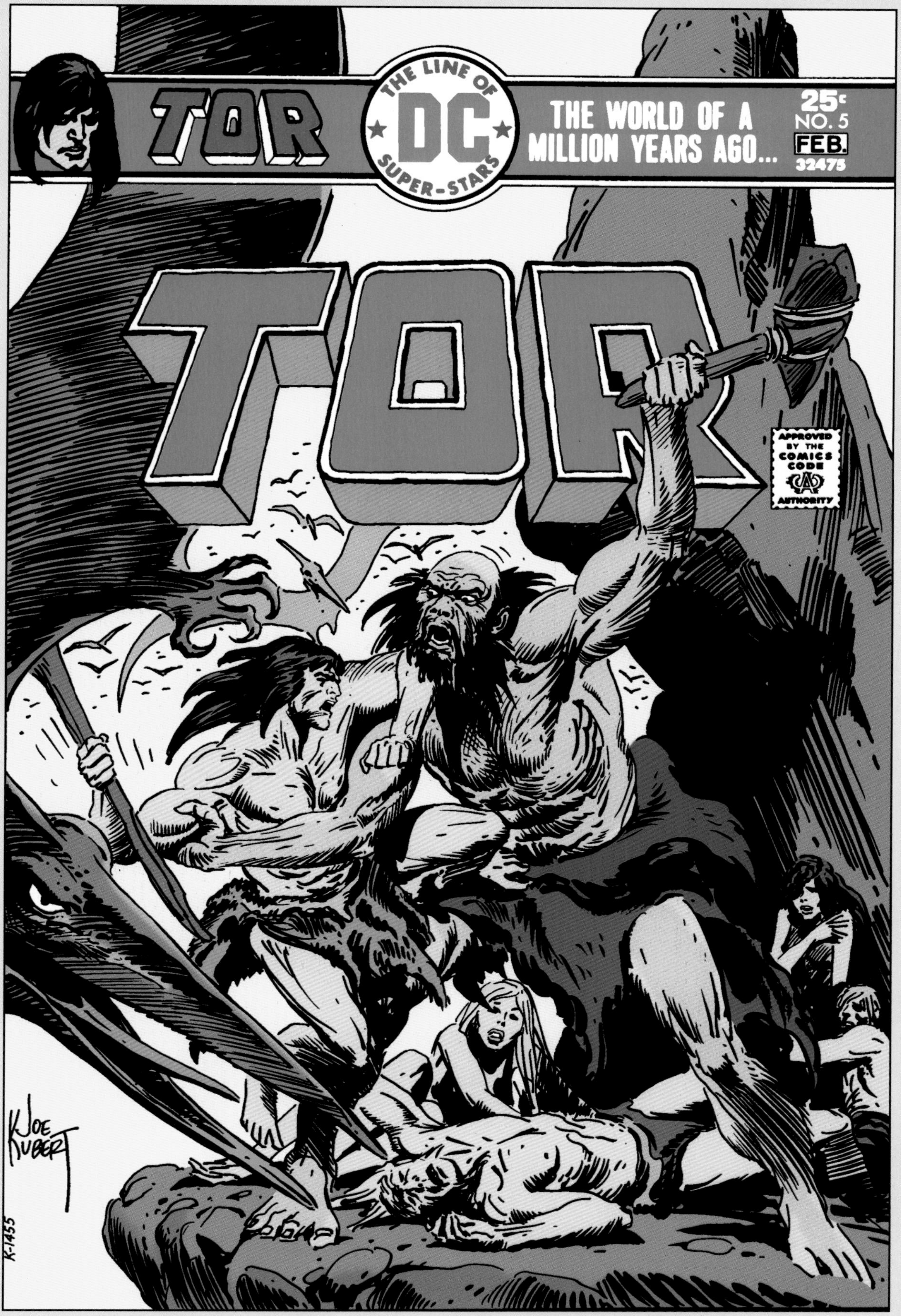
TOR
THE LINE OF
DC
SUPER-STARS
THE WORLD OF A
MILLION YEARS AGO...
25¢
NO. 5
FEB.
32475
TOR
APPROVED
BY THE
COMICS
CODE
AUTHORITY
JOE KUBERT
K-1455

These are the covers I did when DC reprinted Tor. The production staff headed by Jack Adler did an amazing job of converting the interior 3-D illustrations, originally printed in the 1950s, into these publications.

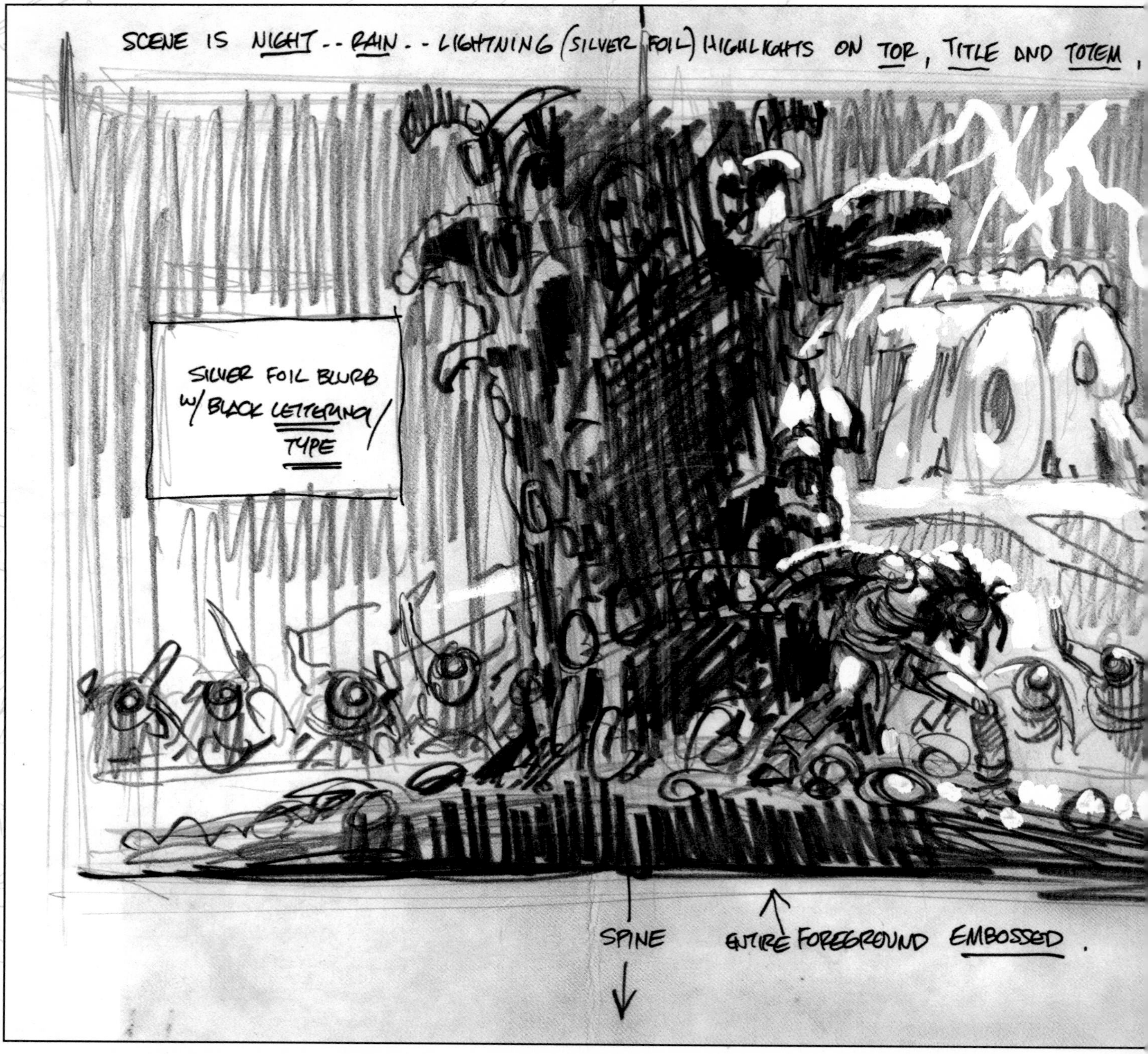
SCENE IS NIGHT -- RAIN -- LIGHTNING (SILVER FOIL) HIGHLIGHTS ON TOR, TITLE AND TOTEM,
SILVER FOIL BLURB W/ BLACK LETTERING/ TYPE
SPINE
ENTIRE FOREGROUND EMBOSSED.

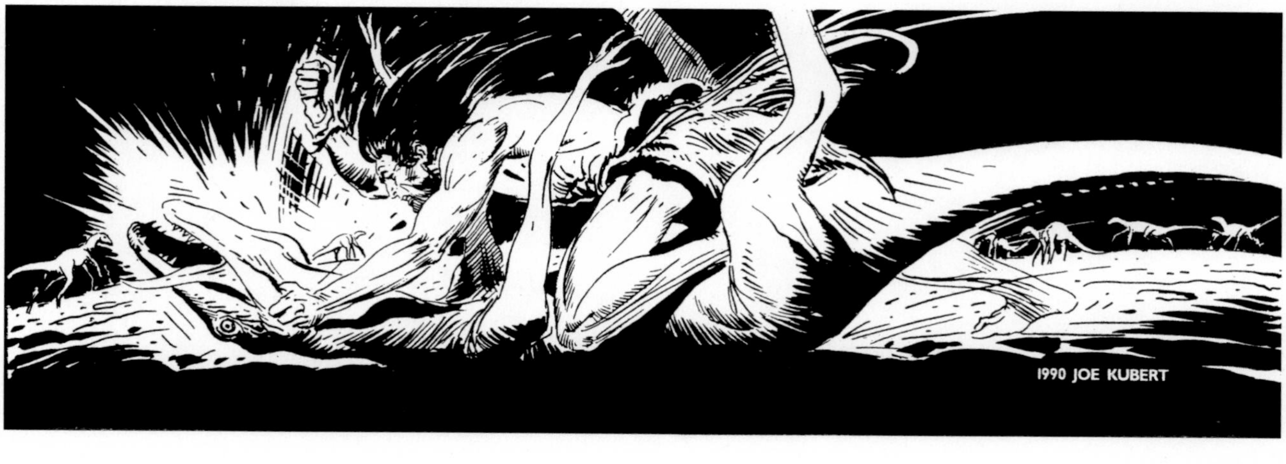
1990 JOE KUBERT

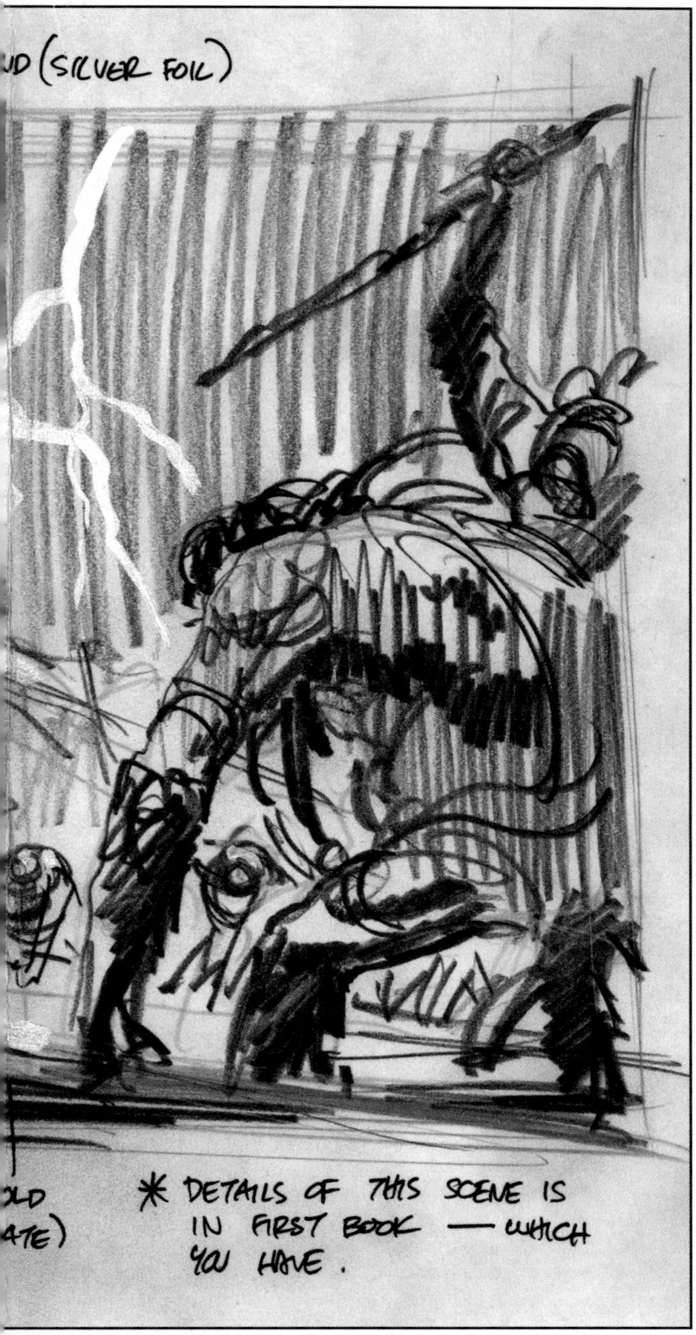
(SILVER FOIL)
* DETAILS OF THIS SCENE IS IN FIRST BOOK — WHICH YOU HAVE.

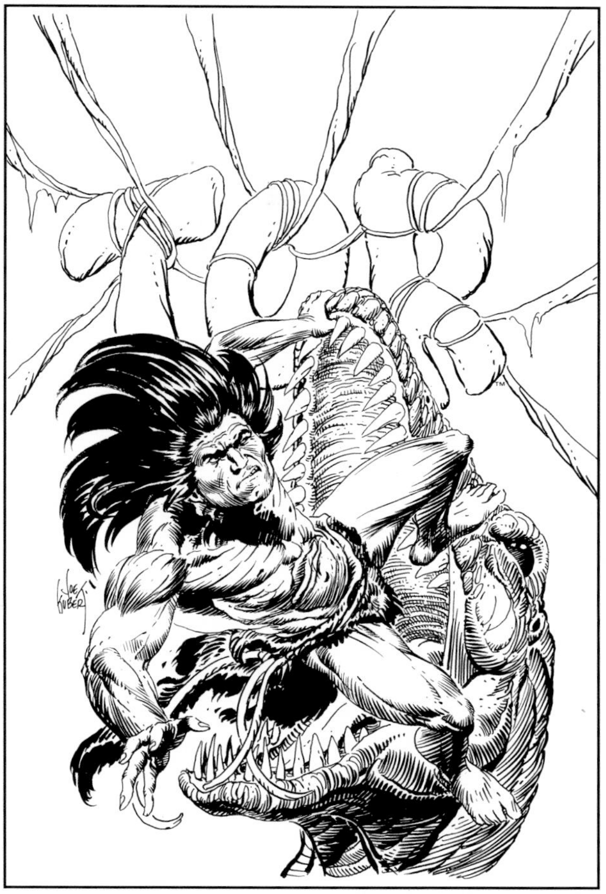

This was the cover art for Tor #2 (Eclipse). Eclipse reprinted Tor stories in 3-D in the mid-80's.

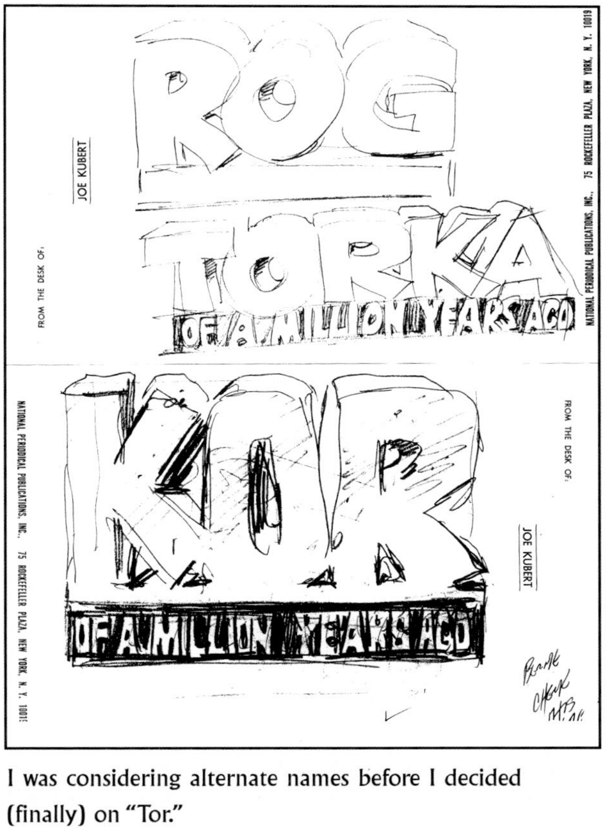
ROG
TORKA
OF A MILLION YEARS AGO
KOR
OF A MILLION YEARS AGO
FROM THE DESK OF,
JOE KUBERT
NATIONAL PERIODICAL PUBLICATIONS, INC., 75 ROCKEFELLER PLAZA, NEW YORK, N. Y. 10019

I was considering alternate names before I decided (finally) on "Tor."

Above: This was my initial sketch for the wrap-around cover of the first issue in which the new Tor stories were published. Note the suggestions for the use of foil and embossing. My idea was also to have a gate-fold on the right side of the cover.
Good ideas, I thought. However, attending costs made them prohibitive. Y'win some and y'lose some.

Left: This illustration appeared originally in the Sojourn publication. I added blacks when we decided to use it on T-shirts.

The Joe Kubert Library

TOR VOLUMES ONE-THREE

The Will Eisner Library

THE BUILDING

CITY PEOPLE NOTEBOOK

A CONTRACT WITH GOD

THE DREAMER

DROPSIE AVENUE: THE NEIGHBORHOOD

FAMILY MATTER

INVISIBLE PEOPLE

A LIFE FORCE

LIFE ON ANOTHER PLANET

MINOR MIRACLES

NEW YORK, THE BIG CITY

TO THE HEART OF THE STORM

WILL EISNER READER

THE NAME OF THE GAME

The Spirit Archives

Will Eisner's The Spirit collected in chronological order
in deluxe, full-color, hardcover editions.